Lugosi as Dracula in a portrait published in the March 1932 issue of *The Cast*.

Bela Lugosi
Dreams And Nightmares

Lugosi as Dracula and Rande Carmichael as Lucy in a 1948 production of *Dracula* at the Green Hills Theatre of Reading, Pennsylvania. *(Courtesy of George R. Snell)*

Bela Lugosi
Dreams And Nightmares

Gary D. Rhodes

with
Richard Sheffield

Featuring Photographs from the Collections of
Bill Chase, Kristin Dewey, Lynn Naron, Dennis Phelps, Gary D. Rhodes,
Richard Sheffield, George Snell, and David Wentink.

Collectables
Narberth, PA

Front cover photo: Lugosi as Dracula circa 1930.
(Courtesy of the David Wentink collection)

Back cover photo: Lugosi as Dracula onstage in Litchfield, Connecticut in 1947.
(Photographed by Samuel Kravitt; Courtesy of Mrs. Samuel Kravitt)

Due to the rarity of many of the historical photographs that appear in this book, reproduction quality may vary.

LIBRARY OF CONGRESS CATALOGING-IN-PUBLICATION DATA

RHODES, GARY D., 1972–
Library of Congress Catalog Card Number: 2006939939
Bela Lugosi: Dreams and Nightmares / Gary D. Rhodes with Richard Sheffield
   p.   cm.
   Includes bibliographical references and index.

ISBN-10: 0-9773798-1-7 hardcover
ISBN-13: 978-0-9773798-1-7 hardcover

1. Lugosi, Bela.
2. Actors—Hungary—Biography.
3. Motion Picture actors and actresses—United States—Biography.
I. Title.

Printed in the United States of America

Collectables® Records Corp.
PO Box 35, Narberth PA 19072
www.oldies.com

Book Designer: Nicole Fichera

Dedication

This book is dedicated to a number of people who in various ways have made it possible:

Edward *(Great Monsters of the Movies)* Edelson, Thomas *(Monsters of the Movies)* Aylesworth, Ian (Crestwood House) Thorne, and John *(The Horror People)* Brosnan, whose books spurred my interests in horror films.

Richard *(The Films of Bela Lugosi)* Bojarski, Robert *(Lugosi: The Man Behind the Cape)* Cremer, and Greg *(Karloff and Lugosi)* Mank, my three favorite Lugosi biographers.

Mario Chacon, Michael Copner, Richard Daub, Michael J. David, Michael Ferguson, Gordon R. Guy, Anthony Kerr, Lynn Naron, Ted Newsom, Dennis Payne, Bill Pirola, and John Wooley, my original friends in all things Lugosi.

Bill Chase, George Chastain, James Clatterbaugh, Bob Madison, Henry Nicollela, Dennis Phelps, Jeffrey Roberts, David Wentink, and Galen Wilkes, all close pals made during the 1990s.

Kristin Dewey, Jack Dowler, Leonard J. Kohl, Michael Lee, Father Mike Paraniuk, John Springer, treasured friends in all this Lugosi madness.

My new friends Gyöngyi Balogh, Noémi Saly, and Florin Iepan.

Forrest J Ackerman, editor of *Famous Monsters of Filmland*, and Bela Lugosi Jr. Both have always treated me as if I was their own nephew.

And of course to my dear friend Tom Weaver, the horror film's best historian. Without his help, I'd never have finally started this book, let alone finished it.

—Gary D. Rhodes, Belfast, Northern Ireland, 2006.

Contents

Lugosi being interviewed in the 1950s.

INTRODUCTION

Years ago, in the early 1980s, I was a young admirer of Bela Lugosi who read that his life had been plagued by an addiction to heroin. Somewhere else I learned that when Peter Lorre and Boris Karloff attended Lugosi's funeral, one of them chided him: "Come now, Bela, quit putting us on."

I already had clouded memories of seeing Lugosi's *Dracula* (1931) at the age of five. Lots of other horror movies, too. *The Wolf Man* (1941), for example. And finally glimpsing some of *White Zombie* (1932). Those were the days just before the video revolution. Those were the days when I would set the alarm clock to wake myself up in the middle of the night to catch a horror film on TV.

Those were also the days when I kept the library's books on horror films checked out so long they'd be ringing the house with admonitions of "Overdue." And when I salivated over the handful of horror magazines and books that I actually owned. My god, *Famous Monsters of Filmland* seemed so unbelievable when I finally got a copy of it in my hands.

Of course, as I hit my teen years I learned that Lugosi had *never* been addicted to heroin. And I learned that Boris Karloff and Peter Lorre did *not* attend his funeral. That was thanks to meeting Forrest J Ackerman, with whom I had endless conversations about Lugosi. It was also thanks to Robert Cremer's wonderful biography *Lugosi: The Man Behind the Cape* (Henry Regnery, 1976). And of course Richard Bojarski, who corresponded with me at length after I wrote to him about reading his terrific *The Films of Bela Lugosi* (Citadel Press, 1980). How well I remember the day I found that book in a shopping mall bookstore, piling all my nickels, dimes, and quarters onto the counter in order to take it home with me.

By 1986, I decided that so much of what had been written about Lugosi's last years was flawed that I considered writing an article myself. At age thirteen, I had just started publishing in a few film magazines like *The Big Reel*. So I began contacting a variety of people who knew Lugosi, including his close friend Richard Sheffield. Then Howard W. Koch and Richard Gordon and Hope Lugosi and Reginald Le Borg and so many others. I also started searching for clippings from film trade publications. Pretty soon, I had compiled enough research that I thought the project should become a series of articles. All for publication in 1986 on the thirtieth anniversary of Lugosi's death.

Things worked out a little differently. Instead of writing those articles, I ended up starting the Bela Lugosi Society, which eventually had close to a thousand memories throughout the US, England, France, Austria, Germany, and Japan. Its primary function was publishing *The World of Bela Lugosi*, a newsletter that added a film to Lugosi's filmography (*Leoni leo* of 1917), that interviewed his friends and coworkers, that published a good deal of previously-unpublished photos, and included contributions from such people as Gregory William Mank, Robert Bloch, and others. Seven issues by the time it ended just before I graduated from high school.

I still gave a lot of thought to writing about Lugosi's last years, but the publication of Rudolph Grey's *Nightmare of Ecstasy* (Feral House, 1992) and the resulting Tim Burton film *Ed Wood* (1994) made me think the market was well-saturated with the Lugosi of the 1950s. So instead I wrote *Lugosi* (McFarland, 1997), which became a reference book on his entire life, a book that added many stage roles, radio shows, television programs, and so forth to the body of knowledge. And my old pal Richard Sheffield provided the foreword.

After that, I wrote and directed *Lugosi: Hollywood's Dracula*, an hour-long documentary film on Lugosi's life. It unearthed all kinds of never-before-seen footage ranging from Hungary to Germany to the US, and featured interviews with a vast array of his friends and family. After making the festival circuit, the film hit DVD. Its two producers were my father Don Rhodes and Richard Sheffield.

Then I penned a book called *White Zombie: Anatomy of a Horror Film* (McFarland, 2002), a scholarly examination of Lugosi's wonderful 1932 movie. That was all in addition to lecturing about Lugosi around the world, appearing on numerous documentary films and television talk shows, doing the audio commentary for a DVD restoration of *White Zombie*, and writing a large number of essays and articles on Lugosi.

When the slate of projects cleared a bit, I began to think again about a book on Lugosi's last years. Hearing about another Lugosi book entitled *The Immortal Count*, though, made me have second thoughts. Surely its author would leave no stone unturned during his research.

But when *The Immortal Count* essentially became a reprint of a 1975 book updated with published information from modern historians like Gregory Mank, Tom Weaver, and myself, I felt differently. There was still room for this book on Lugosi's last years, and so I combined all the unused primary research of years ago with a series of research trips that took me to Hungary, Germany, and across the US. My old pal Richard Sheffield was back to help once again.

Why so much research? Well, the story of Lugosi's last years, the period from 1952-1956, can't be easily cut off from the rest of his life and career. Too much from the past caused three crises by 1952 and 1953: his career, his politics, and his marriage. The past was always encroaching on Lugosi in so many ways. And that fact makes this book a story about his entire life, even if it specifically examines those last five years.

That's all meant that this tale has finally been told, although it's been finished in time for the fiftieth anniversary of Lugosi's death, not the thirtieth as I once intended. I think it is a better book than it would have been two decades ago, so perhaps the delay was worthwhile.

Of course this book would not be possible had it not been for the kind help of so many libraries, archives, and museums around the world. My deepest appreciation to: the Alabama Department of Archives and History, the Andover-Harvard Theological Library, the Annenberg Rare Book and Manuscript Library at the University of Pennsylvania, the Ardmore Public Library–Ardmore, OK, the Arkansas

Historical Association–Fayettville, AR; the Asheville-Buncombe County Library–Asheville, NC; the Augusta Public Library–Augusta, GA; the Bancroft Library at the University of California; the Beverly Historical Society–Beverly, MA; the Birmingham Public Library–Birmingham, AL; the British Film Institute; the Bundesarchiv; the Chickasaw Regional Library System–Ardmore, OK; Cinegraph–Hamburg; the Classic Horror Film Board; Columbia University–Butler Library; the Detroit Public Library; the Durham County Library–Durham, NC; the Fall River Public Library; the Federal Bureau of Investigation (FOIA); the Forsyth County Public Library–Winston-Salem, NC; the Free Library of Philadelphia; the Greenville County Library System–Greenville, SC; the Hayden Library at Arizona State University; the Hillman Library at the University of Pittsburgh; the Historical Society of Pennsylvania–Philadelphia, PA; the Hungarian Film Institute; the Immigration and Naturalization Service (FOIA); the Institute of Contemporary History and Wiener Library Ltd–London; Katy Geissert Civic Center Library–Torrance, CA; the Library of Congress; Live Oak Public Libraries–Savannah; GA; the Margaret Herrick Library; the Maryland Historical Society; the Morristown and Morris Township Library–Morristown, New Jersey; the Museum of History; Ethnography; and Fine Arts–Lugoj, Romania; the National Archives of the United States; the National Library of Budapest; the National Park Service at Ellis Island; the New York Public Library–Lincoln Center; the New York State Historical Association; North Texas University–Denton, TX; the Oregon Historical Society; the Pottsville Free Public Library–Pottsville, PA; the Princeton University Library–Rare Books and Special Collections; the Public Library of Charlotte and Mecklenberg County–Charlotte, NC; the Public Library of Winston-Salem, NC; the Richland County Public Library–Columbia, SC; the Rochester Public Library–Rochester, NY; the Saint Louis Historical Society; the Screen Actors Guild; the Tennessee State Library and Archives–Nashville, TN; the University of California in Los Angeles; the University of Central Oklahoma; the US Senate Historical Office; and the Vasváry Collection at the Somogyi Library–Szeged.

Also, I would like to extend sincere thanks to the following individuals who have helped make this book a reality: Forrest J Ackerman, Tom Amorosi, Robert Anderson, Michelle Andrews Jerry Armellino, Carl Armstrong, Ryan Baker, Gyöngyi Balogh, Buddy Barnett, Wendy Barszcz, Mary Baumann, Doug Bentley, Scott Berman, the late Robert Bloch, the late Carroll Borland, Tom Brannan, Olaf Brill, Sean Brobst, Conrad Brooks, Barbara Browne, the late John Browne, Bob Burns, Steve Buscaino, Bart Bush, Petrina Calabalic, Paolo Caneppele, Allison Carmola, Dr. Juan Jose Camacho Romo, Allison Carmola, Jerry Carroll, Nancy Carver, Mario Chacon, George Chastain, Wiliene B. Chitwood, David Colton, Michael Copner, Tara C. Craig, Robert Cremer, Mária

Gary D. Rhodes in 1986 with the monocle Lugosi used in *Dracula* (1931) at the Biltmore Hotel in Los Angeles. This was the day he met Richard Sheffield.

Cseh, Louise Currie, Daniel Cutrara, Richard Daub, Michael J. David, William Daw, Michael DuBasso, Frank J. Dello Stritto, Patricia Dew, Kristin Dewey, Harald Dolezal, Jack Dowler, Michael DuBasso, Geraldine Duclow, Nancy Dupree, David Durston, Suzie Earp, Don English, Scott Essman, the late Philip R. Evans, Don Fellman, Michael Ferguson, Teddi Figge, Nancy Finlay, Norman Fist, Phillip Fortune, Dolores Fuller, Lawrence Fultz, Jr., Diane Gallagher, Kerry Gammill, Shawna Gandy, Kevin Gardner, Louanna Gardner, Ted Gargano, Michael George, the late Alex Gordon, Richard Gordon, Gogi Grant, Rudolph Grey, Jack Gumbrecht, Gordon R. Guy, Jimmy Haines, Stephen Hall, G. D. Hamann, Jon Hand, Lee Harris, Chuck Harter, Betsy Hendrix, Linda Hocking, David H. Hogan, Tim Hollis, Dawn Hugh, Durham Hunt, Roger Hurlburt, Florin Iepan, Charlie James, Alan Jeffrys, Christine Jochem, the late Steve Jochsberger, Bill Kaffenberger, Steve Kaplan–Collectables Records, Karola, David Katzman, Rose Marie Kerekjarto, Anthony Kerr, Nancy Kersey, Loretta King, Eugene Kirschenbaum, Ken Klosterman, the late Howard W. Koch, Leonard J. Kohl, Mrs. Samuel Kravitt, Michael Kronenberg, Steve Kronenberg, Rosemary Lands, "Larry the Wolf" of the Manimals, the late Reginald Le Borg, Dr. Michael Lee, Kay Linaker, Frank Liquori, the late Arthur Lubin, Tim Lucas, Donna Ludlow, Bela G. Lugosi, Esther Lynn, Leilani McCandless, Steve McFarland, Bob Madison, the late Paul Marco, Peter Michaels, Don Miller, Mark A. Miller, Joe Moe, Hattula Moholy-Nagy, "Baby Peggy" Montgomery, Barry Moreno, Lynn Naron, Jayne Altobell Newirth, Ted Newsom, Henry Nicolella, Margo Nicolet, Dennis Northcott, Noémi Saly, John Norris, Maila "Vampira" Nurmi, Jim Nye, Frances O'Donnell, Gaidos Oliviu, June Ormond, Tim Ormond, László Ottovay, Margaret Papai, Charlene Dodenhoff Patterson, AnnaLee Pauls, Father Mike Paraniuk, Dennis Payne, Sammy Petrillo, Victor Pierce, William Pirola, Michael H. Price, William V. Rauscher, Mike Ravnitzky, Robert Rees, Jeffrey Roberts, George Robinson, Matthew Rodgers, Honey Ryan, Kregg Sanders, Carleton Savell, Becky Scarborough, Robert J. Scheffel, Emile O. Schmidt, Bruce Scivally, Dan Sehested, Daniel Sheahan, the late Ruth Azalea Sheffield, Dr. Robert Shomer, Margaret Sides, Robert Simpson, Don G. Smith, George Snell, Roy Spence, Michael Spencer, Dr. John Springer, Billy C. Stagner, David Stenn, Vera Surányi, Gary Svehla, Elemer Szasz, Dr. Andor Sziklay, Larry Sutliff, László Tábori, Brian Taggert, Brian Taves, Maurice Terenzio, the late Harry Thomas, Mario Toland, Suzanne Troxel, Dallas Turner, John Ulakovic, Richard Valley, JoAnn Van Vranken, Dr. Steven Béla Várdy, Stratton Walling, Jon Wang, Leo L. Ward, Bill Warren, Alexander Webb, Marianne Weldon, Galen Wilkes, Chuck Windley, the late Robert Wise, Clay Withrow, John Wooley, Ann Wright, Valerie Yaros, and Gregory Zatirka.

I would also beg the indulgence of any person (or library or archive) who helped whose name is absent from these lists. For better or worse, the many years of research may have caused a name to slip through my fingers.

Two names that cannot be absent are Bill Chase and Dennis Phelps. Both are important Lugosi collectors, and both have kindly shared many rare images for this book. Dennis was also extremely nice in letting me use materials from the original and authentic Bela Lugosi scrapbook he owns that covers Lugosi movies from *Broadminded* (1931) to *Night of Terror* (1933).

Beau Foutz and Mária Kórász also deserve special mention too. Beau kindly did a great deal of research on Lugosi's 1944 tour of *Arsenic and Old Lace*, as well as Lugosi's 1947 appearance in New Jersey with Bill Neff. Similarly, Mária spent

Richard Sheffield and Hope Lininger Lugosi in Hawaii in 1996.

hour after hour examining all of the theatre publications of Szeged, kindly copying me all of the reviews and articles on Lugosi when he was there in 1910 and 1911.

Gregory William Mank provided much insight, encouragement, and some very helpful proofreading at a late stage in this project. Greg ranks surely as one of the foremost horror film historians.

A very special thank you to Noémi Saly, who is the granddaughter of Lugosi's first wife, Ilona Szmik. She was extremely kind to share the stories that her grandmother told her about Lugosi, which have shed much light on his early years.

Another person whose help I greatly appreciate is the late Hope Lininger Lugosi. We corresponded as far back as 1987, but the high point came when Richard Sheffield and I interviewed her in Hawaii in 1996. Though she spoke to a few other historians over the years, Hope never authorized any of her talks for publication. Not until the interview she kindly gave us, which she approved for use in both my film *Lugosi: Hollywood's Dracula* and this book.

Lugosi collector David Wentink became an enormously important figure in the writing of this book as well. He kindly shared a number of rare Lugosi still photographs. He spent hour after hour squinting at microfilm machines in California chasing after Lugosi in old newspapers. And he conducted two final interviews necessary for the book's completion. One was Maila Nurmi, and the other was Paul Marco, who died mere hours after David finished speaking with him.

And then there was the towering figure of horror film historian Tom Weaver, whose proofreading and fact-checking of every line has been crucial. Research and interviews too. But more than anything else, his encouragement and friendship in every way, shape, and form is the very reason this book has happened.

Thanks also to my parents Don and Phyllis, as well as my fiancée Marina McDonnell. They have all put up with this Lugosi madness for so long, and have kindly encouraged it.

And finally, my deepest appreciation to Richard Sheffield, the man whose name is also on the cover of this book. His memories, his help in arranging interviews, his fact-checking, and his two decades of close friendship. What more can I add, save our ongoing tag line to each other: friends till the end.

Bela Lugosi as Dracula in a 1927 portrait.

CHAPTER ONE

Twenty-Five Years

Autumn. New Haven, Connecticut on September 17, 1927. A chill was in the air when townspeople sat down to read the Saturday issue of the *Journal-Courier*. They saw stories about President Coolidge and General Pershing. Cotton prices, murder cases, and products for sale. Page after page of them. Turning to entertainment news, readers might have noticed an ad for the final evening performance of Louis Bromfield's play *The House of Women* at the Sam S. Shubert Theatre. And if they were movie fans, they might have read a review of the new silent horror film, *The Cat and the Canary* with Laura La Plante.

The New Haven critic praised La Plante's acting, and suggested that the "gruesome and thrilling events follow fast and the mystery becomes more baffling until a sudden stripping of the veil lays bare an astounding plot has failed."[1] The failed plot was described as "astounding" because *The Cat and the Canary* involves an all-too-human criminal in an old dark house that only *seems* to be haunted. Beautifully directed with very eerie sets, *The Cat and the Canary* was emblematic of an entire style of films and stage plays that invoked the supernatural merely as a ruse to scare characters and audience members alike.

Actually, from the Victorian era to 1927, the US stage drama and horror film were largely devoid of the supernatural. Despite popular interest in topics like spiritualism, the idea of the supernatural unleashed remained in the realm of candlelit ghost stories and a few academic studies like Dorothy Scarborough's *The Supernatural in Modern English Fiction* (1917).[2] If the supernatural appeared at all, it was generally introduced to cause laughs, whether in any number of early films featuring playful imps or in, say, a later Will Rogers movie like *One Glorious Day* (1922).

Even these examples are exceptions, though, as the emergent mass media indulged instead in popular tales like *The Cat and the Canary*. In fact, some of the New Haven citizens who went to that movie in 1927 might well have recognized that its story was similar to prior films like *Midnight Faces* (1926) and *The Bat* (1926). They may have also recognized *The Cat and the Canary* from its own earlier stage incarnation. In the back of their minds, audiences probably suspected in advance that no ghosts really walked in the film's old house. A dramatic presentation of the supernatural was, after all, largely unknown at the time.

Whether or not newspaper readers in New Haven were interested in Bromfield's *The House of Women* or *The Cat and the Canary*, they possibly read an advertisement for a play that would open two days later; it would replace *The House of Women* at the Shubert. Presented by Horace Liveright and staged by Ira Hards, it was not just a play, but "The Vampire Play." It was *Dracula*. The ad told of *Dracula*'s three-year success on the London stage, and rather inauspiciously listed eight cast members. One of them was Bela Lugosi.

Wisely chosen for the part, Lugosi was not a young man. Evil needs years. Even if not as old as Dracula's five centuries, Lugosi was on the verge of turning 45. In 1927, he was celebrating his 25th anniversary of being a theater actor, having first performed in Hungary circa 1902. From there it was the Hungarian stage and films in the teens, then German movies, and then arriving in the US in 1921. That meant a few Broadway roles and a number of films before *Dracula–The Vampire Play* really launched his US career. If Lugosi associated himself with any particular roles, it would likely have been as Shakespeare's Romeo, which he had played in Hungary in 1910, and Madách's Adam in *Az ember trajédiája* (*The Tragedy of Man*), which he had staged himself in New York in 1922. Adam, the Son of God, who travels through world history with Lucifer lurking near. Ever near.

By opening night on September 19,1927, New Haven audiences understood that Bela Lugosi would play a character none-too-different than Lucifer. Lugosi had crossed the threshold into evil, imbuing the role with both the Mephistopheles of the past and his own personality of the present. With the Shubert curtain open and the audience silent, Lugosi awaited his cue to step finally onto the stage as Dracula for the very first time. Even with the first performance underway, Lugosi still had to remain backstage. Page after page of dialogue passed as every other character was introduced. Jonathan Harker and his beloved Lucy, who has recently taken ill. Her father Dr. Seward and the erstwhile Van Helsing. Even the fly-eating Renfield, a patient at Dr. Seward's asylum. And then Seward's maid introduces him: "Count Dracula."

Lugosi walked slowly onto the stage, passed the maid and into the full view of the audience. He was polished, continental, and distinguished. His thick Hungarian accent finally echoed into the theater hall; Dracula had arrived. "Gentleman," he said, bowing to Seward, Van Helsing, and Harker. Lucy registers a thrill at seeing him, and in return he asks: "Miss Seward, how are you? You are looking more yourself this evening." The subtle irony becomes clear as the play moves forward. Dracula has already made Lucy in her own words "unclean," and he plans to make her his bride, one of many. He has bitten her, sucking her blood and violating her body, just as he has already done to her friend Mina.[3] As Van Helsing and the others slowly learn, Dracula is a "living corpse, sustained by the blood of the living." Dracula is an offense to God Himself; Van Helsing rightly crowns him "satanic," a prince of darkness.

Only one review of the play appeared in the New Haven press, in the *Journal-Courier*. On the one hand, the critic acknowledged that the Bram Stoker novel *Dracula* had "thrilled two generations of readers with the horror of its story."[4] After all, news of the novel appeared in the US press as early as 1897, and from the time of its first American publication in 1899,

The very first advertisement for *Dracula* that mentioned Bela Lugosi's name. Published in the *New Haven Journal-Courier* on September 17, 1927.

the book had remained in print.[5]

On the other hand, the critic still believed it necessary to mention the character's name is "pronounced Drak-ula," and that the mention of a "Vampire Play" needed clarification. Readers were instructed that it was not the "modern vernacular" usage of the word vampire, as in a Theda Bara-type of female character who bleeds men of money and passion. The vampire Dracula was instead a "supernatural demon or ghost that sucks on the blood of persons asleep."[6]

Overall, the critic believed that the cast was "splendid," and that *Dracula* was "the most weird, thrilling play yet presented to an audience. It differs from all thrillers in that it deals with the supernatural and consequently there is no awkward denouncement–no 'dream' at its conclusion."[7] *Dracula* was definitely not *The Cat and the Canary* or any of its predecessors.

True, Stoker's novel had created *Dracula*, and actor Raymond Huntley had played the character with great success in the 1924 London stage produc-

Above: Lugosi as Dracula in a rare portrait from 1927. *Below:* Lugosi as Adam, the first man. As printed in *Szinházi Ujság* (New York), March 15, 1922.

tion. But things changed for the vampire in America. Through Lugosi, Dracula was born again, and the birthplace was New Haven that September 19th of 1927. It was a new kind of character for the 20th century US stage and cinema. There really was no dream at the conclusion. Only Dracula; only Lugosi. The embodiment of supernatural evil was on display, and popular culture would never be the same.

After four performances in New Haven, the play quickly moved onto three other cities for brief engagements.[8] "The audience was on edge from the very start and under a tense strain," a critic in Stamford, Connecticut wrote.[9] And then by October, New York theatergoers got to see Lugosi on Broadway. Month after month of successes at the Fulton Theatre for well over 250 performances.[10] On one evening alone, eight audience members fainted; that, or eight theater plants did some acting of their own.[11] Either way, Alexander Woollcott felt it necessary to forewarn ticket buyers: "Ye who have fits prepare to throw them now."[12]

While still conquering the Great White Way, Lugosi and some other cast members even gathered at a radio station to offer an abbreviated version of the play in the theater of the air. They performed over Newark's station WJZ on the afternoon of March 30, 1928.[13] At that time, the powerful WJZ could be picked up by radios in various parts of the US, far outside the confines of New Jersey.[14] Lugosi and Dracula and the supernatural had merged for the first time with the mass media.

Then, once the Broadway version closed, Lugosi appeared in the play on the West Coast in 1928, 1929, and 1930. He went on to star in the 1931 Universal Studios film *Dracula*, which ignited a cycle of horror films that essentially lasted until 1945.[15] But of the large number of horror films that came out in that period, only a small number involved the supernatural. Most tended to deal with mad scientists of the Dr. Jekyll and Henry Frankenstein school. Science and religion duelled in film after film, with bad men meddling in things God meant them to leave alone.

Certainly there were a couple of other horror movie characters rooted in the supernatural. The original film version of *The Mummy* had a bandaged Egyptian priest come back to life, but unlike Dracula the character simply wanted to reunite with his long-lost love.[16] There was also *The Wolf Man* (1941), as famously portrayed by Lon Chaney Jr. But while in human form, the character Larry Talbot in that film and others tried to end the supernatural curse on his soul.[17] No, Dracula was definitely unique. As portrayed by Lugosi, the vampire lusted after women and their blood; it wasn't love or guilt that drove his actions. Self-preservation to continue existing century after century guided his actions. Dracula truly was the cinematic sign of supernatural evil.

In September 1952, exactly 25 years after New Haven, Lugosi was still standing in the long shadow of Dracula. By that time, he had played the role some 1,000 times.[18] "I didn't know if you were a success as one kind of character in this country, you're branded," he told a reporter that year. "The play was such a success they haven't let me play any decent characters since."[19] And he was right. That very year he played Dracula onstage in New York opposite the young actress Jan Weber.[20] By that time, he openly wondered whether Dracula had been his curse or his fortune.[21] For a quarter of a century, it had seemingly been both.

Lugosi as Dracula and Hazel Whitmore as Lucy in a West Coast stage version of the play. Photographed in either 1928 or 1929.

That Lugosi was Dracula not only meant a typecasting that limited his artistic outlets, it also meant that he was attached to a film genre that hardly proved to be a consistent source of income. The threat of censors and moral groups and changing tastes always hovered nearby. As a compulsive reader of newspapers, Lugosi perhaps saw a 1952 article in the *New York Times* about the troubles the police in a midwestern town were having with a "nearly hysterical woman," who was "suffering delusions as a result of having seen too many 'horror' movies."[22]

Ever since the 1931 film version of

Dracula, fears of horror movies extended well beyond any shivering spines in darkened theatres. After all, what would they do to the moral fabric of society? What would they do to the children? And what would they do to Lugosi's career, a career that after New Haven became inseparable from Dracula and horror? A career that between 1927 and 1952 *had* to feed off of horror just as Dracula fed off of blood.

By 1932, Hollywood clearly understood the perils of releasing horror movies, with some members of the industry crying out for the studios to stop producing them.[23] The moral groups and churches would protest so strongly as to hurt all of Hollywood, so it was believed. But money, a lot of money, could be made from horror in those days of the Great Depression, and the success of films like Lugosi's *White Zombie* (1932) meant moviemakers would err on the side of the almighty dollar.

Onstage as Dracula in the late 1920s.

A debate over nationalized censorship in 1933 led Roosevelt-appointee Dr. A Lawrence Lowell to discuss the need to curb such movies, given that children suffered "symptoms akin to shell-shock from horror films."[24] And the Payne Fund Studies of the 1930s conducted numerous case studies of youngsters that seemed to reinforce the view that horror films were bad for them:

> What I played after I came home from the movies [was] *Dracula*. I pretended I was the vampire. I played especially good when I had to suck the blood out of the warden's daughter. I loved to play the part where I disappear. I didn't like to have a big nail driven into my heart and make me lifeless, but it had to be done. I am still alive–thanks to god.[25]

Researcher Herbert Blumer recorded those words, a ten-year-old boy's story about pretending to be Lugosi. The boy may have had a lot of fun playing a vampire game, but it was still hardly the kind of tale that made parents happy.

And it wasn't just the children that were said to be affected, even afflicted, by horror. In 1935, one William J. Robinson, M.D., wrote to the *New York Times* worried about films like Lugosi's *Mark of the Vampire*. He suggested that it could have damaging effects on the "mental and nervous systems of not only unstable but even normal men, women, and children."[26] Silly perhaps, but the good doctor wasn't alone. A 1936 study found that "both adults and children find horror pictures bad," since they caused varying degrees of sleeplessness in moviegoers.[27]

Sometime that same year, Hollywood stopped making horror movies. Curiously, though, it wasn't the censors or moral groups or medical doctors in the US that

Lugosi the man in a 1929 portrait.

forced the decision. Instead, it was the result of the British Board of Film Censors declaring that exhibitors in the UK couldn't allow anyone under the age of 16 to see movies given an "H" (for "Horrific") certificate. That effectively meant the end of horror films being shown in England. The loss of such an important overseas market meant that Universal and the other US studios ended horror production.[28]

During that period, Lugosi was virtually out of work. "[Hollywood] branded me with the stamp of an animal," Lugosi said. "I was a horror actor, an animal, and they would not give me a chance."[29] Then in 1938 he and his fourth wife Lillian had their first and only child, Bela G. Lugosi, at a moment when his financial situation had gone from bad to worse. Miraculously, though, the Regina Theater in Beverly Hills booked a triple bill of *Dracula*, *Frankenstein* (1931), and *The Son of Kong* (1933).[30] Three old horror movies that the manager had rented because they were cheap. To everyone's surprise, audiences members drove in from miles away, forming long lines at every screening.

"One day I drive past and see my name and big lines of people all around," Lugosi once said. "I wonder what is giving away to people [*sic*], maybe bacon or vegetables. But it is the comeback of horror, and I come back."[31] A nationwide reissue of *Dracula* and *Frankenstein* took the country by storm. And new horror films like *Son of Frankenstein* (1939) meant new work for Lugosi, as well as a return to financial stability.[32] But the comeback, of course, had been predicated on little more than the chance decision of a single film exhibitor; such was the fragility of a career built on being Dracula.

The return of horror not only meant Lugosi's reappearance on the silver screen, but also the return of the moral outcry. In November 1939, a hundred mothers in Brooklyn argued that horror movies were bad for neighborhood children.[33] By 1941, the head of the "Schools Motion Picture Committee" complained in the *New York Times* about horror films like Lon Chaney Jr.'s *Man Made Monster* (1941).[34] That same year, another *New York Times* article asked the perennial question if movies were good or bad for children, particularly the "delicious terror" films they so enjoyed:

> [An adult witness] says that at horror films some of them hide their heads and whimper, but it is doubtful if any could be persuaded to leave the theater short of force. They foresee what is going to happen before it does, and groan apprehensively. ...During tense moments, several of the children arch their back against the chair and draw their feet onto the seat. Then as the crisis passes, first one leg and then another dangles down, until they are again slumped comfortably chewing their thumbs.[35]

The children, oh the children. They loved the films, even if they did occasionally have to hide their eyes. But the adults, they were even more scared. Scared of what these horror movies would do to junior.

By 1944, older kids seemed to be at risk too. The Baltimore police commissioner announced that horror movies were the cause of the city's rampant juvenile delinquency. A strange notion? Probably, but he developed his hypothesis based on an earlier report from Portland, Oregon. Police there complained regularly that–thanks to scary movies––the streets were "filled with young boys and girls much of the night."[36]

Of course, the attempts of police departments and moral groups to stop horror films were meager compared to what happened in New York City at a 1946 screening of *Dr. Terror's House of Horrors*, a compendium of clips built out of such old movies as Lugosi's *White Zombie* (1932). During a particularly tense scene, plaster on the underside of the balcony fell onto the audience; nineteen injured moviegoers had to be moved to a nearby hospital for treatment.[37] The ceiling had literally come down on the audience, and of course the show stopped.

Lugosi the fiend in a 1929 image posed for *Theatre Magazine.*

That incident seems to be a perfect metaphor for the horror film in 1946, because the ceiling had really come down on the entire genre that year. With the war over, the platelets shifted in Hollywood. The horror movie basically vanished. In 1946, Lugosi made only one film, which was released as *Scared to Death* in 1947. Despite being shot in color, it was little more than a relic of an earlier era. Like Lugosi, its director Christy Cabanne dated back to the silent film days.

Why did the horror film simply go away at the end of the war? That Hollywood suffered a great deal economically in the late forties is true, but disaster didn't hit until 1947. Horror films virtually disappear in 1946, a year in which the studios actually garnered large receipts.[38] In a 1946 essay, Curt Siodmak–who wrote such films as *The Wolf Man* (1941) and *Frankenstein Meets the Wolf Man* (1943)–claimed that the sheer number of horror films that emerged during World War II were inextricably linked to it. "Like sickness being fought with toxins of the same virus, people flocked to see horror pictures, to find release from [their war] nightmares, though they were frightened at the same time."[39]

Perhaps Siodmak's theory is correct; maybe audiences no longer needed the toxins of Hollywood horror. After all, once Germany was defeated, the term "horror film" made front page news time after time when reporters used it to describe

An advertisement promoting the Realart reissue of *The Raven* (1935) and *Murders in the Rue Morgue* (1932).

footage that *wasn't* shot in Southern California. "Horror film" instead meant emerging images of Nazi atrocities. In response to their first public appearance in New York, the "camp horror films" were described as featuring the "most frightful pictures of death and woe ever exhibited in American news-reels."[40] The horror film and war newsreel had become one and the same, at least for the press.

Towards the end of 1952, Curtis Harrington–later a noted film director–published a study on horror films in which he discussed how quickly their popularity had diminished after the second world war, expressing his surprise that "even Universal gave them up."[41] Once again Lugosi's film career was disrupted. That the 1952 *New York Times* account of the woman suffering delusions was blamed on horror films added insult to injury, as Hollywood really wasn't even making those kinds of films any more.

A quarter of a century had passed since New Haven, and supernatural evil was definitely not en vogue. As the *LA Times* wrote in 1951, "Horror movies have been scarce of late."[42] To the degree the horror film continued in Hollywood at all, it was of a new breed. It was modern. And it seemed to have been creeping up on Lugosi ever since the fifties had begun. Slowly, but surely.

In 1951, Lugosi toured England in a disastrous production of *Dracula—The Vampire Play*.[43] In rather shoddy style, the production went through the motions of 1927.[44] Certainly a surviving Pathe newsreel does show Lugosi smiling on that trip. And he must have appreciated the attention from, say, the throngs of children that awaited him at the stage door in Belfast.[45] But as Richard Gordon–who helped arrange the tour–recalled, the show "smacked of 'poverty row' and the disappointment of being surrounded by such amateurish elements crushed Bela's hopes and reduced him to desperation."[46]

In those old lines of dialogue, the character Van Helsing calls Dracula by various names, but he once refers to him simply as "the thing." Lugosi heard that description

As Dracula in the 1931 Universal Studios film.

Even wearing a sweater, Lugosi appears menacing in this portrait from the early-to-mid 1930s.

throughout the 1951 tour, but perhaps he didn't realize how it resonated with new meaning in Hollywood. Scarcely had Lugosi left the US for England when "The Thing" became attached to a new kind of monster, one from outer space, via RKO Studios. Walter Winchell actually wrote in 1951 that "previewers say *The Thing* makes *Dracula* look like a petunia."[47] Out with the old; in with the new. True or not, *The Thing From Another World* reinvigorated the horror film that died after World War II, bringing with it a kind of contemporary relevance that the science-fiction/horror film of the fifties would feed on. Flying saucers and the atomic age. In 1952, Louis Berg of the *LA Times* wrote:

The thriller-chiller specialists out on the coast never got much further than the quaint 19th-century notions of Frankenstein, Dracula, vampires and zombies. When this limited Gothic vein threatened to peter out, they resorted to clumsy sequels. *Destination Moon* [1950] got away from the philters and potions, it abandoned the old-time chemical laboratory for the supersonic, electronic, atomic science of tomorrow. Others followed suit.[48]

Berg was right, of course. A new cycle of films was underway, one where viewers had to keep watching the skies. Movement through the clouds, caused by our rockets or their ships.

At times, Lugosi's own films of the thirties and forties had tried to give a hint of Things to Come. The comedy film *International House* (1933) with W. C. Fields and the low-budget mystery movie *Murder By Television* (1935) both had plots revolving around the topic of TV. The following decade in *Voodoo Man* (1944), Lugosi's Dr. Marlowe had a televisor on hand to watch passersby at his house of horror. At that time, his films sported technology that wasn't present in any average person's home. Spurned by Hollywood as the 1950s approached, Lugosi desperately tried to break into the small screen that he had once controlled in his old films.

But his appearance on *Suspense*, the radio show hit-turned-TV program, in October 1949 hardly caused a favorable reaction. *The Billboard* lambasted his performance, in which they believed he "failed to bestow an iota of reality on what appears to have been a fine and meaty part. ... Lugosi almost seemed to walk into the spot [of the climax] with alacrity, and the tension which had been established ... was vitiated."[49]

Later that same month, Lugosi was reunited with comedy team Olsen and Johnson—with whom he had appeared 18 years earlier in the film *Fifty Million*

Frenchmen (1931)–on the *Texaco Star Theatre* with Milton Berle.[50] Reviews of that show were okay, with *Variety* mentioning that the skit "came off well." "Well," despite Berle's improvised line bemoaning Lugosi's comedic skill. "You kill people on the screen; you also kill jokes," he jabbed.[51]

At any rate, by January 1950, Lugosi and Anne Russell appeared on the television show *Versatile Varieties*.[52] That same month, he and Arlene Francis appeared on *Celebrity Time*.[53] In May 1950, he showed up on *Starlit Time*.[54] Ventriloquist Paul Winchell hosted Lugosi on his evening program in October 1950.[55] And then in April 1951, he was on the *Charlie Chester Show* in England.[56] Even "Mrs. Bela Lugosi,"Lugosi's fourth wife Lillian, made her TV debut, appearing on WABD's program *Okay Mother* in October 1950.[57]

Along with TV, Lugosi continued to make numerous guest appearances on radio shows of the era. In 1950, Allen Funt included Lugosi in a stunt to scare a woman on his *Candid Microphone*; listeners heard her banter with Lugosi, but it took the press to describe what radio couldn't show: the *LA Times* claimed she "clutched her throat protectively" when it was revealed who Lugosi was.[58] The following year, in 1951, Lugosi played an arsonist on *Crime Does Not Pay*.[59] And most curious of all was the time that Lugosi "discarded a Dracula outfit for a kitchen apron" when he visited the

Betty Crocker Magazine of the Air in January 1951. A newspaper account claimed "Mr. Lugosi told his air audience of several Hungarian delicacies–also of how he and Mrs. Lugosi, now celebrating their 18th annivesary, first met."[60]

The collective performances seemed to prove that Lugosi was suited for early television. In January 1952, the syndicated column "In Hollywood" even announced that Lugosi would "face the TV film cameras in a new horror and shivers series."[61] He had just arrived back in New York after the British Dracula tour, and the thought of having his own TV show must have been heartening. But nothing finally came of the idea; it just faded into the airwaves.

Ensconced back in Hollywood in May 1952, Lugosi happily told a reporter that, "Now I am filming *Bela Lugosi Meets the Gorilla Man*, which is not bad publicity."[62] It was his first US film in four years, and this time his name was in the title. That had only happened once before to a Hollywood horror actor, with *Abbott and Costello Meet the Killer, Boris Karloff* (1949). Boris Karloff of *Frankenstein* (1931) fame, often considered Lugosi's rival. The

An advertisement heralding the reissue of
Dracula and *Frankenstein*.

Onstage in Reading, Pennsylvania in 1948 with Greg Rodgers as Renfield (left) and Maury Hill as Van Helsing (right). *(Courtesy of George R. Snell)*

stuff of Hollywood legend. The stuff that dreams–and nightmares–were made of.

Rechristened *Bela Lugosi Meets a Brooklyn Gorilla*, the result was a crazy film that had Steve Calvert running around in a gorilla suit.[63] But it meant that Lugosi was back in Hollywood movies, being directed by his old friend William Beaudine.[64] And he was the star, or at least the costar along with the comedy team of Duke Mitchell and Sammy Petrillo.

The duo's schtick was nothing more than imitating the reigning kings of Hollywood comedy, Dean Martin and Jerry Lewis. Petrillo bore such an uncanny resemblance to Jerry Lewis that Lewis had once featured him on his television show.[65] But this new Lugosi film was different; Petrillo represented a unique kind of cinematic plagiarism. By the end of July 1952, Martin and Lewis's producer Hal Wallis had demanded to see a print of the film. One gossip column warned that "there could be a restrainer."[66]

Regardless, not many audiences saw the film that autumn. In October, it did play Los Angeles on the bottom of a double bill with *Untamed Women*.[67] The *LA Times* thought Lugosi was "growing more sinister with age," but the few other critical notices were generally negative.[68] The press was also reporting that Mitchell and

Petrillo were "currently being sued by Martin and Lewis for infringement on their act."[69] Outside of its legal problems, the movie hardly generated any buzz.

In the autumn of 1952, a *New York Times* crossword puzzle featured "Mr. Lugosi" in one of its word games. The correct answer was "Bela," number eighty across.[70] Perhaps Lugosi saw it while reading the *Times*; perhaps a friend pointed it out to him. Maybe not. Anyhow, Lugosi was trying to work out another puzzle at that moment. It had to do with many other times his name was in the newspapers that year. The past few years, really. His name was showing up with extreme regularity, but not in any way that was helping him or his career.

In New York in 1949, for example, a theater played *The Invisible Ray* (1936) with Karloff and Lugosi.[71] That same year in Chicago, a theater screened Lugosi in *The Gorilla* (1939).[72] In Los Angeles in December 1950, audiences could catch Lugosi in *Black Friday* (1940) or *The Ghost of Frankenstein* (1942).[73] In Dallas in 1951, a ticket buyer could easily see a double bill of Lugosi in *The Raven* (1935) and *The Wolf Man* (1941), or catch his *Murders in the Rue Morgue* (1932) paired with Karloff in *Bride of Frankenstein* (1935).[74] And his old B-movies like *The Devil Bat* (1940) appeared countless times in small towns during the late forties.[75] Even the old theater gimmicks were still trotted out; at a "witching hour" double feature of Lugosi horror movies in Ohio in 1949, free smelling salts were available for "those who can't take it."[76] Revivals of old Lugosi films were happening over and over again in city after city, town after town.

Most notable of all was a major reissue of the original *Dracula* (1931).[77] Throughout 1952, the film, paired with *Frankenstein*, turned up across the country. Three different Los Angeles theaters played the double bill that year.[78] The double bill came from the same source as several of the other films, Jack Broder's Realart Re-Releasing Company. By October 1952, Broder had grossed $18,000,000 by reissuing a variety of old Universal films.[79] But none of this brought Lugosi any royalties.

And given the predominance of science fiction, the horror revivals often took place at either small theaters or drive-ins. An example of what was happening can be seen in the *Washington Post* in September 1950. A large ad for the fifth record-breaking week of *Destination Moon* jumps out from the page, while a reader has to squint to find an announcement for the reissue of Lugosi's *Night Monster* (1942).[80]

Television was also a part of the same problem. In 1952, for example, a newspaper reader in Texas may have noticed the article "Mr. Lugosi Featured in Chiller" in the *Dallas Morning News*. "Mr. Horror himself," the newspaper claimed, would be the first attraction on the Channel 8 program *Mystery Manor*. And the year before,

Captured by photographer Edith Sherman in a portrait as Dracula circa 1950.

Lugosi in England in 1951, as photographed by a Pathe newsreel cameraman.

another newspaper listed Lugosi as appearing on a program hosted by Freddie Bartholomew. But Lugosi was only on these programs via his old movies; Bartholomew was just introducing the 1935 Lugosi film *Phantom Ship*.[81]

Over and over again throughout 1952, they appeared on TV: *The Death Kiss* (1933), *The Mysterious Mr. Wong* (1935), *Invisible Ghost* (1941), *Return of the Ape Man* (1944), and *Scared to Death* (1947).[82] That same year, Washington D.C.'s WTOP accidentally advertised "Bela Lugosi is at his horrifying best in *Light Zombie*," when of course they really meant *White Zombie* (1932).[83] And every one of these films had been broadcast before, as had others like *Shadow of Chinatown* (1936), *The Devil Bat* (1940), *The Corpse Vanishes* (1942), and *The Ape Man* (1943).[84]

In 1952, Lugosi turned seventy years old. At that age and with the financial need for more work, he was not only competing against the lack of new horror film production and the dominance of science-fiction, but he was also competing against himself. His old self, in the form of constant reissues of his old movies in theaters and television. To the degree there seemed to be room for the actor at all—this symbol of the cinematic supernatural and all things gothic—it was generally for the way he used to be.

The film *Bela Lugosi Meets a Brooklyn Gorilla*—despite its poor reviews, limited screenings, and threatened legal action—does prove that Lugosi wasn't completely invisible in 1952. After all, he still rated mention in an occasional gossip column; for example, James Copp's "Skylarking" in the *Los Angeles Times* mentioned he had been spotted at LA's "House of Murphy."[85] More importantly, though, the press soon announced Lugosi would get yet another chance at the movies.

To bring Lugosi back to the screen and situate him in the sci-fi world of the fifties, his friend and admirer Alex Gordon crafted a story that linked the laboratories of old mad scientist films with the atom age. "[Bela and I] spent much time together, finally evolving a script entitled *The Atomic Monster*," Gordon said years later.[86] Shooting would start at the end of October 1952, with Helen Gilbert playing the female lead.[87] It would be the first of three Gordon-produced Lugosi films that Jack Broder would release through Realart.[88] But Gordon recalled that, "for various reasons, *The Atomic Monster* did not get off the ground."[89]

Attorney Samuel Z. Arkoff later remembered that Broder agreed to read the script, but soon told Gordon that interested in moving forward. Then strangely, a few months later, Broder's Realart company released a film called *The Atomic Monster*. It was a reissue title tacked onto an old Lon Chaney Jr. movie, *Man Made Monster* (1941), the one that the "Schools Motion Picture Committee" had railed about on its original release. Arkoff also recalled Gordon's outrage at the fact Broder stole his title. When confronted, Broder pled innocent. He and Gordon did reach a monetary settlement, but that was of little help to Lugosi.[90]

BROOKLYN CHUMPS BECOME ISLAND MONKEYS IN A JUNGLE FULL OF LAFFS !

JACK BRODER PRODUCTIONS presents

BELA LUGOSI *meets a* **BROOKLYN GORILLA**

Introducing

DUKE **MITCHELL** · SAMMY **PETRILLO**

with **CHARLITA** · MURIEL **LANDERS** AND **RAMONA**, THE CHIMP

Associate Producer HERMAN COHEN · Produced by MAURICE DUKE
Directed by WILLIAM BEAUDINE · Screenplay by TIM RYAN

From the press sheet for *Bela Lugosi Meets a Brooklyn Gorilla* (1952).

So despite Alex Gordon's best efforts, in late 1952, Lugosi was left without a film title, let alone a new film. He was left to look back over 25 years of *Dracula*, a quarter-century of vampires that haunted his every move since New Haven. He looked back over the five decades since his stage career began in 1902. But to make money, to make ends meet, Lugosi had to look to the future as well. And he did that knowing he would have to carve out a place for himself in an era increasingly known as the Space Age. An era that could replay the supernatural evil of the past through Realart Re-Releasing or late night TV.

CHAPTER TWO

Are You Now or Have You Ever Been?

Bela Lugosi had more troubles in the early 1950s than his crumbling career. A Red Scare burned its way across America, scorching Lugosi while leaving so many others charred beyond recognition. At times, it seemed as if the entire movie industry was in flames.

The dangers of infiltration. Communists were in Hollywood, allegedly encrypting the Wrong Ideas into their art. They were everywhere, it seemed: in the closet, and under the bed as well. Those science fiction films that kept Lugosi out of work thrived on rampant xenophobia. But if anything, the surreptitious Reds were a lot scarier than flying saucers landing at movie theatres. Hence Joseph McCarthy and McCarthyism. Hence HUAC, the House Committee on UnAmerican Activities. And hence the Hollywood Ten, a group sentenced to prison time for contempt of Congress.[1]

By the autumn of 1952, a time when Lugosi was hoping to star in *The Atomic Monster*, the US government was looking into whether or not he should be deported.[2] After all, at a 1949 hearing of the Senate Subcommittee on Immigration and Naturalization, undercover FBI agent John J. Huber named Lugosi as having contributed services to the "Communist front."[3] The Reverend Steven E. Balogh identified him as a member of the "Communist movement," as did Paul Nadányi.[4] And the most extensive and damning testimony came from the Reverend George E. K. Borshy.[5] All of these allegations still carried weight some three years after they were spoken.

But were they true? Was Lugosi a Communist, or a Communist sympathizer? The questions are easy and quick to ask, but the answers are convoluted and complicated. And they're rooted in the long history of Lugosi's political philosophy. Roots all the way back to Hungary, twisting and turning since the early days of his career.

Lugosi's interest in politics and unions stems to at least 1907, when he helped start an "Actor's Federation" to fight discrimination against Hungarian actors by Romanian theatre management.[6] Where did those inclinations come from? Though it's difficult to say with any certainty, he had to have been aware of the organized movements and strikes led by peasant Hungarian farmers in the 1890s and early 20th century.[7]

Then Lugosi enlisted in World War I, serving from 1914 to March 1916 on both the western and eastern fronts.[8] He later claimed he was the strongest man in his regiment.[9] And it was likely patriotism for Hungary that led him to fight, rather than any sense of obligation to the reigning Hungarian bourgeoisie or the country's semi-colonial dependence on Austria and Germany. After all, the desertion rate

Lugosi in the hospital in 1916 recovering from
wounds received during World War I.

among Hungarians in the Austro-Hungarian army grew rapidly, and many Hungarian troops had to be driven into battle with guns at their own backs.[10] No, Lugosi likely fought for the Hungarian peasants, the Hungarian worker.

During the war, the plight of Hungarian workers worsened, fomenting further distrust in their leaders and cultivating a climate where the number of strikes increased greatly during 1915 and 1916. The October Revolution in Russia intensified workers' demands in Hungary. Even more strikes followed, including a major 1918 stand against the war. Workers' councils set up to demand peace, as well as universal suffrage. The general mood of the masses was to solve problems from the left side of politics. And when the government in Budapest essentially fell apart in 1918, a bloodless revolution took place. Insurgents took command of what became a new "republic" by Halloween of that year.[11]

So after four hundred years of the Habsburg Empire, power was lying in the streets. The Social Democrats grabbed it, with Count Michael (Mihály) Károlyi taking up the office of Prime Minister and then President. Leftist to be sure, with reform plans drawn up to give land to the workers; Károlyi even gave away his own estate. But as he later admitted, the situation had changed too radically for his own leadership to work. The fact that Károlyi was in charge of the government when Allies took Hungarian lands in March 1919 eroded what little power he had.[12]

Lugosi's own political involvement during the brief Károlyi period was apparently limited to the theatre. In one publication, he wrote:

> Right before the revolution of October 1918, the prevailing atmosphere in the IV district to which I belonged was so tense and heated that I decided the time has come for the organization of the community of the nation's actors on class basis, its centralization into a syndicate and awakening to a proletariat mentality. I knew that essentially enlightenment and socialist education was needed, since the actors' community had been lacking the socialist point of view only because it has not dealt with social sciences at all. It has been blinded by the false glamour and diverse lies surrounding it.
>
> Therefore its self-consciousness and sensitivity to socialism had to be awakened by exposing it to poverty. That the awakening of the actor slave was at all possible is in great part due to the revolution of October 1918 and the related event that the self-conscious socialist members of the Opera House did not join the antisocial organization of the capitol's actors.[13]

Comments like these suggest that the Lugosi of autumn 1918 was already committed to Communism.

By December 1918, Lugosi was one of nine members who made up the "National Union of Theatre Employees," and quite possibly its key member.[14] Later, Lugosi admitted the union nearly dismissed him in late February 1919 until he gained the support of the "whole company of the Opera House." That was in addition to his backing from the Union of Public Servants and the "country movement" centered in Szeged, where Lugosi had performed with great success in 1910-1911.[15] His leftist rhetoric apparently resonated with all of those groups.

Lugosi in the film *Az ezredes* (1917).

Lugosi's triumph with the actors' union came just as Count Károlyi's grip on power loosened. And so there was another bloodless revolution. The newly-formed Communist Party of Hungary took the reins of government on March 21, 1919. The seeds of Hungarian socialism dating to the end of the 19th century flowered into Bolshevism and the "Dictatorship of the Proletariat."[16] That brought a new leader to power, Béla Kun. And that brought Lugosi into politics in a more formal way than ever before. Within ten days of Kun taking charge, Lugosi held an important position in the Communist government.[17]

A leading Hungarian theatre publication spoke of Lugosi's "new responsibility," claiming:

> The main organizer of the Budapest Union of Actors is Bela Lugosi, who has been released from the National Theatre by the People's Commissar on Education to participate in the Communization of theatres.[18]

Lugosi was no mere lackey or dupe or administrative secretary; he headed a major department within the Kun government.[19] That he was chosen for this position so very rapidly suggests that he already knew many Communists and agreed with their agenda, at least in some measure. After all, Lugosi was a Communist party member, and may have been even during the Károlyi period.[20] In turn, the Kun government must have been aware of Lugosi's successful unionization efforts in the latter days of the Károlyi regime.

All of this makes his appointment in the new government understandable. That Kun and the Communist Party trusted Lugosi seems clear; they placed importance on the tasks he had before him. No less than Lenin noticed Kun's emphasis on such matters, questioning: "What sort of dictatorship [of the proletariat] is this you've got, socializing the theatres and musical societies? Do you really think that this is your most important task now?"[21] Apparently Kun believed that it was.

As for Lugosi, well, he quickly laid out his own agenda in a March 1919 publication.[22] Four key aims for the how and why of nationalizing the performing arts, fleshed out in some detail. First was the economic benefit to all theatre employees, rather than to private theatre directors. Secondly was the idea that state-run theatres would return drama to an end in and of itself, motivated by culture rather than profit. Thirdly, the quality of drama would increase, with academies accepting students with talent rather than students with tuition money. And lastly, theatre employees would see an improvement in their pay, their health care, and their pensions.[23]

Changes to the theatre industry also meant changes to a typical evening's entertainment. "The Working-men's International" was sung at the beginning and end of every performance, and the program often included Communist lectures and poems.[24] Theatres operated not only by, but also for (and in favor of) the Kun government. Whether tacitly or enthusiastically, Lugosi must have approved of these changes.

As head of the National Union of Actors, Lugosi also signed one order of major proportion, an edict prohibiting Kun's Red Army from entering actors' homes to confiscate their clothes.[25] This was a highly important issue, as soldiers were commandeering a portion of every Budapest man's wardrobe for the benefit of disbanded soldiers.[26] Lugosi was trying to protect actors, perhaps even placing them above other citizens. Whether it was fair or not, though, that Lugosi signed the order suggests he had some power within the government.

Even if the order was unfair, it would have seemed insignificant compared to Kun's rampant "Red Terror." Soldiers terrorized the bourgeoisie and perceived enemies of the state. Virtually no one's home was safe from being entered and looted. The clergy was stripped of the right to vote.[27] A terrible situation, and one that Lugosi must have known about, even if he disapproved of it.

Then, once again night became day. Kun abdicated after a reign of only 133 days; under moderate pressure, his "Bolsheviki" failed. A counter-revolutionary government had begun in Szeged in April 1919, placing the right-wing conservative Miklós Horthy at the head of their armed forces. He marched into Budapest on August 6 of that year, spreading "White Terror" against the Communists and Jews in retaliation for Kun's "Red Terror."[28] Like so many others, Lugosi fled. After all, imprisonment was likely. Perhaps even death at the hands of Horthy's brigands. They would hang quite a few Communists, and Lugosi having held a government post would have made him an attractive target.[29]

What to make then of Lugosi's political life in Hungary? His writing of the period seems very idealistic, but a similar kind of idealism was shared by many Europeans who desired better governments at the end of the War to End All Wars. In particular Lugosi hoped for a better life for Hungarian actors. Perhaps he even hoped to benefit personally.[30]

But none of that means that Lugosi didn't honestly believe in the Communist cause; his writing clearly suggests otherwise. And Lugosi—with his interest in

Count Michael Károlyi.

politics—would not have been so naïve to be unaware of the speed with which the Károlyi government came to power as the longstanding Habsburg Empire fell apart. Or the speed with which Kun displaced Károlyi. The political ground in wartime and post-war Hungary shifted quickly; Lugosi had to have understood the potential for more political upheaval when he assumed the position that caused him to flee first to Vienna and then to Berlin.

After that, Lugosi made his way to the United States in late 1920, travelling on the *Graf Tisza Istvan*.[31] Ironic, really, given that the ship was named for a man

Béla Kun in his study.

who had twice been Prime Minister of Hungary. Tisza exemplified so much that Lugosi would have disdained; he had been murdered in the same October 1918 Hungarian revolution that apparently caused Lugosi to form plans for unionizing actors.[32] All of this is made even more ironic given that Lugosi claimed that he faced trouble on *Tisza Istvan* from royalists who disapproved of his politics.[33]

Arriving in the US in December 1920, Lugosi made his way from the port of New Orleans to New York City.[34] By March 1921, he reported to Ellis Island.[35] Lugosi told an immigration agent that he was a sailor who was originally from Romania. After all, he had been a member of the crew on the *Tisza Istvan*, and his Hungarian hometown Lugos had become a part of Romania after border changes resulting from World War I. So what he told them was basically true. And outside of standard questions inquiring as to whether he was an anarchist, politics just didn't come up at the interview.[36]

But Lugosi's arrival in the Hungarian community of New York meant some actors began to circulate stories of his work for Kun. After only eight months, Lugosi had the First Hungarian Literary Society of New York write a letter to immigration officials. They tried to explain that gossip about Lugosi's activities in the "Council's Republic" was based on too little information. Their letter claimed on the one hand that Lugosi was not involved in politics and was merely a paid secretary; on the other hand, they suggested that actors elected him to his post. It reads as if they were vaguely referring to his work at the National Union of Theatre Employees during the Károlyi regime, omitting his governmental role in the National Union of Actors under Kun.[37]

And so this became Lugosi's recurrent tactic. When asked, focus on Károlyi, and never mention Kun. Take his activities under Kun and recast them as having been with Károlyi. In fact, go even further and eliminate Kun from history by implying that Horthy's White Terror ended Károlyi's regime. In 1931, Lugosi claimed:

> When the war ended, the revolution in Hungary took place. Count Károlyi seized the government, and because I was a friend, he gave me a ministerial post. Soon the royalist party regained control, and where they could find a Károlyi adherent they hanged or shot him.
>
> … It was the post-war penalty for being on the wrong side of politics.

I'm told they use the same method in Chicago occasionally. Well, I didn't want to be 'taken for a ride.'[38]

On another occasion in 1931, he said much the same, with a syndicated columnist reporting that "when Károlyi's government enjoyed its brief regime, Lugosi was Minister of the Theater." All of that came to a swift end thanks to a "monarchical party" that seized power.[39]

Why was he trying to conceal his past? Newspapers in the US had spoken at length about Béla Kun in 1919; newsreel footage of Kun appeared in theatres that same year.[40] That was all during the first Red Scare that swept across America following Russia's October Revolution. Though it had peaked before Lugosi arrived at Ellis Island, fears of Communism continued. After all, Lugosi played a Bolshevik spy in the film *Daughters Who Pay* (1925).[41] And with his penchant for keeping up with news, Lugosi must have been well aware of the general xenophobia that led to the 1927 executions of Sacco and Vanzetti. He also might well have known about the specific anti-Kun feelings that existed throughout the Roaring Twenties. One 1927 newspaper article claimed:

> Kun was cruel and depraved and his sins found him out. Thousands died while he was riding the whirlwind and the social, economic, and industrial fabric of Hungary was blown to shreds. That he was insane all the while is a reasonable view, for no man, in his senses, could be so cruel as was Béla Kun.[42]

In 1929, Kun released a statement claiming, "You know who I am. I am a Communist–that is explanation enough." His words hit newspapers as they wrote about Russia's hopes to overthrow the Horthy regime.[43]

That's not to say that Károlyi's own connections to Communism were unknown. In 1925, the *Chicago Daily Tribune* spoke of him as a man without a country, a man whose "only backers" were Communists.[44] But the press made little of his leftist inclinations as compared to Kun and the "Bolsheviki." And invoking Károlyi meant invoking someone whose anti-Kun sentiments were well known. As late as 1929, for example, an exiled Károlyi charged the Hungarian government with slander over a Budapest mural depicting him and Kun together when Kun took over the government.[45]

When the US government granted Károlyi a temporary visa in 1929, the press described his rule in Hungary as "President" of "the independent people's republic."[46] Among other places, Károlyi visited California, implying in his memoirs that he saw Lugosi on that trip.[47] Their rekindled friendship could only have furthered Lugosi's aims to connect his past with Károlyi's

Lugosi in Hungary in the late teens.

Lugosi (pictured to the left of center) at a 1919 political march.

government rather than Kun's.

As time went on, Lugosi clouded his version of prior events with even more vague language. By 1936, he spoke in generalizations of having been with "one of the several revolutions" that followed the collapse of the Habsburg Empire.[48] By 1944, Lugosi claimed he "fled after the war when [Horthy's] White Army overthrew [Károlyi's] new republic."[49] After all, the word "republic" had positive connotations in the US.

The way in which Lugosi rewrote his history suggests a rather savvy approach to the anti-Communist climate of 1920s America. And it definitely helped when Lugosi decided to apply for US citizenship in 1928. He enlisted witnesses to testify on his behalf, ranging from an optometrist named Irving Adler to Joseph Diskay, whose singing voice was dubbed into Warner Oland's mouth for *The Jazz Singer* (1927). He took a special course to help him with the citizenship exam. And he submitted to a lengthy interview with an immigration agent, at which he likely didn't mention Béla Kun.[50]

What he did talk about was his love of the United States. As one syndicated newspaper column wrote, "Few immigrants are as enthusiastic over the prospect of American citizenship as Bela Lugosi. Lugosi's admiration of American ideals and customs creeps constantly into his conversation, making American listeners ashamed of themselves."[51]

Lugosi was naturalized on June 26, 1931, ten years after telling Immigration Services at Ellis Island that he hoped to become a citizen.[52] Saying he wasn't sure whether Lugos was part of Hungary or Romania, Lugosi renounced allegiance to both countries.[53] "America," he said, "with more freedom than any country in the world, offers more opportunity for self-culture than any other by virtue of this freedom."[54] Self-culture. Virtue. Freedom.

Curiously, Lugosi seems to have experienced his first difficulties with branches of the US government just months after becoming a citizen. In early 1932, Hollywood studios panicked at impending Congressional legislation that attempted to ban all foreign-born stars from appearing in US movies.[55] A list of actors in jeopardy hit newspapers in February and March of that year, with Lugosi's name featured prominently among them.[56]

Though that legislation certainly didn't become law, it apparently did spur Murray W. Garsson to travel to Hollywood in early 1933.[57] Garsson was the US Department of Labor's "trouble shooter on aliens," and he was on special assignment to investigate foreign stars in the movie business. Again the press mentioned Lugosi's name.[58] Within a week, though, Garsson recanted, announcing that Lugosi wouldn't investigated. By January 24, 1933, Garsson had learned he was a naturalized US citizen.[59]

Perhaps this was an important moment for Lugosi, who would already have learned of the protections provided by the US Constitution and the Bill of Rights when he was studying to take his citizenship exam. Then, he quickly saw his name erased from a federal investigation; his citizenship papers had protected him.

It's possible that situation helped embolden him to join the Screen Actors Guild at the beginning of July 1933.[60] He was among the earliest members of the newly-formed union, particularly interesting given that–unlike SAG's founders–he wasn't a member of the Masquers Club or the Hollywood Cricket Club. Likely, it was founding member Leon Waycoff who lobbied Lugosi to join.[61]

Once he signed up, Lugosi made no secret of his membership. In May 1934, he

Taking the citizenship oath in 1931.

appeared as part of a three-day engagement of the SAG-sponsored Film Star Frolic; newspapers clearly listed Lugosi as a SAG member.[62] He and SAG founding member Boris Karloff appeared in newsreel footage mentioning the event.[63] Then in 1936 Lugosi and his wife Lillian appeared at SAG's annual dinner and ball, with Lugosi even reserving a special theatre box to see the evening show.[64]

He also took an active role in SAG administration. In July 1934, Lugosi successfully ran for election to the SAG advisory board.[65] Meeting after meeting for nearly two years, while other advisory board members came and went.[66] Lugosi also tried to propose changes to the guild, once feeling so strongly about the plight of film extras that he sent SAG secretary Kenneth Thomson a telegram at four in the morning.[67] Later he offered rather detailed suggestions to help actors who worked freelance for studios rather than under contract.[68] This was all in addition to lobbying for new members, recruiting four fellow actors during the making of his 1935 film *The Raven*.[69]

Not only did he actively participate in SAG, Lugosi clung to his membership even during the British ban on horror films when he worked so little.[70] He had also become a member of the AFRA, the American Federation of Radio Artists.[71] And why not? Unions had become part of the fabric of the American workforce during the Great Depression, and as a citizen Lugosi had a right to involve himself. As he said in 1935, "The idea is that I myself feel the most loyal to America that you can imagine. But I feel that way if somebody does something I do not think is right, I am like a mother going to spank."[72] After all, unions had always been the way Lugosi fought against perceived injustice.

Dire economic troubles of the time also meant the rise of political left and the growing acceptability of more radical movements. One million people voted for a socialist candidate in the 1932 presiden-

Lugosi during the early years of his involvement in SAG.

tial election, for example. The ranks of the US Communist Party swelled that decade.[73] Voices of protest like Huey Long and Father Coughlin gained widespread support.[74] And Franklin Roosevelt's New Deal reconstructed much of American life.[75]

That US politics moved to the left must have excited Lugosi, who spoke about his support for FDR during World War II:

> I am an avowed Roosevelt disciple and I think without a doubt the President is the greatest outstanding personality of the day. I am a firm believer in his ideas and ideals and you can put that down in spades.[76]

On another occasion, Lugosi described himself as an "extreme liberal democrat."[77] An extreme liberal democrat who tried to help in the war effort.

"Can't Uncle Sam place Bela Lugosi in the Ghost Guard?" Jimmie Fidler joked in 1942.[78] That same year, Lugosi appears as a Nazi plastic surgeon that is mixed up with a Japanese Spy Ring in *Black Dragons*, one of the first anti-Axis films of World War II. It also happened to be the first Monogram Studios film to feature a closing trailer promoting the sale of defense bonds and stamps.[79] A year later and Lugosi was portraying a Nazi in *Ghosts on the Loose* (1943). The fascists, they were the enemy; Soviet Russia, on the other hand, was an ally.

To assist in the cause, Lugosi gave a pint of blood to the Hollywood blood bank in 1943, along with donating a carved ivory figure to a British War Relief Society auction.[80] A year later, he was present at a United Nations show in Pasadena that sold $2.5 million in war bonds.[81] That was right after Guy Lombardo's patriotic party on the *Hollywood Barn Dance* radio show played

Lugosi's "favorite tune": "I'll Walk Alone."[82]

Even the end of World War II didn't halt Lugosi's efforts. As late as 1949, Lugosi met with paralyzed war veteran Vinnie Shelton in Syracuse, New York while he was appearing in a summer stock version of *Arsenic and Old Lace*. Lugosi remarked on the sacrifice that Shelton had made, as well as commending Shelton's wife for standing by him. Then he gave them both free tickets to his show, making special arrangements for Shelton's own chair to be moved to his theatre.[83]

But it was Lugosi's *other* activities during World War II that created questions. In 1940, he told Hedda Hopper, "every naturalized American and every person born here should kneel every morning and utter a prayer for being an American."[84] That same year, Hopper wrote at length about the "Un-American Left in Hollywood":

> Any actor whose words or actions indicate that he is friendly to Communism is very soon going to be asked to stand over with the professional Reds and share in what is coming to them.[85]

Hopper added that the "finger of suspicion" would certainly be directed at the "large foreign group" in Hollywood.[86]

The finger of suspicion. The foreign group. In 1942, the Hungarian-American Council for Democracy (HACD) began to develop in Chicago out of two previous Hungarian organizations.[87] By the time of their first convention in June 1943, the HACD–dubbed an "anti-Fascist organization" in the press–was in place with Bela Lugosi as its first President.[88] Lugosi had actively competed with "New Bauhaus" artist László Moholy-Nagy for the position; Lugosi won, with Moholy-Nagy becoming the leader of the group's Chicago chapter.[89] For their "honorary" president, the HACD elected Count Károlyi.[90]

The perceived need for the HACD came out of the war's impact on Hungary.

Lugosi, a self-described "extreme liberal Democrat."

Conservative Miklós Horthy, whose "White Terror" caused Lugosi to flee Hungary and who still led the country, had signed the Tripartite Agreement with Nazi Germany and Fascist Italy. Thanks to Horthy, the homeland of people like Lugosi and Károlyi was in league with the Axis powers.[91] The desire was to help the Allies and thus to help the Hungarian people. Another aim was to see Károlyi returned to power after the war for the "democratization" of Hungary.[92]

Of course the war might have placed some pressure on what was already a kind of dual national identity for Hungarian émigrés to the US.[93] But deciding what political philosophy should guide that effort was an even more problematic issue. In the Hungarian-American community of the time, a conservative approach was the majority view, a view espoused by the American Hungarian Federation (AHF) and its leader Tibor Kerekes.[94] During the

Publicity portrait for Monogram's *Black Dragons* (1942), in which Lugosi plays a Nazi plastic surgeon who changes the appearance of Japanese spies.

war, the AHF was the largest and most influential Hungarian-American organization.[95] Very much in the minority was the kind of leftist approach adopted by Lugosi, by Károlyi, and by the HACD.

Why had Lugosi been able to spearhead the new group? Clearly he knew Károlyi and many of the Hungarian émigrés in the US, and just as clearly he had name value among the general US population that Moholy-Nagy lacked. [96] But it was more than that. In 1940, Lugosi had taken a leading role in sending a message to the Chairman of the House Committee on UnAmerican Activities, pledging that Hungarian-Americans were loyal to the US and against the Axis powers.[97] Two years later, Lugosi appeared before the United Nations Committee of Southern California with the same message.[98]

Then, in the Spring of 1943, Lugosi wrote a series of articles for the *Hungarian Future* newspaper. The publication was leftist in philosophy and allegedly owned by a Communist Party member; Lugosi's writing revealed his own hard left political stance.[99] And he had also decided to start a "Károlyi Movement" among Hungarian-Americans.[100] Others in the emergent HACD were likely aware of his published views, and perhaps even his involvement with Béla Kun's government.

Within just a few months of its development, the HACD gained a great deal of notoriety, eventually becoming the most renowned Hungarian leftist organization in the US.[101] They began a drive to set up chapters of the HACD throughout the US, Central and South America, and Canada.[102] They gathered endorsements from a number of US Senators.[103] And they collected a huge number of signatures in an unsuccessful petition drive to gain Károlyi another US visa.[104]

Buying a war bond from Rose Friedman (left) in Pasadena in May 1944.

What else did the HACD want? For one, Lugosi spoke at a mass meeting about helping to save the Jews in Hungary and Europe.[105] And at the end of 1944, they issued a statement calling for a "free and democratic provisional government on liberated Hungary soil." A democratic government that could join the Allies in fighting the Fascists. In the same breath, they also suggested the "Hungarian people should break forever with the feudal past and provide land for the landless people."[106]

They pursued some very specific projects as well. For example, when the war came to an end, HACD Executive Secretary Dr. Mózes Simon handled a major effort to raise and transfer donations to Hungary. In particular, the HACD hoped to funnel money into Hungary to help Hungarian children, as well as to assist about 150 who were orphaned and then living in Paris. To this end, Simon tried to enlist the Unitarian Service Committee.[107]

Lugosi's own involvement was very hands-on, and does not seem at all affected by his busy wartime career. "Into this project he packs all the power of his political conviction," one reporter wrote.[108] His surviving HACD letters illustrate the depth of his involvement and his grasp of the issues.[109] After all, a high-ranking HACD member said, "He sat out to work with enthusiasm and achieved unexpected success."[110] If anything, at times he placed his HACD responsibilities above his career. For example, during a tour of *Arsenic and Old Lace*, he cleared his schedule for March 15, 1944, when the HACD held events across the country.[111] He secured radio time through the Office of War Information (OWI) for the HACD to make broadcasts to Hungary, and he once spoke eloquently on a US radio show with William S. Gailmore.[112] And he even let the HACD hold a major event in his California home.[113]

As part of his leadership, Lugosi stayed in regular communication with Károlyi. On a radio interview, Lugosi once made an impassioned plea for Americans to see Károlyi as "Hungary's own Abraham Lincoln."[114] The two men exchanged cables of mutual admiration and esteem.[115] And

Meeting paralyzed veteran Vincent Shelton and his wife in July 1949.

their surviving letters show the extreme depth of their "confidential" discussions and their shared trust, again making clear that Lugosi was no mere figurehead. In one letter, Károlyi spoke to Lugosi about the need for "serious leftist politics" despite the "Károlyi bogey" that sat beside the "Bolshevik one."[116] He also appealed to Lugosi to join forces with Oscar Jászi and Rustem Vámbéry.[117]

Károlyi also sent Mózes Simon a telegram hoping he could "Please ask Lugosi and Chicago Hungarian Council in my name to put aside difference and collaborate with Jászi [and] Vámbéry."[118] He sent Jászi and Vámbéry a similar request the same day, telling Jászi, "In face of collapse of Mussolini it is of paramount importance you should immediately invite Lugosi and all progressive Hungarians to conference serious and close collaboration."[119]

Who were these two men? Neither Jászi or Vámbéry were Communists, but they had hard left political views; they were also notable Hungarian figures living in the US.[120] Jászi had been part of Károlyi's 1919 government before becoming a naturalized US citizen in 1931. By the time of the war, he was a political science professor at Oberlin College.[121] Rustem Vámbéry was an attorney who had defended Károlyi in a Hungarian court years earlier. When Horthy took over the Hungarian government, Vámbéry fled to the US.[122] He was particularly against a popular front organization like the HACD, which he told Mózes Simon in no uncertain terms.[123] And he was also against circulating petitions for Károlyi's visa, knowing that conservative Hungarian-Americans would be able to get far more signatures in opposition.[124]

Jászi had similar feelings. "As with regards to my joining the Chicago movement, I am afraid I must say it is impossible," he wrote to Lugosi.[125] Lugosi continued to lobby Jászi, but to no avail.[126] Though Jászi and Vámbéry did speak at a mass meeting that also headlined Lugosi, neither aligned with themselves with the HACD.[127] Why? There may have been several reasons, including a possible clash of egos. But what is certain is that Jászi and Vámbéry were both worried about the HACD's involvement with Communists.[128] Jászi even wrote to Lugosi about his fears of those members in the HACD hierarchy whom he did not know.[129]

What can be said of the HACD membership? Certainly during the thirties and early forties Honorary President Károlyi was a known admirer of Joseph Stalin.[130] Executive Secretary Mózes Simon was an associate editor of the same *Hungarian Future* which had published Lugosi's articles in 1943. Simon had previously been a legal advisor to the Communist Party in the Ukraine and later a member of the Sudeten Communists; he was also a close friend of Károlyi's.[131]

Other key members of the HACD Board of Directors included John Roman, editor of *Hungarian Future*; the US Office of Strategic Services (OSS) believed he was a "functionary" of the Communist Party in the US. [132] And there was Ferenc Göndör, the editor and publisher of a New York-based Hungarian publication called *The Man*; the OSS believed he had been "won over by the Communists."[133] There was John Gyetvay-Nagy, one of the founders of *Hungarian Future*. And then there was Imre Békéssy, whom Lugosi likely knew in Hungary; Békéssy had been close to Béla Kun, and under Kun's authority ran a government news agency in 1919.[134]

There was also Julius Emspack, well-known trade unionist and suspected Communist. Though he was not in the HACD hierarchy, Emspack and the National Council of Hungarian-American Trade Unionists co-sponsored a joint full-page ad in newspapers like *The Washington Post* to recruit new HACD members.[135] He also spoke at the same mass meeting that included Lugosi, Vámbéry, and Jászi.[136]

This is to say nothing of Lugosi's many close friends in the organization, including the Reverend Géza Takaró, whose wife Irén had become the sister-in-law of

Lugosi's first wife. The Reverend Steven Balogh later told a Senate Subcommittee that Takaró was the "Hungarian Red Dean," a man who wrote for "Communist newspapers" and was an "organizer of and representative of various suspicious leftist organizations."[137]

And then there were Lugosi's long-time associates in the Los Angeles HACD. That chapter's president was Melchior Lengyel, who penned the story that became *Ninotchka* (1939), a film in which Lugosi appeared as a Soviet Commissar. Other key HACD members included director Michael Curtiz, who directed Lugosi in the film *99* (1918) and fled Hungary when Kun's government fell. Also actor Nicholas Bela, who appeared in *Dracula* (1931) and who was reportedly a Communist.[138]

Lugosi's father-in-law Stephen Arch, president of the United Hungarian-American Defense Federation, also got involved.[139] He was also Vice-President of the LA branch of the HACD, an office he

Having a drink during World War II around the time he was president of the HACD.

shared with László Vadnay, Hungarian screenwriter of such films as *Tales of Manhattan* (1942).[140] That Lugosi's own father-in-law was involved did not go unnoticed by the FBI and the Immigration and Naturalization Service.[141]

Of course, it was Lugosi himself that the government began to watch most closely. Certainly the OSS and the State Department kept track of the HACD, which at times they called the "Dracula Council."[142] The Immigration and Naturalization Service maintained a file on Lugosi as well. So did the Federal Bureau of Investigation.

For example, only days after Lugosi became president of the HACD, an unknown informant wrote to the FBI field office in Washington DC claiming that Lugosi had been a Communist in Hungary and

A newspaper ad sponsored by the HACD in April 1944.

had worked for the Kun government. A couple of weeks passed, and an apparently different informant relayed the same information. The Los Angeles and Chicago FBI offices began keeping records on Lugosi, but didn't undertake a formal investigation because the Washington office learned he was not a past or present member of the US Communist Party.[143]

By 1944, however, J. Edgar Hoover felt differently. He personally signed a letter to the Los Angeles field office seeking assistance "in conducting an investigation concerning the activities" of Bela Lugosi.[144] Hoover was likely concerned about Lugosi and the HACD, but anything more specific seems lost to time. Was it the HACD's activities? Lugosi's associates in the group? His own support of Károlyi? Or a combination of these reasons? Difficult to tell, but the FBI and Hoover very definitely wanted Lugosi to be monitored.

And so they kept track of some of his movements. One item in his file is an a pro-Lugosi article published in the May 31, 1945 issue of the Canadian Federation of Democratic Hungarians' magazine.[145] The FBI believed that organization was Communist-inspired. That the Canadian group was praising Lugosi's political efforts hardly looked good.

After the war ended, the FBI and the Immigration and Naturalization Service continued to keep tabs on Lugosi. Both groups traded information about him on several occasions during 1947 and 1948. In particular, Immigration and Naturalization was trying to determine if there was enough cause to revoke Lugosi's citizenship.[146] Being a US citizen was no longer enough to keep Lugosi safe.

Their key concern, which they shared with the FBI: "A report has been furnished this office to the effect that the subject is a Hungarian Communist."[147] And then an unknown man who had served as an administrative secretary to Lugosi at the HACD informed Immigration that Lugosi had a "long record of Communist affiliations here and abroad."[148]

Even though Immigration and Naturalization ended their investigation in early 1948 due to "insufficient evidence," they continued to compile information about him, including that 1949 Senate testimony by Huber, Balogh, Nadányi, and Borshy. Given everything else that they and the FBI had in their files, the words of those four men must have looked pretty bad. Borshy, who didn't actually know Lugosi, was the most damning of the group; he even read from an article in a Hungarian Catholic church weekly:

> Thus the chairman of the so-called Hungarian-American Democratic Council, Dracula Lugosi is proven by a Budapest paper that he is not democratic but extreme leftist, that is, Communist—as we always knew it.[149]

The (now unclassified) letter signed by J. Edgar Hoover regarding an FBI investigation of Lugosi.

The article—which suggested Lugosi might soon be travelling to visit his sister in Hungary—hoped he would permanently stay in Budapest with the "Mátyás Rákosis." The reference was to the Hungarian leader of the time, a man who was also General Secretary of the Hungarian Communist Party. The article's complete text was entered into the Senate Subcommittee record as "Borshy Exhibit 3."[150]

Anti-Lugosi sentiment wasn't confined to Hungarian-language publications like Borshy Exhibit 3. As early as April 1946, one newspaper article claimed that President Truman's war relief board favored Reds, and it singled out Lugosi and the HACD. They were "affiliated with the Institute for International

Democracy, which is a federation of half a dozen or more Communist fronts."[151] In 1947, the press carried a list of organizations that were "disloyal." The HACD was listed alongside groups like the "Black Dragon Society" that was the subject of Lugosi's 1942 film.[152] Subversive and UnAmerican. And by 1949, the press ran the words of the same John J. Huber who testified before that Senate Subcommittee; papers like the *Chicago Tribune* quoted him as naming Lugosi as part of a group of "show people who have been connected with fronts or who have contributed their services to the Communist front."[153]

Examining the testimony that Borshy and the others gave in 1949 shows an attempt to damage Lugosi's reputation. Perhaps they believed everything they said

Lugosi in the 1940s.
Communist, or victim of unfair accusations?

and that it was their patriotic duty to inform the Senate of what they knew. But there is also the fact that enough hatred existed between the right-wing and left-wing Hungarian groups that they blackened the names of each other to US authorities after the war.[154]

The increasingly conservative US climate in the late forties and early fifties meant that Lugosi found himself on the wrong side of a political debate. And his detractors weren't limited to conservative Hungarian-Americans with an axe to grind. When Lugosi was scheduled to speak at a New Jersey reception in his honor, Congressman C. R. Howell contacted the FBI.[155] Was Lugosi subversive? Howell was eager for an answer.

Of course, Lugosi was likely unaware of the degree to which people like Howell or government agencies were keeping tabs on him. Immigration and Naturalization knew he wrote to Károlyi as late as 1949, for example.[156] But he knew well enough that accusations against him were coming from a great many people. Enough that he wrote a letter to László Dienes, editor of the publication *California Hungarians*, dated December 27, 1950:

> I herewith emphatically say–I AM NOT NOW, NOR HAVE I EVER A MEMBER OF THE COMMUNIST PARTY. I HAVE NEVER ATTENDED ANY COMMUNIST MEETINGS–I HAVE NEVER ENTERTAINED AT ANY COMMUNIST GATHERING–I HAVE NEVER DONATED ONE CENT TO ANY COMMUNIST CAUSE.[157]

Lugosi added he had suspicions of the HACD's Communist leanings in March 1945; at that time, he dropped out of the organization and requested an FBI inquiry. He was told that it had been a Communist front, but that it had folded.

But those words weren't true. An HACD letter from July 1945 survives in which Lugosi wrote to and scolded then-US Representative Clare Boothe Luce about a speech she gave on the floor of the US House.[158] He was still involved at least months after he claimed. Indeed, his name remained as president on HACD stationery until at least September 1945.[159] And there was also the fact that the HACD continued operations until some point in 1947; it hadn't folded in 1945.[160]

His denials continued when he sent a January 1951 letter to John S. Wood, Chairman of the House Committee on UnAmerican Activities. The HACD had deceived him, he claimed. He repeated some of the statements he made in the Dienes letter, adding that "actors are usually too busy to pay much attention to organizations that request their sponsorship."[161] In Lugosi's case, that wasn't quite true. At any rate, Wood does not seem to have responded.

On March 15, 1951, an upset Lugosi visited Andor Sziklay, their meeting set up by a noted New York doctor, Pál Kauffman. Kauffman believed that Sziklay might be able to arrange for Lugosi to testify before HUAC.[162] That might help clear his name. Sziklay later wrote that when Lugosi appeared at his office, he said:

> 'I have become the target of accusations,' he said. 'Unknown slanderers are accusing me of being a Communist in Hungary, following the first World War.'
>
> 'I want to meet the HUAC,' said Lugosi. 'I want to present them my past and present and also what has already been presented by a series of magazine articles: that I have urged the procurement of American war-bonds at meetings and factories, with a considerable success...'
>
> But where was I from being able to make this possible...? I was barely a department head, meaning that you could perhaps observe me amidst the pyramids of bureaucracy in sunny weather and with strong spectacles... I explained this to him, not mentioning that, even if I could contribute somehow to his meeting with the dark lords of HUAC, I would not do it for the sake of myself and him. This strong, high-spirited Transylvanian guy would probably start throwing committee members out of the windows of the building of the House of Representatives.'[163]

And so Lugosi never testified before HUAC. Even if Sziklay was joking about Lugosi's possible physical reaction to the congressmen, he was likely correct that an appearance might only further damage Lugosi's reputation.

A tarnished reputation, certainly by that time. Was it deserved? It's possible that the HACD was never all that Red.[164] And yet, Lugosi in his own words admitted there was a Communist component in the HACD. At a minimum, Lugosi, like Rustem Vámbéry, doesn't seem to have avoided working with Communists in the interest of Nazi defeat. Nor did the US government for that matter, which was allied with Soviet Russia during the war.

Was Lugosi just the kind of dupe the Communists were hoping to find: a naïve actor to be an HACD figurehead, unknowingly helping savvy and insidious Reds? No, surveying all of the existing evidence shows a highly-involved Lugosi who was well-aware of what was going on. An intelligent and articulate correspondent and author: hardly a dupe.

As for the rest of the HACD membership, perhaps many were unfairly maligned in an era when allegations were all-too-commonly confused with facts. But regardless of

With his friend Duci de Kerekjarto, who performed at a Socialist Workers Party event in 1952.

who was and was not a Communist, these were people who in many cases Lugosi had known for years. Close associates, fellow entertainment figures, and even his father-in-law; if a great many key members were Communists, they were hardly shadowy puppet masters of a naïve Lugosi.

What can be said with certainty is that Lugosi was a Communist in Hungary who showed his belief in that political philosophy even before Kun came to power. And then he became a part of Kun's government. Lugosi tried to suppress that history once he arrived in the US, where he stayed out of all manner of politics until becoming a citizen. After the war in Europe began, he rather vigorously pursued his goals.

But were his goals subversive and UnAmerican, as so many believed? Lugosi's political beliefs had perhaps changed since the Kun era; to imagine his thoughts were completely static over the decades would probably be an oversimplification. At the same time, his writing in *Hungarian Future* is more than tinged with Communist philosophy and nothing at all suggests he disavowed the basic beliefs he held during the Kun era.

And while his associates' views were not

With Martha Dodd-Stern in New York in the early 1950s.

necessarily his own, Lugosi was certainly involved with numerous persons and publications whose alleged tendencies were very Red, and this extends beyond the HACD hierarchy. Lugosi's close friend, violinist Duci de Kerekjarto, was performing for a Socialist Workers Party event as late as 1952.[165] And one photograph from the early fifties pictures Lugosi with leftist Martha Dodd-Stern, who fled the US in 1957 when a Russian counterspy pegged her as being "part of the Soviet apparatus."[166]

That still doesn't really answer whether Lugosi was an avowed Communist, or, as he claimed, an "extreme liberal democrat." In 1945, Lugosi had signed a petition to keep labor leader Harry Bridges from being deported as a threat to the US.[167] The government failed in the end; among other things, Bridges hadn't been careless enough to actually sign Communist Party membership cards or other documents.[168] Lugosi perhaps had similar strategy in mind. Don't join the party, because it was party membership and government position that caused him to flee Hungary. But pursue political goals aligned with Communist philosophy.

Or perhaps by the 1940s Lugosi's views were somewhere in between Communism and the hard left of the US Democratic Party. Some ill-defined gray area where both met. After all, Lugosi's support for the liberal policies of FDR may well have been very genuine. In fact, it isn't difficult to presume that he voted for FDR, rather than for a socialist candidate.

Was Lugosi blacklisted? An appropriate question, given the allegations surrounding him. After all, his last major film role came in *Abbott and Costello Meet Frankenstein* (1948). Work dried up as the allegations mounted. But there isn't any evidence to form a causal link between his career problems and his politics. Blacklists weren't written down, of course, but in Lugosi's case there isn't even anecdotal evidence (say, the memories of others in Hollywood) to give any credence to that claim.

Indeed, there's far more evidence supporting the idea that he *wasn't* blacklisted. This would include the fact he signed a long-term agreement with the William Morris Agency in November 1949, two months after the damning Senate testimony against him.[169] They scarcely would have signed him to a new agreement if he had been blacklisted.

What about a Lugosi blacklisting after 1949? That seems extremely difficult to believe as well. Along with continuing to appear on television and radio, Lugosi did star in *Bela Lugosi Meets a Brooklyn Gorilla*. Low-budget and inauspicious, yes. But its producer Jack Broder was making millions from reissuing old films through his Realart company. To think he would have jeopardized all of his own success and reputation by hiring a blacklisted actor whose name even appeared in the *Meets a Brooklyn Gorilla* title just doesn't stand to reason. And in the years that followed were more network TV appearances and a 1956 film role at United Artists. Others who were blacklisted had to wait far more years to return to work, if at all.

In the end, Lugosi wasn't even pursued by HUAC, let alone blacklisted. This was not because he was seen as too insignificant a figure, a star whose career was fading. Many lesser-known persons were blacklisted, including actress Dorothy Tree and Lugosi's friend Nicholas Bela, both of whom appeared in *Dracula* (1931).[170] The difference was that Lugosi never joined the Communist Party in the US, and his years of strategic lying about his Kun days clouded the accusations that were made about his life in Hungary. Rather than refusing to talk, he also made vigorous denials of wrongdoing, as in the letter to Dienes.

But that hardly meant Lugosi didn't suffer. His reputation with Hungarian-Americans eroded, a particularly horrible blow for a man who clung so tightly to that community. The entire situation was an irritant for many years that bordered on a crisis.

After all, on March 12, 1953, the Immigration and Natualization Service once again considered cancelling Lugosi's citizenship.[171]

CHAPTER THREE

Yellow Eyes

Fan magazine writer Gladys Hall was in the film business for nearly two decades before meeting Bela Lugosi. She got her first work around 1910, and within five years she was writing for *Motion Picture Magazine*.[1] By the twenties, she was on the payroll of *Motion Picture Classic*, where she gossiped about Hollywood, interviewed the stars, and even authored some poetry. At that same time, she was writing under seven pen names for other magazines.[2]

Long after the movies began to talk, Hall kept writing about them. *Photoplay*, *Modern Screen*, *Silver Screen*, *Screenland*: she ended up working for most of the movie magazines at one time or another. "One of the most popular girls in this town," columnist Hedda Hopper said about Hall.[3] And by 1950, *Flair* magazine dubbed her, "one of the principal architects of the wondrous Hollywood myth," adding that she was the "undisputed queen of the cozy confession."[4]

How many times did Hall meet Lugosi? It's hard to know, really. Presumably they were together on at least five occasions, but maybe more.[5] He was certainly with her in February 1930 at a party for the Women's Association of Film Publicists, for example. It was Hall along with a fleet of other female writers like Mollie Merrick and Hedda Hopper. Lugosi and film director Woody Van Dyke were among the few men present.[6]

With Hall and Lugosi, though, how much time they actually spent together was far less important than what she wrote about him. Four different articles published at key moments in Lugosi's career. The first came before he made the film version of *Dracula* (1931), and the second just as it was being released. The third came in 1935 when he was firmly entrenched in the horror film; the fourth in 1941, not too long after his comeback in *Son of Frankenstein* (1939).

Why so important? Well, throughout his Hollywood career, Lugosi was the focus of only about a dozen movie fan magazine articles.[7] They ran plenty of Lugosi film reviews, of course, and also still photographs from the same. But only rarely did they print entire articles on Lugosi, and the work of Gladys Hall represents about a third of them. More than any other Hollywood magazine writer, she seems to have taken a great interest in his life and career.

All of her articles touched on his connection to horror, but all of them also spoke of his love life, often drawing links between the two. At times this meant a discussion of the sexual magnetism Lugosi had over women in the audiences of his films. In that way, Hall was part of a tradition of critics in his early years who commented on his

True Hollywood Ghost Stories

II---The Case Of The Man Who Dares Not Fall Asleep

By GLADYS HALL

MOLDERING grave-yards and shrieks in the night. The drip-drip-drip of blood. The odor of Death that comes from the secret places. A man with a pale green face and stretching hands. Ghouls. Unspeakable things. The worm that never dies.

A bloodsucker in human form—*Dracula!*

You have read the book, "*Dracula*"? By Bram Stoker? You have seen the play of "*Dracula*"?

I have seen the—let us say the man, *Dracula*.

He is here. He is in Hollywood. He walks the streets by day with pallid face and preternatural hands. He works in the studios. He lunches at the Montmartre. He is to be seen in a forthcoming Corinne Griffith production, "*Prisoners*." Watch for him. Scrutinize his eyes.

By nights, he never sleeps. He never sleeps lest—but hush! S'h'h! This is another matter.

One I dread to tell lest this sleepless man—this man who cannot love as other men love—but hush! S'h'h!

You've never believed in vampires? You've thought them figments of disordered imaginations? Mordant fancies? You are wrong—there are vampires. In human form. Disguised by day. And dread beyond description by night. The fancy shudders away from the writing of such a tale. The flesh creeps and crawls. The little lonely human spirit whines in its thin envelope. It crouches in its pitiful lair and whines, as the banshee whines about the house of the newly dead.

ARE THEY EACH OTHER?

Dracula is Bela Lugosi. Is Bela Lugosi *Dracula*?

Bram Stoker's awful hero. The black mountains where dwell those vampires who kiss human beings into a semblance of death. It is true. It is done. The mountain folk will tell you so themselves. It is done time and time again. Bela Lugosi has seen the very funerals of these vampired dead. And then, nights later, when they awaken in their dread resting places, the vampires who have marked them as their own—are waiting.

So often and so frightful is this practice that in the town of Lugos they keep their dead for days and sometimes weeks to make sure they have died the sweet death of the Church and not the horrible, half-death of the vampires.

I have said that Bela Lugosi comes from Hungary.

No, no, no, he doesn't come from Hungary. He was driven from Hungary by a——. He fled the place, emaciated, a skeleton, drained of blood and nerve and sinew. He fled

Many men have from time to time been called male vampires. But Bela Lugosi is one in more than a figurative sense it, the part which has made him famous—and fearful lest the fiction bring a dread reprisal upon him. Lugosi comes to the screen from playing the title rôle of "*Dracula*," the bat-like man who drew both blood and souls from his victims

Or is he himself the victim of a *Dracula* in—but of that, more later.

Bela Lugosi is intimately aware of vampires. For Lugosi comes from the town of Lugos, in Hungary. The black mountains of Hungary where dwelt

Gladys Hall's article on Lugosi from the August 1929 issue of *Motion Picture*.

good looks and charm. The difference was that the discussion now included horror as part of his sexual allure.

In 1931, for example, Lugosi spoke to Hall about "The Feminine Love of Horror." In it, he talked at length about his theory that women were overly interested in all things morbid. They "gloat over it," Lugosi said. "Feed on it. Are nourished by it. Shudder and cling and cry out—*and come back for more.*" How to support this theory? He claimed that women gloat over death, whether recounting the last hours of men they knew or visiting loved ones at cemeteries. And they savored getting to the front lines during the Great War, witnessing lynchings in the South, or attending executions of prisoners. He also drew the link between death and sex, claiming that women who saw him in *Dracula* onstage "knew an ecstasy dragged from the depths of unspeakable things."[8]

Of all of Hall's stories, this one seems to have actually been information Lugosi believed, or at least that he said for fan consumption. He repeated the idea to the *Los Angeles Evening Herald Express* in 1935, claiming that murder trials were always overrun with women because of their delight in the gruesome side of life.[9] And he said much the same in a syndicated column that same year.[10] Women were drawn to his Hollywood persona in part because they were inherently drawn to things like vampires.

But Hall's more curious articles about Lugosi are the two where she claimed Lugosi had in fact been pursued by a real vampire. A clever narrative inversion, really, to suggest that the famous Dracula of stage and screen was not in control of the supernatural, but rather a victim of it. This Lugosi that Hall created in her writing was a figure made tragic due to love and passion and desire.

"The Case of the Man Who Dares Not Fall Asleep," published in 1929, was the first of Hall's articles. In it, she wrote that Lugosi had fled Hungary because he had become "a skeleton, drained of blood and nerve and sinew. He fled with the ghastly mark of the vampire on his throat."[11] A female vampire; a "nameless" actress with pale skin and pointed teeth. He dared not stay away from her, but he had to escape. Not to return, not while she was there. Even in faraway Hollywood, he only felt safe sleeping in the day. And of course, this Lugosi could "never love again." As Hall said, "he told me so." Thus it was True.

And then in 1935, Hall returned to the same theme in her aptly titled article "Do You Believe This Story?" This time, Lugosi claimed to believe the wild stories of vampires that ran rampant in the "black mountains of Hungary" where he grew up. "Folklore gone mad," he thought, until he met an actress whose skin was: deathly pale at times; at other times it was a blood, blood red–that was when she had been fed. Her mouth was thin and ravenous. Her teeth were tiny, and pointed. She had been married many times. There had been many other loves. One never asked what had become of them. Men feared her–and went to her at her command. Husbands left their wives because of her.[12]

A dapper Lugosi from his days at the National Theatre in Hungary.

This article, in which Lugosi falsely claimed to have left two sons in Hungary, again cast him as the prey of an alluring succubus who drained his passions.

Hall's fourth and final article was the longest of the group; its byline claimed the story was "told to" her by Lugosi. "Memos of a Madman!": Every word was allegedly his, and he spoke at length about so many aspects of his life and career. And the stories certainly seem to contain much more truth than any of the other Hall articles. This time, he claimed that as a young boy he was a "brute" with other boys, but a "lamb" with the ladies. "The minute I came into company with girls and women, I kissed their hands, I kissed their hands again."[13]

Near the end of the article, Lugosi recalled a woman he met in Hungary who had eyes like an "owl's ... like two ornaments hung on her face." He admitted such a deep "urge to see her, to make it to see that woman that I became desperate. I looked for ways to accomplish it, just like a criminal." Lugosi claimed he climbed her balcony to see her, and she came to him "without a word, as wordless as I."[14] Then he references an earlier fan magazine article about him by saying:

> It was the story of this woman that was told by a writer in Hollywood some years ago, as my experience with a vampire ... she was not a vampire, she was a woman of flesh and blood. But she did to me what the vampire is imputed to do. She drained away much of my youth. When she said, "Drop the curtain, now, and let it end, as I do," I was not as I had been before.

It is almost as if, in the final Gladys Hall article, Lugosi disavows what she had written in her first, "The Case of the Man Who Dares Not Sleep."

Or perhaps he was referring to a very similar story about "the woman with yellow eyes," published by *Modern Screen* in 1932. It featured the byline J. Eugene Chrisman, but reads so much like Gladys Hall that it may have been her writing under a pseudonym. Whoever wrote it, though, placed an author's note at the beginning of the story claiming the article "is not a fabrication." No, the "woman with yellow eyes" was real:

> Four times she has come into his life; first when a mere youth, to give him three weeks of romance so passionate, so vivid as to make him her unwilling slave for life. Three times more she has appeared, once following each of his marriages and although she spoke to him but once, the mystery which lies in those yellow eyes tore him from the woman he loved. Bela Lugosi will never marry again. He is afraid—afraid of the woman with yellow eyes![15]

Her name was Hedy, and she forever haunts this cursed Lugosi. Forever fearing marriage, forever fearing love with another woman.

Fanciful stories of that kind offer a fictitious Lugosi foredoomed to a life without love thanks to the supernatural. But the real Lugosi seems to have had little difficulty in having affairs with German after woman. His success with the opposite sex dates to at least the beginning of the 20th century, if not earlier. During his acting apprenticeship in Szabadka, during his work in a Temesvár repertory company, and during his days on the stage in Szeged. Over and over again, audiences and critics alike responded to Lugosi's handsome features and his commanding presence. He was particularly popular in Szeged, but even in Budapest he had a large array of female admirers.[16]

If Lugosi is to be believed, there were many, many affairs. Fevered passion, without interference from yellow eyes. If there was trouble, it was that Lugosi had to fight duel after duel with irate husbands who found him in their bedrooms with his hands on their wives. Seventeen in total, he later claimed, and then there were all the occasions when he wasn't caught.[17] Was all of this any more true than Hall's female spectres? Maybe, maybe not. But what is certain is that once Lugosi met Ilona Szmik, she was not the woman for a brief affair.

Ilona Szmik's parents weren't quite upper class economically, but they were extremely well-situated. Her father Lajos was an attorney who worked for a bank; his own father had been a mine inspector. Lajos had been married twice, his first wife dying at a young age. His second wife, Ilona Voigt, was from a very old and noble Hungarian family. Together they made their life on the Buda side of Budapest in a large, two-story home.[18] Thirteen years separated their ages, and for the first seventeen years of their marriage there were no children. Then in 1898, when Lajos was 50 and Ilona was 37, their daughter Ilona was born.[19]

As a child, young Ilona had everything. Puppets and dolls and toys filled her room. She went to a very good Protestant school for girls. She studied French and German, along with taking piano and singing lessons. By the time Ilona was sixteen, she decided to leave

Stars at Swords Points, All in Fun
Telling on Hollywood.

BELA LUGOSI fought 17 Duels

WON	LOST	PCT
17	0	1,000

As printed in the *Dallas Morning News* of March 26, 1932.

school, wanting to see the world. And her parents agreed. She travelled, and she enjoyed the life and culture of Budapest.

Sometime near the end of 1916, Ilona met Bela Lugosi at a ball, and immediately they fell in love with one another. Deeply, madly in love. "A very big love, a very big love for both of them. The biggest," Ilona's granddaughter Noémi Saly later remembered.[20] Within a matter of months, Lugosi and Ilona married; that was in June 1917. Lugosi was nearly 35 years old; Ilona had just turned 19. The existing wedding photo of the two together teems with happiness and love.

But Ilona's parents were only able to share part of the joy. They had nicknamed Ilona "Baby," and she was indeed their baby girl. Lajos had hoped for someone from Budapest's upper class to marry his daughter, not an actor from a small country town. Lugosi's affiliation with the National Theatre was another sore point; Lajos knew how much the women in the audience loved Lugosi, and he had heard rumors of affairs. But in the end, Lajos couldn't say no to Ilona's marriage; after all, he had never really said no to her.

After their wedding, Lugosi and his new bride went to Abbazia, a coastal town on the Adriatic Sea. A popular summer resort, and the site where the "woman with yellow eyes" met the Lugosi of fan magazine lore.[21] There the newlyweds arrived amongst the remains of medieval walls and the splendor of villas built by Hungarians in the nineteenth century. But the serenity of the honeymoon was disrupted. At 35, Lugosi had been sexually active for over two decades.[22] Ilona was not only a virgin, but she knew nothing about sexuality. The first night of the honeymoon was a major shock.

Returning to Budapest, they lived in a separate flat within the large home of Lajos Szmik. They were tremendously happy, with Lugosi gaining more film roles and with Ilona staying at home. And Ilona's

Top: Ilona Szmik, Lugosi's first wife.
Middle: Lajos Szmik, Lugosi's father-in-law.
Bottom: The wedding photo of Lugosi and Szmik. *(Courtesy of Noémi Saly)*

mother grew more and more fond of Lugosi. But whatever ground he made with her family over the next 21 months was lost when he became involved in the actor's union in 1919. That he was moving in Communist circles was hardly welcome news.

Of course the real disruption came when the Kun regime fell apart, and the White Terror of Horthy spread through the streets of Budapest. "Lugosi was afraid.

He was genuinely afraid for his life," Noémi Saly claimed.[23] And when he fled to Vienna, Ilona went with him. Their rapid and unexpected departure from Budapest could hardly have helped their marriage. That Lajos's baby was torn from him thanks to Lugosi's Communist leanings drained him of whatever good feelings he had for his son-in-law.

But even worse things seemed to happen after Lugosi and Ilona settled in their new city. Lugosi and Ilona lost their unborn child. Whether due to a failed pregnancy or to an abortion is unknown; Ilona later spoke of the matter only in hushed tones to her granddaughter. The loss escalated their problems, which included Lugosi's inability to find work in Vienna. The city was full of other unemployed actors, and so Lugosi groped for a solution. And for him, that was heading to Berlin.

Making their way to Germany was only the first part of his plan, though. A place to work for a short time, mainly to make money. After all, Lugosi already had his sights set immigrating on the United States. And that became the trigger for the marriage to fail. It wasn't their having to flee their home country. It wasn't even the unsuccessful pregnancy. "At the word America," she later said, "that was when I came home."[24] Ilona felt her parents would die if they lost her to the US, so far, so very far away from Budapest.

Above: Two unknown women, likely Hungarian or German, pose in this photo that Lugosi had kept in his own collection. Perhaps he had a love affair with one or both of them?
Below: Lugosi (third from left in the front row) in his swimming outfit in Abbazia in the 1910s.

Lugosi wrote to Ilona from Vienna, and then from Germany. Even Lugosi's affair with film actress Violetta Napierska in Berlin didn't diminish his deep love for Ilona.[25] For her part, though, Ilona was shattered when Lugosi would not return to Budapest for her. She couldn't believe it. And so as the weeks turned into months,

Ilona finally divorced him in July 1920. Lajos had helped convince her to move forward legally, clearing the way for Ilona's second marriage in December 1920. The groom was Imre Francsek, a reputable architect who was closely associated with the mayor of Budapest. Like Lugosi, he was very good looking. But that was where the similarities ended. Francsek was everything Lajos wanted for his daughter, everything that Lugosi was not.

Even before Lugosi had married Ilona Szmik, though, he almost certainly knew the name of the woman who would become his second wife. Another Ilona actually: Ilona Von Montagh, the most mysterious of all of Lugosi's wives.[26] An actress, a singer, a prima donna. She was born in Hungary, circa 1899, making her roughly the same age as Ilona Szmik.[27] She had black hair, dark eyes, and stood 5 feet, 9 inches. As a teenager, she performed to great acclaim in the play *Polish Blood* at Budapest's Royal Theater.[28] And in 1916, she also appeared in two Hungarian silent films.[29]

Sometime around 1919, Von Montagh moved to Germany, planning to do studies in acting. But her career took off quickly after she performed at the Metropol Theater. She then took on the lead role in the opera *Königin der Luft* (*Queen Of The Sky*) at the Lessing Theater, with Berlin newspapers praising "her gracefulness, fresh and energetic movement, [and] sophisticated and clear voice."[30] That she was a Hungarian and playing lead roles in German opera was also much talked about at the time.[31]

The following year, she acted in her first and perhaps only German film, *Juck und Schlau*.[32] While the movie hardly seems to have made much of an impact, Von Montagh continued to gain praise at various opera performances in Berlin and Dresden.[33] And of course her success in Germany came exactly during the period in which Lugosi was in Berlin in 1919 and 1920. Just as he likely knew of her work in Budapest a few years earlier, he had to have become reacquainted with Von Montagh's work. Perhaps the two even met in Germany.

By December 1920, Lugosi arrived in the US, having

Ilona Von Montagh in Hungary, on the cover of *Szinházi Élet* for August 17, 1917.

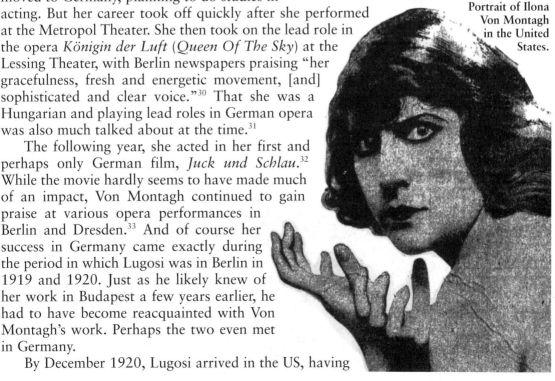

Portrait of Ilona Von Montagh in the United States.

MONTAGH ILONA
MAGYAR SZARMAZASU BERLINI PRIMADONNA
ANGELO FOTOGRAFIA

Photographed during Von Montagh's
theatrical success in Berlin.

sailed from Trieste to New Orleans. He was fulfilling the plans he had shared with Ilona Szmik. By January 1921, he made his way from Louisiana to New York. And then Ilona Von Montagh arrived in New York on January 6, 1921, having sailed from Hamburg on the *Manchuria*. At a glance it almost seems as if she followed Lugosi from Hungary to Germany and then to the US. A story fit for Gladys Hall.

But all of this seems to have been mere coincidence. A US immigration officer recorded that a "Director Amberg" had paid her fare, and that she would be staying with Julius Kessler in New York City.[34] Who were they? Well, Gustave Amberg regularly presented German opera to New York City audiences; one of his most famous had been a performance of Strauss's *Die Fledermaus* (*The Bat*) in 1911.[35] As for Julius Kessler, he was a Hungarian who by 1895 had become a dominant figure in the US whiskey business. By the time of prohibition, he devoted his time to philanthropic activities. He and Amberg were close friends.[36]

Presumably Amberg had heard of Von Montagh's success in Berlin and wanted to present her to US audiences. And Kessler offered accommodations to a fellow Hungarian. But whatever their exact plans, everything was disrupted by Amberg's death on May 23, 1921. He left his entire estate to Kessler.[37] As for Von Montagh, it is difficult to say. Perhaps she continued to stay at Kessler's home, but her stated reason for being in the US had crumbled. "Bad luck began to decorate her with all sorts of jinx-insignia," one journalist later wrote.[38]

Her acquaintance (or, as the case may have been, re-acquaintance) with Lugosi came fairly quickly. And it came out of a need for work. By June, she and Lugosi appeared in a Hungarian-language version of *Little Miss Bluebeard* in New York.[39] Its success with audiences meant other plays followed. In September 1921, for example, she starred in the play *Törvény* (*Law*), which Lugosi directed and presented in Bridgeport, Connecticut.[40] Then they were top-billed together in a New York presentation of Molnár's *Liliom*, with

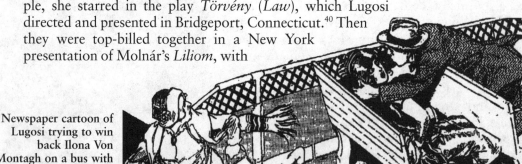

Newspaper cartoon of Lugosi trying to win back Ilona Von Montagh on a bus with her fleeing. As published in the *Indianapolis Star* of December 28, 1924.

Lugosi playing the title role and Von Montagh as Juli.[41]

They both received strong reviews and publicity in the Hungarian-American press, and they were both drawn to each other romantically. In the same way that Lugosi liked to claim that his father was a Baron, Von Montagh dubbed herself a "Countess." That they both loved the theatre and were trying to make their way in a new country may have only increased their passion for one another. A rapid engagement led to a wedding and honeymoon. In September 1921, the couple married.[42]

"A prospect of bliss which seemed too good to be true," a newspaper article soon recounted. "It was." [43] Years later, Lugosi recalled that they were together for only fourteen days.[44] Von Montagh claimed it was for two months.[45] But they appeared with each other on stage in Madách's *The Tragedy of Man* in April 1922, with Lugosi as Adam and Von Montagh as Hippia; Lugosi doubled as director.[46] In it, Madách wrote that "joy is but a fragile flower, foredoomed to fade." Divorce proceedings don't seem to have started until October 1924, a little over three years after Lugosi and Von Montagh had married.[47]

Given that Lugosi rarely spoke of his second wife, the surviving account of their marriage and breakup comes largely from Von Montagh. A story she gave to a newspaper in 1924 while awaiting the final divorce decree that came in February 1925.[48] In her eyes, their marriage didn't work from the start because Lugosi wanted her to retire from the stage. "Marriage and a career?" Lugosi once asked. "No; the Hungarians believe that the man should take care of the woman. Her divine profession is motherhood."[49] His demands led to an eventual separation. They reconciled at some point in 1922, after which things got worse, rather than better.

An X-ray allegedly showing Estelle Winwood's rib that Lugosi was said to have broken in a close embrace. As printed on December 28, 1924 in the *Indianapolis Star*.

In a rare portrait as Fernando in *The Red Poppy* (1922). *(Courtesy of David Wentink)*

Alleged affections between Lugosi and Estelle Winwood, his costar in a New York stage production of *The Red Poppy*, became too much for Von Montagh to bear. Perhaps it was the concocted publicity surrounding *The Red Poppy* that claimed Lugosi broke one of Winwood's ribs after holding her so tightly; perhaps it was something else. Whatever was or wasn't happening between Lugosi and

Winwood is difficult to say. Von Montagh did hire a private detective, learning that Lugosi was definitely seeing another woman.[50] A newspaper reporter wrote, "So deep proved the dent that Bela inflicted on the core of her affections that she demanded a divorce."[51]

Lugosi didn't want to end the marriage, with Von Montagh claiming he started a bizarre campaign to win back her affections. At first he kidnapped her beloved dog Fleurette, returning the pet apparently as an opportunity to speak to his estranged wife. Then things got even stranger:

> No sooner had Ilona recovered from Fleurette's vanishing that she began to act as an unwilling shock-absorber for other strange attentions. Weird voices informed her over the phone at unearthly hours that she had better hurry and mend her absent husband's heart as soon as possible, or else!
>
> Ilona was more perturbed when the New York press began to develop a strange interest in her private life. Not once, but a half a dozen times, reporters pled for interviews, and she politely admitted them. But they threw off all pretense of being news-gatherers, and candidly told her that they were emissaries from her desolate mate.
>
> Shortly after this Ilona embarked for the theatre—alone. At the corner a strange man sprang out at her, uttering incoherent words and making peculiar gesticulations. The gist of his mumbled discourse was that Madame should, must, would take back Bela Lugosi.
>
> Scared out of her senses, Ilona was about to yell for the police when, to her astonishment, the stranger accomplished the equivalent of a quick nocturnal shave by feverishly snatching off his facial decorations.[52]

The facial decoration was a beard, a "bogus set of whiskers," and underneath was Lugosi, a disguised advocate for himself. Von Montagh stormed off, apparently unimpressed with him or his disguise.

But the "end was not yet." A week later, while Von Montagh was riding on the top of a bus, she felt her ankles go cold. Reaching down, she found her legs had just been shackled together by some kind of cord. Apparently Lugosi had been in the seat behind her, crouching onto the bus floor to reach her legs. Caught in a moment of shock when he sat beside her, Lugosi proceeded to tie her wrists together. "Would she come back to him? Would she have mercy?" But she tore loose from him and the quickly-tied bindings, fleeing from the bus and disappearing into the night.[53]

Is any of this true? Perhaps, but it certainly smacks of the kind of wild tabloid journalism of the Roaring Twenties that fostered the fake story about Lugosi breaking Estelle Winwood's rib. It may also have been an attempt to build a case against Lugosi to obtain the divorce. After all, some years later Von Montagh allegedly described her marriage to Lugosi as "two months of boredom."[54]

From the New York *Daily Mirror* of November 5, 1929.

Of course, in the end Lugosi and Von

Lugosi in a provocative photograph from the Broadway play
Arabesque (1925). *(Courtesy of David Wentink)*

Lugosi at his home in the 1930s. The nude portrait of Clara Bow
still hangs on his wall.

Montagh were officially married for over three years. Wherever he was in the autumn of 1924 (whether New York or Chicago or LA), Lugosi didn't respond to the summons and complaints from the Superior Court for New York County.[55] The divorce proceeded without him, and there is no record that the two ever spoke again.

But Lugosi clearly spoke to other women. He presumably had relationships with a variety of women during the mid-to-late 1920s. Once he secured fame on Broadway with *Dracula* in 1927, the eyes of women were upon him as never before. As he told Gladys Hall, "It is a biological thing. … it was the embrace of Death their subconscious was yearning for. Death, the final, the triumphant lover."[56]

Whatever admirers, whatever affairs, though, none would become as famous as Lugosi's romance with film star Clara Bow. Remembering an evening in 1928, actor Jack Oakie later wrote that:

> Suddenly [Bow] came running out. "Come on, everybody! We've got tickets!" she said. "We're going down to the Biltmore to see *Dracula*." She was so excited that she didn't stop to dress. She just threw a great long mink over her swimsuit and we all got into her chauffeur-driven black Packard limousine.
> He couldn't speak English, but no language barrier could hide his thrill at meeting Clara Bow. He was overwhelmed with the redhead. …Bow invited him to her home and they became very good friends.[57]

Lugosi did of course speak English when he met Bow. Perhaps Oakie was referring to his limited skills with the language. Perhaps Lugosi even gave the appearance of being less adept at English to appear more exotic.

Little is actually known of Lugosi and Bow's relationship, but it does seem to have gone beyond simply being "good friends." Marion Schilling, whose father Peter had invested money in the 1928 West Coast version of *Dracula*, remembered:

> Clara Bow, then at the peak of her fame, attended at least two performances a week during the two months run. She'd sometimes come directly from her beach house wearing a fur coat over her bathing suit. The play's attrac-

tion for her? Bela Lugosi! She had a terrific crush on him.

Bela liked to tell my father that if I were a bit older, without question he'd marry me. I'm certain this was a bit of blarney. In competition with the scintillating Clara, what chance would poor green little Marion have had![58]

The story of Bow wearing nothing but a swimming suit under her fur coat only fuelled the imagination of later film historians. A torrid affair of legendary proportions. Fevered passion unleashed between the Vampire and the It Girl.

Well, maybe. Certainly Lugosi's name became romantically linked with Bow's in the press. Some of this came in scandal-laden newspapers like the New York *Daily Mirror*. And to be sure, some of it was in more reputable newspapers. For example, the *Los Angeles Times* claimed that "Morley Drury and Bela Lugosi each had a brief inning in Clara's affections."[59] Much of it directly or indirectly seems to have come from stories told by Clara's secretary Daisy DeVoe.[60]

One of the other key memories of Lugosi and Bow comes from Tui Lorraine Bow, who remembered when Lugosi visited Clara's Malibu cottage. Three bedrooms and full occupancy, but it was Tui and not Lugosi who shared Clara's bedroom.[61] That situation may speak to the state of Bow and Lugosi's relationship at that moment, as well as the fact other house guests were present. But stories suggesting the more torrid aspects of their affair stem from fairly spurious accounts. And given that Lugosi had serious problems with career-oriented women, he could scarcely have built a successful long-term relationship with Clara Bow any more than he had with Von Montagh.

Whether they ever spoke during the 1930s or after is unknown. But they certainly parted with fond feelings for one another. They both kept mementos of one another till their deaths. Lugosi had a large painting of Bow in the nude (which was almost certainly painted by artist's imagination rather than posed by Bow). And Bow always kept a signed picture of Lugosi in her collection of photographs.[62]

At first glance, the next woman in Lugosi's wife was very different than either Clara Bow or Ilona Von Montagh: Beatrice Weeks. Beatrice Woodruff Weeks, actually. She didn't work, for example, and came from a family wealthier than Lugosi's; in those ways, she was similar to Ilona Szmik. But like Clara Bow, she was American, a modern woman of the Roaring Twenties. And also like Bow, Weeks met Lugosi as a result of his West Coast version of *Dracula*.

Beatrice Woodruff Weeks.

It was Luigi Stilliti, an Italian Consul-General, who introduced Lugosi to Weeks at a reception in late summer 1928. Lugosi was then performing in the "Vampire Play" at San Francisco's Columbia Theatre for a three-week run. He must have quickly learned that she had recently become a widow; only five months

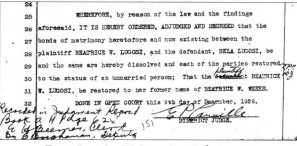

24
25 WHEREFORE, by reason of the law and the findings
26 aforesaid, IT IS HEREBY ORDERED, ADJUDGED AND DECREED that the
27 bonds of matrimony heretofore and now existing between the
28 plaintiff BEATRICE W. LUGOSI, and the defendant, BELA LUGOSI, be
29 and the same are hereby dissolved and each of the parties restored
30 to the status of an unmarried person; That the plaintiff BEATRICE
31 W. LUGOSI, be restored to her former name of BEATRICE W. WEEKS.
32 DONE IN OPEN COURT this 9th day of December, 1929.

From *Beatrice W. Lugosi vs. Bela Lugosi*, filed December 9, 1929 in Washoe County, Nevada.

earlier, her husband Charles Peter Weeks had died in his bed.[63]

Charles Weeks had been a noted architect, designing buildings in San Francisco, Sacramento, and San Jose. He had even drawn up the plans for the famous Loew's State Theatre in Los Angeles. And that was all after studying in Paris years earlier. A worldly figure who was twenty years older than Beatrice. But certainly neither of them was naïve when came to relationships; both had been married once before.[64] In fact, Beatrice had only been legally divorced from her first husband for one day when she and Weeks took their vows.[65]

At the time Beatrice met Lugosi, though, she was no longer married. That fifteen years separated their ages was hardly a worry. A wider age gap separated Beatrice from her then-deceased Charles Peter, just as it had in reverse for Lugosi and both Ilonas. And Lugosi would have seemed even more the worldly man than Beatrice's recently-deceased husband. Perhaps she was even fascinated by his role in *Dracula*; presumably she saw the play at least once in 1928.

By the autumn of that year, Lugosi left Beatrice and San Francisco to return to Los Angeles. They corresponded, but it's impossible to know how close of a relationship that they had developed at that stage. Or how frequently they corresponded, for that matter. It would seem logical that she told him of her father's death in January 1929.[66] John Woodruff—an attorney, naval commander, and member of the US Shipping Board—had died after a relapse of influenza; he was only 58 years old. Whether Beatrice made it to his interment at Arlington Cemetery two days after his death in unknown.[67]

Lugosi meets Chief Thundercloud circa 1930 with an unknown woman at his side.

But what is certain is the fact that Beatrice was alone. Her husband and father dead. No siblings at all. And her mother living thousands of miles away in Washington, D.C.[68] Alone, that is, until *Dracula* arrived back in the Bay Area. Lugosi—who in 1929 was in Los Angeles rather than touring with a *Dracula* roadshow—decided to star in a San Francisco production. The show came almost a year after the 1928 stage *Dracula* when he met Beatrice. And *Dracula* had now brought them back together.

Within a week of the play's opening in late July, the couple wed at a courtroom in Redwood City.[69] No honeymoon, of course. Lugosi had to continue appearing in the San Francisco *Dracula* for another two weeks, then one week in Oakland.[70] After that, maybe a honeymoon would have been possible before the two would make their home in Hollywood. In the short term, they'd stay in a group of rooms on the top floor of the Hotel Mark Hopkins in San Francisco; curiously enough, it had been designed by Charles Peter Weeks.[71]

But in the end, there never would be a honeymoon, or a home together in Hollywood. If anything, it doesn't seem like they remained together for those last two weeks of the San Francisco run of *Dracula*. Lugosi once said the marriage lasted only three days; Beatrice said it had lasted four and a half.[72] What could have gone so horribly wrong in that short amount of time? Lugosi later complained of Beatrice's dancing with other men, her smoking, and her lack of help with his hangovers.[73] He was also distressed by the fact that she drank gin at eight in the morning.[74]

Lillian Arch in a 1931 photo taken at Witzel Studios in Los Angeles. Inscribed to Lugosi.
(Courtesy of David Wentink)

As for Beatrice, well, her version was wildly different. She claimed that he had a violent temper and was inhospitable to their guests and servants.[75] The New York *Daily Mirror* quoted her as saying:

> [Lugosi] slapped me in the face because I ate a lamb chop which he hidden in the icebox for his after-theatre, midnight lunch. ... His table manners were terrible. ... He constantly used his fingers in place of a fork and was addicted to similar habits that simply frayed my nerves. [And] he told me that he was King, that in Hungary a wife and all she possessed were placed at the husband's disposal, that, in effect, she was nothing but a servant.[76]

On that final point, she added that Lugosi demanded her checkbook and the key to her safe deposit box on the third day of their marriage.[77]

Beatrice's claims about the checkbook seemed even more dastardly alongside her stories about Clara Bow. "I don't know when they will be married," she said of Lugosi and Bow. "But before I left my husband he told me he and Clara had been engaged; that they had agreed to remain away from each other a year to test their love."[78] The implication was that he married Beatrice for her money, while waiting for the right moment to reunite with Bow.

The story becomes more confused when the *Daily Mirror* suggests Lugosi (whom they refer to as "Count Lugosi") had actually "jilted" Bow to marry

Beatrice. Did Beatrice say any of this? Certainly the *Daily Mirror* claimed their information came from Beatrice when she filed for divorce. Even if that's true, though, it is possible that some of what she said was only to illustrate the legal necessity for a divorce. Or, given that the bar for obtaining a divorce in Reno was so low, perhaps if she actually said such things, she was speaking out of anger.

As with the divorce court proceedings with both Ilonas, Lugosi didn't appear in Reno to say anything on his own behalf. But he did speak his mind to the press in December 1929 while doing an interview about his new film, *The Thirteenth Chair*. When the *Hollywood Citizen-News* "timidly" asked "You were married recently for just a few days, weren't you?" Lugosi responded affirmatively, adding:

> I cannot accustom myself to the modern girl. She is a creature of impulse. She has found a new liberty in thinking for herself. She has discovered all things are possible for her, and she is forgetting there is a greater happiness in consulting and thinking things over with friends, husband, family. She will never be completely happy until she once again takes her place by the side of a man as his companion and helpmate. It is her natural place and she will be unhappy, restless, and doing things she is sorry for until she adjusts herself to this place.[79]

With all the rancor in the press, though, Lugosi told another interviewer that he did see Beatrice after the divorce. "And why not?" he questioned. "Two people who failed at marriage may still find each other enjoyable and entertaining persons."[80]

Lillian and Lugosi in the early 1930s.
(Courtesy of Dennis Phelps)

For reasons that aren't entirely clear, Beatrice became increasingly unhappy. Perhaps it was because of drink, perhaps it was being sad at the loss of Charles Peter Weeks. Beatrice even reached out in vain to Lugosi, asking him to take her back.[81] And whatever depression she was experiencing, Beatrice also had increasing medical problems. Pulmonary disease. She moved to Colon, Panama, where she died in May 1931 at the young age of 34. Her official obituary in the *New York Times* didn't mention Lugosi at all, Lugosi who years later regretted the divorce.[82]

Despite Beatrice's alleged statements, Lugosi and Clara Bow did not get engaged. By the time the divorce was final, it is very possible Lugosi wasn't even in contact with Bow. He did have affairs after the divorce, apparently; a woman accompanied him to the set of *Dracula* in 1930, for example.[83] But Lugosi claimed that he "learned" a "lesson" about marriage after his experience with Beatrice.[84]

Lugosi learned a lesson about the press, too, at least when it came to his love affairs:

> That part of my life is my own. My romances have been the subject of much publicity. Oftener than not, the press reports have been more fictional than otherwise. I prefer not to discuss it.[85]

He also told the same reporter that readers would have to content themselves by looking at back issues of old tabloids to learn about his affair with Bow or his wives.[86] On another occasion, he was even less kind to a prying reporter. His friend Andor Sziklay recalled that he once "bodily threw a reporter out of his anteroom" when the reporter was trying to collect "spicy episodes" of his life.[87]

After the film version of *Dracula* became a success, though, Lugosi wasn't worrying about either Bow or

Lillian with one of Lugosi's beloved dogs. Could the shadow on the lower right be Lugosi?

the women he married in the US. The failed relationships of recent years made him think about the one that apparently still held the most meaning for him: Ilona Szmik. In a January 1932 magazine interview, Lugosi spoke of his lost love:

> In all his life a man finds only one mate. Other women may bring happiness close to him, but there is just one mate. This girl was mine.
> …That was years ago. We have thought of remarriage. But she has children. One can forget many things, but not when children are there as reminders of old, deep wounds. They would always come between.[88]

Some of what Lugosi said in the interview about Ilona was definitely false. He said that she hadn't left Budapest with him, when in fact she had. He also claimed she divorced him as the way to convince her father to intervene in his impending execution. Along with the fact that Lugosi had fled to Vienna, Lajos Szmik simply didn't have that kind of political influence.[89]

But presumably for reasons of rebuilding his own pride, the most noticeable error he committed in telling the story was the moment when he said, "we have thought of remarriage." Remarrying was Lugosi's idea, not Ilona's. He may have been thinking, hoping that the two could reunite for years. Whatever she felt about America, by the release of *Dracula* (1931) he was conquering Hollywood in a way that was definitely beyond his stage success in Hungary. And by the time of *Dracula*'s release, Lugosi had learned that Lajos Szmik had died in 1927.

Of course he had also learned about Ilona's new husband, Imre Francsek.

Though Francsek was highly successful, he had lost everything in 1929 when economic depression hit Hungary. He looked to Iran for work, moving to Tehran that very year; many doctors and pharmacists and architects were moving there at roughly the same time. All looking for work in a country where the Shah of the time welcomed Europeans. Ilona joined him in 1930, bringing with her the couple's two children.

How did Lugosi learn all of this? Curiously it was through Imre's own sister, Irén Takaró, who had become well-known in the Hungarian-American community after moving to the US with her husband, the Reverend Géza Takaró. Sometime in 1930, Irén gave Lugosi Ilona's address in Tehran. He had written to her many times since they parted ways in earlier years, but this time his envelope included a one-way boat ticket. Lugosi begged her to use it to reunite with him in the US.

Ilona threw the ticket out and didn't respond. By that time she had already burned everything to do with him, except for just a few photos. She would stay with Imre and her two children in Iran. America was still not a word she wanted to hear, even if for different reasons than in 1919. As for Lugosi, he continued having affairs in Los Angeles with women like Lulu Schlange.[90] Maybe affairs were easier for him to deal with, at least at that stage in his life. After all, in August 1931, the *Los Angeles Record* claimed that he always liked "a lady better if she's stupid."[91]

Affairs or not, though, Lugosi apparently fell in love again sometime in 1931.[92] She was Lillian Arch, and in some ways she seems to have been similar to Ilona Szmik. In fact, perhaps—at least at first—she was a replacement for Ilona, who just months earlier had spurned his invitation to America. After all, Lillian was much younger than Lugosi; the 29-year age gap between them was even larger than it had been between Lugosi and Szmik. Though she had been born in the US, she was of Hungarian descent. And though she did work as a secretary, including for Lugosi in the early thirties, Lillian like Ilona was not a career woman.

But Lugosi must have appreciated the fact that her family was very different than the Szmiks. Both Lugosi and Lillian's father Stephen Arch had somewhat similar views on marriage and gender roles.[93] And they both were in agreement on his leftist politics, with Arch becoming Vice-President of the Los Angeles branch of the HACD during World War II.[94]

At the same time, Stephen Arch was against Lugosi dating or marrying Lillian when he learned that Lugosi wasn't rich.[95] Arch and his wife Mimi became so intent on keeping them apart that Lugosi and Lillian had to sneak around together. To break free of Arch's dictates permanently, Lugosi convinced Lillian to go

Photo by Porter S. Cleveland

MR. and MRS. BELA LUGOSI, with their new **1935 BUICK**
STRAIGHT 8 DeLuxe, 7 Passenger Sedan, purchased from

PHIL HALL
Branch Manager
HOWARD AUTOMOBILE CO. OF LOS ANGELES
HOLLYWOOD STORE
Sales   6157 Hollywood Boulevard   GRanite 3181   Service

The movie colony is more **B U I C K** and **P O N T I A C** minded than ever before

Lugosi never drove a car himself, which might explain why Lillian is behind the wheel in this advertisement from *The Screen Guild's Magazine* in May 1935.

to Las Vegas with him at the end of January 1933. They would elope, and be together forever. After a quick ceremony, Lugosi and Lillian immediately took a plane back to Los Angeles. They were now impervious to her family's interference.[96]

Perhaps Stephen Arch—who served as manager of the Magyar Athletic Club's sports teams and was also owner of a Hungarian restaurant—renewed his worries over Lugosi's financial situation when he read about Lugosi being sued for back rent.[97] That was in early February 1933; the story hit newspapers less than a week after the newlyweds had eloped.[98] Hardly a perfect beginning to his new life with Lillian.

What was their relationship like? Given that it would last so much longer than any of his other marriages or affairs, it is impossible to understand its complexities and to chart all its

Lugosi with Lugosi Jr.

many peaks and valleys. But it is fair to say Lugosi tried to create a home life with Lillian that was impossible with Beatrice or Von Montagh. One New York journalist quoted Lugosi as saying that Lillian was "a perfect wife, a perfect housekeeper, a perfect woman."[99] And of course there was what he told Gladys Hall in "Memos of a Madman":

> I pick out everything my wife wears. I like to see her in simple things. I do not like exotic things on women. When we were first married, I stopped my wife from using make-up. I did it, she will tell you, very gradually and very delicately. First the lipstick… "Do not use it," I said, "You have natural color in your lips; I like natural color." …then the rouge, then the powder… I told her, "When you wear make-up, you look just like the rest of them."
>
> I allow her to wear no jewelry and no perfume. I took the curls away from her face. I push her hair back of her ears all the time saying, "Now, this is the way you are the loveliest…" Men like natural women, I submit; it is a natural instinct.
>
> …Now, when my wife will tell that I am the Master of the House, when she tells, "I do what he says, oh, definitely," when it is known that I must have my house run perfectly, like machinery, everything, to the last pin, in its appointed place, and people raise eyebrows and shudder a little….[100]

Decades later, Lillian recalled the kind of domineering behavior that Lugosi described to Hall, mentioning that he tried to "mold" her to his own satisfaction.[101]

Their first several years together may have well been quite happy, at least in large measure. Having parties, singing songs, and enjoying the best that Hollywood

Lugosi and Lillian, presumably from the early forties.
(Courtesy of Bill Chase)

could offer.[102] That Lugosi spent money with reckless abandon may have unnerved Lillian at times, but at least temporarily the money kept coming in. And even with all of his bad moods, Lugosi could also be so fun, so charming.[103]

Perhaps in the summer of 1935, the two of them read the news about one of Lugosi's earlier wives. Wearing an expensive gown, the "Countess" Ilona Von Montagh was caught shoplifting in New York City. She and her friend Irene Humphrey were then sharing a penthouse; both were caught stealing dresses at the same department store. Von Montagh claimed it was a publicity stunt for a book she was writing; in another story, she said it was a kind of prank, done as part of a "bet."[104] Despite the fact she appeared in court draped in diamonds and a silver fox, Von Montagh couldn't afford bail. And only months later, a trust company in New York went after Von Montagh and Humphrey for money they owed.[105] Humphrey soon married, but what finally became of Von Montagh is unknown.[106]

The Countess certainly didn't encroach upon Lugosi and Lillian in any way, of course. Nor did any other woman in their early years together. No, their first major problem seems to have been financial woes brought on when the studios stopped making horror films. But Lugosi and Lillian fought through that period together. And they did so as a growing family.

In January 1938, Lillian gave birth to their son, Bela Jr. Actor's Relief had to help pay the bills, but the couple were still overjoyed. It was Lugosi's only son, his only child, and he lavished attention on him. In 1939, Jimmie Fidler wrote about how the happy parents spoke Hungarian to Bela Jr., hoping he'd learn the language.[107] In another column, Fidler also joked about the diet that the Lugosis fed their son.[108] And the *LA Times* spoke about how Lugosi hired a gypsy orchestra to play at Bela Jr.'s second birthday party.[109] Nothing was too good for his boy in those days.

By 1940, Lugosi told Hedda Hopper that because his wife was an "angel," he didn't "think anybody could be happier."[110] But it was during World War II that increasing difficulties between Lugosi and Lillian transformed into major issues. His beliefs about marriage and being the "Master of the House" had benefited from Lillian's youth and naiveté; by the 1940s, it was behavior she increasingly understood to be mental cruelty. There were also his mood swings when Lugosi seemed to want to argue with her. There was his drinking, which became more and more of a problem as the years wore on. There also was his intense jealousy.

And curiously, the press talked about Lillian's second pregnancy. More than two months before Bela Jr. was born, Ed Sullivan had announced the upcoming birth in his newspaper column.[111] In that same way, Jimmy Fidler wrote in the summer of 1941 that there would be an "heir-rival" at the Lugosi home that October.[112] A mistake? Perhaps, but only a month later Fidler repeated his claim that the "stork" would be paying the Lugosis a visit, this time changing the expected date of birth.[113] And then nothing more was printed. Was Lillian in fact expecting a child that became a failed pregnancy?

Whatever problems existed, Lillian left Lugosi in 1944; she took their son and moved in with her sister.[114] Some weeks, probably even months later, she filed for divorce in August 1944.[115] She claimed (presumably through her attorney) that he had made her life "unbearable," and even asked for a restraining order that was not lifted until November of that year.[116] The reason? Lugosi and Lillian had reconciled. Lugosi told the press that he:

Lugosi in a publicity photograph for the play *Three Indelicate Ladies* (1947)

> became a careless husband. I guess I just expected [the marriage to be] too much my own way instead of operating on a 50-50 basis. The divorce suit was a good thing; it made us realize how much we loved each other.[117]

By that time, the press also mentioned that Lillian had enrolled their son in a local military academy.[118] He soon earned the nickname "The Field," thanks to his success at playing ball.[119]

The reconciliation wasn't permanent though. For reasons unknown, Lillian quickly left Lugosi a second time. And after a matter of weeks, she returned again; in March 1945, the *LA Times* announced their "second reconciliation within five months."[120] That led to Lillian's formal dismissal of her divorce suit.[121]

What changed? Presumably Lugosi made a good faith effort at altering his ways, but other factors must have soon weighed heavily on the marriage. Lugosi's screen career began to decline shortly after the reunion. Lillian had returned to grapple in the ensuing years with a Lugosi that was likely harder to deal with than ever before. Money grew tighter, and Lugosi's endless personal appearances often included Lillian onstage as the woman he hypnotized. He once tried to force Ilona Von Montagh off the stage; now he had to convince Lillian to do the opposite.

After 1948, Lugosi also grew more depressed as film roles decreased to a point of nonexistence.[122] Without the movies, he felt like he had been reduced to "freak status," which was something he "just couldn't stand."[123] His health declined. His drinking increased. And his bad habits that he tried to correct after the separations came back. Bad moods, domineering attitudes, and intense jealousy.

Lugosi and Lillian on board the *RMS Queen Elizabeth*
in 1951. *(Courtesy of Bill Chase)*

Perhaps the jealousy came in part from the fact he may have had affairs with other women during his marriage to Lillian. Certainly there was a rumor that Lugosi had an affair with a script girl at Universal Studios in 1939; another bit of gossip claimed he had fathered a child with someone other than his wife.[124] No proof supports such tales, and they may well not be true at all.

Certainly Lugosi did notice other women, though. Actress Suzanne Kaarén, Lugosi's costar in *The Devil Bat* (1940), noticed that "he had an eye for the ladies—in fact, he was a bit of a flirt."[125] And there was the time in 1948 that actor David Durston saw a young female fan approach Lugosi wanting an autograph. As Lugosi's eyes circled around her prominent bustline, he offered to take her "around the world." Not understanding the sexual undercurrent of his joke, the young lady responded, "Oh Mr. Lugosi, my mother wouldn't let me go that far!"[126]

But there are also more clear instances of attempted infidelity. While working on a production of *Arsenic and Old Lace* in 1949, Lugosi gave costar Helen Richman the impression that he and Lillian were separated, which wasn't the case. Later, Richman said:

> I remember one night when I was changing into my different costume backstage, I felt these cold lips up and down my back. And I realized that Mr. Lugosi was kissing my back, and I said to myself, well, I'm not going to say anything because he's the star, but he must have had a strong feeling for me to be doing this.
>
> The next thing I know, the next day he said, "I would like you to tour with me in *Dracula* as Lucy. Of course you would have to be my baby." And I said to myself, that's an expression I haven't heard before, but I think I know what he means.[127]

Richman didn't accept Lugosi's advances. But the questions remains very open as to whether this was the only time he tried to cheat on Lillian.

By the 1950s, their relationship grew worse. Near the beginning of that decade, Irén Takaró wrote to Ilona Szmik, who had returned with her children to Budapest in 1942. Her second husband Imre had disappeared after trying to deliver payroll checks to some oil field workers in Iran. Years later, Ilona learned he was in a Russian *gulag*. Takaró included a few lines about Lugosi in her letter. She had remained in touch with Lugosi over the years; her husband had even been involved in the Hungarian-American Council for Democracy.[128] In her letter, Irén told Ilona that Lugosi was with a good woman who was taking care of him.[129]

And then, when a reporter in 1952 asked Lugosi who scared him, he responded with a list that included Lillian. "She's not afraid of me," he said, "I do what she says."[130] But that comment, however humorous, wasn't true. Sometime in late February 1953, Lillian left Lugosi again.[131] He called; he wrote letters. In one of them, he promised he was a "completely new Bela." [132] A Bela who had achieved so much thanks to Alcoholics Anonymous. A Bela who cared about her happiness, and loved her very much.

But his loudest overture was phoning (or perhaps having a friend phone) the police department, claiming that he was going to commit suicide. Reporters from the *Los Angeles Examiner* and the *Herald and Express* made it to his apartment while the police officer was still there, perhaps because they were tipped by the authorities. Or, more likely, because Lugosi (or a friend of his) called them. With a smile on his face and an arm around the policeman, Lugosi said:

> Gentlemen, some foul creature from the Rue Morgue is playing a joke on me. It is all a mistake. Who wants to commit suicide? Why, I'm a happy man. I'm just beginning to live. [133]

The scheme succeeded in getting him newspaper publicity, a signal to Lillian that he existed. And simultaneously, he sent the same message to the Hollywood film community; after all, he told reporters that Alex Gordon's movie *The Atomic Monster* would "soon" start production.[134]

Lillian as a hypnotized maid with Lugosi's Dracula.

But the suicide scheme didn't benefit his career or his relationship with Lillian. When she actually decided to divorce Lugosi is unclear, but newspapers covered the story at the beginning of June 1953. Journalists claimed that their latest separation had begun on May 1, 1953. Either that was in error, or it speaks to some minor reconciliation that occurred between February and May.[135]

When the case actually went before Superior Court Judge Samuel R. Blake in mid-July 1953, Lugosi didn't appear.[136] Lillian attended with her sister, Valeria. Her testimony was not all that different from the complaints she lodged in 1944. She told the judge:

> He was extremely jealous. He kept me under his thumb 24 hours a day. He'd listen in on an extension phone when I talked to my mother; he checked up on me when I went to the dentist's office; he charged me with infidelity.[137]

On the latter point, Lillian added, "He frequently accused me of associating with other men, knowing that the charges were untrue."[138] Who were these men? They could have been all kinds of different people she knew; they possibly included actor Brian Donlevy, for whom she was doing some secretarial work.[139]

Lillian also explained to the judge that Lugosi hadn't worked for months, and

Above: Lugosi and police officer R. W. Hastings, who investigated Lugosi's alleged suicide attempt.
Below: Lugosi in late February 1953, laughing off reports of his suicide attempt.

that she was not asking the court for alimony or child support for the 15-year-old Bela Jr. "I know if conditions change, Bela Lugosi will support his son without any order to do so," she said.[140] But Judge Blake still ordered that Lugosi should make child support payments if his future income would allow it.[141]

As far as the property went, the court awarded Lillian ownership of their 1947 Buick. They would share the plots of land they owned at Lake Elsinore. And Lugosi had to continue making payments on two life insurance policies, with Lillian remaining as the beneficiary.[142] It had really ended.

Whither the woman with yellow eyes? Had she reappeared? No, not unless she was a metaphor for Lugosi's personality problems that affected all of his wives. And it had happened again. If Ilona Szmik had been his greatest love, Lillian Arch had been his most important relationship. Twenty years of marriage, good times and bad. It had begun at the height of Lugosi's Hollywood fame. And now, all of it was over in the midst of his corroded career. A tragic tale.

By the time Lillian divorced Lugosi, Gladys Hall was no longer writing for film magazines. She had retired from journalism in 1949 to breed springer spaniels. The little she did write was about pet care for dogs.[143] The days of crafting stories about Bela Lugosi were long in the past. The days when she wrote that he was:

the man to whom no woman can stay married–why not?

No answer. No answer. No answer. There are questions better not put to Bela Lugosi. There are answers far better not heard. There are secrets better–much better–left interred.[144]

CHAPTER FOUR

Screen Classics

Bela Lugosi prided himself on how much he read each day. World events, mainly. Newspaper after newspaper.[1] And at the beginning of December 1952, just
a short time before Lillian left him, Lugosi likely read a story that was printed in just about every newspaper in the country. It was the story of Christine
Jorgensen.

Someone who definitely read those newspaper stories was exploitation filmmaker George Weiss. By the end of 1952, Weiss had produced at least four films, only
one of which featured anything close to a recognizable star, *The Devil's Sleep* (1949)
with Lita Grey Chaplin. His films made money largely because he ripped news stories right out of the headlines and made movies out of them. Artificial insemination,
for example, and illegal drug rings.[2] Seeing the articles on Christine Jorgensen at the
end of 1952, Weiss wasted no time in mobilizing a film production.

Christine Jorgensen. Who was she? Well, the question might just as well be who
was *he*? George W. Jorgensen, Jr., born in the Bronx and a two-year veteran of
World War II, had at the age of 26 become "transformed by medical science into a
normal, happy, beautiful woman." A successful sex-change in Denmark performed
by the "world famous Professor Hamburger," which Jorgensen's parents divulged to
the press after two years of complicated treatments came to an end.[3] Her story was
perfect for an exploitation film, and so Weiss quickly tried to hire her.

And, not surprisingly, she just as quickly turned Weiss down. In the days after
the press first broke the story, she was buried under all kinds of offers. The *LA
Times* wrote, "US and European showmen, theatrical producers, and agents have
offered her big sums... They say they do not care how shapely she may be, whether
she can hum a simple tune or not, or even act." But Jorgensen–who was thinking of
writing a book–initially turned down every offer, and many of them were likely for
a lot more money than Weiss could have mustered.[4]

Another factor was that Jorgensen didn't even make it back to America until
mid-February 1953.[5] By that time, she had an agent in New York who began booking her into venues like the Los Angeles Orpheum.[6] But none of this would have
suited Weiss, who acted on the initial publicity as fast as he could. Strike while the
iron is hot. He almost certainly produced *Glen or Glenda* in January 1953 at the
latest, before Jorgensen had even landed back on US soil.[7]

For his new project, Weiss hired cinematographer William C. Thompson, a
largely overlooked figure in film history, whose work allegedly went back to the

Lugosi the avid reader. Note his pipe collection
on the table next to him.

Edison studios.[8] Following his first feature film *Absinthe* (1914), Thompson spent most of his career shooting exploitation films, ranging from silents like *The Woman Untamed* (1920) through such talkies as *Maniac* (1934), *High School Girl* (1934), and *Tomorrow's Children* (1934). As time went on, Thompson also shot burlesque movies like *B-Girl Rhapsody* (1950), as well as Weiss's own film *The Devil's Sleep* (1949). For decades, he was the eyes behind exploitation.

Most famously, of course, Weiss hired Edward D. Wood, Jr. as the film's writer and director. Ed Wood. The famous, the infamous Ed Wood. A transvestite who fought in World War II wearing women's underwear under his uniform. A filmmaker whose career was virtually unknown until after his death, when it appeared at the vanguard of new kind of screen celebration: movies so bad they were good. A celebration of artistic failure.

By the time Weiss hired him, Wood's only notable credit as writer or director was for a television drama called *The Sun Was Setting* (1951). For *Glen or Glenda*, Wood not only wrote the script and directed the proceedings, but he also hired the bulk of the onscreen talent, ranging from his real-life girlfriend Dolores Fuller to noted screen actor Lyle Talbot. Wood cast himself as well. He then tried to hire Bela Lugosi, perhaps out of a love for his films, perhaps out of a desire for his name value, and perhaps out of a plan to forge a relationship that could help his future projects.

How did Wood even get to know Lugosi? Through a mutual friend, Alex

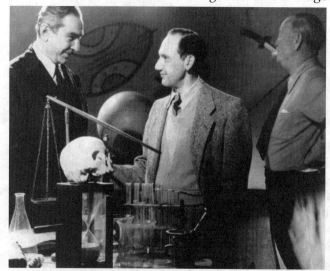

Lugosi, George Weiss, and William C. Thompson
on the set of *Glen or Glenda* (1953).

Gordon. Sometime after Lugosi made it back to California following his 1951 stage tour of *Dracula* in England, Gordon introduced the two, presumably in 1952.[9] As Wood remembered, "Alex Gordon and I had an apartment together. He knew Bela and I didn't."[10]

Wood later claimed that Lugosi didn't particularly like him in the early days of their relationship.[11] This was in contrast to future *Glen or Glenda* co-star Dolores Fuller, who quickly won Lugosi's heart with a goulash dish made from her Hungarian grandmother's recipe.[12] With Fuller by his side, Wood pitched the Weiss project in

Lugosi and "Tommy" Haines in *Glen or Glenda*.
Did Lugosi know what the film was really about?

December 1952 when they were dining with the Lugosis.[13]

"Well, Lugosi just turned the thing down flat," Wood claimed. "He didn't want to go with the independents. He knew it was going to be about the Jorgensen thing."[14] Makeup man Harry Thomas later agreed, saying, "of course he knew that it was going to be about sex-changes and stuff like that."[15] And actress Evelyn Wood added, "I just assumed that Bela knew what the film was about, because we all sat and talked [about it]."[16]

But not everyone remembered it that way, with co-star Conrad Brooks later claiming, "Ed got Lugosi in the thing without actually letting him know what the film was going to be about."[17] And one friend of Lugosi's believed that Lugosi may have only had a vague idea of the storyline.[18] Memories and oral histories regularly conflict with one another, but they seem particularly embattled when it comes to all things Ed Wood.[19] That Lugosi understood that the film was about Jorgensen would explain why he initially turned it down. At the same time, Wood gave him such cryptic dialogue that it seems equally possible that Lugosi was kept largely in the dark.

The Lugosis soon reconsidered, perhaps out of financial desperation. "Now I remember Lillian saying that it would be okay if it were to be $1,000," Wood said. "I gave Lugosi the script at that point."[20] With everything finally in place, Wood shot the movie at the Jack Miles studio in only four days, probably in January 1953.[21] Lugosi's footage took only a day to shoot, perhaps less. One day and one thousand dollars. After all, not many people would ever hear about it, let alone see it.

To Aline Mosby of the United Press, George Weiss announced that his new film was a "documentary. We talked to hundreds of people and psychiatrists. We had doctors supervising the operation scene."[22] He also spoke to the *Oakland Tribune*, who in turn wrote:

> Christine Jorgensen, who has been a little coy about doing her life story on the screen, may regret that she did not take the original offer of agent Al Rosen.
>
> The story is being filmed, willy-nilly, by producer George Weiss, one of the more successful of the Poverty Row independents of Hollywood, and will hit the screen under the title *I Changed My Sex*.
>
> [It] is about ready for the market. It will have Bela Lugosi as a name, and such unknowns as Tommy Haines, a woman musician, as Miss Jorgensen, Wood and Dolores Fuller in support.[23]

Above: Lugosi with Conrad Brooks, an actor and friend of Ed Wood's who appeared in *Glen or Glenda* (1953).
Below: Lugosi on the set of *Glen or Glenda* (1953).

I Changed My Sex. Glen or Glenda. I Led 2 Lives. He or She? Weiss later claimed that different titles emerged for different markets, with exhibitors choosing the one that they thought would work best for their audiences.[24]

Though it was "ready for the market," the question was really whether the market was ready for it, regardless of whatever title it carried. *Glen or Glenda* certainly played some theatres in 1953, but not too many. It took years for many cities to see the film. For example, Oakland–whose newspaper ran the 1953 production story on the film–didn't end up screening it until 1957, sandwiching it between *Screen Burlesque* and *Undraped Lovelies*.[25] A year later in Ohio it was double-billed a drive-in theatre with *White Slavery*; they openly promoted it as the "film version" of Christine Jorgensen's story.[26]

To the degree *Glen or Glenda* registered much at all in 1950s culture, it was strangely thanks to Charlie Chaplin. In his film *A King in New York* (1957), Chaplin plays a king who arrives almost broke in New York City after escaping a revolution in his own country. Visiting a movie theatre, the king is puzzled by

Some sequences in *Glen or Glenda* (like this one) smack of sexploitation, while others play out like documentary or avant-garde filmmaking.

coming attraction trailers that include a parody of *Glen or Glenda*. "A problem play …At last the screen reaches maturity in *Man or Woman*?" A brief scene shows a pretty blonde who in a dubbed male voice tells her nearby lover, "It's no use, honey. Our love has no place in this world."

As for the real *Glen or Glenda*, it's certainly far stranger than Chaplin's parody. It's even strange when compared to most exploitation movies.[27] Actor Conrad Brooks later wrote, "They just made up that blank verse as they went along," a remark that doesn't seem hard to believe.[28] The film famously features Ed Wood playing the transvestite Glen, who as "Glenda" wears women's clothes, something he finally confesses to his fiancée Barbara (Dolores Fuller). That Wood really was a transvestite and really did date Fuller transforms these scenes into an odd combination of realistic autobiography and unconvincing fictional filmmaking.

Background music swells as Glen's tale comes to an end, suggesting the movie is nearly over. But it's just the end of Wood's own story, really, before the movie launches into another. It's the one Weiss had wanted to tell, the Jorgensen story. For it, Wood found "Tommy" Haines to star as Alan, whose sex-change operation turns him into Anne. And Alan is indeed Jorgensen by any other name, ranging from the character's sex-change to his having been a soldier in World War II.

Though *Glen or Glenda* is built on those two major sections, it's far more fragmented than that description would suggest. Stylistically, the movie functions like a kind of bizarre, post-modernist collage. Some of it seems like a Christian education-al film, featuring biblical allusions ranging from "Judge ye not" in the opening text to dialogue that uses John Bradford's quotation, "There but for the grace of God, go I." A dream sequence features footage of one woman playfully whipping and tying up another one, right out of a bondage short subject. And then there are some extreme close-ups of faces and ears, which all smack of an experimental art film.

While *Glen or Glenda* certainly wasn't a documentary, some of it does have the veneer of nonfiction filmmaking. Wood uses extensive stock footage from World War II with sound effects only, for example. Two characters ("Dr. Alton" and Police Inspector Warren) end up talking at times directly into the camera as television news reporters might, and they both are in an office that features the requisite charts on the wall and library books on shelves. Alton's voice is heard as documentary-style voiceover throughout, and both characters function as a framing device.

But that framing device has its *own* framing device. Enter Bela Lugosi, whose role is credited as being a "scientist," but–short of the fact that he mixes a couple of chemicals in a cheap laboratory set–the character seems more like an omniscient kind of god. The bulk of his footage has him seated in a chair and spouting lines like the now famous, "Pull the string! Dance to that which one is created for!"

Some of this enigmatic dialogue is actually in keeping with Wood's opaque sto-rytelling, but some of it definitely works against any "documentary" aims. Part of this results from Lugosi himself, whose mere presence evokes his entrenched repu-tation for fictional films and horror, an association that hardly seems helpful in cre-ating sympathy for the subject matter. And his most curious dialogue comes in lines like "No one can really tell the story. Mistakes are made, but there's no mistaking

"Pull the string! Dance to that which one is created for!"

the thoughts in a man's mind." Comments like that hardly inspire trust in Dr. Alton, the film's other storyteller.

Strangely, *Glen or Glenda* wasn't the first film Lugosi had made with a man wearing women's clothing. Only two years earlier he had co-starred in *Mother Riley Meets the Vampire* (1951), with comedian Arthur Lucan in drag, playing, as he did in so many films, the lovable old Mother Riley. That film was a come-dy though, with Lucan a part of the English music hall tradition of men dress-ing as women for laughs. And in *Genius at Work* (1946), Lugosi's costar Lionel Atwill appears in drag. But *Glen or Glenda* was something altogether differ-ent. Different in story, different in budg-et, and different in target audience. Lugosi had crossed a line, a new bound-ary, traversing into a cinematic region where his film career had never gone.

During Lugosi's career in talking pic-tures, the "Big Five" studios (MGM,

Warner Brothers, Paramount, Fox, and RKO) reigned in Hollywood alongside the "Little Three" (Universal, Columbia, and United Artists).[29] The breakdown into two groups resulted in part from their prestige and operating budgets, but also from industry power: the Big Five were powerful for theatre chains they owned in addition to the production studios they ran. Collectively, the eight corporations represented the Hollywood studio system.[30]

Many actors of that era became associated with a given studio, whether, say, James Cagney at Warner Brothers or Clark Gable at MGM. The same is true of Lugosi at Universal, who produced *Dracula* and the bulk of the classic horror films of the Great Depression and World War II. Of course, he did work for all of the other major studios as well. Between 1923-1952, Lugosi appeared in ten films at Fox, five at RKO, four at Warner Brothers, three at MGM, three at Paramount, and three at Columbia.[31]

A cartoon of Lugosi in *White Zombie* from the August 6, 1932 *New York American.*
(Courtesy of Dennis Phelps)

But his perceived affiliation with Universal makes sense even beyond the fame of *Dracula*; he acted in 19 films for them over the course of two decades.[32]

During those same years were Lugosi's independent films. B-movies. Poverty row. "*Skid* row. That was skid row, those little companies," remembered Johnny Lange, musical director for such Lugosi films as *Invisible Ghost* (1941), *Spooks Run Wild* (1941), and *The Corpse Vanishes* (1942). "They weren't even really studios, if you know what I mean." [33] And so even their names of course belie their operating budgets, distribution abilities, and artistic achievements: Majestic, World-Wide, Imperial-Cameo, Republic, and Victory, all of whom hired Lugosi.[34] Others had names that smacked of more importance within the industry than they had, like Producers Releasing Corporation (PRC) and Screen Guild Productions; Lugosi worked for them as well.

And of course there was Monogram Studios, where Lugosi made ten films.[35] The word monogram suggests an identifying mark to distinguish a product's individuality. In the early forties, Hollywood columnist Jimmie Fidler dubbed Lugosi the "Creeper of the B's."[36] A new moniker, an identifying mark, thanks to associating at length with one of the most famous low-budget studios.

By the time of *Glen or Glenda*, Lugosi had worked for poverty row companies

Lugosi as *The Mysterious Mr. Wong* (1935).

20 times in the US, as well as an additional three in England.[37] These movies accounted for something like forty percent of Lugosi's output between 1932 and 1952. Whatever their reputation, these studios didn't necessarily treat Lugosi unfairly. They gave him steady employment, and they certainly gave him top-billing far more often than the major studios ever did. Of those 23 poverty row films, he was top-billed in 20.[38] This is in sharp contrast to the majors, who gave him top-billing in just four films out of the 44 he had made from 1923 until the time of *Glen or Glenda*.[39]

What can be said about all of those independent movies? Certainly a good deal has been written about them, and the reputation of many has actually increased over time.[40] Shot quickly and generally released truly as B-movies, meaning the second film for double features, these films—especially by World War II—were popular fare among school children.[41] Like B-Westerns, they came and then they went. "Programmers," the industry sometimes called them, suggesting that they existed simply to round out a movie theater's program. At the time of their release, they were part of a mass of B-movies that would have seemed indistinguishable from one another.

As for the 23 that Lugosi made, under scrutiny they show a gradual decline in production values as the years wore on. His first, *White Zombie* (1932), became the most successful independent film of the 1930s.[42] Thanks to rented sets and props, the film has in many ways the look of a major studio film. His other independent

Lugosi played two roles in this 1935 Imperial-Cameo film.

projects of the early thirties like *The Death Kiss* (1933) and *The Return of Chandu* (1934) also show a relatively impressive use of sets and optical printing, such as in the use of wipe transitions. The same could even be said for the much-maligned *Murder By Television* (1935); sets in it representing business offices and home dining rooms appear much more impressive than what followed.

By World War II, the Lugosi B-movies featured cheaper sets and storytelling devices. More montages, more stock footage, and more prop newspaper headlines move the action forward in these films. There may be a few exceptions, of course. *Scared to Death* (1947) sported "natural color" film stock, whereas the serial *Shadow of Chinatown* (1936) appears more threadbare than much of what followed. But overall, it was a slow descent in production values during the two decades from *White Zombie* to *Bela Lugosi Meets a Brooklyn Gorilla*, a film that looks as if it was about the cheapest of them all.

That wasn't the only evolution. Early on, the B-movie scripts were pretty straightforward and simple, whether the fairy-tale structure of *White Zombie* or the crime story in *The Mysterious Mr. Wong* (1935). As the production values went down, the stories became increasingly outlandish.

A winged monster that kills anyone wearing a particular aftershave in *The Devil Bat* (1940), or a professor / crime boss in *Bowery At Midnight* (1942), whose drunken cohort can inexplicably raise the dead. The stories also became progressively more cryptic and incoherent. *Invisible Ghost*, for example, and particularly *Scared to Death*.

By the time of *Glen or Glenda*, Lugosi had made 23 films at the poverty row studios, as well as 44 films at the majors. But working with Wood and Weiss was something entirely different. This went well beyond the

Above: **A publicity still for *The Corpse Vanishes* (1942).**
Below: **As Dr. Marlowe in *Voodoo Man* (1944).**

extremely low budget, which was so cheap that now the prop newspaper headline shown onscreen was obviously just pasted on top of a real one. No, this film wasn't part of a slow decline, but a sharp break with the past. With *Glen or Glenda,* Lugosi had truly stepped outside of the Hollywood mainstream. As Madách's Adam bemoaned in *The Tragedy of Man,* "The constellations have been left behind us."

Not only did *Glen or Glenda* represent the underbelly of cinema, it was Lugosi's first exploitation film. From George Weiss to William C. Thompson, it was exploitation. From story topic to visual execution, it was exploitation. From publicity materials to target audience, it was exploitation. And it was all made under Weiss's ironic company name: Screen Classics.

Lugosi apparently did watch at least part of *Glen or Glenda,* but it's hard to

Lugosi with a fan letter in 1944.

imagine he was happy with anything he saw.[43] A horror film would have been better. Any horror film, which is exactly what Wood decided to write for him. A script that could help both of their careers. And for a twist, Wood decided to combine a horror story with elements of the western.

He developed a mad scientist character for Lugosi, a role fairly similar to so many Lugosi had already played. But he also thought about co-starring Lugosi with horror film star Lon Chaney Jr. Together they would make for twice the publicity, and Chaney's appearance would actually help to blend the two genres. Wood wrote the part of a ranch foreman named Marty for Chaney that played off of his roles in westerns like *High Noon* (1952).

On July 20, 1953, Wood wrote a letter to Lugosi, claiming that since they had become "close friends" he had:

> been trying to come up with a story which would deserve your fine talent. I think I now have that story in a thing called *The Phantom Ghoul*, which I plan to start in 3-D Wide Screen production within the next few weeks. ... I enclose a script for *The Phantom Ghoul* and hope you will enjoy the role of Professor Smoke as much as I enjoyed writing the character strictly for you.

To help persuade Lugosi, Wood mentioned the strength of their two-year friendship, though it seems unlikely that by summer 1953 they had known each other for more than twelve months.[44]

As for the script, it featured not just a ghoul, but a Phantom Ghoul. And actually there were two of them, named Tanz and Karl, first seen at the beginning of the film robbing graves in an old western town:

> As the camera pans a small, western-style cemetery to show rough crosses, wooden head boards, a scattered granite head stone here and there and one or two big marble monuments. The cemetery holds the stillness of the dead except for the soft scraping of a spade as it digs into the earth. As the camera comes to rest on the action the scraping changes to the sound of a spade hitting then scraping on wood. The camera moves in until, clearly, we see a giant of a man over six feet tall and weighing perhaps three hundred pounds.
>
> He is holding a lantern over an open grave. He sits the lantern down and tosses a rope into the grave. For another long moment, he looks deep into the grave where his accomplice works. The man who at this point comes out of the grave is a giant some eight feet tall. He tosses the spade to the ground and dusts his hands together. Both men move one on each end of the grave and lift up the ropes readied there for them.[45]

They're stealing bodies for the ominous Professor Smoke, who is busy conducting experiments at the nearby MacGregor castle. His plan is to create not only more ghouls, but ghouls more easily controlled than Tanz and Karl; after all, both have to be regularly drugged to obey commands. Succeeding in his experiments could generate untold wealth, paid for by whatever country might wish to control an unstoppable ghoul army.

Nat Pendleton, Angelo Rossitto, Lugosi, and Gladys Blake on the set of *Scared to Death* (1947).

Investigating the goings-on are Chance, the local sheriff, and his deputy Tom. When listening to the cemetery caretaker talk about "them ghouls," Chance realizes that the giants aren't locals. So who can they be, and where are they hiding? The urgency to find out builds when Chance's girlfriend Sally goes missing.

So Chance enlists a few friends to help pull off a plan that will finally reveal the villains. Ranch foreman Marty will "kill" Chance in a gunfight, and the caretaker will bury him with an oxygen tank: a clever ruse that would mean the body snatchers would dig him up. The only problem is that the old caretaker quit after the ghouls made their last appearance. His replacement is none other than Professor Smoke, who simply puts a different body in the grave and carts Chance off to his castle.

In the meantime, the townspeople develop into a lynch mob that's after Marty's blood; after all, they think he actually killed their beloved sheriff. Deputy Tom has to fend them off until Chance's grave is unearthed. Finding a body where Chance should be, Tom realizes that all the evil-doing must be coming from the old castle. He races there with some help, including the town doctor.

By that time, Smoke describes how hard he has worked to perfect his experiments:

SALLY

He is mad…

PROFESSOR

Mad – my experiments have been a success twice – Tanz, whom you subdued – and Karl, who now gazes upon you. Is that the work of a mad man? I am sorry that I've had to do things the way I did – but medical science frowns upon such as my work. But then this past work was so much easier…I had to kill the victims myself in the early days to produce the likes of Tanz and Karl – but one little thing stands in my way of complete success – and that is the reason for the bodies of late. – Even with all my profection [*sic*] I have no control over my two subjects without the use of hypnotic drugs that I slip into their arms once every forty-eight hours…Strange isn't it – To perfect one such as he and still not be his complete master without the use of drugs…But such are the rewards of a scientist.

CHANCE

How long do you think you can get away with this…?

PROFESSOR

I've been – getting away with it – a good many years. Of course I will not be able to return to our little town – but there are others – and the people in it will be constructed just the same … Take him, Karl.

The giant moves in towards Chance and Sally…

DOCTOR (o.s.)

That's far enough…

All eyes turn towards the door to the organ room.

With the Doctor, Tom, Ed, and Skimpy – their guns held in readiness, levelled on the off scene group.

DOCTOR

Nice story, Professor…

As Chance moves for the giant, Karl slams him a quick one with his forearm that send Chance crashing against the wall. The Professor grabs Sally's arm and pulls her in front of him…

PROFESSOR

Get him, Karl…

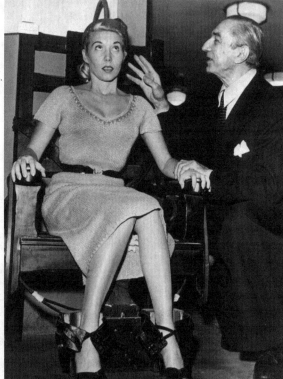

Above: **With Dolores Fuller at the Hollywood Historama.** *Below:* **Fuller sits in a prop electric chair once used in** *Angels with Dirty Faces* **(1938).**

Get him, Karl, so the professor can make his getaway. Smoke quickly makes for his vehicle, creating a car chase when Chance follows right on his heels. But instead of the Law catching him, Smoke dies horribly when his car crashes over a cliff. Not wasting any time, Chance then makes his way back to town, where the yokels are still about to lynch Marty. That Chance is alive startles all the town folk, thus saving Marty and of course returning Sally to his loving arms.

Wood was hoping to shoot this new script right away, as soon as he shot and finished a different film, a crime thriller called *The Hidden Face*.[46] And he had a role for Lugosi in that one too: Dr. Boris Gregor, a plastic surgeon who makes over a criminal's face to conceal him from the police.[47] Gregor would echo elements of Lugosi's role in *The Raven* (1935), as well as allow Lugosi to play the father of Dolores Fuller's character Marilyn.

As summer turned into autumn, though, neither film went into production, making Lugosi increasingly desperate for work. He needed money, for himself and his estranged son. Even if not in films, he needed some kind of work. His agent, Lou Sherrell, hadn't come through with anything in the second half of 1953.[48] And the brief mention of a J. Arthur Rank-produced sequel to Lugosi's 1932 *White Zombie* never got off the ground.[49]

But thanks to Wood, Lugosi did get to make a personal appearance at the Hollywood

A page from the script of *The Phantom Ghoul*.

Historama on Hollywood Boulevard. The Hollywood Chamber of Commerce had started it as a non-profit exhibit to celebrate the "50th anniversary" of filmmaking.[50] Along with some celebrity appearances, the Historama featured screenings of various silent films supplied by collector Charles Tarbox.[51] It also sported such a wide array of early movie equipment, props, and posters that the *LA Times* wrote that only one thing was missing: "popcorn."[52]

Sometime between late November and Christmas of 1953, Lugosi made his appearance.[53] Accompanying him was Dolores Fuller, with the two clowning around a couple of old movie props: a bed of spikes (actually made of rubber) and an electric chair that had been used in *Angels with Dirty Faces* (1938). Wood was particularly happy with the picture of them taken at the electric chair. He held onto it, thinking that some day soon it might make for a good publicity photo.[54]

But as for any major publicity, none really happened; Lugosi had been only one of many movie stars that showed up at the exhibit. That's when Wood started thinking about some other kind of venue for Lugosi. Something that would put the spotlight on him, and something that would make them both money. After giving it some thought, he decided pitch an idea to a theatre manager in San Bernardino. Wood later wrote:

> At the time, I was presenting a western stage show, which had shown some minor success at motion picture theatres throughout the area, owned by Mr. Albert Stetson. It was then an inspiration hit me.
>
> I mentioned to Mr. Stetson that Bela Lugosi had decided to go on tour and meet his public in person.
>
> "What kind of an act does he have?"
>
> There was the horrifying question again.
>
> "None."
>
> What else could have I said.[55]

Lugosi of course had performed several acts through the years, ranging from performing scenes of *Dracula* and reading Poe's *The Tell-Tale Heart* to clowning with Arthur Treacher in a 1940 variety show.[56] Some of these were staged at major venues; others may have only been seen at second and third-rate regional theatres. But he certainly always had *Dracula* at the ready, on large or small budgets, in condensed or more extended form. He was well used to performing a scene from it sandwiched between other films or acts, as he had done at least as early as 1936 with Rochelle Hudson at LA's *Night of 1000 Stars*.[57]

Was Wood unaware that Lugosi had performed in so many live acts? After all, Lugosi could presumably have acted a scene of *Dracula* with Dolores Fuller. Perhaps not, though. Given that the theatre hadn't featured live talent in some time, perhaps they didn't have needed stage lighting or props to mount a scene of anything. Or perhaps Wood's memory of the event was flawed in some way.

Regardless, he also claimed that Lugosi made several trips to San Bernardino in the days before the show, which was scheduled for Stetson's West Coast Theatre on New Year's Eve.

> [Lugosi] held press conferences, gave interviews over radio stations, and presided as toastmaster at ladies' clubs, men's organizations, and cocktail parties—all to boost ticket sales and audience attendance. Bela [also] prized a photograph taken during this period. It was taken as he presented [a] ticket to "admit one" to Mayor Blair, then mayor of San Bernardino.[58]

While all of this might be true, none of it appeared in the local press. The only coverage of the event was paid advertisements.[59]

When it was finally New Year's Eve, Wood, Lugosi, and Dolores Fuller drove to San Bernardino together in Fuller's new Chevy. Wood later remembered on more than one occasion that Lugosi was very nervous. Worrying about his cape being steamed, not pressed. Worrying about whether the audience would like him. Worrying about the fact that he was "guest host" on a bill with five movies.[60]

After over five decades on the stage, would Lugosi have been so nervous at this kind of an event? He had, after all, made a large number of personal appearances at theatres

Lugosi's Christmas card to Dolores Fuller and Ed Wood.
(Courtesy of Dennis Phelps)

before. Everything from *The Raven* (1935) to *Abbott and Costello Meet Frankenstein* (1948), promoting his own movies at major theatres.[61]

This is all in addition to Lugosi making live appearances at all kinds of other events. He attended the premiere of the film *Seed* in 1931, and a preview of Deanna Durbin's *Spring Parade* in 1940.[62] He attended benefits for Lieutenant Hugh Crowley in 1932, as well as for the Mount Sinai Home for Invalids in 1935 and 1936.[63] He was Master of Ceremonies at a stamp collecting conference in 1940, and was

Lugosi flanked by an unknown couple (left) and Dolores Fuller and Ed Wood (right).

"Ghost of Honor" when the Mystery Writers of America met in 1950.[64] And of course he was featured at all kinds of Hungarian events as well, ranging from opening the Los Angeles Hungarian National Day in 1936 to starting a program of speeches at a Hungarian press festival in 1939.[65]

Would Lugosi have been so nervous over giving what Wood claims was only a one-minute speech in San Bernardino? Maybe he was, given the state of his career at that moment. Or then again, perhaps Wood's recollection was faulty. At any rate, Wood claimed the show was a huge hit, with manager Stetson sending him a personal note of congratulations.[66] Dolores Fuller remembered that the "crowd went wild" when Lugosi in his cape walked onto the stage that night.[67] And Lugosi himself? Shortly after the event, he wrote:

> It did my heart good to see so many thousands of people who remember me and see my work. Every seat was filled and many more people waited in lines. I talked to many of those people in person that night. But to the point. A very lovely young lady came to me and said, "So you are Dracula?" I replied, "I am Bela Lugosi."
>
> The young lady was startled, then with a big smile she asked the never-ending question: "What do I have to do to be an actress?" I told her at great length of the studies, the hard work and perseverance that must be taken into consideration to be a successful actor. Her words were, "You mean you have to study to be an actor? Why, I thought you just had to wait for a talent scout to see how pretty you were, then they put you in front of the camera, and well – just say your lines...."
>
> The poor misguided young lady is in the position of so many others who must necessarily fall along the wayside unless they learn now. Success is the payment for Hard Work and study, no matter what the profession. Acting is a profession.
>
> Yes, I am a trained actor. Bragging? No! It is my profession – and I know and am proud of my profession.[68]

A trained actor proud of his profession. But during 1953, he was a trained actor who had stepped out of any semblance of legitimate filmmaking into the world of *Glen or Glenda* and Ed Wood. And it was all on the heels of career problems, political controversy, and a devastating divorce.

CHAPTER FIVE

Shapiro

In 1952, the "Celebrity Service" organization—a group that helped funnel letters to movie stars—told a newspaper reporter that they still got requests to locate Bela Lugosi every October.[1] For Halloween, of course, but apparently not the rest of the year. And certainly not at the beginning of Spring 1953. Sometime during February of that year, Lillian had left Lugosi and their separation was underway. The apartment was quiet, and not just from the lack of her voice. In the days and weeks after shooting *Glen or Glenda*, the phone wasn't exactly ringing with offers of more work.

The irony of all of this is that there was one person who desperately wanted to find Lugosi, a young 14-year-old named Dick Sheffield. He hoped to speak to Lugosi, to meet his hero, and he knew that they didn't live all that far from one another. But for months, he just didn't know what number to call, not until March 1953 anyhow. And when he finally made contact with Lugosi, it spurred a friendship that changed both of their lives.

Who was this Dick Sheffield? Well, he was officially Frank Richard Sheffield, Jr., born on July 22, 1938 in Culver City, California to parents Frank and Ruth. And he was immediately exposed to the world of the cinema. His mother's obstetrician was a doctor at the MGM studio hospital, and his father made a living as a film technician at Paramount Studios. At an early age, Dick even played at the Paramount lab on Sunset Boulevard.[2]

But the war changed all of that. Frank went into the military as a naval photographer in February 1942, and Ruth went to work at the Adell's defense plant. Dick stayed with whatever family friend or relative could keep him. Soon there were even more changes. Frank divorced Ruth, who then remarried in 1944. Dick's new step-father was Lewis Jenkins, a former bronco buster in the rodeos who was then working with Ruth at Adell's. For Dick, that meant yet another home; step-grandparents Edgar and Inez Jenkins took him in at their small farm in Pacoima. It meant a cow and chickens and a strawberry patch in the backyard. It meant long, quiet days in a small town.

Sometime in 1944, though, just months after moving to the farm, Dick's maternal grandfather Fred Fisher and his great aunt Flora came to pick him up. From that point on, Dick lived with them in LA, just a few blocks off of Wilshire Boulevard. Pretty soon, Ruth and Lewis moved into the house too. It gave Dick a chance to spend more time with his mother, and more time to get to know the stepdad, who tried hard to build a bond with him.

Dick Sheffield (right), his friend Tony Bass (left), and the Schneider sisters (Dick's neighbors) in the 1940s.

On Saturdays when Lewis wasn't working, he regularly took Dick to the Hitching Post movie theater on Hollywood Boulevard. It specialized in B-westerns, so all the little kids came wearing their cowboy outfits. The Post even had pegs on the back wall of the ticket booth for hanging up toy gun holsters. On the screen, it was Gene Autry and Tim McCoy and Tex Ritter; for a few hours, double features allowed cowboys to ride the range and do What Was Right.

Then in 1945, Dick fell in love with *The Purple Monster Strikes*, a serial playing at the Hitching Post. Week after week, Dick saw each new chapter, hanging on the edge of his seat. It was science fiction and horror and for Dick it was completely new. An introduction, really, to the kinds of stories that would fascinate him more and more as time went on.

All of his neighborhood pals loved the movies, too. Ruth even chaperoned Dick and his pal Joe Dassin, son of film director Jules Dassin, to a midnight spook show at an area theater in the late forties.[3] More than anything, the late forties and early fifties meant reissues of old horror films, and Dick and his friends saw one after another. Old stars like Boris Karloff quickly became their heroes.

Dick was seeing even more horror movies across the street thanks to a neighbor who had converted his basement into a theater. A small number of seats and two 16mm projectors; all the wall space not used by the screen was covered in 8x10 film stills and one-sheet movie posters. Thanks to him, Dick even began a one-sheet collection of his own. And so did Dick's pal, Norman Fist.

Dick in makeup for the horror film he made with Mike Spencer and Norm Fist.

Of all the neighborhood kids, Norm was one of Dick's favorites. A kind of odd, unique kid with an equally unique father. Norm's dad was an obstetrician who really pioneered the use of hypnosis over anesthesia; he was also an amateur magician. Dick spent hour after hour with their family, and best of all was the fact that Norm also loved horror movies. Together they carved marionettes with the faces of the Frankenstein monster and others; then they charged the neighborhood kids admission to their show. They also experimented at length with the food blender belonging to Norm's mother. She caught them after they had liquefied about every piece of food in her kitchen, and then she made them drink every drop. Waste not, want not.

Though Norm had gone to a different grade school, he and Dick both ended up at John Burroughs Junior High. It was an old, brick, two-story on South McCadden. Soon they met a young Dustin Hoffman, who attended school there. They also met Tony Curtis's younger brother, whom Curtis picked up each day after school. Lots of new people and lots of new faces, and a couple of them became close friends with Dick and Norm.

There was David Katzman, a quiet student who hated gym class and sports. His passions were things like music, teaching himself to play a variety of instruments. And science too. In fact, that's how Dick met him. A

(From left to right) **Roland Kent, Dick Sheffield, David Katzman, and Richard Morgan, playing on the steps of John Burroughs Junior High.**

teacher named Philip Ferguson started a science club, and Dick and Katzman were among the first to join. Katzman wasn't really a horror buff, but he shared plenty of other interests with Dick, including paleontology.

Thanks to the science club, Dick also met Mike Spencer. He was a talented pianist, giving his first public concert at the age of 14. He also had a Patrician sound system, the best to be had in the early fifties. The group often took it easy listening to classical music at Mike's house. Best of all, though, Mike shared Dick's love of old movies. Everything from Sergei Eisenstein to Laurel and Hardy. And horror stories too, from literature to movies, from Lugosi to Karloff.

As for Dick, if anything his interests in all things fantastic and macabre deepened. He memorized parts of *The Raven* and dug into Poe's short stories. Darkness and decay and the Red Death held illimitable dominion over all. He read Ray Bradbury's novel *The Martian Chronicles* and a Modern Library edition of Bram Stoker's *Dracula*. *Dracula*'s spine quickly developed cracks from being opened so many times. Dick was especially taken with the early part of the novel, when Jonathan Harker visits Transylvania and arrives at Dracula's castle. "Enter freely and of your own will!"

Of course by 1950 there were the EC horror comics, and Dick collected all of them. Every issue of *The Haunt of Fear* and *The Vault of Horror* and *The Crypt of Terror*, which was soon rechristened as *Tales from the Crypt*. The covers featured werewolves in cemeteries, ghosts materializing at séances, and hands erupting out of the ground. They captured Dick's imagination, just as the horror programs on the radio did. The creaking door of *Inner Sanctum*, and *I Love a Mystery*. The only one that initially disappointed him was Red "Skelton," who turned out not to be the "skeleton" Dick hoped for. As for the shows he loved, he listened to them under the sheets with the volume turned low and the lights off. Bedtime in those days did mean bedtime.

And so Dick and his pals were filling their minds with horror movies, radio shows, and comic books. "These out-of-school activities do exert great influence

Dick dressed as Dracula for the Halloween of 1949.

over the adolescent's development," Dr. Alice P. Sterner announced around that time in a study released by Columbia University.[4] Though she grudgingly admitted that bright students might be attracted to horror movies just as much as poor students, Dr. Sterner still believed that it was incumbent upon parents and teachers to channel children toward more fruitful pursuits.

But for Dick, Norm, and Mike, horror did bear fruit. By the time they saw a 1951 reissue of the old film *WereWolf of London* (1935) with Henry Hull, the trio were so taken with horror films that they decided to make their own. In the tradition of Lon Chaney Sr., Dick doubled as the star and as makeup man. Mike played the hapless victim; Norm was director and cinematographer. With 8mm camera in hand fully loaded with color film stock, Norm rolled on Dick's interpretation of a man inflicted with the curse of the damned, the curse of the werewolf.

Around that same time, Norm heard about the Los Angeles Science Fantasy Society, and so he and Dick went to one of their meetings in the basement near the old Mayflower Hotel in downtown LA. Walking in that first afternoon, Dick was struck by an enormous photograph of one of his favorite actors: Boris Karloff as the Frankenstein Monster, imprisoned and chained to a chair in a scene from *Bride of Frankenstein* (1935).

Once they joined the group, the duo met Forrest J Ackerman, literary agent and future editor of *Famous Monsters of Filmland*. Hitting it off with him from the first moment, they spoke endlessly about old horror movies. Through him and the society, Dick and Norm met Ray Bradbury and A.E. Van Vogt and so many other writers. They made the journey time after time to the meetings, even though getting to that side of town was no easy feat in the days before they got driving licenses.

Together, Dick, Mike, Norm and Katzman explored their interests in really everything that seemed unknown. Occult phenomena, the atom bomb, outer space, and dinosaurs: those subjects dominated their time when they weren't talking about music. They experimented with hypnosis at school, which once landed them in the Vice Principal's office. They attended séances and read about reincarnation. They created Tesla coils and built rockets. They sought out everything Old as an antidote to the New, ranging from antique cars and guns to haunted houses and ancient fossils.[5]

Lugosi in 1953 on the day that he and Dick Sheffield first met.

For Dick, though, the interest in all things unknown and fantastic crystallized most clearly around Bela Lugosi. Onscreen, Lugosi was the intersection of so much that interested him, ranging from the supernatural to mad science to hypnotism. Lugosi dominated much of Dick's conversation during recess at the junior high, and as time went on he became more and more fixated on the idea of meeting him. To be with Dracula in the flesh.

Dick's initial fascination with Lugosi began in 1948 when he saw *Abbott and Costello Meet Frankenstein* at the Fox Ritz on Wilshire Boulevard. It was the first time he had seen Lugosi in any movie, and it was Lugosi playing Dracula. The movie was a new release, and it even featured new kinds of props. The film's flapping bat was allegedly built out of airplane parts and materials.[6]

As a film, *Abbott and Costello Meet Frankenstein* is a wild and crazy farce; character motivations

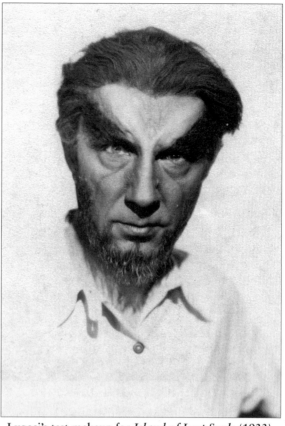

Lugosi's test makeup for *Island of Lost Souls* (1933). One of the many still photographs Lugosi showed Dick Sheffield and Norm Fist.

hardly exist. With no explanation as to why, Dracula (Lugosi) believes he must have the Frankenstein Monster (Glenn Strange) restored to full strength, and risks his life by traveling across the ocean in a shipping crate to make this happen. Lawrence Talbot, the Wolf Man (Lon Chaney Jr.), somehow learns about this in London and inexplicably feels obliged to stop Dracula's plans. And of course this largely takes place at a gothic castle that sits conveniently outside of a modern town in Florida.

Rather than making the film into a fragile story, the absurdities create a kind of wonderful nonsense. All of it possesses the feel of something improvised, something that just happened; at one point, Lou Costello even calls Bud Abbott by his real name instead of his onscreen character Chick Young.[7] And it seems so current, at least for 1948. Some of this is because of the clothing fashions. Some of it stems from the plot point about European police hunting for Dr. Mornay (Lenore Aubert), a vague allusion to war crimes. The entire film seems fresh, even though the monsters and Abbott and Costello had gone through similar routines in so many prior films.

That the comics and the villains were teamed together in the same film explains some of the freshness. But some of it is also Lugosi's Dracula, whose appearance registers growth as a character in a way that Chaney's Wolf Man and Strange's Monster do not. Lugosi's own aging creates some of this change from when he played the vampire in the 1931 film; the lines in his face during close-ups show a rather appropriate appearance for an ancient vampire. The emphasis on Dracula's ring and crest

Dick Sheffield and Bela Lugosi.

is also definite addition, as is the more physical side to Dracula, who engages in combat with the Wolf Man. And the animation of Dracula into a vampire bat is executed much more skillfully than anything seen in prior horror movies.

But aside from all of those factors, Lugosi deserves credit for intentionally altering his approach to the role. Repeatedly he conceals the lower part of his face by holding a small part of the cape over his nose and letting it drape downward. The effect is not one he used in the original 1931 *Dracula*, nor does it seem to be one he used in stage revivals.[8] The striking visual is coupled with his new approach to Dracula's dialogue. Gone are the unusual cadences and pauses he used in the 1931 film. Here Lugosi offers a distinctively old world delivery while exhibiting complete command of the English language. In far fewer lines than he had in the 1931 film, Lugosi's Dracula expertly shifts his tone of voice from the threatening to the conversational to the darkly comic when describing Wilbur's (Lou Costello's) brains and blood.

For Dick in 1948, of course, these flourishes weren't really concerns. What was on his mind was the fact that Lugosi was unlike any actor or character he'd ever seen. He dragged friends with him to see the film a second and third time. And after gushing over and over again about the supernatural vampire to his family, Dick's Aunt Florence sewed him a Dracula cape just in time for Halloween that year. At last his attempts to mimic Lugosi's mesmerizing hand gestures felt right, what with a black cloak draped over his back.

From that point onward, Dick watched carefully for old Lugosi films to appear in theater revivals or on late night television. Some of them he loved, like *The Devil Bat* (1940), *Bowery at Midnight* (1942), *The Ape Man* (1943), and *Voodoo Man* (1944). Dick particularly got a kick out of *Spooks Run Wild* (1941) and *Ghosts on the Loose* (1943), the two films that paired Lugosi with the East Side Kids, who always gave him a chuckle. Others like *Invisible Ghost* (1941), *Phantom Ship* (1935), and *Scared to Death* (1947): well, he didn't like every Lugosi film he saw at the time, that's for sure. But he always enjoyed Lugosi's performances, and his particular mannerisms. The voice, the eyes, and the hands; Dick studied them closely.

The fever pitch came in the autumn of 1952. Dick saw *Bela Lugosi Meets a Brooklyn Gorilla* at the El Rey Theatre on Wilshire Boulevard. Lugosi seemed so much older than he had in the Abbott and Costello film, and certainly more so than any of the old films he had caught on TV. But Dick and his pals thoroughly loved the movie. They thought it was funny, and they particularly enjoyed seeing Lugosi on the big screen in a new release.

"If you like him so much, why don'tcha meet him?" That thought rattled around Dick's head over and over again in late 1952. Dick knew from newspaper stories that Lugosi was living in the LA area. The more he thought about it, the more he was determined to shake Lugosi's hand, to see those eyes staring right at him in person. But how does a 14-year-old kid find a Major Star, a Legend? By March 1953, Dick finally got his answer.

Amazingly, Tony Kemp, one of Dick's friends at John Burroughs, came up with a phone number through an uncle that worked for *The Hollywood Reporter*. But who

Mike Spencer and Bela Lugosi.

should make the call? And what would they say? Dick was too nervous, so he passed off the responsibility to David Katzman, who really wasn't even that big of a Lugosi fan. As a result, he'd be less prone to get the shakes. So Katzman rehearsed his speech and then had the operator dial Hollywood 5-2241. But in the end, he didn't have to say very much at all, because as it turned out the number was actually for Lugosi's nephew Béla Loosz.

Loosz kindly passed on his famous uncle's correct number, but once again Dick was too nervous to take the next step. This time he decided to get his paternal grandmother Cora Bee to make the call. She was a journalist for the *Pasadena Star News*, so she could ask Lugosi for an interview. Once it was set up, Dick and the others could go along. The perfect plan. Except for the fact that when Cora Bee phoned Lugosi, he politely told her that he was too ill to do an interview. Maybe some other time.

For a few days, this was a particularly sore subject. Slowly, however, nerves turned again to steel and Katzman picked up the receiver once more. Why not just try him again, using the angle that they were fans? So when Lugosi answered the phone, Katzman introduced himself as a young admirer and then moved the conversation to Dick. Decades later, Katzman remembered the conversation:

> "My friend Richard Sheffield here is a tremendous fan of yours and has seen almost all your movies."
> "This fellow Shapiro ... he is a big fan of mine?" Lugosi asked with a tinge of excitement to his voice.
> "Uh, yes sir. His name is *Sheffield*. Richard Sheffield. He's probably your biggest fan."

"That's very kind. This fellow Shapiro ... is he with you now?"

"Yes ... yes sir, but its Sheffield. *S-h-e-f-f-i-e-l-d.* You should really talk to him."

"Ahhh, *Sheffield.* Hmmmm. Very good. Please put this young man on the line."

"Uh, Mr. Lugosi, well, yes, I'm Dick Sheffield. You know, we're a small group of your most devoted fans here, and we've seen all your movies. Or, at least all we've been able to. We'd love to meet you and get your autograph. We really love your films. ... how's that? And that's 4601 Rodeo Lane, Apartment 2? Indeed. Well, we'll see you then. Thank you, sir."[9]

By the end of the brief conversation, Lugosi had invited Dick and Katzman to his apartment. They had a meeting set up for the following Saturday afternoon.

Days at John Burroughs Junior High passed slower than normal as Dick waited impatiently for the weekend. But when it finally came, Katzman had something else he had to do, so Dick went with Norm Fist instead. At ages fourteen and fifteen they needed transportation. Although it was a sunny day, 4601 Rodeo Lane was much too far to walk.

The Fist family Dodge zipped along to Lugosi's address, and Norm's mother said a cheerful goodbye as she let the duo out at the curb. There they were, and there wasn't any going back. The two hesitantly made their way to the door of his apartment, and with a bolt of newfound courage Dick quickly knocked on the door.

When the door creaked open, they both looked upward at the elderly actor who towered over them from a height of six foot one. He was dressed comfortably in a short sleeve shirt, and he wore a welcoming smile. "Enter freely and of your own will!" Well, no, he didn't say that. He just kindly asked them into the apartment. There wasn't any cape, any candle, or any children of the night. The apartment was no House of Horrors.

After the introductions were over, Dick's confidence grew and he began to ask questions about *Dracula* and about horror movies. He also got out his collection of 8x10 still photographs of Lugosi's films. The actor sat down and examined each one carefully through his reading glasses, making occasionally comments about certain images from the old movies. The pupils of his eyes brightened as Norm released the flash of a camera, adding a new picture to Dick's collection.

A few minutes later, Lugosi led Dick and Norm into another room where he kept a large filing cabinet next to his bed. It housed his own enormous collection of photographs, and he happily gave them several 8x10s. And then after a little more conversation, it was time to leave and meet

An advertisement from the *Chicago Daily Tribune* announcing the joint live appearance made by Lugosi and Vincent Price on February 29, 1940.

Norm's mother back on the street. Another smile, another handshake, and the door closed behind them. And so they had met Dracula.

A short time later, and Dick and Norm made another appointment to see Lugosi. They had forgotten to get his autograph on the first visit, which became the excuse for the second. Once again, Norm's mother acted as cabdriver and delivered them to Rodeo Lane. This time Lugosi greeted them in a suit and tie, and this time he invited them to join him for lunch.

Dick and Norm scanned over the living room after he went into the kitchen. A large oil painting of Lugosi towered above an old love seat. A charcoal sketch of a nondescript Hungarian hung unevenly on a nearby nail. All of the furniture was old, all of it antiques. Newspapers, some in Hungarian, were stacked on the floor.

Lugosi soon reappeared with coffee and a plate piled high with toast. Dick didn't even drink coffee, and he certainly didn't like it at room temperature. The toast was pretty stale too. But somehow it still seemed like a feast, and in between munching bread they spoke again about Dracula. This time, Lugosi offered an example of the hand movements he used in his films to hypnotize victims. His fingers bent at their joints in a strange rhythm right in front of Dick's eyes, just as they had in front of Lou Costello's in *Abbott and Costello Meet Frankenstein*.

Then Lugosi spoke of an advertisement he had seen in one of his newspapers. Socks were on sale at a nearby Hollywood shop on Wilshire Boulevard's "Miracle Mile" of stores, and he asked the boys to go with him. He thought they were priced pretty cheaply, and that he should buy at least one pair while he could. The three waited for Norm's mother to drive up.

"Hello, mother," Lugosi said before kissing Mrs. Fist's outstretched hand.

Above: Lugosi leads a gorilla (Steve Calvert) into the Paramount Theatre for the "Premathon" of *House of Wax* (1953). *Below:* Lugosi drinks milk instead of blood at the Paramount Theatre during the "Premathon" of *House of Wax* (1953).

Lugosi and gorilla from an unidentified show.

She was too surprised by the unexpected meeting with Dracula to say much more than quiet, "Hi." After they parked the car and entered the store, Lugosi drew a few stares from some of the other shoppers. But just as Norm and Dick grew comfortable, Lugosi bowed out. He and his new socks would walk home alone, but he appreciated their offer to drive him back. After bowing slightly and kissing Mrs. Fist's hand again, he said he hoped to see Dick and Norm again. And off he walked. They not only knew Dracula, but they had helped him buy footwear.

It was on the third visit to Lugosi's apartment that Dick and Norm went with Mike Spencer. All three of them, and for another of Lugosi's lunches. This time it was cold bouillabaisse that was at least a day old. It looked like a gelatinous mess, and the fish heads poking up through it hardly seemed appetizing. So much for vampire food. And Mike had to shovel sugar cube after sugar cube into the strong coffee to be able to drink it. Mike also got to see Lugosi with his ever-present cigar, a cheap Italian brand that he called his "El Ropo, El Stinkos." It looked like he was smoking the dried branch of an old tree.[10]

Before leaving that day, the trio convinced Lugosi to get one of his Dracula capes out of the closet. He tried it on for them, and then followed the group outside where cameraman Norm snapped pictures of Dick and Mike with Lugosi. For one of them, Lugosi put the cape on Dick's shoulders, which gave Dick the chance to show Lugosi his own hypnotic fingers. They were in, all three of them. This went well beyond reading horror comics or attending séances. Now they all knew Bela Lugosi.

Dick and Lugosi hit it off so well that Dick began to keep a scrapbook about the actor. And by mid-April 1953, he clipped an article about *House of Wax* premiere at the Paramount Theatre in downtown LA. A remake of the 1933 film *Mystery of the Wax Museum* with Lionel Atwill, *House of Wax* was in color and 3-D. It wasn't science fiction; it was an old-style horror film, none-too-different than so many Lugosi appeared in years before. But this time the star was Vincent Price. And Lugosi was one of literally dozens of famous names who attended what became a "Premathon" where the film premiered and was then shown again and again during a 24-hour period.[11]

Price had actually done a brief bit as the Invisible Man in an audio-only cameo for the ending of *Abbott and Costello Meet Frankenstein*. But Lugosi likely knew him best from a live joint appearance that they made in Chicago in 1940. Curiously, it was for a movie premiere too. Actually, it was for *two* movie premieres at the same theater: the first Chicago showings of *The House of the Seven Gables* (1940) and *Black Friday* (1940) on a double bill. Price and Lugosi appeared live at four different performances of the films.[12]

As for Dick, he was a little hurt that Lugosi didn't offer an invitation to

Immediately after appearing at the Oriental Theatre in Chicago in early May 1941, Lugosi appeared with a gorilla onstage at the Palace in Fort Wayne, Indiana on May 10-11, 1941. *(Courtesy of Margo Nicolet)*

go to the Paramount with him; after all, they were pals. Later he learned that Lugosi was unhappy about the premiere as well. Warner Brothers had called and asked Lugosi to make the appearance, but the results were disastrous. At a booth in the theater, Lugosi was supposed to take a photograph drinking milk instead of blood. But when he tried to grab a nurse by the neck, she spilt milk all over him. An interviewer asked him questions on the air, but varied from a pre-arranged list of questions; the increasingly deaf Lugosi had memorized his answers in order and ended up giving the wrong responses to every question. After the movie finally began, Lugosi got up; he was in no mood to stay.[13]

When Alex Gordon later remembered having gone to the event with Lugosi, he mentioned that the studio sent a limousine to pick them up. The trip to the Paramount was actually a bit more difficult than any snafus with the Red Cross or radio-TV interviewers. Gordon recalled:

> The limousine made a stop at a large hotel, and Bela immediately asked what the stop was for. I timidly told him it was time to pick up a gorilla. At first it seemed he hadn't heard right, then he roared "*Gorilla!*" It took all my powers of persuasion to keep him from taking a taxi home.[14]

This time the man in the suit was Steve Calvert, who had performed the same duties for *Bela Lugosi Meets a Brooklyn Gorilla* (1952). But for Lugosi, it was just another gorilla; over two decades of his horror career had been checkered with men in monkey suits. First *Murders in the Rue Morgue* (1932) with Charles Gemora as the ape, then *The Gorilla* (1939) with Art Miles, then *The Ape Man* (1943) with Emil Van Horn. There was also someone dressed as a gorilla at his live stage show in 1941, and then someone else again for his appearances on the East Coast in 1950 and 1951.[15]

Whatever problems happened, though, going to the *House of Wax* premiere meant that Lugosi appeared in a Pathe newsreel covering the event. Released on April 27, 1953, the newsreel showed everyone from Shelley Winters to Danny Thomas at the Paramount. And a wonderful image of Lugosi wearing sunglasses and entering the theater with Calvert in costume is captured on film too. In fact, that brief bit was the only new footage of Lugosi to play on mainstream theater screens in either 1953 or 1954.[16]

Even though he didn't get to go the premiere, Dick kept in touch with Lugosi as much as he could without becoming too much of a bother. He also talked about meeting Lugosi to Forrest J Ackerman, one of his friends from the LA Science Fantasy Society. Dick arranged for a meeting at Lugosi's apartment, with Ackerman taking his wife Wendayne and a houseguest named Tetsu Yano. Along with being a literary agent, Ackerman was already a renowned collector of horror and science fiction memorabilia. And so he took with him an item from his collection, one of the sound discs to *Murders in the Rue Morgue.*

More apes. But Lugosi cupped his hand over his ear and listened patiently to his own voice crackling from the needle in the groove. It was a speech he gave in the film about being "Dr. Mirakle," who was not the "usual sideshow charlatan." After the record ended, Lugosi gave a laugh and left the room. When he re-entered, he was wearing his Dracula cape and twitching his hypnotic fingers towards Yano while Ackerman took a photograph. Lugosi had more new friends.[17]

Above: Lugosi with Forrest J Ackerman and his wife Wendayne at Ackerman's home. *(Courtesy of Forrest J Ackerman) Below:* Lugosi as Dr. Mirakle with Charles Gemora as the gorilla in *Murders in the Rue Morgue* (1932). *(Courtesy of Kristin Dewey)*

In fact, Lugosi soon visited Ackerman at the agent's home. On June 19, 1953, he saw the massive amount of horror books and posters and props that Ackerman had collected. They filled the shelves and floors too. Lugosi saw himself on yellowing old lobby cards and still photographs. That someone cared so much about his work left Lugosi amazed, which is exactly how he signed Ackerman's guest book. When Ackerman later drove him on an errand, Lugosi admitted his surprise that young people were so nice to him.[18]

Young people like Dick and Norm, whom Lugosi soon invited to be in the live audience of the television show *You Asked For It* with Art Baker. The gimmick of the program was to give the audience what they truly wanted, and a woman named Harriet Frazier in Springfield, Massachusetts asked for Lugosi; in a letter to Baker, Frazier wrote that she had missed seeing him in new films. And so on July 27, 1953, Norm's mother gave Dick and Norm a lift to the old Mack Sennett Studios where the program was broadcast.[19]

Lugosi was already there for the rehearsals. Though the final divorce papers with Lillian were filed only ten days earlier, they found Lugosi to be in a great mood. That day, the fact that he was working seemed to mean everything to him.[20] If Dick found anything surprising, it was that Lugosi was going to play an illusionist on *You Asked For It*. He didn't realize then that the evening's TV performance invoked Lugosi's various associations with magicians and magic acts.

Lugosi had certainly played a magician in the movies. He did in the color film *Fifty Million Frenchmen* (1931) with Olsen and Johnson. And publicity in

Dr. Bill Neff and Lugosi at a live appearance at the end of 1947.

the mid-thirties claimed that an old Houdini trick had solved a production problem for *Mark of the Vampire* (1935) in a scene where Lugosi and Carroll Borland had to walk through a spider web without disturbing its strands.[21] But what Dick knew best was *Spooks Run Wild*, that East Side Kids film he loved so much; in it, Lugosi's plays a magician named Nardo.

But by the 1940s, Lugosi occasionally tried to incorporate magic into his live appearances as well. This may have happened the first time in the summer of 1945 as his film career was slowing down. On an episode of the ABC radio show *County Fair* with Jack Bailey, Lugosi sawed a woman in half.[22] On the radio, he sawed her in half. The wonderful days of old-time radio, when audiences could hear but not see actually see the talents of popular ventriloquist Edgar Bergen.

And then there were the midnight spook shows like the one that Dick had gone to with Joe Dassin. Horror-themed stage shows that included liberal doses of magic acts alongside actors dressed as monsters, pretty women in peril, and usually a horror movie onscreen to round out the evening. Over and over again, the films at these shows were old Lugosi movies. Take the spook show at the Capitol in Washington DC in August 1946 as an example. Magic and monsters billed with Lugosi in *The Ape Man*.[23] Shows like this became extremely popular in the late forties and early fifties.[24]

By 1947, the spook shows included Lugosi not only on the screen, but onstage as well. In February of that year, Lugosi starred in *A Nightmare of Horror* in San Diego.[25] And by December 1947, Lugosi made a number of live appearances with

STANLEY B'WAY & MARKET

TOMORROW NITE AT MIDNITE

DOORS OPEN 11:45 P. M. SHOW STARTS 12 MIDNITE

ONE PERFORMANCE ONLY!

ON STAGE! THE ONE AND ONLY! THE ORIGINAL DRACULA!

IN PERSON 'MR. HORROR' HIMSELF BELA LUGOSI AND COMPANY with his HORROR & MAGIC STAGE SHOW

13 BREATH-TAKING SCENES TO HOLD YOU SPELLBOUND! A CARLOAD OF SCENERY!

SEE! BELA LUGOSI COME TO LIFE FROM HIS COFFIN!

SEE! THE BEAUTY and THE MONSTER!

SEE! GHOSTS - GOBLINS - IMPS OF DARKNESS FLY THRU THE AIR!

SEE! BEAUTIFUL GIRL BURNED ALIVE!

SEE! VAMPIRE MAIDENS VOODOO MAGIC!

SEE! LUGOSI AND THE BLOODY GUILLOTINE!

SEE! THE BAT MAN AND THE MONSTER IN DEATH STRUGGLE!

• PLUS ON OUR SCREEN • BELA LUGOSI in "THEY CREEP IN THE DARK"

TICKETS NOW ON SALE AT BOX-OFFICE • ALL SEATS $1.00 INC TAX

BREATHE ON THE VAMPIRE'S EYE—IF IT TURNS RED YOU WILL BE ADMITTED FREE TO SEE THIS SHOW

Above: Magician Alexander the Great and Lugosi clowning around in the late forties.
Below: An advertisement for Lugosi's "Horror and Magic Stage Show" when it appeared in Camden, New Jersey. From the *Camden Courier-Post* of March 16, 1951.

Dr. Bill Neff, a magician whose "Madhouse of Mystery" ranked among the most popular of spook shows. When they worked Newark together, Neff handled all the magic tricks, including making one of his eight well-endowed female assistants levitate, held up only by the bristles of a broom. As for Lugosi, he mainly answered questions from Neff at the microphone before offering a scene from *Dracula*.[26] The duo allegedly even appeared together in a filmed trailer promoting Neff's show.[27]

The fact that Lugosi and Neff didn't work together for very long didn't keep Lugosi from thinking about other magicians.[28] In 1948, he planned to do a spook show with his old friend Loring Campbell, who worked at Abbott's magic store and appeared onstage as the magician "Alexander the Great" and "Kim Key."[29] The idea never became more than just an idea, but Lugosi did allegedly go on to make a guest appearance with Dr. Silkini's "Asylum of Horrors," another spook show that incorporated magic tricks.[30] And he also seems to have appeared at Hubert's Museum in New York, a venue that focused on magic acts, sword swallowers, and the like.[31]

Most famously, at the end of 1950, Lugosi headed his own "Horror and Magic Stage Show," which promised thirteen "breath-taking scenes" that ranged from terrifying events like Lugosi emerging from a coffin to magic tricks like a beautiful girl being burned alive. There was even something called "Lugosi and the Bloody Guillotine!"[32] *Variety* claimed that the show was similar to Silkini's and Neff's, and the photomontage that Lugosi used for publicity even included a picture of Neff.[33] Lugosi performed the show only a small number of times before the end of 1950, canceling a string of dates due to illness; then, in February and March 1951, he appeared in the show for a few final performances.[34]

Even later, Lugosi seems to have made at least one 1952 appearance with Kim Yen Soo, the magician who changed his name from Kuma during World War II in order to sound Chinese instead of Japanese. But his most famous trick remained the "Kuma Tubes," in which he produced a brass bowl and small animals out of very narrow metal tubes; then he pulled scarves from the tube and finally a huge sheet of silk that covered himself and his female assistant. After coming

Lugosi onstage for a performance of his "Horror and Magic Stage Show," from late 1950 or early 1951.

out from underneath it, they both were dressed in different clothes.[35] Close curtain.

Lugosi's tangential, but recurrent work with magicians and magic acts is preserved in the surviving kinescope of 1953's *You Asked For It*. As the *Los Angeles Times* promised, he played the "Master Illusionist."[36] The setup was a Transylvanian castle with fog, and Lugosi was certainly wearing his full Dracula attire. But the act was as much magic as horror. After hypnotizing the female victim (Shirley Patterson) with his tapering fingers, Lugosi has her locked inside a large wardrobe.[37] After it's rotated, the wardrobe is reopened and the victim has disappeared, leaving in her place a vampire bat. *Voila!* The Master Illusionist Lugosi had succeeded with his "Vampire Bat Illusion," in front of a live studio audience no less.

And then for Halloween 1953, Dick put off donning his own Dracula cape and going out with his buddies just long enough to catch on the *Spade Cooley Show* at 8PM on KTLA.[38] Lugosi was on TV again, though apparently not doing a magic act. He was guest-starring on the program along with comic Ukie Sherin, who had been the Dialogue Director for *Bela Lugosi Meets a Brooklyn Gorilla*. Cooley, a western swing bandleader, had one of the hottest shows on the West Coast in the early fifties; he later became infamous for violently murdering his own wife.[39]

Of course these two TV appearances hardly overshadowed all of Lugosi's old B-movies that were continuing to air on stations across the country; if anything, this problem of competing with himself had gotten worse. After all, the most visible national article written about Lugosi in 1953 came in a summer *TV Guide*, which

Bela Lugosi and Dick Sheffield.

bemoaned the fact that Lugosi could have been king. "The King of Terrorvision," anyhow. If only he had bought up the rights to his old movies like Bill "Hopalong" Boyd had done, Lugosi would have been making thousands. "The rental rights would be stupendous," they speculated. And like Hoppy, they thought he could have gone into product merchandising too.[40]

Of course none of that had happened, and Lugosi wasn't making a penny from the rebroadcasts of the old movies. And the infrequent new TV appearances weren't bringing that much money either. So at the end of October 1953, Lugosi moved to a cheaper apartment. And he phoned Dick and Norm and Mike to help him move. The new place was located near Sunset Boulevard and Laurel Canyon, just around the corner from Schwab's Drug Store.

The boys couldn't drive, but they helped pack as many of his things as they could into Béla Loosz's car. Box after box. Among other things, Dick spotted a pistol with an engraving that said, "Bela Lugosi, Honorary Sheriff of Hollywood." And then there was that painting of Lugosi in a Prince Albert-style costume. And another framed painting of Clara Bow in the nude. All of it went into Loosz's car for what became several trips to the new apartment.

Carrying the boxes that day, it seemed like quite a bit of stuff, but it was less than Lugosi had when he first met Dick earlier that year. Lillian had gotten some things before the move, and then Lugosi had auctioned some of the other stuff near the end of October. He needed the money, but he also needed to conserve space; the new apartment only had three rooms.[41] But it did have more than enough space for Dick and Mike to visit, which they tried to do every few weeks.

And so in a matter of months, Lugosi had become friends with Dick. They weren't really close yet; Lugosi wasn't an easy person to get to know. It would take more time. But they were fast becoming good friends, and Dick proceeded to help him out at the new place by delivering those cheap cigars or cleaning up his apartment. Spending time with him as he drank beer at room temperature or even from one of his beer warmers.

After all, Dick had only seen his real father Frank once since the 1944 divorce, when he showed up briefly at Dick's eighth birthday party with his new wife and his new convertible. And as for step-father Lewis, well, Lewis cared deeply about Dick; he even unsuccessfully tried to convince Dick to change his last name to Jenkins. But the fact that Lewis pronounced Bela Lugosi's name as "Bella Lagoosey" hardly helped.

No, in 1953 Lugosi was not only the living embodiment of horror and the unknown, but also as something of a father figure to Dick, who was still at the onset of puberty and his teen adventures. And as for Lugosi, well, the fact he hardly mentioned Lillian didn't change the fact that she was gone. Or the fact that he told Dick that his suicide attempt was just a publicity stunt. Aside from anything else, maybe they both just needed a new pal that year.

CHAPTER SIX

Rugged Peaks

Just before he graduated from John Burroughs Junior High in June 1953, Dick's family moved into a house on Formosa Street, one block from Hollywood Boulevard. A new home, and within a few months Dick would be at a new school. But between junior high and high school was a beautiful California summer, during which the 14-year-old could put up his feet and bask in the sun. Lazy, hazy, crazy days.

As it turned out, though, thanks to Lugosi, Dick's feet scarcely stopped moving that July and August. By that time, he and his friends had spent a number of afternoons with Lugosi in his apartment. The actor patiently answered all their questions about the Old Days in Hollywood. He was, after all, a dramatic storyteller. Reflections of former glory, but even an aging Hollywood vampire isn't supposed to cast reflections. Lugosi realized he had to look to the future. Not only did he need to work for financial reasons, he wanted to act.

Ever the reader, Lugosi had seen a clipping earlier in the year that had stuck in his mind. "U-I Plots Movie About a Vampire," the *New York Times* had written in late February. In it, he learned that the studio was "in the market" for "Dracula-type hijinks." They were even thinking about filming in "3 Dimensions." Universal put DeWitt Bodeen—noted screenwriter of such films as *Cat People* (1942) and *The Seventh Victim* (1943)—in charge of penning the story. In the meantime, producer Ross Hunter was searching for an actress to play the lead part, a female vampire.[1]

By summer, discussion of the project disappeared in the press, but the sheer fact it had been announced meant that Universal could still muster an interest in vampires. And Lugosi had an idea that wouldn't even require a new story: the studio could remake the original 1931 *Dracula* in color and 3-D. The classic could be modernized, recrafted for a new generation of filmgoers. Starring Bela Lugosi, too, of course. After all, he had worked in more than one color film, and he had been acquainted with 3-D as early as 1949, when he and stage actor Hampton White were supposed to star in the movie *Strange Deception*. Had it been produced, it would have become the first feature film using the process.[2] And of course Lugosi had also been inspired by the use of color and 3-D film in the *House of Wax* (1953) with Vincent Price.

So a remake of *Dracula* was the perfect choice for a new horror film; after all, it was the father of all talking horror films. And who else could star in *Dracula* but him? True, different Universal films of the prior decade had featured other actors in

Having already scared Norm Fist (center) into shock, Bela Lugosi tries to hypnotize his good friend Richard "Dick" Sheffield (right).

the role, but Lugosi had been the *first* to the play the role at the studio. And the most recent, too, what with his success in *Abbott and Costello Meet Frankenstein* (1948).

Lugosi explained the idea to Dick with dramatic flourish. After all, audiences flocked to see *Dracula* every time it was revived. He even told Dick something that he said several times during his later years, that the original 1931 film *Dracula* was so popular that it was revived in every city in America every year. That wasn't exactly true of course. Universal had themselves reissued the movie only twice, in 1938 and in 1947; a third major reissue came in 1952 by the company Realart.[3] But while Lugosi was wrong about the frequency of its revivals, he was not quite as wrong as those few reissues might suggest.

While *Dracula* certainly wasn't seen in every city, every year, it did make many appearances at individual theaters outside of the major reissues. One or two screenings, here and there. In 1934, for example, a "travelling exhibitor" showed up in at least a few rural towns with a battered *Dracula* print in hand. A press account in Utah spoke about how *Dracula*'s "final triumph" was that everyone in the rural area loved it even though the ragged print "was so cut up that no one knew what it was all about."[4]

Regardless of the reality, Lugosi seems to have convinced himself about the annual *Dracula* screenings. He said it to a television reporter in 1951, broadcasting it over the airwaves.[5] He said it to a famous US Senator while under oath in 1955.[6] And he told it to Dick in 1953, along with his ideas for a remake. Dick had already organized the Bela Lugosi Fan Club, made official by Hollywood columnist Betty Burr. They had a membership card; Lugosi himself had signed at least a hundred photos for members.[7] But now they had major purpose during those summer months: persuade Universal to remake *Dracula*.

How does a group of five or six teenagers who can't even drive a car yet convince a major Hollywood studio to spend hundreds of thousands of dollars? Dick, Norm, Mike, Katzman, and another pal named Jack Mattox met for a strategy session at Dick's new home; his mother Ruth made the refreshments. It was all dollars and sense, meaning that Dick believed if they could prove audiences *wanted* to see a new version of *Dracula* with Lugosi, then the studio would see it as a good financial investment. As for Lugosi, well, it would mean a come-back of major proportions.

After developing a quick sales pitch to tell people what they were attempting, the group fanned out for days and days. They knocked on doors in residential districts around Hollywood. They caught movie audiences walking out of theaters. They even hit up some businesses. And they did it with pen and paper in hand. A petition drive to get Lugosi back on the screen as Dracula.

After wearing out a fair amount of shoe leather, the gang had collected literally hundreds of signatures. They regrouped at Dick's home one afternoon, satisfied they had knocked on about as many doors as they could. All of the signatures were gathered into a single group. As Fan Club President, Dick wrote a letter to the studio chief, pecking out the sales pitch on an old typewriter, Then he packed all the fruits of the summer labor into an document envelope and marched to the nearest post office.

Ironically, even though Dick had watched many Lugosi movies, he didn't see the original 1931 *Dracula* until some time after meeting Lugosi the man. Somehow he had missed it at its LA revivals in 1947 and 1952. When he finally did catch it at a theater around 1955 or so, he could hardly contain his excitement. The projector snapped on and the credits of the old movie appeared as an art deco bat filled his eyes. And then came the first line of dialogue, from a tourist reading out of a travelogue while bumping through the Transylvanian countryside: "Among the rugged peaks that frown down upon the Borgo Pass are found crumbling castles of a bygone age." The rugged peaks frown down.

For Lugosi, *Dracula* had begun onstage at New Haven in 1927, just before taking Broadway by storm. Then success in Los Angeles and San Francisco during the summer of 1928. Success enough that the farewell Los Angeles performance in 1928 meant a big society party for Lugosi and the rest of the cast at the Sea Breeze Beach Club.[8] Only a year later, he was back in Los Angeles for another stage revival; that meant another big society party, held this time on opening night to welcome Dracula back.[9] Excitement over Lugosi's return to the role meant that Hungarian artist Géza Kende completed a three-quarter length portrait of the actor to hang in the lobby of the Music Box Theater.[10] Dracula had been captured in California not by stake, but by oil and canvas. And the celluloid was still to come.

In a comical 1927 "interview" with the *New York Herald-Tribune*, a journalist asked "Count Dracula" if he had ever visited Hollywood. "'Never,' declared Count Dracula firmly, 'to my certain knowledge.'"[11] But the fictional vampire was wrong. *Dracula* had been discussed as a Hollywood film at least as early as 1925. The *Los Angeles Times* wrote that a producer was looking for a proper vehicle for Arthur Edmund Carewe, with Stoker's *Dracula* being one of the key projects being considered.[12] Arthur Edmund Carewe, stage and screen star, was Svengali in the 1923 *Trilby* and Ledoux in

Bob Shomer's original membership card for Dick's "Bela Lugosi Fan Club."
(Courtesy of Dr. Robert Shomer)

Above: Advertisement from the April 1, 1931
San Francisco Chronicle.
Below: A signed portrait of film director
Tod Browning.
(Courtesy of David Wentink)

the 1925 *Phantom of the Opera*.[13] Later he appeared in *The Cat and The Canary* (1927), *Doctor X* (1932), and *Mystery of the Wax Museum* (1933).

Rumors of other possible films circulated in the movie industry before the Broadway play. In 1928, Lugosi himself spoke about the need for the play to make the transition to film. Though he believed it would be effective, Lugosi did admit a belief that the play would always have an advantage, because "picture audiences are apt to shake off any alarmed feeling which results when the emotions are excited by reminding themselves they are at a movie."[14]

Most famously, of course, director Tod Browning wanted to make a film version starring Lon Chaney Sr. The duo had worked to create a fake vampire for *London After Midnight* (1927), one of their many film collaborations. But Chaney died of throat cancer in late August of 1930, shortly after Universal decided to produce *Dracula*. Browning alone had to carry on; such is Hollywood History. In reality, of course, Universal studios pursued other Draculas for a few months before Chaney's death.

While Lugosi was appearing as Dracula at the Fulton Theater in Oakland in the summer of 1930, he likely saw a press account announcing actor John Wray would probably portray the vampire in Universal's film. It appeared on the *very same page* as an ad for Lugosi's stage version of *Dracula*.[15] Startling, shocking, unbelievable to think that anyone other than Lugosi could have been cast in the role, especially given the list of other possibilities.

Well, maybe. It's certainly shocking when the person thinking about it is having those thoughts anytime after the movie's 1931 release. Fixed forever into cultural memory, films like *Dracula* starring Bela Lugosi are moments in the cinema, moments in time, really, that just *had to be*. In retro-

In the role he hoped to play again at Universal Studios in the 1950s.

spect, to think that the studio wavered on whom to choose seems hard to fathom.

Funny though how different things would have seemed in 1930, and how every other choice Universal could make would actually have been safer. True, Lugosi starred in the role onstage each year between 1927 and 1930. He had also gotten a fair amount of press coverage. But he had starred in no national tour of the play; the bulk of his performances had been limited to Broadway, Los Angeles, and San Francisco.[16] Whatever effect he held over audiences who saw him, Lugosi was a virtual unknown to most US moviegoers.

Lugosi had been in a number of US films, but none of these pre-1931 appearances made much of a lasting impact. Though he appeared in about 13 films between 1923-1930, it's a marker of how little impact he made in so many that, for example, the *Los Angeles Times* claimed his first US movie was going to be *The Veiled Woman* of 1928. In reality, that film came five years and five films after his US film debut, *The Silent Command* (1923).[17] Even later, Lugosi himself even answered a written questionnaire by suggesting his first film was *Dracula*.[18]

By contrast, Universal's other possible choices were all better known to the moviegoing public of 1930, even if some are now forgotten. Along with having performed onstage in *The Spider*, longtime film actor William Courtenay had just been seen prominently in *Evidence* (1929), *The Sacred Flame* (1929), and *Three Faces East* (1930) with Constance Bennett. Conrad Veidt was well-remembered not only for *The Cabinet of Dr. Caligari* (1920), but also Universal's own *The Man Who Laughs* (1928) and *The Last Performance* (1929). Along with playing John Wilkes Boothe in D.W. Griffith's *Abraham Lincoln* (1930), Ian Keith was the male lead in Universal's *The Boudoir Diplomat* (1930); both of those films were only the latest in a movie career dating to 1924.[19] And John Wray, who may have come closest of the group to playing the role, had been one of the three male leads in Universal's Academy Award-winning *All Quiet on the Western Front* (1930).[20]

Universal could scarcely have hoped to sell the film *Dracula* to moviegoers based upon genre alone, as no talkie horror film genre yet existed. That the story had been a success onstage, as well as in print certainly would help. But Hollywood marketing was heavily-reliant on the use of famous names

Advertisement from the March 6, 1931
Kansas City Star.

Lugosi as Dracula, circa 1930. *(Courtesy of David Wentink)*

and faces. All of these other choices would actually have been safer than Lugosi in terms of their recognizability to movie fans of 1930. From a marketing standpoint, Wray in particular would have made sense due to *All Quiet on the Western Front.*

After all, Lugosi didn't even have the role to himself onstage; there seemed to be Draculas everywhere in 1930. Romaine Callender successfully played the role onstage in Washington D.C. in June 1930. Victor Jory was the Count onstage in Pasadena in August.[21] Courtney White did the same in Wilmington in September.[22] This is to say nothing of Raymond Huntley, the star of the 1924 London production of *Dracula*, who played the vampire again in Philadelphia in 1930.[23] The studio doesn't seem to have considered any of these other Draculas, but they did prove one thing: you didn't have to be Lugosi to get applause as the vampire. And so why not choose a rising star like John Wray?

Certainly Lugosi had supporters in areas where he had performed in the play, supporters who urged the studio to cast him. The *Hollywood Filmograph* printed a number of articles lobbying for Lugosi to get the role in August and September 1930.[24] And the *San Francisco Call-Bulletin* claimed that "if Lugosi isn't picked for the title role, there won't seem to be any justice."[25] Lugosi also lobbied for the role, a role that he wanted to play in 1930.[26] After all, it was the title role in a major Hollywood production.

Finally of course, after all the waiting and worry, Universal chose Lugosi. Perhaps it was a result of his screen test in late August 1930. Perhaps there were other reasons

A cartoon of Lugosi as Dracula from a 1930s issue of *Vanity Fair*. Instead of a romantic figure, Dracula had become an image of horror. Also pictured are Boris Karloff from the 1935 film *The Raven* (lower left), Charles Laughton (middle left), John Barrymore from the 1931 *Svengali* (left of Dracula), Henry Hull from the 1935 *WereWolf of London* (right of Dracula), Warner Oland as Fu Manchu, (beneath Dracula), and Peter Lorre from the 1935 *Mad Love* (right of Oland).

too, given that Universal didn't announce him for the role until a couple of weeks after the test.[27] Whatever the case, he got the role, against odds that were much greater than they would appear years later when names like John Wray faded from memory.

Lugosi's admirers have balked ever since that received only $500 a week for seven weeks work. But Universal was after all gambling approximately $400,000 during the Great Depression on a relative unknown. This was a very different thing than hiring, say, Helen Chandler as Mina and David Manners as Harker. Both were fresh from major film successes in 1930, which meant audiences knew who they were.

At the onset, producer Carl Laemmle, Jr. knew that Tod Browning would direct *Dracula*. Along with his successful productions with Lon Chaney, Browning had directed *The Thirteenth Chair* (1929), which included a seventh-billed Lugosi. That they had worked together previously seems not to have impacted Universal's casting for

Dracula in any particular way. No evidence exists that it helped get Lugosi cast, nor did it preclude him from getting the role.

As for Browning himself, he once declared that he was very sentimental. "You have to be sentimental," he said, "to be sensitive to impressions of terror, mystery, or the occult. After all, sentimentality is nothing more or less than an overactive imagination, a tendency to try to dramatize impressions."[28] Though Browning became known as a mystery man after his death, screenwriter Maurice Rapf once remembered that the director was "extremely friendly and not at all mysterious. He and my Dad [Harry Rapf] and some other fellows used to play cards at our house all the time. It wasn't as if he was some secretive hermit or anything."[29] Mysterious as a person or not, in 1930 Browning would have certainly been considered the master of mysterious films.

At the beginning of October 1930, a trade publication wrote, "After puzzling for a week as to whether *Dracula* should be a thriller or a romance, Carl Laemmle Jr. and Tod Browning decided to make it both."[30] Certainly ads just before the film's release played up this angle, featuring the tag line "He lived on the kisses of youth."[31] These kinds of slogans can be found in numerous city newspaper advertisements, including "His Kiss Was Death–Yet No Woman Could Resist It!"[32] Studio posters and publicity materials heightened this with the tag line "The Story of the Strangest Passion the World Has Ever Known." A truly gothic story, horror and romance intertwined. And with all the passion and kisses, Lugosi in late 1930 and early 1931 could easily have envisioned moving into romantic parts in other films.

Once shooting finally began, Browning shot in sequence, presumably to allow the actors and crew to feel the story's progression more acutely. Few tales from the set emerged in 1930, but a journalist for the *Exhibitors Herald-World* did record a visit

From the Rocky Mountain, North Carolina *Evening Telegram*, February 25, 1931.

to Universal that coincided with an important scene. He witnessed the Transylvanian introduction of Dracula and Renfield:

> I arrived on the Universal stage one day in time to see [Lugosi] walk up the dingy stairs of his deserted castle, and down again, holding a candle.
>
> His black mane sweeps back above his forehead. His black cloak droops about him. His black eyes turn at a given moment to show the clear white beyond the rim of his pupils. The candle flickers eerily as the camera cranks. The dull tread of his feet echoes through the silent stage.
>
> Few men can walk up and down a flight of stairs while telling a story, but he has accomplished it.[33]

Seeing footage in the days and weeks that followed the staircase scene, Universal agreed that Lugosi had accomplished a great deal. They decided to increase the size of his name on publicity materials for the film. Make him *seem* like more of a name star even if he wasn't yet.

Once released, *Dracula* was greeted with a variety of critical reactions. Some reviews claimed it was better than the play; some claimed it was worse.[34] Some praised Browning; others did not.[35] Some praised Karl Freund's cinematography, but at least one thought his work was "faulty."[36] One review praised the use of sound, while a second claimed the film could have benefited from music. A third even questioned the quality of the sound recording techniques.[37]

The *New York Times* called *Dracula* "far superior to the ordinary mystery drama," but *Time* magazine said it was "not as good as it ought to be."[38] What does all of this critical response mean? Not very much of course. Films often get a mixed response from critics, with thumbs going up and down. An exhaustive survey of 1931 *Dracula* reviews does show more positive than negative, which suggests little more than the fact that some trade press and city newspaper critics believed the film was an artistic success.[39]

As for audiences, some in the industry had feared that it might be "bound to dis-

With an unknown Santa Claus.

turb many a young kid and prove distasteful to many grownups."[40] But its success at the box office quickly eased those worries. In Virginia, *The Bee* declared that "no other talking picture ever shown in Danville has created such a furor of comment, or has so powerfully gripped the emotions of local theatergoers."[41] A critic in New Orleans heard audience "gasps, screams, and startled exclamations" throughout the film.[42] The *Binghampton Sun* claimed that two women fainted after initial film screenings in the city.[43] And the renowned *New York Times* critic Mordaunt Hall wrote that, when Van Helsing held a cross up to Dracula, the audience responded with "a no uncertain round of applause—handclapping such as is rarely heard during the showing of a motion picture."[44]

Motion Picture Classic, a popular fan magazine of the time, ran the extended response of a moviegoer in San Diego, who told readers that:

> [*Dracula*] made me feel I was there in the scene, hushed and still, while horrible things were being done, while drama and tragedy and life flowed past. It made me realize the artistry of acting so flawless that I forgot it was acting.
>
> I've knocked around the world considerably, done nearly everything in my life from flying a plane to being secretary of a Christian endeavor group, had enough experience to make me think I was fairly blase against movie 'spooky' plays–but *Dracula*, folks, really and truly gave me a thrill!"[42]

Did everyone respond the same way? No, certainly not. Audiences reactions and their intensity are impossible to gauge accurately; even within a single auditorium a excited viewer can be seated right next to someone who is falling asleep. And both have bought tickets, which add equally to the film's gross. But it is true that the film was a major box-office success, suggesting at least some strong word-of-mouth advertising, repeat viewers, and extended theatrical runs.

And Lugosi's name value—as well as his connection to *Dracula*–had grown considerably. If he wasn't already attached symbiotically to the vampire before the film was released, he certainly was after it. On at least one occasion, he told Dick what he said so many times: Dracula had been a blessing and a curse. In *The Tragedy of Man*, Madách's Adam questions if he should be "free to shape my destiny, And to destroy again what I might build, Uncertain of myself and my design." To escape from the very film role he had lobbied so hard to get, to escape the horror movies that it spawned. He had played so many roles in three different countries; now it was time to reshape his destiny once again.

That Hollywood regularly typecast actors by genre was something Lugosi had to have understood. Some actors became known for comedy, some for westerns, and some for horror. But during his time in Hollywood, he also must have noticed that an actor like Fredric March moved easily into nonhorror roles after winning an

Academy Award for *Dr. Jekyll and Mr. Hyde* (1932). It could happen, and occasionally it did.

His struggle is visible immediately after the film version of *Dracula*. In 1931, Lugosi costarred as a red herring in a mystery called *The Black Camel*. Because he was Dracula in a prior film, he had become a suspect for Chinese detective Charlie Chan. At about the same time, he also appeared as a Mexican in the Joe E. Brown comedy *Broadminded*.[46] But some critics responded to Lugosi's role in it by mentioning that his work even in it

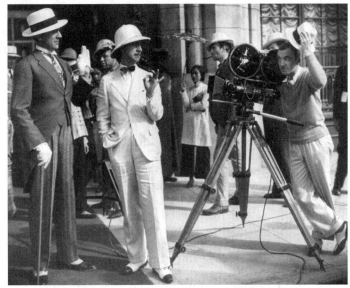

Lugosi (left) in the film *International House* (1933).

smacked of *Dracula*. The following year, Lugosi's three released films featured him in three horror roles.[47]

But 1933 would have been one of those periods where he could have seen some hope. Out of his five films released that year, two weren't horror stories. To be sure, *The Devil's in Love*, a French Foreign Legion drama, gave him only a small role as a military prosecutor. And for whatever reason he didn't receive billing in a cast that included Victor Jory, David Manners, and Loretta Young. But it was something other than Edgar Allan Poe, H.G. Wells, or Haitian zombies.

That same year, in *International House* (1933), he was a Russian in a film comedy. Four years after that, in *Tovarich* (1937), he was a Russian in a stage comedy. Another two years, in *Ninotchka* (1939), he was a Russian in another film comedy. Certainly in the first two instances he was able to reveal a flair for comedy, sparring with W.C. Fields in the movies or Osgood Perkins on the stage. In the third, he played a small straight role opposite Greta Garbo in Ernst Lubitsch's classic comedy.

For each of those performances, Lugosi received some strong reviews. And certainly he hoped for more of the same. Enough more, and the tide against his typecasting could change. But what he may or may not have realized is that these roles depended on his being "foreign" as much anything else. Eastern European, Arab, Indian, Russian: on the rare occasions when he was outside of horror films, Lugosi was cast in these kinds of ethnic roles, roles that also found him playing a "heavy." Take as another example *No Traveler Returns*, a brief 1945 stage drama with Lugosi as an Indian criminal named Bharat Singh. The character spends the whole of the play knifing and poisoning other characters until he's shot and killed.

A curious exception was when Hunt Stromberg Jr.—producer of *Treasure Island* (1934), *The Great Ziegfeld* (1936), and the *Thin Man* movies—hired Lugosi to headline the cast of a new play, *Three Indelicate Ladies* in April 1947. A trio of women find themselves in the detective business, with Lugosi playing an Irishman named Francis O'Rourke. *Variety* was unimpressed, though, thinking that Lugosi was "overwhelmed" by the character's ethnicity and that it gave him "no opportunity to capitalize on the horror angle."[48]

Regardless, Lugosi was overjoyed at starring in the play. Some of this may have come from working with high-calibre costars; some of it may have been the chance to make money. But certainly he enjoyed the opportunity to play a character so very different than the norm. All of this is confirmed by his costar Stratton Walling, who remembered:

> Bela was tremendous. His wife Lillian was there with him. I remember her wearing a gold bat on her dress. And they were having fun with the play and the cast, people like Elaine Stritch and Ray Walston. The mood changed a bit when the bad reviews came, and the writer even stormed out yelling.
>
> In particular, I remember that in one scene of the play, someone punched their fist through Lugosi's hat. They went through this in rehearsals and then performances, so the busted hats started piling up. And in Boston, we saw this guy, we never knew who he was, who took out the busted Lugosi hats and went away. This happened more than once.
>
> Eventually we learned that it was a burlesque comic, a friend of an actor in the play named Joey Faye. Faye himself had done some burlesque I think. Anyway, after we learned this, Faye arranged for us all to go down to the burlesque club where the hats were being used in a comedian's act.
>
> Lugosi was there, Ray Walston, and a few of us. And that was when the comedian got Lugosi to come up onto the stage. The audience wasn't told who he was, and so they may not have even known. The comedian made him the butt of a few jokes, of course, because he was a comedian. Then, wouldn't you know it, he punched his fist right through Lugosi's hat!
>
> Lugosi of course was a very nice guy, and he took all of this in good humor. He was really enjoying himself the whole time of the play, I think.[49]

All of the fun came to an end, though, when *Three Indelicate Ladies* closed within a month of its opening. Hopes of getting to Broadway died.

Lugosi had a final opportunity of this kind just a few years later in June 1950, when he was signed to the cast of *The Devil Also Dreams*, a play starring Clare Boothe Luce and Francis L. Sullivan. Set in England in the late 19th century, the story features has-been playwright Quill (Sullivan) involving himself in everything from plagiarism to murder in an effort to hang onto his actress/mistress Effie (Luce).

As Petofy, Lugosi played an out-of-work Hungarian actor who makes a living as Quill's butler.[50]

The character was a magnificent one, with butler Petofy always acting, as if even dusting the mantle was a role in a play. He regularly cribbed lines from Shakespeare, and even spoke of how they benefited from being translated into Hungarian. Lugosi and Shakespeare again, and in a comedy where he thrived on the laughs. "Having threatened people for the last 23

A cartoon of Lugosi (left), Melville Cooper (center), and Osgood Perkins (right) in *Tovarich* (1937). From the *San Francisco Chronicle* of March 28, 1937.

years," he said, "I'm having the time of my life making people laugh."[51] It was a part that fit Lugosi perfectly. And it was all in a new play, with a well-known cast and one last chance at Broadway.

Lugosi got a number of strong reviews, and some critics seemed surprised that he had could do comedy so well.[52] But the play's story, as well as Sullivan and Luce, received poor notices, and the show folded after only about a month. With it closed not only Lugosi's final hope for Broadway, but also his last real chance to escape Dracula's clutches. A blessing and a curse.

These particular roles are only part of the story, of course. Lugosi's hope for change were founded on more than just four films and four stage plays. As in any actor's career, there was always plenty of talk about proj-

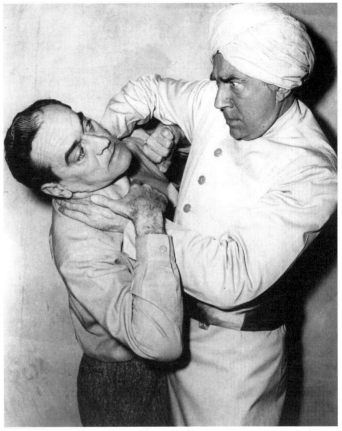

Lugosi as Bharat Singh in *No Traveller Returns* (1945).
(Courtesy of Bill Chase)

ects that never happened. In 1935, Lugosi tried to set up his own production company to make historical dramas, but he never could get financial backing.[53] He did an unsuccessful screen test for *The Charge of the Light Brigade* (1936). And in 1941, producer Alexander Paal wanted him to costar with Rudy Vallee in the Melchior Lengyel story *Gala Performance*, but the film never went into production.[54]

The same was true of a number of stage plays. Three nonhorror plays with Lugosi were slated in the 1930s—*Conception* in 1933, *Pagan Fury* in 1934, and *Ferrari* in 1937—but none of them were staged. For *Pagan Fury*, Lugosi would have acted as producer as well as actor. That seems to have been his answer at times in his career: if no one else will cast you, cast yourself.[55]

In the late forties, Lugosi tried that approach again. It was an "Evening of CHARACTER SKETCHES," for which he even had a promotional flyer printed. Sporting several photos of him from different roles, it read "Mr. Lugosi, who has given command performances before the King of England, is considered to be one of the Greatest of Shakespearean Actors. His varied program consists of excerpts from *Hamlet*, *King Lear*, *Richard III*, Edgar Allan Poe's *The Tell-Tale Heart*, and others from his extensive repertoire."[56] This was a separate program from Lugosi's touring production of *The Tell-Tale Heart*, and it seems very possible it was never publicly performed.[57]

And then of all things there was actually Mary Chase's play *Harvey*. Lugosi as Elwood P. Dowd, costarring with an imaginary 6-foot tall rabbit. A radical break

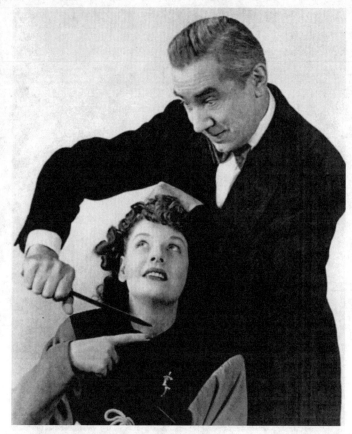

Lugosi as Francis O'Rourke in *Three Indelicate Ladies* (1947).

from his horrific past. Columnist Hedda Hopper first printed the announcement at the end of January 1948, saying he'd do four weeks in the play later that year.[58] And then Bob Thomas's syndicated column repeated the same story in March 1948, claiming that the play would be staged in the coming autumn. "I will give a slightly different interpretation of the role," Lugosi told Thomas, who called his comment "the understatement of the week."[59] Regrettably, *Harvey* with Lugosi didn't move out of the planning stages.

Was Lugosi wrong to keep hoping year after year that he might be able to leave horror behind him? Perhaps, but his career after the 1931 *Dracula* included regular opportunities outside of horror movie roles. Some were produced, some weren't. But they appeared with just enough frequency to fuel his ongoing hopes. Tantalizing but deceptive. In the end, he just wasn't free to reshape his destiny.

All of this creates a great irony. In a way, Lugosi couldn't escape Dracula for Elwood P. Dowd. Dracula was the role for which he was always identified, a role that became his middle name in publicity that so often dubbed him "Bela (Dracula) Lugosi." Lugosi was forever Dracula. And yet, he wasn't, not in Hollywood anyway.

The role that in the end consumed nearly three decades of his life was one that he only played *twice* onscreen, in the original 1931 film and then again in *Abbott and Costello Meet Frankenstein* (1948). Sometimes writers have claimed he also appeared as Dracula in a 1933 short subject called *Hollywood on Parade*, but he really didn't. He played a wax figure of "Bela Lugosi as Dracula" that comes to life at a Hollywood museum along with some other stars; the short subject inadvertently under-scores this very irony.

Lugosi did appear as "Count Mora" in *Mark of the Vampire* (1935), Tod Browning's MGM film in which the Count and his vampire daughter Luna are revealed to be nothing more than actors hired to catch a murderer. And to a lesser degree his role as Dr. Carruthers in *The Devil Bat* (1940) built on the vampire con-nection. But neither of these were even vampires, let alone Dracula.

Not only did he make a mere two appearances as Dracula onscreen, he played only one other actual vampire role. It was for Columbia's film *The Return of the Vampire* (1943), in which he appeared as a bloodsucker named Armand Tesla. Aided by a werewolf manservant, Tesla spent his time terrorizing two female characters played by Nina Foch and Frieda Inescort. The film's title sounds a bit like a

Clowning around while starring in *The Devil Also Dreams* (1950).

Dracula sequel, but in reality the vampire Tesla makes his first appearance *and* his return within the same movie, thanks to a story that takes place in 1918 and in World War II.

More famously, of course, *Dracula's Daughter*–Universal's sequel to the 1931 *Dracula*–didn't end up casting Lugosi, even though that had been their hope. One trade publication wrote that, "*Dracula's Daughter* has been withdrawn from production at present ... Bela Lugosi is without a role but the studio hopes to get one [for him] soon."[60] A proper role wasn't worked out though, and the film went ahead without him. Dracula appeared only as a dummy, set ablaze by his vampire daughter. When Lugosi visited the set to create some publicity, he was indeed a visitor.[61]

After these missed opportunities, gossip columnist Jimmie Fidler wrote that he "wish[ed] some film factory would give Bela Lugosi another one of those vampire roles. They always knock me for a ghoul."[62] For awhile it looked as if Fidler was going to get his wish. Between 1939-1945, Edwin Schallert's column in the *Los Angeles Times* claimed Lugosi would appear in five different vampire films; in the end, only one was produced, and it was produced without Lugosi.

In 1939, Schallert announced that Lugosi had "a rather definite commitment in England for a film called *The Vampire*, said to resemble his success[ful] *Dracula*."[63] A year later, Schallert wrote that Lugosi had "signed a two-picture deal with Paul Gordon, formerly producing in England, first to be *Poison Gas Over Manhattan*, a horror yarn, and secondly probably *Foruthun*, a vampire story by H. R. Barnett."[64]

Lugosi and Glenn Strange in *Abbott and Costello Meet Frankenstein* (1948).

None of these projects seem to have ever been mentioned again.

A few years later, hot on the heels of Columbia's *The Return of the Vampire*'s "highly favorable" reaction, Schallert wrote about a possible sequel that would star Lugosi. Writer Griffin Jay of *Return of the Vampire* and a number of other horror films was hard at work on a script for *The Bride of the Vampire* in December 1943.[65] The studio planned a smaller budget, which meant neither Frieda Inescort and Nina Foch would appear in the new film. But in the end neither did Lugosi, because the project was shelved.

General vampires aside, by mid-1939 Universal Studios started to plan another *Dracula* sequel, but the *Los Angeles Times* wrote that they were having "problems" with the fact a stake had been driven through his heart. "How to bring Dracula to life again" was the question, at which the "occult expert" Manly P. Hall proposed an answer. His treatment rewrote the ending of the 1931 film to claim that Van Helsing had staked Dracula one minute after sundown which hadn't in fact killed the vampire at all. Instead, Dracula simply moved on to new blood in Buenos Aires. [66]

Then Schallert claimed in 1944 that Universal was planning another opportunity for Lugosi to play Dracula, this time in *Wolf Man Versus Dracula*. Bernard Schubert would be the writer, Ford Beebe the producer, and Lon Chaney Jr. the Wolf Man. And in February 1945, Schallert's column headlined the fact "Bela Lugosi enlisted for *House of Dracula*," an apparently rechristened *Wolf Man Versus Dracula*. [67]

By the time *House of Dracula* (1945) finally went into production, John

Carradine played the vampire count. He had already appeared as Dracula in Universal's *House of Frankenstein* in 1944. The year before that, Lon Chaney Jr. took on the role in *Son of Dracula* (1943). Combined then with the brief moments of the dummy in a casket in *Dracula's Daughter,* the character made four appearances in Universal horror films after being staked in the catacombs of Carfax Abbey. Carfax Abbey, with the word Carfax being a corruption of "Quatre Face": four faces. And none of those four Universal faces of Dracula after 1931 belonged to Lugosi.[68] Instead, he had to wait until an Abbott and Costello comedy in 1948 to finally reprise the role. By that time, one reviewer claimed Dracula seemed to "creak a bit with arthritis."[69] Maybe that was why Universal's announcement of remaking *Dracula* with Lugosi in 1948 went nowhere.[70]

At the Universal commissary with Gloria Holden (seated, right), who played the title role in *Dracula's Daughter* (1936). *(Courtesy of Bill Chase)*

A number of planned stage productions of *Dracula* fell through over the years too. Producer Ben Lyon wanted Lugosi for a Washington DC production in early 1938, but things never got past the planning stages.[71] A press announcement in 1941 claimed Lugosi had "been inked for a two-year tour of 124 cities," but the monumental tour never took place.[72] Announcements of a Chicago performance of *Dracula* came in 1939, 1942, and 1943.[73] None of them materialized, even though the 1942 show was so close to happening that Lugosi travelled there to begin rehearsals.[74] In 1948, he was supposed to go to England for a tour of the play.[75] In 1949, Lugosi was supposed to travel the US in the play with actor Hampton White.[76] In 1951, *Variety* claimed Lugosi might even appear in an Australian tour.[77]

And yet there was a major difference between Lugosi's experiences with Dracula on stage and in film. Even though a number of attempts to stage *Dracula* failed, Lugosi still appeared in the play with a frequency that could never have been matched in Hollywood. There was a Portland, Oregon production in 1932.[78] A condensed version for vaudeville in New York and Washington D.C. in 1933.[79] A wartime tour ten years later that not only streamlined the Deane-Balderston play, but also updated it with dialogue that mentioned atom smashing and likened Renfield to a "Flying jitterbug."[80] This is to say nothing of the variety of vaudeville and spook show acts in the forties where Lugosi incorporated moments from the play, sometimes with wife Lillian even playing Lucy.[81]

And then, wonderfully, there was summer stock after World War II. Summer stock, an "American theatrical phenomenon" where independent theaters established resident companies to stage plays on a regular basis during the warmer

With Manly P. Hall (center), who wrote a treatment for a
1939 sequel to Universal's *Dracula* (1931),
and R. K. Bennett (left).

months of the year. To draw audiences, the companies often hired a single name performer to join the cast for the short run of the show. And after the war, a rise in the use of star performers coincided with the decline in Lugosi's own film roles.[82] Between 1947-1950, he was able to appear in the three-act version of the 1927 play over and over again. Work, good pay, and sometimes wonderful experiences. But these were still the appearances of a Dracula in decline, battling not only Van Helsing but also marital problems and old age.

In September of 1947, Lugosi also played Dracula for a week at the Litchfield Summer Theatre in Connecticut.[83] Leonard Altobell, later associated with the 1950 Lugosi play *The Devil Also Dreams*, directed the show, which included Gene Lyons as Renfield and Saralie Bodge as Lucy.[84] Not only was Bodge generally the lead actress in the company, she was also Altobell's wife. The two had opened the theatre in 1940 and ran it for some seventeen years.

Allan Jefferys, himself an actor and later a theater critic, constructed the 1947 *Dracula* set to accord with Lugosi's blocking, which Lugosi had sent in advance of his arrival. Jefferys remembered that:

> Among other things, I built the set to meet Lugosi's needs. The result was my seven-door set (including a hidden door). Four were for him ... three for me.
> Lugosi wasn't particularly talkative. It was actually a good thing that the Dracula role only had something like eight sides of dialogue, because he was pretty beat in those days. His wife was there, and, to help him not miss his cues to move out onto the stage, she gave him little nudges on the back. I remember seeing that from backstage.[85]

Capturing Jefferys' sets and Lugosi's vampire was noted filmmaker and photographer Samuel Kravitt, who snapped a variety of pictures during the dress rehearsal. They remain the best images of all of Lugosi's many summer stock appearances as Dracula.

When the show finally opened, Altobell's daughter Jayne sat excitedly in the audience. Meeting Lugosi that week, Jayne thought that he was "gentle and calm offstage," and she loved his performance as Dracula. In particular, she found his "cape twirling technique mesmerizing as he made his entrances and exits."[86] The *Litchfield Inquirer* gave strong notices to Altobell, Bodge, Lyons, and Jefferys, but mustered a little less enthusiasm for Lugosi than Jayne had. Of his Dracula, the critic wrote that he "is well-acquainted with his characterization, if that's a compliment."[87]

During Lugosi's own life, very little had been written about his Draculas outside

As Dracula in the 1940s.

Onstage as Dracula in the 1940s.

As Dracula in Litchfield, Connecticut in 1947 with Harald Dyrenforth as Van Helsing.
(Photograph taken by Samuel Kravitt; Courtesy of Mrs. Samuel Kravitt)

of newspapers, fan magazines, and industry trade publications. An exception was the Reverend Montague Summers, an eccentric writer and intellectual who studied such topics as witchcraft, demonology, and vampirism. In his 1928 book *The Vampire: His Kith and Kin,* he quickly mentioned Lugosi as headlining the play in New York, misspelling his name as "Lugoni." It was likely the first thing close to an "academic" mention of Lugosi in print.[88]

But the first time anyone close to a film historian or theorist tackled the 1931 film version of *Dracula* in any depth seems to be in October 1953, when George Geltzer published a Tod Browning article in *Films in Review.* "Today *Dracula* seems weak," he wrote, "but its opening sequences of Count Dracula's castle still create an eerie atmosphere."[89] In January 1954, William K. Everson's essay "Horror Films" appeared in the same publication, echoing Geltzer's praise about the opening sequence but damning the rest as "plodding" and "talkative."[90]

Dracula had surely excited so many audiences in 1931, but by the fifties so many viewers would have felt a collision between the film's incredible fame and all the things about it that at that time would have seemed increasingly old-fashioned and out of date.

In the autumn of 1953, around the time Geltzer's *Films in Review* article was published, Dick Sheffield came home one afternoon from Hollywood High to find a letter. Universal had finally responded to the petition. Dick quickly tore open the envelope, and read what seemed almost like a form letter. No remake in color and 3-D. No new *Dracula* film at all, with or without Lugosi. Dick and his gang were

With Rande Carmichael as Lucy in a 1948 production of Dracula at the Green Hills Theatre of Reading, Pennsylvania. *(Courtesy of George R. Snell)*

thanked for their time and interest in Universal Studios. The rugged peaks of Hollywood frowned down upon them.

A little time passed, and then Dick came up with a new idea. Norm Fist's uncle owned a wire recorder that could make recordings from the radio, records, or live events. That meant *Dracula* could happen once more without any studio or any camera. After setting it up one afternoon in his bedroom, Fist turned it on and cued Lugosi. The actor's eyes brightened as he began to speak Dracula's dialogue from the 1927 play, talking as if to a maid at the Seward Sanitarium. "Hear and obey. From now on you will carry out any suggestion that reaches you from my brain instantly without question."

Then, with a copy of the stage play in hand, Dick took on the role of Renfield: "Yes master, I want lives, I want blood—but I didn't want human life." Lugosi's Dracula answered: "You betrayed me. You sought to warn my destined bride against me." And then Dick again: "Mercy, mercy, mercy, don't kill me!" The wire continued to thread from one spool to another, preserving every word of an unholy alliance between the fly-eating servant and the King of the Vampires.

It's actually difficult to tell with certainty when Lugosi last played Dracula in front of a public audience; it was certainly before Dick met him in the Spring of 1953. But Lugosi's last performance as the vampire count—his last reading of dialogue that he first performed in New Haven, Connecticut—was with his friend Dick in the privacy of Norm Fist's bedroom. The only audience was Fist, who quietly shut off the recorder when the two actors finished.

CHAPTER SEVEN

He Said I Looked Like Boris Karloff

It was cold when Lugosi pulled into St. Louis. He had spoken to Dick before leaving Los Angeles, and regretted that Lillian was no longer able to drive him across country. The train ride was fine, but January weather in the midwest could be pretty cold. January 1954 in Missouri. Lugosi wasn't discontent, despite the winter chill. An inauspicious location and time for a major career moment.[1]

For Lugosi, it was the latest incarnation of a role that he had portrayed more than any other in his entire career except for Dracula. Jonathan Brewster, the murderous nephew of two murderous old ladies in the black comedy *Arsenic and Old Lace*. January 19-24 at the Empress Playhouse, with the haughty and reserved British actress Velma Royton and the more bubbly Danish actress Ruth Hermansen costarring as the Brewster aunts.

At the train station was Emile O. Schmidt, a member of the resident company of the Empress Playhouse. Along with acting in their productions, Schmidt helped with spiriting guest performers like Lugosi around St. Louis. Not only did this mean transporting Lugosi to and from his hotel and the theater, but also getting him to local interviews.

Joseph and Louis Ansell formed the resident company at the Empress after running several movie theaters in the city. The theater had 1,500 seats, and they needed it to be pretty full to turn a profit. Many seats were taken by subscription tickets, but plenty more had to be sold to the walk-in crowd. The lead actors cost a great deal of money, and the company itself had a payroll to make. Their other guest performers like Miriam Hopkins and Fay Bainter drew strong crowds, but Lugosi posed a challenge.[2]

As Emile helped with the publicity, he kept hearing the same question from reporters and potential ticket-buyers: "Is Bela Lugosi still around?" Once Lugosi arrived, though, excitement grew, thanks in part to local newspaper, radio, and television interviews. Though at times that week Lugosi seemed very old and tired, Emile noticed how vibrant he appeared at the interviews, smiling and puffing smoke from a cigar that occasionally caused him to have to spit out bits of tobacco leaf.[3]

Everything was working as smoothly as it possibly could have. Director Robert Perry was a patient and pleasant fellow whose style meshed well with Lugosi. Lugosi took a particular joy in working with Royton and Hermansen. Ken McEwen as Mortimer Brewster and Gena Bantle as Elaine Harper were well-suited for their roles. And Emile played the small but very important part of Mr. Witherspoon. By

131

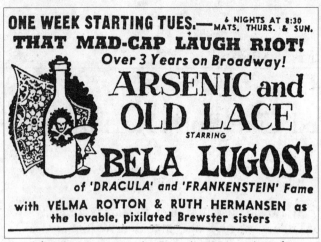

ONE WEEK STARTING TUES.— 6 NIGHTS AT 8:30
MATS. THURS. & SUN.

THAT MAD-CAP LAUGH RIOT!

Over 3 Years on Broadway!

ARSENIC and OLD LACE

STARRING

BELA LUGOSI

of 'DRACULA' and 'FRANKENSTEIN' Fame

with **VELMA ROYTON & RUTH HERMANSEN** as
the lovable, pixilated Brewster sisters

Advertisement promoting Lugosi's 1954 version of
Arsenic and Old Lace in St. Louis.

opening night, tickets were selling almost as fast as they could.[4] Lugosi had good reason to be happy, but he didn't realize that *Arsenic and Old Lace* in St. Louis that week would be an important event in his career.

How many times had Lugosi performed in the play? As with his Draculas, it's difficult to come to any exact number, as some of his *Arsenic* productions continue to rise up out of the pages of musty newspapers and theater magazines. Something akin to Jonathan Brewster and his sidekick Dr. Einstein counting their murder victims and the cities where they occurred.

For Lugosi, there was that successful *Arsenic* in Saratoga Springs, New York in 1947.[5] Saratoga Springs, where he also guest-starred on one television program, two radio shows, and was then driven to Schenectady for yet another radio show.[6] That was in addition to meeting with Robert Ripley aboard a yacht and then doing some live entertaining at Delmonico's in New York.[7] He was treated like a king.

There was a week in summer stock at New Hope, Pennsylvania in 1947; maybe even a week that same year in Beverly, Massachusetts.[8] Also a run in Deer Lake, Pennsylvania.[9] The following summer meant a week in Sea Cliff, New Jersey in 1948.[10] One more summer, and he was Jonathan again at the truly famous Famous Artists Country Playhouse in 1949, and then at the lesser known Lakeside Summer Theatre at the Landing, Lake Hopatcong in New Jersey. The Lakeside, where a smaller theater meant a bigger response; *The Daily Record* there spoke about how he was "hailed enthusiastically by the audience."[11]

And then there was a week in Reading, Pennsylvania in 1949, where the *Eagle* wrote: "We saw *Arsenic and Old Lace* with Bela Lugosi at Green Hills last night, and it scared hell out of us."[12] George Snell, director of that version, remembered, "Here was a 360 degree turn from the horrible vampire to the comedian. What a pleasant surprise is his ability to do comedy. It was fun—it was rewarding."[13]

All of those performances came after World War II when Lugosi's career relied heavily on summer stock theaters, particularly those in the New England area. But his history with Jonathan Brewster had much deeper roots. They went back to 1941, in the days of the original New York production that starred Boris Karloff. The tale had taken the Great White Way by storm. Its tenure on Broadway outlasted so many other plays, including the original 1927 *Dracula* with Lugosi.[14]

In the stage play, two kindly old aunts poison a variety of men with elderberry wine mixed with arsenic. Nephew Mortimer, a drama critic who hates melodramtic plays, learns about their murderous ways in between trying to control his crazy Uncle Teddy and marry his impatient fiancée. Everything grows more complicated when another nephew appears: Jonathan, a wanted murderer travelling with an accomplice named Dr. Einstein. Einstein has disguised Jonathan through plastic surgery by giving him a face he'd seen in a movie, the face of film star Boris Karloff.

Lugosi in *Arsenic and Old Lace* at the Famous Artists County Playhouse in Fayetteville, New York in July 1949. On the far left is Florenz Ames as Dr. Einstein, at the top of the stairs is Tom Reynolds as Teddy Brewster, at the table are Catherine Cosgriff as Abby Brewster and Florence Beresford as Martha Brewster, and on the far right are John Larson as Mortimer Brewster and Helen Marcy as Elaine Harper. *(Courtesy of Burry Fredrik)*

Ongoing comparisons to Karloff ignite Jonathan's rage, which caused the most talked about humor in the play: a postmodern joke in which the real Boris Karloff played Jonathan who looks like Boris Karloff.

In March of 1941, with Karloff in New York, a journalist pointed out that a second company was being formed to play Chicago. In that version Erich von Stroheim played Jonathan, which necessitated a change of dialogue. Rather than looking like the actor Boris Karloff thanks to plastic surgery, he now looked like the actor von Stroheim. The columnist anticipated that "from the looks of things, this successful farce will no doubt be represented on the road by as many duplicate companies as the producers can find famous villains to take this particular role. So don't be surprised if … you'll be seeing Bela Lugosi, looking like nobody else but Lugosi."[15]

Only months later, columnist Jimmie Fidler announced Lugosi had been approached to play Jonathan in a lengthy roadshow version of *Arsenic*, a "swell offer" that Lugosi was tempted to sign until he read a clause "compelling him to stick for 'the run of the play.'"[16] The indefinite time schedule meant Lugosi feared being gone from Hollywood too long. After disappearing almost completely from the screen in 1937 and 1938, he didn't inadvertently want to cause a repeat of that problem. He may have also initially bristled at playing a role made famous by Karloff.

That changed in 1943, when Lugosi starred in a production of *Arsenic* in San Francisco for two weeks and then Los Angeles for five. He had not seen Karloff onstage in the play, which he believed was fortunate in that he wouldn't be influenced in his portrayal.[17] After seeing his initial interpretation of the role, the *San Francisco Chronicle* predicted that "Lugosi has in him the makings of a Jonathan

Brewster which is the equal or perhaps the superior of Boris Karloff's masterful reading."[18] They hardly could have known, though, that he'd still be appearing in the part over a decade later.

The LA performances were even more successful, with Lugosi telling the press that the play was his "first break since the Dracula curse hit me."[19] He must have felt the distinction between vampires and comedy clearly at that moment, as during part of the LA production he was actually shooting a Columbia film called *The Return of the Vampire* (1943), a notch below Dracula as the returning revenant was only something of a Stoker imitation.[20] He even confided to the *LA Times* that he was so eager to do comedy, the producers "could have got me without [a] salary."[21]

By the time Lugosi first played Jonathan Brewster, he had already built up a resume of horror film spoofs that included *The Gorilla* (1939), *Spooks Run Wild* (1941), and *Ghosts on the Loose* (1943). He had also acted in horror comedy skits on the radio with Walter O'Keefe, Ken Murray, and Fred Allen.[22] Lugosi claimed it was fun "burlesquing" horror films, but in *Arsenic* and these other appearances, much of his work depended on playing straight against more comical characters. Humor erupted out of contrast.

In 1944, he finally appeared in a roadshow version of *Arsenic*. It was actually a tour that starred Karloff, who had to bow out to make his way to Hollywood for a role in Universal's *The Climax* (1944). Jonathan once again looked like Bela Lugosi; cast and crew quickly scribbled the change onto script pages. Lugosi himself made his way from the West Coast to join the company in Oklahoma City. This time, he travelled not only in a play made famous by Karloff, but in a roadshow that included Karloff amongst its investors.[23] With each

Above: Advertisement for Lugosi's appearance in *Arsenic and Old Lace* in San Francisco in August 1943.
Below: Lugosi (center) during a performance in Reading, Pennsylvania in August 1949 with William C. Cragen and Maurice Nugent (left) and Virginia True and Theodora Landess (right).

performance, Lugosi earned money not only for himself, but for Karloff as well.

It was January as Lugosi travelled east. Oklahoma City was cold; winter was in the air, and Lugosi must have felt a chill as he made his way to a hotel on January 28, 1944. He had two shows ahead of him at the Shrine Auditorium the next day. While he was eating at the local Huckins coffee shop, newspaper photographers took his picture hypnotizing a pretty cashier who "never did meet a movie star before."[24] Talking to the local press before the evening performance, Lugosi extolled the virtues of green salads, fruit, orange juice, and milk before wishing he had a "good rare steak."[25]

By the next day, the cast moved onto Tulsa, appearing at the city's Convention Center and getting an extra day's layover before travelling to their next show in Little Rock. Lugosi complained about the suit he had worn onstage; he didn't believe it was shabby enough to give the effect of a fugitive criminal on the run. Taking advantage of their extra time in Oklahoma, Lugosi proceeded to tour Tulsa's pawn shops. After

Above: **Boris Karloff in a stage production of** *Arsenic and Old Lace.* *Below:* **Bela Lugosi in the same pose for the 1944 tour of** *Arsenic and Old Lace.* **To the left are Jean Adair (Abby Brewster) and Ruth McDevitt (Martha Brewster). To the right is Henry Sherwood (Dr. Einstein).**

getting strange looks for refusing to look at their "better merchandise," he finally decided on an old blue suit that was two sizes too big, a used black hat, and an old pair of shoes. Baffling the pawn shop owner, Lugosi knotted up the suit to cause wrinkles. After first thinking he was a "real mental case," the shop owner finally learned his customer was the real Bela Lugosi.[26]

With his costume finalized, Lugosi left with the cast for Arkansas and what would be over thirty more cities by the time the tour finished in early June 1944. A rigorous, even gruelling schedule, with matinee and evening performances in many a city before quickly moving onto the next. A rather strange image, Lugosi stalking the streets of Louisiana and Alabama, Georgia and the Carolinas before trekking north. In each town, though, Brewster looked like Lugosi, and Lugosi looked at success.

Lugosi and Ann Lincoln (Elaine Harper) in the
1944 roadshow of *Arsenic and Old Lace*.

In Savannah and in Roanoke, waves of audience applause erupted from the first moment he walked onto the stage.[27] In Birmingham, he thanked reporters for the interview after he was surrounded by a group of high school kids begging for autographs.[28] In Winston-Salem, he met reporters in casual attire and discussed his belief that Lon Chaney Sr. was the "master of horror," and how Boris Karloff had a "fortunate face" to be working in the genre. Lugosi added that he wasn't afraid of the dark, "just cautious." [29]

The costume was his own, and the dialogue sported his own name. But theater programs were another matter. That Lugosi had taken over for Karloff during the tour meant that, while programs changed to feature his name, the artwork remained Karloff's face.

Dracula had hovered ever near Lugosi, a blessing and a curse that haunted him for almost three decades. But Lugosi was also haunted by Boris Karloff, at least a version of Karloff constructed out of his unhappiness, resentment, and even a kind of irony. His agent Don Marlowe once remembered Lugosi signing an autograph for a child who believed his name was Boris Karloff.[30] And in the early 1950s, Lugosi told a journalist that "every time I get into a cab—and this is without exception–the driver looks at me and says, 'Aren't you Boris Karloff?'"[31]

On one level, the mixup wasn't strange. Karloff himself once admitted that he received a number of fan letters addressed "Dear Bela Lugosi."[32] But for Lugosi to be mistaken for Karloff suggests how Karloff towered over the horror film, as well as so many aspects of Lugosi's career. It was 1943 when Lugosi finally appeared in *Arsenic and Old Lace* in the role Karloff had made famous. That same year, Lugosi also appeared in movie theaters as the monster in *Frankenstein Meets the Wolf Man* (1943). Lugosi had famously refused to play the monster in the original 1931 film version of *Frankenstein*, showing disdain for the makeup and the lack of dialogue. But he donned the makeup for the 1943 release; he tantalizingly did have some dialogue, but it was taken away during the production, leaving the monster silent.[33] The situation was the same as 1931, the same except that the new film was merely a sequel to *The Wolf Man* (1941).

The tale of Lugosi turning down the role of the Frankenstein monster for the 1931 film has been retold countless times since the early thirties. It's probably been written about much more often than the story of how Lugosi got the famous role he did play: Dracula. At times Lugosi himself discussed the Frankenstein situation, picturing himself as a victim of his own making. As the decades moved along, writers and historians seized upon the story. A story of mythical proportions; a drama of winners and losers.

Lugosi balked at being the monster, either due to its makeup and lack of dialogue or to his inability to visualize the potential of the role. He fought for release from the project, or was pushed out. The director assigned to the film, the French expressionist Robert Florey, was also dismissed. Both were given a "consolation" prize, a film version of Poe's *Murders in the Rue Morgue*. The new director James Whale came on after Lugosi had left the project, or helped push him out of it. Either way, Whale then cast the unknown William Henry Pratt, stage name Boris Karloff.

Like so many myths, fiction intermingles with nonfiction. At every step of the story a great deal of "or" can be mined. This happened "or" something else did. An accurate account, or at least a complete and objective account, now seems impossible. The result gives latitude for storytellers to sculpt the event to meet their own needs. Some Lugosi admirers suggest that the monster role was different in Florey's script, so of course Lugosi saw little possibility in it. After all, he would have been perfect in the role he preferred, Henry Frankenstein. Some Karloff fans suggest Lugosi was simply unable to grasp the monster's inherent potential. Whale's adherents claim Whale wanted nothing to do with Lugosi. On each retelling, the myth invariably serves the better good of whomever is preferred by the storyteller, conveniently leaving out the "or" and whatever other possibilities should follow that word.[34]

That Universal saw Lugosi as being appropriate for the monster is not only a typical example of Hollywood typecasting, but also of a particular desire among Hollywood studios at the time. Lon Chaney Sr., the silent screen's "man of a thousand faces," died of throat cancer in 1930. One of the biggest stars in Hollywood, Chaney bedazzled and horrified audiences with his makeup effects in films like *The Hunchback of Notre Dame* (1923), *The Phantom of the Opera* (1925), and *London After Midnight* (1927). His death created a perceived missing link amongst Hollywood stars, and so filmdom watched and waited for a replacement.

In September 1930, the *LA Times* announced that Wallace Beery would be "groomed to take the place Chaney filled and the characterizations that would have been his."[35] By the following month, columnist Rosiland Shaeffer announced that it would actually be Lugosi who would "get many of the horror and mystery stories of the sort Chaney used to do."[36] A few months later, a January 1931 article in *Silver Screen* asked, "Is He the Second Chaney?" The fan magazine proclaimed that "Lon is gone but his art lives after him. May Lugosi be worthy of following in the path he made so thoroughly

Lugosi as Jonathan Brewster.

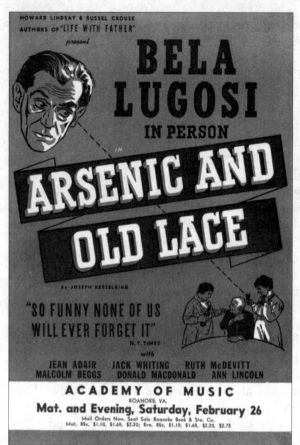

HOWARD LINDSAY & RUSSEL CROUSE
AUTHORS OF "LIFE WITH FATHER"
present

BELA LUGOSI
IN PERSON

in

ARSENIC AND OLD LACE

by JOSEPH KESSELRING

"SO FUNNY NONE OF US
WILL EVER FORGET IT"

N.Y. TIMES

with

JEAN ADAIR   JACK WHITING   RUTH McDEVITT
MALCOLM BEGGS   DONALD MACDONALD   ANN LINCOLN

ACADEMY OF MUSIC
ROANOKE, VA.
Mat. and Evening, Saturday, February 26
Mail Orders Now. Seat Sale Roanoke Book & Sta. Co.
Mat. 85c, $1.10, $1.65, $2.20; Eve. 85c, $1.10, $1.65, $2.20, $2.75

Though Lugosi had taken over the role of Jonathan from Karloff on the 1944 tour, Karloff's image remained on some of the publicity. The program from the Roanoke, Viriginia performance on February 26, 1944.

his own."[37] Talk of this type continued at least as late as July 1931, when *Variety* suggested that "two candidates for successor to Lon Chaney honors have developed suddenly on the coast. They are Edward G. Robinson and Bela Lugosi."[38]

A second Chaney was needed, and thus the Frankenstein monster was created. But the myth of *Frankenstein* that has emerged in histories speaks more about the acceptance of the completed James Whale and Boris Karloff film than it does about Universal's plans before it began production. For example, the first mention of any Lugosi followup to *Dracula* was definitely not *Frankenstein*. It was instead *The Red Mystery*, a German story that Carl Laemmle Jr. had recently purchased.[39]

The Red Mystery appeared on the horizon due to the studio's happiness with Lugosi's Dracula performance at the end of October 1930. Mention of him in it or any other Universal film then largely disappears until the spring of 1931. Though the studio was happy with his work in *Dracula*, they were likely waiting to see its box-office receipts, which began in mid-February of 1931 and continued for weeks and even months afterwards as the film made its way to US cities and small towns.[40]

By April 1, 1931, Lugosi was in Hawaii shooting a Charlie Chan film for Fox called *The Black Camel*. In between shoots, he enjoyed himself on the beach. It seemed that he had good reason to relax, as *Variety* wrote that he would probably sign a term contract with Universal once he got back to California. "The studio has other parts in mind," they said that day, "one of them being in *Frankenstein*, a medical melodrama."[41] This is likely the earliest published mention of the studio planning to make *Frankenstein*.[42]

A week later, on April 8, *Variety* wrote that Universal "has horror cycle all to self," claiming that they would produce Poe's "*Murders in the Rue Morgue*, then *Frankenstein*."[43] Several days passed, and then the *Los Angeles Record* claimed that Universal "has *Frankenstein* for Bela Lugosi and is considering *The Murders in the Rue Morgue* for him."[44] A similar story appeared in the *Hollywood Reporter* on April 20.[45] And during the middle of May, the *Hollywood Filmograph* claimed that *Frankenstein* was moving forward with Robert Florey as director.[46]

By the last week of May, however, the *Los Angeles Times* claimed that "due to a change in production schedules, Bela will play the leading role in *Murders in the Rue Morgue* before he goes into *Frankenstein*."[47] At the beginning of June, the *Los*

Angeles Evening Express wrote that, given Lugosi would make a film at another studio, "It will be some time before Lugosi starts work in the leading role of *Murders in the Rue Morgue*. Following this comes *Frankenstein*."[48] The indecision over which film to produce first suggests that Universal, even as late the beginning of June, did not necessarily view *Frankenstein* as a more important project than *Rue Morgue*. Likely they were more concerned with simply getting Lugosi into another Chaney-esque role in any film, continuing to build publicity around him, and generating much-needed revenue.

As June moved forward, the tide turned away from *Rue Morgue*, perhaps due to Robert Florey's interest in and work on *Frankenstein*. But that is almost all that can be said with certainty of June 1931, a month that seems even more worthy of the word "or." Robert Florey directed a screen test with cinematographer Paul Ivano, Lugosi in makeup, and two actors from *Dracula*, Edward Van

Lugosi as Jonathan Brewster in the 1944 roadshow of *Arsenic*, complete with the crumpled jacket he bought in Tulsa, Oklahoma.

Sloan and Dwight Frye. It was a great test that meant other directors wanted *Frankenstein*, or it was an awful one that caused Florey to be removed. Lugosi's makeup was laughably bad, or it was reminiscent of the silent film *The Golem* (1920), causing Lugosi to thank Paul Ivano for capturing his profile so well. Lugosi happily gave the cameraman a cigar, or he fought with studio boss Carl Laemmle Jr. Story after story persist about the lost screen test, how it was made and how the studio reacted. Contradictions in the existing data collide with the motivations of historians to favor one party or another.

It can be said with certainty that towards the end of June, the ground beneath Robert Florey quaked; James Whale replaced him as director on *Frankenstein*. The myth reaches a pivotal moment, deserving of a background score featuring brass instruments heralding Whale's arrival, or mysterious tympani underscoring the curious turn of events. On June 29, the *Hollywood Daily Citizen* claimed that "just as James Whale has finished *Waterloo Bridge*, he will start working out plans for *Frankenstein*. Bela Lugosi, you know, will be starred in this production."[49]

Lugosi remained attached to the film after Florey had been replaced, but for only for two weeks, more or less. In mid-July, though, the *Oakland Tribune* claimed that "Bela Lugosi is to have the chief role in *Murders in the Rue Morgue* instead of *Frankenstein* for Universal. ... As yet an actor has not been assigned to *Frankenstein*. The role calls for a dumb monster."[50] Like Florey, Lugosi was now working on *Rue Morgue*; unlike Florey, Lugosi was perhaps happy about the change. Again the myth deserves appropriate background music when retold.

A week after he was gone from *Frankenstein, Variety* purported that Lugosi would soon do a "talker version of *The Hunchback of Notre Dame*," a curious suggestion if makeup alone had caused all of the problems with Lugosi on *Frankenstein*.[51] Regardless, at the beginning of August another announcement claimed that Lugosi would likely be starred in a film based on the book *The Real Rasputin*. Neither film went into production, but *Rue Morgue* moved ahead.

That *Frankenstein* became a major hit for Universal and transformed Boris Karloff into a star is etched into the foundation of Hollywood history. The role was not a "dumb monster." Not at all. Examining the Karloff phenomenon, the *Los Angeles Times* said, "it took such a very intelligent fellow to play *Frankenstein*. When Universal offers us an horrific monster, a creature concocted in a scientific laboratory, grafted with the brain of a criminal, who, throughout the story never utters a word, yet somehow conveys wild emotional distortion, and even in truth, arouses a semblance of human sympathy, it calls for a rather superior brand of intellect."[52]

Universal's new star Boris Karloff certainly did not appear with Lugosi in *Murders in the Rue Morgue*, but the influence of *Frankenstein* looms large over that film. That the two bear some stylistic similarities might stem from Florey's involvement on both films. It might also stem from the fact that both Florey and Whale were well-acquainted with German Expressionism and *The Cabinet of Dr. Caligari* (1920). Regardless, they both owe a great deal to the dark fantasies of Weimar cinema.

More curious though is the narrative influence of *Frankenstein* on *Rue Morgue*. Poe's version of "Murders in the Rue Morgue" is a detective story, but for the Florey film it became a mad scientist tale. Dr. Mirakle, a character that does not exist in Poe, emerges as the lead role. Driven by inexplicable obsession, Mirakle tries to create new life. He attempts to play God, mating an ape with a woman by mixing their blood. Eventually, though, the ape runs amok

Above: Artwork of Boris Karloff from 1932. *Below:* Publicity from the 1932 screening of *Frankenstein* in Oklahoma City, Oklahoma. The film allegedly "out-Draculas *Dracula*."

and kills Mirakle. The basis of the film is not Poe or detective fiction. It is instead a kind of retelling of *Frankenstein*, with Florey as director and Lugosi as Henry Frankenstein.[53]

If anything, *Rue Morgue* had the potential to be more horrifying, or at least more offensive, to audience sensibilities than *Frankenstein*. To use dead bodies as source material for new life was frightening; to mate a woman with a gorilla through mixing their blood invoked bestiality and rape. Mirakle wasn't just playing God and meddling in things best left alone; he was set up in firm opposition to the very idea of God, preaching Darwin at his carnival show by day while experimenting by night. To be sure, Lugosi's Mirakle offers a good deal of insight into how he might have played Henry Frankenstein.

But *Frankenstein* proved far more successful at the box-office,

Lugosi flanked by director James Whale (seated on the far left) and James Flavin (standing behind Whale) and (right of Lugosi) Carl Laemmle Sr. and Tom Mix (far right). *(Courtesy of the Academy of Motion Picture Arts and Sciences)*

and had an effect on many more films than *Murders of the Rue Morgue*. It became the key influence on the US horror film from 1931-1945, if not longer. The genre that erupted out of 1931 was not one that dwelled on the supernatural landscape of *Dracula*. The narrative and thematic debates of these films were generally not religion's crucifix held up to an evil borne out of Satan; the debates revolved instead around the uncomfortable coexistence of God and science. In film after film, it was the scientist who went stark, raving mad. He became the recurrent character of the golden age of horror, as the horror film trended towards *Frankenstein* instead of *Dracula*. The result went beyond the fact that Karloff became a more successful star than Lugosi. The genre became Karloff's kind of horror, not Lugosi's.

Throughout the rest of his own film career, Lugosi played a mad scientist repeatedly, far more often than he did any supernatural characters. He starred in some fourteen mad doctor film roles.[54] That was in addition to a stage play and a handful of radio shows where he did the same.[55] So much was this the case that when Lugosi played Dracula for the final time in a feature film, it was in *Abbott and Costello Meet Frankenstein* (1948); Dracula co-stars with the Frankenstein monster, whose scientific needs occupy Dracula's thoughts far more than his usual bloodlust.

When Lugosi became particularly distraught at being trapped in horror movies in 1935, he decided to start his own production company. The master of his fate,

Lugosi as Dr. Mirakle in *Murders in the Rue Morgue* (1932).

planning, according to one press account, "ten or twelve historical romances." The first story though would be *Cagliostro*, "who stood the courts of Europe on their heads in the eighteenth century." Lugosi's intensive research was turned into a script by Andre de Soos, but the project never got off the ground. The attempt to get away from films of the Karloff/horror school failed, but on one level Cagliostro would never have fully archived that aim. After all, Nina Wilcox Putnam, screenwriter of *The Mummy* (1932), had earlier penned a script of *Cagliostro* for Karloff that Universal had planned to produce in 1932.[56]

All of that was after 1931 though, a year in which Universal decided that Karloff would inherit Chaney's crown. They needed one actor to promote to that position, and it became an actor who generated more money with *Frankenstein* than Lugosi had with *Dracula*. An actor who did not pose the kinds of personality difficulties that Lugosi did in the spring/summer of 1931 when his *Dracula* success perhaps translated into obstinance. And an actor who would willingly wear the makeup of monsters, a thousand faces other than his own.

In January 1932, the *Hollywood Citizen News* announced that the "whisper is around that this Karloff is to be Hollywood's new 'man of a thousand faces.'"[57] Later that same month came the word that "Universal fondly hopes [Karloff] is a successor to Lon Chaney."[58] By summer of the same year, the *Los Angeles Times* remarked that the answer was Boris Karloff, who was already "well on his way to being Lon Chaney's successor." As late as 1933, the same newspaper followed up by asking, "What would Universal do without Boris Karloff? The principal activity of the studio seems to center around the man who has taken the place left vacant by the death of Lon Chaney."[59]

And so to heighten his mystery, Boris Karloff became transformed. By face, to be sure. After *Frankenstein* (1931), it was the bearded and mute butler of *The Old Dark House* (1932). It was the aged bandages of *The Mummy* (1932). Loaned out to MGM, it was Sax Rohmer's Asian madman in *The Mask of Fu Manchu* (1932). His face, though, was only part of the transformation.

In the early thirties, Universal rechristened him simply "Karloff," largely dropping his first name. In the same way Greta Garbo was featured so often by last name alone, as if to heighten her mystique, so it became with Karloff. Even a gossip columnist in the early thirties called Karloff one of Hollywood's "male Garbos."[60] But the studio went further, though, offering an adjective as part of his new name. He was more than "Karloff," he was "Karloff the Uncanny."

"The Uncanny." It evokes various thoughts or definitions. Though most movie-goers would not have known or cared, "The Uncanny" was also the subject of Freud's famous essay that investigated a particular kind of horror and dread and fear. For him, the uncanny ("das unheimliche") was at least in part that which seemed to us familiar but was twisted into the unfamiliar. Something we recognize, but still find disturbingly unrecognizable. Freud, for example, described seeing an old man once whom he studied visually for several moments from a distance before realizing it was himself in a mirror.

Along with the roles Karloff played, he possessed a degree of otherness by his almost Russian-sounding name and his distinctly British accent. He also certainly did not cut the figure of Hollywood's handsome leading man. His were not the looks of most movie stars. Though his roles presented things unfamiliar to audiences, he himself resonated with more familiarity than Lugosi. His name was easier to say; his accent was easier to understand. The degree of otherness was far less than Lugosi's. He was indeed uncanny. And "Karloff the Uncanny" became the emblem of horror.

Does the fact that Karloff succeeded so well mean that Universal Studios intentionally treated Lugosi badly during his various tenures with them from 1930-1948?[61] No evidence exists of that, none at all.[62] They were a profit-driven company begun by Carl Laemmle, Sr., a man who had helped unleash the star system on film companies even before the studio era actually began. Prior to creating Universal Studios, Laemmle hired Florence Lawrence, a woman whom audiences knew only by her face in Biograph films. Lammle's Imp film company promoted her face *and* her name, helping to create the star system. [63]

In the case of Universal in the 1930s, an era in which like

Lugosi and Karloff at their first meeting in 1932.

all of Hollywood they battled declining movie attendance and the Great Depression itself, the studio needed a horror film star, not necessarily two horror film stars. After all, there hadn't been two Chaneys in the 1920s. Their decision to promote Karloff was what they saw as an intelligent business decision.

That said, they had no apparent interest in sabotaging Lugosi intentionally at any point during the years he worked for the studio. At times they could have paid him more money, but that could be said of much of the talent they hired. At times they could have given him more film roles or better parts, but likely the bulk of Universal's actors in that era would have made similar complaints.

It's also important to remember that the "they" under discussion was hardly consistent during the years Lugosi worked for Universal. Laemmle Sr. sold the studio in 1936, and so Universal was run by a very different group of people when Lugosi worked for them from 1939-1943. This was also true when Lugosi returned in 1948 for one film, by which time even the studio's name had changed to Universal-International, reflecting a merger that helped stave off financial ruin after World War II.

If any Universal regime might have borne a grudge against Lugosi, it would likely have been the Laemmles, resenting Lugosi's behavior after *Dracula*. But the Laemmles did not force Lugosi into *Frankenstein*, and they also apparently respected some of his stated desires. During the Laemmle years at the studio, Lugosi never had to wear heavy makeup. Some curly hair in his *Murders in the Rue Morgue*, perhaps, but there was no mummy bandaging, no werewolf hair.

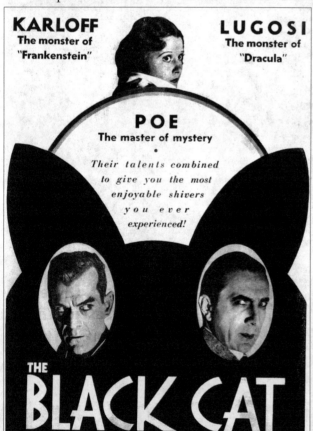

An advertisement for *The Black Cat* (1934) from *Universal Weekly*.

Consider also the plight of other stars that Universal promoted. In January 1932, ads suggested what a "brilliant" personality Genevieve Tobin was, "ready to pump blood into your box-office."[64] The same ad touted Karloff and Lugosi as well. They built Tobin up as a star, and yet stardom didn't come. She continued in a wide variety of films through 1940, though most of them for other studios. But that hardly means Universal conspired against her. Did they owe her better or did she deserve more films or money from them? Perhaps, but again this was the reality of a star system, not an individual vendetta against Tobin any more than it was Lugosi.

It was also the reality of individual actors making individual choices, such as moving onto other studios, taking other roles, and being in control of their careers. Lugosi had done this by avoiding *Frankenstein*. The same could be said of actors from Universal's 1930 film *All Quiet on the Western Front*. Lew Ayres was not highly-prized by the studio, with his long career built out of many roles at many studios. John Wray quickly found his way to other studios and numerous B-movies.

And then there was that short but important item in *Variety* in February 1932, "U's Three Buildups."[65] In it, the trade claimed that Karloff (along with Sidney Fox and Tala Birell) were the three new players that Universal "will build for stardom this season." This article is particularly crucial to understanding what occurred. Whatever reason or reasons led them to this decision, it was a decision that meant Universal's focus became Karloff. Similarly, they decided to promote Sidney Fox as a star.

While Fox made numerous films, received some good reviews, and certainly had some fans, she did not really become a star; Karloff did. Whatever their plans, Universal was to a degree at the mercy of filmgoers. Their ticket purchases, their letters, their comments to the local theater

Karloff and Lugosi judging black cats to appear in their film *The Black Cat* (1934).
In front of them is contestant Norman Salling. Walking behind the duo is Salling's father.

manager: the audience played a key role in the behind-the-scenes drama of Hollywood. During the spring of 1932, theaters polled their patrons on what stars brought them to the theater. The questionnaires showed enormous response for stars like Marie Dressler, Janet Gaynor, Joan Crawford, and other expected luminaries of Depression-era Hollywood; all three of those stars were mentioned in at least 75% of the returned questionnaires. Karloff was mentioned in 5.6%; Lugosi in less than 1%.[66]

By the summer of 1932, *Motion Picture Herald* presented a tabulation of the "Ten Biggest Money Makers" in Hollywood, on which neither Karloff or Lugosi appeared.[67] In calculating the box-office appeal of other stars over the 1931-1932 season, Karloff rated a 4.3%, and Lugosi again rated at less than 1%. The disparity in their numbers seems even more stark when considering that Karloff's *Frankenstein* did not appear in theaters until the end of 1931. Another poll of exhibitors that summer placed Karloff in the top fifty draws for theater attendance; Lugosi wasn't even in that number.[68] What this means is that various tabulations results of box-office draw, however suspect they might be mathematically, ranked Lugosi far lower than Karloff.

It is highly possible that these kinds of numbers (and Universal's own accounting of, say, how much money *Frankenstein* generated) led them to create a situation for Lugosi that meant less prominent roles, films, and publicity, which meant in turn the likelihood that his financial draw with audiences would decrease. Decrease it did, as the *Motion Picture Herald* tabulations of the top money makers of 1932-33 included Karloff at 1.2% and Lugosi not at all.[69] The same tabulations for the 1934-35 season had Lugosi registering a 2% rank, but Karloff at 34%.[70]

For a 1935-36 poll, exhibitors had to calculate the stars who made their theaters the most money. Karloff scored in the ten percent rank of responses. Western film favorite and future Ed Wood star Tom Keene received a 1.6% ranking. Talent like the forgotten Ned Sparks, Henrietta Crossman, Pert Kelton, and Dorothea Wiek received a one percent ranking. Lugosi, however, was not even listed with those names; he didn't register at all in the poll.

Tabulations of these kinds may be suspect in their accuracy, but the data was certainly printed and presumably understood at the time as mathematical fact. Lugosi's poor ratings certainly does not mean he was unknown, or that he didn't possess box-office appeal. Clearly he was famous and had a following of fans, but after *Frankenstein* it was never to the degree of Karloff. That meant Universal–fighting off the Great Depression and acting as a business entity–made decisions in their own economic interest in promoting Karloff more heavily.

To the degree Lugosi was a casualty of Hollywood meant that he suffered the trajectory of so many stars: rise and fall. In Lugosi's case, though, a comeback followed the fall. And after the comeback another decline. All of this beginning in 1931 at the time of *Dracula*'s release when Lugosi was already 48 years old. What he was really dealing with was something more powerful and more callous than an individual grudge or a studio that disliked him. He was grappling with Hollywood stardom, meaning everything from larger studio trends and economic decisions to the fickle tastes of millions of US moviegoers. That he fought a battle is true, but the enemy wasn't really Universal or Karloff.[72] It was bigger than either of them.

As for Lugosi and Karloff, their relationship in Hollywood truly became "KARLOFF and Bela Lugosi." They made eight films together at two different studios.[73] They jointly appeared in two newsreels and two radio shows.[74] Horror's duo, with Karloff's name first.

Their first two films together, *The Black Cat* (1934) and *The Raven* (1935), presented bold narratives to Depression-era audiences. *The Black Cat* offers a tale of murder, torture, incest, and Satanism. *The Raven* merges a story of a mad doctor's penchant for torture devices with elements of the gangster movie, the only Hollywood film genre that had alarmed censors and moral groups more than horror. Though he becomes a sympathetic character in the film, Karloff's gangster is after all fairly sadistic himself, having once burned a victim with an acetylene torch.

Like Chaney's masked face in *The Phantom of the Opera* (1925), Karloff's image is concealed in both films as the top-billed star is held back from audience view, building suspense. When will he appear, and what will he look like? *The Black Cat* tantalizes the audience with opening credits that show each star onscreen with their name; Karloff though is only seen from the back, playing an organ. Later, in his first scene, Karloff is shown behind a bed curtain in silhouette, still hidden. Only a slowly opening door, with tympani drumming on the soundtrack, finally reveals his face.

The Raven keeps his gangster character Bateman at bay even longer, and when he's finally in view his head is facing downward, slowly moving upward to let audiences glimpse his face. The unveiling repeats with even more suspense as Lugosi's

Lugosi and Karloff (with Peter Lorre in the center) in a publicity still for *You'll Find Out* (1940).

mad doctor changes Bateman's appearance, allegedly to help him go unnoticed by the police. The soundtrack music swells as the bandages are carefully removed to unmask Bateman's now-hideous face.

While this device in both films gives Karloff's characters a degree of mystery and builds a level of suspense as the audience waits for him to be seen, that doesn't necessarily hurt Lugosi. The result actually gives Lugosi's characters more screen time in both films. This is particularly true in *The Raven*, where Karloff's character is not seen or even mentioned until the beginning of the film's second act. With his screen time Lugosi evokes much sympathy in *The Black Cat*, which takes place in his native Hungary. And in *The Raven*, his mad doctor dominates the film even after Karloff's Bateman is introduced.

The Invisible Ray (1936), their next major film, did shift from this pattern.[75] It seems endemic to the story the studio purchased that there was not a prominent second character, and Karloff being the bigger star received the lead part. One syndicated newspaper column wrote, "Bela Lugosi is without a role at present but the studio hopes to get one [for him] soon."[76] His minimal role and screen time probably stem from story development that had to force in a part for him. In the 1950s, Dick Sheffield stared aghast at the disparity between Karloff and Lugosi's roles and billing, a reaction shared by Lugosi fans for decades thereafter. Interestingly, though, *The Invisible Ray* is a film that Lugosi himself seemingly appreciated on some levels, with a syndicated journalist in 1936 remarking that he was happy to return to sympathetic roles.[77]

By the end of the decade, things continued to change. When the two appeared in *Son of Frankenstein* (1939), they were both credited onscreen by their full names; "KARLOFF the Uncanny" was now "Boris Karloff." His name was still above Lugosi's, but it was also under Basil Rathbone's. As in *The Raven*, Karloff doesn't show up until the beginning of act two. This time, though, he doesn't really become active until the beginning of act three. Instead, the film is Rathbone and Lugosi's throughout, with Lugosi really outshining the rest of the cast as Ygor. In the post-Laemmle era, he was now covered in makeup, from a broken neck to a beard, rotting teeth, and mussed hair.

In the fifties, Dick Sheffield and Lugosi spoke at length about Ygor. The first *Frankenstein* had introduced a cinematic concept of the monster that became the way everyone saw him, from the bolts in the neck to the flat head. The second film had offered the *Bride of Frankenstein* (1935), an indelible screen image of the bride with her bandaged arms and electric hair. *Son of Frankenstein* fulfilled the promise of the first two by yet again providing a character that would exist permanently in US culture. For the general public, the memory of lab assistants Fritz in the first film and Karl in the second were erased; Ygor *was* Frankenstein's assistant. The power of Lugosi's performance etched the name forever into film history.

In 1940, Karloff and Lugosi appeared together in *Black Friday*, a mad doctor film that combined elements of *Frankenstein* and *Dr. Jekyll and Mr. Hyde*. Director Arthur Lubin was a longtime friend of Lugosi's, having first met and worked with him in 1922 as the actor's dialogue coach for the play *The Red Poppy*. Curiously, *Black Friday* inverted the roles Karloff and Lugosi played in *The Raven*. Now Karloff was the mad doctor, and Lugosi was the gangster. Actor Stanley Ridges appeared in a third role, that of a kind professor who is given a criminal brain by Karloff's doctor character.

Apparently the original idea was for Karloff to play the old professor with the new brain, and Lugosi to play the doctor who implants it. Roles were switched, which gave Lugosi far fewer lines and screen time. Exactly how, why, and when this happened is somewhat hard to untangle. That it occurred has been the source of conspiracy theories that suggest Universal was trying to hamper Lugosi's career.

Several problems emerge in trying to attach very much meaning to the change of roles, however. For one, Arthur Lubin later suggested he hardly remembered that it had even happened.[78] For another, there is the question of why Universal would not have just given Lugosi the smaller role initially if their intention was simply to saddle him with a small part. By contrast, a kind of logic may have existed for eventually giving Lugosi the gangster character. A few years earlier, he had played criminals in the film *Postal Inspector* (1936) and the serial *SOS Coast Guard* (1937). He had also just appeared as a gangster in RKO's *The Saint's Double Trouble* (1940). Though still playing a heavy and certainly in a small part, Lugosi's role as the gangster gave him an opportunity to portray something other than a typical horror film character.[79]

Most damning to the argument that Universal switched Lugosi to mistreat him is the publicity campaign for the film. Thanks to the studio's contrivance, the spotlight of media attention focussed almost solely on Lugosi. Karloff did get more screen time, and his name was as always top-billed. But once Universal decided that Lugosi would be allegedly hypnotized to perform his death scene, it became Lugosi's show. Coverage of the stunt appeared throughout the country in newspaper after newspaper, small town and large city alike. The studio's own coming attraction

Karloff and Lugosi (with Russell Wade on the far left) in a scene from *The Body Snatcher* (1945).

trailer for the film centered on Lugosi's performance. If anything, *Black Friday*—the final Karloff and Lugosi film at Universal Studios—became the one film where Lugosi dominated the publicity, something that seems all the more of an achievement given his small role.

After working together in RKO's comedy *You'll Find Out* (1940) with bandleader Kay Kyser and fellow movie villain Peter Lorre, the two paired for a final time in *The Body Snatcher* (1945). The coming attraction trailer for the film suggested the duo robs graves together, but the Val Lewton-produced and Robert Wise-directed film actually features Lugosi in something more of a cameo role. To draw on the marketing of the old Universal films, RKO decided to create a character for Lugosi simply to include his name for publicity purposes.[80] As with *The Invisible Ray*, a role was created for Lugosi for no other reason that to give him a part and benefit by whatever marquee value his name possessed.

They share only two scenes, the last of which would forever mark the end of their screen time together. It becomes a highlight of the film, and a highlight of both of their careers. Lugosi as the simpleton Joseph tries to blackmail Karloff's murderous body snatcher John Gray. Gray quietly suggests that the two join forces in business. A calculated ruse, as Gray murders Joseph under the pretense he is merely going to demonstrate how an enterprising body snatcher can create a new corpse. Their final onscreen moments achieve a tremendous subtlety, exemplifying an acting style more subdued than either would have given years earlier when their collaboration began. The Karloff-Lugosi collaboration thus ended with rather quiet aplomb.

Issues like their screen time in films, who kills who in each, and the like stir the larger and ongoing debate of whether or not they were rivals. As early as July 1932, the *Los Angeles Times* wrote that "Constance Bennett has her Bette Davis, and Boris Karloff his Bela Lugosi (or is it vice-versa?)."[81] Of *The Black Cat*, a syndicated column wrote: "It looms as a contest — which will outspook the other?"[82] For *The Raven*, another journalist wrote, "I bet Boris Karloff wakes up screaming after seeing Lugosi's pictures."[83] For a 1948 double bill revival of *Son of Frankenstein* and *Bride of Frankenstein*, a Chicago theater proclaimed their "Phantom Horror Show" meant that it was "Bela Lugosi Vs. Boris Karloff."[84]

Then there was an array of columns that suggested that the two were good pals. One 1938 article claimed that, "Karloff and Lugosi, say their friends, are really two of the most amusing companions in Hollywood."[85] The next year, writer Jimmie Fidler quipped that the two "aren't jealous of each other, but they do want to scare and scare alike."[86] As late as November 1945, Walter Winchell jokingly wrote that the duo met "the other middle-of-the-night" and compared notes:

> "I had a wonderful day," said Karloff. "I picked up three more corpses!"
> "Y'don't say,'" said Lugosi. "That's wonderful. You must come to my house some time and see my bathtub of blood!"
> "I'd love to," Boris exclaimed. "What's your phone number?"
> "Call me anytime," giggled Bela. 'I'm at PLazma-9-2259.'[87]

Silly columns and studio publicity alike then tended to pronounce them as either spooky rivals or spooky friends.

What was the reality? Certainly it doesn't seem that there were many occasions outside of film sets when the two were together. They both did appear at the dedication of an international Christmas tree at the Hotel Christie in Hollywood in December 1932.[88] Both also attended actor Henry Armetta's 1934 "spaghetti party" at his Hollywood home.[89] And in 1940, the two accompanied Edward G. Robinson, Spencer Tracy, and others to a gala ball at the Coconut Grove.[90] Dining and dancing all night to the rhythms of Guy Lombardo. They also did a joint interview in 1940.[91]

With their film collaborations boiling the cauldron of Dick Sheffield's imagination, he asked Lugosi about Karloff on more than one occasion. Looking back at over two decades, Lugosi explained that they had not really been friends or enemies, just generally friendly coworkers. How to explain? How to attach some meaningful anecdote to encapsulate their films together? Lugosi thought about it a bit more, and summed up their association by complaining about Karloff's demands for afternoon tea breaks. Whatever was occurring, whatever tight schedule or artistic momentum, Karloff stopped for the tea break. Everything halted. Everybody waited. Lugosi had to wait as well.

By the time Dick asked his question, eight or nine years had passed since Lugosi had worked with Karloff. It had been two or three years since he had seen the actor.[92] But soon he told Dick that they would be on a radio program together. It never happened. He spoke even more about a possible film collaboration. A new Lugosi-Karloff, or rather Karloff-Lugosi movie.

Alex Gordon, who had previously tried to get *The Atomic Monster* off the ground in 1952, was trying to produce a new film with Karloff and Lugosi. Gordon recalled

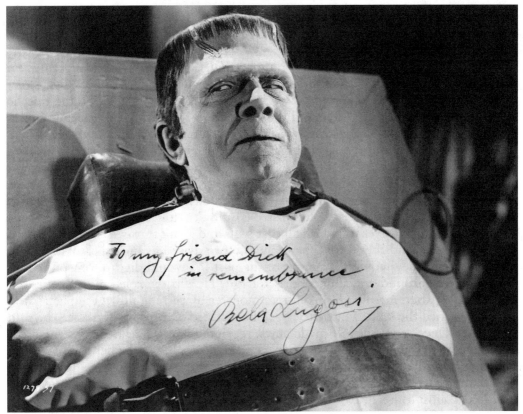

Lugosi as the Monster in *Frankenstein Meets the Wolf Man* (1943), signed to his friend Dick Sheffield.

his conversation with Karloff: "Karloff became sort of very thoughtful and said, 'Well, they really want me and Bela together again.' I said, 'Yes, Boris... I don't know how you feel about it.' He said, 'Well, all right.' But there was a slight hesitation." [93]

Of course, the history of Karloff and Lugosi was rife with unrealized projects. They were to costar at Universal in Robert Louis Stevenson's *The Suicide Club*, in *Mystery of Edwin Drood*, and in *WereWolf of London*.[94] By the forties, the duo was supposed to be in a horror-comedy at RKO with Kay Kyser and Peter Lorre called *Star-Strangled Rhythm*, as well as *The Monster of Zombor* at Universal.[95] A Jack the Ripper movie with Karloff, Lugosi, and John Barrymore.[96] Even as late as 1952, George Minter was allegedly going to reteam the duo in two films to be made in London.[97] But none of these were produced.

Why would Karloff have hesitated about working with Lugosi again in the early fifties? Though they weren't friends, they don't seem to have ever been enemies or rivals in any negative sense of that word. To the degree that anyone saw resentments, they seemed to be more from Lugosi than from Karloff. So what could have made Karloff somewhat skeptical? No definite answer can be given, but one thing is clear: a longtime story about the 1931 *Frankenstein* reached more ears in 1952 and 1953 than ever before. A story that Lugosi told that Karloff didn't believe. A story that Karloff may well have disliked.

In 1935, the *New York Daily News* published Irene Thirer's interview with Lugosi. In it, he claimed that he got out of playing the monster in the 1931 film by supplying someone else who would. Lugosi personally "recommended" Karloff, and the rest became history.[98] This echoes what Lugosi told his fourth wife Lillian and the stage director George Snell.[99] And he continued to tell the story again and again in the early 1950s.

Though Karloff never outwardly claimed that Lugosi was being untruthful, in 1940 he did try to set the record straight. He told Hedda Hopper that "When director Whale saw me in *The Criminal Code*, he thought I might just be the one he wanted for *Frankenstein*."[100] He said those words in front of Lugosi during a joint interview. He said those words without any thank you to Lugosi for any alleged help in getting the role. Nor did Lugosi chime in with his anecdote about having suggested Karloff for the part.[101]

Forgetting Karloff's comments, Lugosi proceeded to tell his own version as time went on. "They wanted me to play the part of Frankenstein's Monster," he recalled in May 1952 to a syndicated columnist. "[I] didn't want to do it. I figured they could get any truck driver to put on all that stuff and grunt through the part. At first they were angry, and then I told them my doctor advised against such a strenuous part. They said they would let me out of the part if I would dig up someone to do it. So I looked around and found Boris Karloff. He did the role, and of course, it was a hit. I created my own Frankenstein monster by turning down the part."

He repeated the story again in 1953. "I suggested Karloff for the role," he told one writer. Once again the tale made news, reprinted in a syndicated column across the country in large and small newspapers at Halloween.[102] Whether the repetition of this apparently falsified account bothered Karloff or was responsible for his hesitance about working with Lugosi is difficult to say. But it hardly could have endeared Lugosi to his heart.

Around 1953, Lugosi told the now well-rehearsed tale to Dick Sheffield. He didn't want the Frankenstein monster role due to the makeup and lack of dialogue. He had seen Karloff at the studio and felt his facial characteristics would be perfect for the part. Bringing Karloff to the attention of the studio allowed him to escape from the film. This was one of the few times that Lugosi uttered Karloff's name in front of Dick, who thought Lugosi actually believed the story.

During 1953 and 1954, Dick often helped out Lugosi by doing odd jobs around the apartment. Cleaning up papers; cleaning up the closet. Lugosi had held onto many things through the years, including a small number of clothes he had worn in his old films. One day a smoking jacket practically leapt out of the closet into Dick's eyes. It was the smoking jacket from *The Raven*. Later, Dick found a robe that Lugosi wore in the same film. Then the pants and vest from the film. He hadn't kept any other costumes or props from the other film collaborations with Karloff. Only those items from *The Raven*, a movie in which he dominated the story and screen time. It was one of Dick's favorite films, and in time Lugosi gave him the various costume pieces for helping him.

Lugosi also autographed a photo around that time for Dick. He signed many during their friendship, but this one was unique. It was an 8x10 of Lugosi playing the Frankenstein monster from *Frankenstein Meets the Wolf Man*. Dick loved the movie, thinking it was a tremendous performance, particularly when Lugosi grinned slightly at the moment the monster's power is re-energized. The still he bought in Hollywood was a closeup of the monster sporting that same grin. Lugosi, who apparently never signed another photo of himself as the monster, took the photo quietly and penned down his name with an inscription. He didn't comment on the picture or the monster or Karloff. He just quietly signed it.

Nor did he really ever say much about *Arsenic and Old Lace* or Jonathan Brewster. He certainly knew it, like the Frankenstein monster, was a Karloff role. Whether Lugosi considered that a murderous criminal angry about plastic surgery smacked similar to Karloff's Bateman role in *The Raven* is unknown. Whatever costume hung in his closet or Dick's, the roles had reversed. And Lugosi was in St. Louis in the winter of 1954.

Lugosi did enjoy himself during his time in Missouri, even though Emile noticed he wasn't always feeling well. He smelled the alcohol too, and he noticed how Lugosi's accent seemed to get ever thicker the more he drank. But when Lugosi was around other people, Emile saw him rise to the occasion. "Lugosi was wonderful with his fans, and you know, despite the age and everything he seemed like a kind of Lothario with the women," Schmidt remembered. "I don't mean young ones, but mature women, ones working around the theater. He really charmed them; you could tell he loved every minute of that."[103]

Despite a fair bit of publicity, neither the *St. Louis Post-Dispatch* or the *Globe-Democrat* reviewed the play. It didn't really matter, though, because the show was very profitable, taking in $11,000 for the week with the most expensive seats selling at only $2.50 each.[104] And even though no reviews appeared, the play generated a fair amount of publicity in the media. Along with TV and radio, Lugosi had given a lengthy interview to Mary Kimbrough at the *Post-Dispatch*. The resulting article showed how he had charmed yet another St. Louis woman. "I'm just back from a date with Dracula," she gushed, "and what's more he kissed my hand. ... He has a soft voice and his blue eyes crinkle at the corners when he laughs."

Kimbrough proceeded to write a biography of his career in several paragraphs. From Hungary to the stage to films. Ups and downs. And in it she quoted Lugosi as saying, "I was originally scheduled to do the Frankenstein monster in the first Frankenstein film, but I turned it down. I didn't want to wear that heavy makeup and that mask. So I suggested my friend, Boris Karloff, be given the role. You see, I created a Frankenstein monster for myself."[105]

On the afternoon of January 23, 1954, Lugosi took an envelope out of the hotel drawer. Thumbing through the documents he had brought in his luggage, he found Dick Sheffield's address. After quickly scratching down the 1544 N. Formosa address, he stuffed Kimbrough's article into the envelope and sealed it. There wasn't time to write a note; Emile would be over soon to pick him up. Two shows remained in St. Louis, two more big audiences. The evening of January 24 was closing night. Special, very special, though Lugosi would not have really understood why, and certainly not to express it to Dick. It was another stage show, one of so many over the decades. True, it was a play that Karloff made famous, a play that Lugosi had performed at far more important venues. But the performance of January 24, 1954 was special because it was the last time Lugosi would ever appear in a legitimate stage production.

CHAPTER EIGHT

Las Vegas Nights and Hollywood Mornings

Don English famously captured everything Las Vegas, from photographing a mushroom cloud from atop a downtown Vegas drugstore to cheesecake showgirl pictures of Miss Atomic Bomb. What he saw in Vegas, much of the world saw too. And what he saw in the early fifties was a wild town:

> It was a fantasy land, really. There was neon everywhere, and there were the great casinos, the pretty girls, the great performers and bands. And mobsters, though we didn't see their guns, you know, but all of this meant that you got the feeling anything could happen.[1]

The Flamingo, the Sands, and the Sahara. Gambling, drinking and laughing. Hedonists cavorting under the desert sun.

In the early fifties, the Silver Slipper at the Last Frontier Saloon was one of the most popular places in town. "Everybody went there, you know, Sinatra, all of them did," Don English said. "And it was a quite a place."[2] Longtime burlesque comedians Hank Henry and Sparky Kaye held sway with their straight man and writer Bill Willard; the three of them were regularly billed as the "Beau Jester Revue."[3] Jimmy Cavanaugh was emcee, and George Redman's four piece band provided the music.

Of course there were the showgirls. Last Frontier manager Herb McDonald remembered, "I had girls dancing on the [Silver Slipper] bar with powder puffs. If you were sitting at the bar, a very pretty girl, almost naked, would give you a powder puff in your face. You'd have to explain that to your wife when you got home. But the people loved it."[4] Sometimes the girls even dipped their toes into the men's drinks, while the likes of Sally Rand and other strippers disrobed onstage.[5]

A strange scene for Bela Lugosi? In some ways, it certainly seems to have been; Vegas was at the vanguard of the new and the happening, whereas Lugosi's vampire was increasingly old-fashioned. But at the same time, he had already worked in venues not too different from the Silver Slipper. Famed gossip columnist Dorothy Kilgallen wrote in February 1950 that Lugosi was "currently doing his Dracula act in night clubs," joking, "that ought to kill the bar business!"[6]

Transforming the "Dracula act" into a comedy was something that increasingly made sense as well. When Lugosi played Detroit in 1948, a reviewer claimed his scene from *Dracula* was "more humorous than horrifying."[7] In Miami that year, another critic said his act "was supposed to be a scary bit, but [it] just [didn't] come off, inspiring giggles instead."[8] Playing Dracula for the sake of horror wasn't having the desired

effect in post-war America. Inspiring giggles intentionally, though, was another matter, as the success of *Abbott and Costello Meet Frankenstein* showed in 1948.

Talk about Lugosi and Las Vegas began in 1953. Sammy Petrillo, the Jerry Lewis
look-alike from *Bela Lugosi Meets a Brooklyn Gorilla*, developed plans for himself,
his Dean Martin-styled partner Duke Mitchell, and Lugosi. Petrillo later recalled that,

> Well, Duke Mitchell and I played Vegas, three times a year at the Flamingo.
> And I went and I pitched the idea us together with Lugosi. We'd come out
> onstage, singing "Its Mitchell! Its Petrillo! And Lugosi!" And then the lights
> would flash and thunder, like a Frankenstein-type thing, and here'd be
> Lugosi in a white coat, performing surgery. "Give me the suture!" And
> sound effects, you know. And he'd say "Ahh, congratulations my friends.
> You no longer look like those other two comedians. No longer will people
> bother you and stop you and ask you if you are... Abbott and Costello!"
> And we would do all kinds of other bits too.[9]

Petrillo tried in vain to get the William Morris Agency to take on the act for a Vegas
booking, but they weren't interested.

By 1954, on the heels of his *Arsenic and Old Lace* performance in St. Louis,
Lugosi did make his Vegas debut at the Silver Slipper, and it was without Mitchell
and Petrillo. Writer/straight man Bill Willard later said that Lugosi was chosen
because the Slipper was "doing shows that were spoofs on popular films." Publicity
man Eddie Fox "knew Bela's agent [presumably meaning Lou Sherrell] and said he
could get him."[10] Alex Gordon later mentioned something similar, saying that "we
ran into these people who had an idea to put on this show in Las Vegas."[11]

On one occasion, Ed Wood said much the same, that Eddie Fox had contacted
Lou Sherrell.[12] But at other times Ed Wood remembered things pretty differently,
claiming that he had the idea and that he had taken the initiative to contact Fox.[13]
Complicating things further is Dolores Fuller's memory that Wood and Sherrell
jointly "landed" Lugosi the contract.[14]

Wood also claimed to have designed the act with Hank Henry; he even told

A postcard promoting the Silver Slipper in Las Vegas.

Lugosi in a still photograph allegedly from the *Bela Lugosi Revue.*

Edwin Schallert at the *LA Times* that he had directed the rehearsals.[15] But Bill Willard later said he didn't remember Wood "being there at all."[16] Perhaps Wood made some contributions, perhaps not. It does seem likely that he did help Lugosi with his dialogue; Wood referenced something to this effect in a 1954 letter he wrote to Lugosi.[17]

Memories clash on the business arrangements as well. Willard believed Lugosi was hired for a full six weeks; Wood claimed that it was for one week only, with an extension coming only after Lugosi proved himself.[18] In Wood's version, Fox was even ready to cancel the act before it opened, but Wood saved the day by working to help Lugosi.[19] Whatever really happened, some changes were definitely made to the act during the first few days of its run.[20] And Wood does seem correct that the show received an extension; in a letter he wrote to Lugosi in 1954, he congratulated him on getting "the holdover of three more weeks."

What does seem certain is that Lugosi flew to Vegas with Wood and Fuller for the rehearsals.[21] Fuller remembered that to save money the trio rented a car to avoid taxi fares.[22] How long Wood and Fuller remained in Vegas is difficult to determine. Fuller accidentally left her purse in Vegas, but Wood didn't ask Lugosi about it until March 11 in a letter from Los Angeles. Either the bag had been forgotten for days and days, or perhaps Wood really had spent a fair amount of time with Lugosi.[23]

Whatever went on before opening day, the *Bela Lugosi Revue* certainly began on February 19, 1954, with a cast featuring Hank Henry, Sparky Kaye, Jimmy Cavanaugh, and Bill Willard. There was also Texas singer Virginia Dew, who ended up in Vegas after travelling in an Earl Carroll show.[24] And there was singer and dancer Joan White, who continued on at the Slipper even after a bad accident injured her eye. The entire revue cost about $4,500 a week, with one thousand going each payday to Lugosi.[25] Together, the troupe performed four times a night, at 9PM, 11PM, 1AM,

Lugosi with Dolores Fuller (right) and an unknown female (left).

and 2:30AM. Free parking. No cover. No minimum. No ticket charge.[26]

For the show, Lugosi appeared in what *Variety* called "familiar horror makeup" with a "big cape around his dress suit to elicit screams in a vampire skit with Joan White, who plays a hypnotized femme in a sheer nightdress."[27] After that, the cast came together to perform "Dragnet," a sketch written by Bill Willard and Hank Henry.[28] It began with Bill, Hank, Jimmy, Virginia, and Joan onstage to sing:

> We love a mystery show
> A mystery show is great
> Each night by our Video
> We quiver and quake and wait
> For the plot to thicken and to boil
> Will the hero win or the villain foil?
> We love a mystery show
> A mystery show is great
> Jimmy: WE GET GOOSE PIMPLES
> All: A mystery show is great!

Willard chose a *Dragnet* parody not only because of the show's popularity on TV, but because it gave him a chance to cast Lugosi "as the butler, because the butler was always suspicious."[29] And, with what Willard called a "funny gleam in his eye," Lugosi played it generally straight against the antics of Hank and Sparky and the others.

The fairly loose sketch featured three brief acts centered around the murder of Lord Ashley (Willard), with Lady Ashley (Dew), the maid (Kaye in drag), and

Lugosi's butler left as suspects. Joe Friday (Cavanaugh) and two other officers (Henry and White) arrive to investigate. The middle act offers an flashback that has Lord Ashley exploring Africa with Kaye in a second role as a native.

Lugosi had appeared as butler in such horror comedies as *The Gorilla* (1939) and *One Body Too Many* (1944), but the *Revue* certainly gave him more unusual opportunities for comedy. With be-bop sounds from George Redman's orchestra behind him, for example, Lugosi spouted some beatnik jive worthy of Del Close:

> You must be flipping your ever-lovin' wig
> I'm the real gone ghoul the cats all dig
> The chicks dig me most like Errol Flynn
> So don't beat your chops man – just give me some skin.

And then Hank Henry slapped five down on Lugosi with a hearty, "Well – Daddy O!"

While some of the comedy was a simple play on Lugosi's horror persona ("I'm an expert at murder, you know"), much of it featured double meanings relevant to the Vegas scene. That the butler's name was "Boris Kozloff" not only played off of Boris Karloff, but also off of famed Slipper manager Bill Kozloff, who was also Vice-President of the Last Frontier.[30] There was dialogue like, "I have an appointment to haunt the El Cortez," a joke about the quality of that hotel. And there was Henry's line, "Dracula? I remember Dracula. Best stripper the Embassy ever had," a jab about the appearance of women at that particular venue.

The timeliness of the humor is also something easily lost reading it today. Sparky (along with playing the maid) was a native that looked like Beldon Katleman, part owner of the Last Frontier and Silver Slipper. That Kaye's native wore a diaper was a joke on Katleman's troubles over a paternity suit.[31] That Willard's British "Lord Ashley" actor was after uranium in Africa referred not only to the atomic age, but a then-current UN plan on uranium exploration.[32]

Other topical jokes referred to ongoing newspaper stories on the anti-white Mau Mau terrorists in Kenya that spilled over to the British colony of Tanganyika; the Mau Mau leader was hanged in a Nairobi prison the very week that the *Lugosi Revue* opened.[33] Willard's British "Lord Ashley" character came out of that situation. That the Mau Mau were making front page news during the *Revue*'s run meant Eddie Fox worked the phones to help make sure the newspaper reporters understood just how incredibly topical the show was.[34]

Along with the two sketches, Virginia Dew

Advertisement from the *Las Vegas Sun* of February 19, 1954.

sang a couple of blues songs with Redman's orchestra. And then of course there was stripper Terre Sheehan (sometimes spelled "Tere" Sheehan), who had arrived at the Slipper after having just created her act at Larry Potter's Supper Club in LA; Potter even visited the Slipper to see how her she was coming along.[35] Sometimes compared to Lili St. Cyr, the six-foot tall blonde with blue eyes emerged onstage from an enormous champagne glass full of bubbles. After moving through the audience to give away a pair of champagne bottles, Sheehan returned to the stage to strip off the few bits of clothing she had on.[36] End curtain.

So that was the show. That was the *Bela Lugosi Revue*. Well, not quite. Not really. The surviving copy of the script shows marks through some dialogue, and it is certainly dated before the changes made once the *Revue* was underway. And Bill Willard remembered that, "Sometimes with the added schtick the show would run ten or twenty minutes over." He also mentioned that he wrote additional one-liners for Lugosi, so "he could break off in the middle of the show and go free-lance for a few minutes."[37] Even though Lugosi generally wasn't given much credit for improvisation, *Variety* applauded the fact that "Lugosi is no mean adlibber, along with Henry." All of this together meant that the *Las Vegas Sun* claimed that it was a "show you can see again and again for a new experience every time."[38] The *Bela Lugosi Revue* was something vibrant and alive, something that resonated with the crowds.

And the crowds crowded in. The Slipper's official capacity was 200, though Willard later remembered that sometimes three or four hundred people jammed through the door.[39] "A much desired sense of intimacy," singer Gogi Grant recalled.[40] Willard also claimed that, "it was a full house for most of the [Lugosi] shows."[41] At the Slipper that full house meant other actors and singers and dancers in the audience, especially at the late 2:30AM show. "The big business," *Variety* wrote, "comes from other performers dropping in after their shows."[42] And this time they were stopping by to see the "ghost with the most, man!"[43]

The show's rapid popularity also meant the newspapers gave regular reports on all the goings-on. When Lugosi told Eddie Fox he was "taking my cape home; it needs mending," the *Las Vegas Sun* called it one of the remarks of the week.[44] And when a columnist for the same newspaper and Eddie Fox were trying to figure out what film Lugosi made that

```
"DRAGNET" - 2

                              Sparky:

Yes,  there is something wrong in this house.   Ever since you've been here.
Say -- haven't I seen you somewhere before?

                              Lugosi:

(Bloodcurdling laugh)   BOO!

                              Sparky:

(Big.  Scurries away)

                              Virginia:

(As Lady Ashley,  slinks in dressed in tight gown a la Charles Adams,
 heavily made up around the eys, and carries a long cigarette holder)

Ah, there you are, Boris.

                              Lugosi:

Madame -- do not call me Boris.   Call me Kosloff.

                              Virginia:

All right -- Boris Kosloff.   Where is my husband?  I'm terribly worried.

                              Lugosi:

Perhaps you'd like a cup of tea, Lady Ashley?  With a pinch of cyanide?

                              Virginia:

Why not?  I haven't been feeling myself lately.

                              Sparky:

Then why don't you give him a crack at it?

                              Willard:

(As Lord Ashley, dressed in khaki shorts, shirt all bloody, mustache and
 sideburns, with helmet.   Offstage bloodcurdling yell, then reels on
 clutching breast)

                              Lugosi:

Why master -- have you been shaving yourself again?

                              Willard:

No, of course not.  Can't you see I've been poisoned?
```

A page from the script to the *Bela Lugosi Revue*.

had "a lot of coffins, Lugosi thought a moment, [and] said: 'All my pictures had lots of coffins in them.'"[45]

At a dress rehearsal, a fake deodorized skunk, made by "Air Tron Electric Deodorizers," showed up on the stage to "startle" Lugosi.[46] About the same time, the press jokingly reported that Kaye had inadvertently shot himself while trying to put a bullet through a fly buzzing around his dressing room.[47] Once the show was underway, an unnamed cast member switched the water in teetotaler Henry's prop gin for real whisky.[48] Some unexpected talent interrupted one performance to pay tribute to Lugosi in early March.[49] And when the cast celebrated Cavaugh's four thousandth live appearance, Lugosi dubbed him the "Rock."[50] This was it, one of the most talked about shows in town, one that had the Vegas newspapers covering its every move.

Above: Lugosi and Hank Henry in the *Bela Lugosi Revue*, as published in the *Las Vegas Sun* of February 27, 1954. *Below:* Terre Sheehan in a picture taken while she was appearing in the *Bela Lugosi Revue*.

After Ed Wood left Vegas, Lugosi did want him to return. By mid-March, Wood wrote to him saying that he and Alex Gordon both hoped to make it to Vegas soon, but only if he could "raise any money at all. But if all works out well I will try and make it next weekend— if not, I'll let you know in time. Of course I'd only be able to stay the one day as if I can even raise 20 that will be about it."[51] A week later, on March 21, Wood told Lugosi that he:

> Put about 7 bucks into gas and getting the car ready to go (it was completely repaired by the Nash Co., so it's in good shape now), then the rains came and the snows in the mountains and Alex busy down at the studio. He called me again around ten last night and was still in a meeting with Ford Beebe and Harold [Mirisch] at Allied Artists. This is very important to all of us, so I didn't press the issue of getting up there.
>
> I've been checking all the [Los Angeles] newspapers and haven't found any of the writeups yet – buying all these newspapers every day gets rather expensive – but we need every bit of publicity on you we can get."[52]

Finally, a few days later, Wood and Fuller made it to the show without Alex Gordon.[53] "We drove the long and in those days arduous journey over terrible roads," Fuller recalled. Seeing the show in full swing meant Fuller was impressed with how well Lugosi and Hank Henry worked together.[54] Impressed and surprised.

Who could have foreseen it? Lugosi and Vegas, Lugosi and Burlesque, Lugosi and a champagne glass stripper. Well, the *Las Vegas Sun* had gazed into the crystal ball, saying before the show opened, "Actually, mah fellow constituents, this one has all the earmarks of a

Lugosi scared by a fake, deodorized skunk at a rehearsal of the *Bela Lugosi Revue*. The skunk was a "representative" for Air Tron electric deodorizers.

socko, boffo show all the way."[55] Later of course they heralded it as a success, saying it was a "show that'll be hard to top."[56] *Variety* called it "hilarious," adding that Lugosi "scores big with patrons no matter what he does," and "there is no doubt he has the affection of the audience."[57]

Socko, boffo all the way. Whatever hitch caused some changes early on, the only problem once it was underway was the one time Lugosi "took ill."[58] Just once though, no big deal. Years later Willard wouldn't even remember that he missed a performance. When the show finished its sixth successful week on April 1, 1954, the Slipper cast started a new show with Buster Keaton and extra added attraction Gogi Grant.[59] Lugosi went back to LA. Willard said that the Slipper never made him a return offer.[60] Apparently no other Vegas clubs did either. The *Las Vegas Sun* believed Lugosi had found a "new career"; in the end, though, that prediction didn't come true.[61] In fact, Lugosi may have even given back most of his salary; later, he claimed he had "lost it all gambling."[62]

What did happen thanks to the Silver Slipper was a closer association with Ed Wood. During the six weeks in Vegas, Wood took care of all kinds of errands for Lugosi. He responded to some fan mail that arrived in Hollywood.[63] He sent Lugosi four new collars as requested, claiming that no one paid for them as far as he knew, so "let's not mention it until we get a bill."[64] By special delivery, he sent Lugosi "Enzypan tablets" within a half hour of receiving Lugosi's letter asking for the popular indigestion medicine.[65]

Once Lugosi was back in Los Angeles, Wood continued helping him with errands and problems. When the Burke Electric Company repaired a light switch at Lugosi's Hollywood apartment on North Laurel, they billed him for more than twice the expected amount. He had Wood type a letter to offer them a smaller amount, with an added warning that he might turn them over to the Better Business Bureau.[66]

But of course the help that he really wanted from Wood was work. More roles. New films. And Wood was involved in a flurry of activity that even predated the Vegas show. For example, in a letter in late 1953, Lugosi and Wood inquired about gaining the rights to Walter C. Brown's novel *The Six Arms of Siva*, probably seeing it the November 1952 issue of *Short Stories*. *The Six Arms of Siva*... "and the horror they brought." A peculiar choice, since it was neither the more romantic or comedic kind of storyline Lugosi craved, nor was it really a horror story.

It was really an adventure story, a thriller featuring the exploits of Dan Mellody and his crew. Stealing a well-guarded Shikanoi Siva from a sacred shrine, they arrive back in the US to deliver it to Colonel Pottermax, a collector of rare "Orientalia." But visiting his "Dreamer's Rest" estate, they find only a butler named Loring. The fact they can't get paid means they wait, but waiting only brings the "six arms," guards of the sacred and valuable Siva. In the chaos that follows, Mellody learns that the butler really is Pottermax. But the revelation helps no one, as Dreamer's Rest burns to the ground when the six arms attempt to reclaim what is rightfully theirs.

Jimmy Cavanaugh and Hank Henry, with Lugosi creeping up behind them, in an image from the *Bela Lugosi Revue*.

Of the variety of characters in the story, it's difficult to see who Lugosi wanted to play, other than perhaps Pottermax, which basically meant yet another butler role. At any rate, Lugosi suggested a kind of speculative joint effort with Brown that would lead to a film version of the novel. The result would be a movie that would stir the emotions, as well as stir the memories. Lugosi told Brown in his letter believed that Hollywood had forgotten him. *The Six Arms of Siva* could change all of that.[67]

While seeking out Brown may have been partially or wholly Wood's idea, Lugosi had a long history of trying to obtain film rights. Along with gathering ideas for his ill-fated production company in 1935, he later bought a number of stories from writers, hoping to keep a ready supply on hand. When he purchased Barkley Davis's werewolf story "The

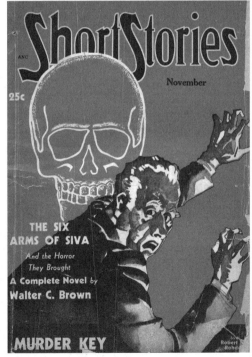

Howling Death" in 1939, the *LA Times* announced that Lugosi already owned six of his other stories, including "The Sect of the Assassins"; Lugosi had even collaborated on some of them.[68] Later that same year, he also purchased Georgia Albert's story "Prince of Hell."[69]

Lugosi with his friends Richard Gordon (left) and Alex Gordon (right).

Why did he buy these? At that time, it wasn't to produce them himself; he had tried that to no avail in 1935. Lugosi was hoping to interest the studios in some of the stories, which would result in him starring in the productions. He pitched "The Howling Death" to Universal, for example, but they didn't go for it.[70] In fact, nothing came of any other stories he bought; not a single one of them. The stories themselves seem to have disappeared completely, along with their authors.

And at the end of 1953, it became apparent nothing would happen with *The Six Arms of Siva* either. Brown wrote a polite response from his home in Pennsylvania, reminding Lugosi that no one had forgotten him. "Just the other day, for instance, one of our local theatres had a Lugosi double bill, *The Raven* and *Rue Morgue*. So the general public hasn't forgotten you."[71] Of course Lugosi knew that these reissues were partially the problem; competing with his own old movies was never easy.

As for the rights to his novel, Brown told Lugosi that he would:

> much rather make an outright sale of the movie rights to a film company than enter into any speculative arrangement. I too have to make a living, and my business is writing. I am not in a position to handle complicated financial arrangements that are centered hundreds of miles away.[72]

In the story, the Siva is valuable because a storehouse of jewels are hidden inside it. But with flames engulfing the house, the jewels become useless. "A momentary break in the billowing smoke brought out the face of Siva, triumphant." No dice.

Maybe Lugosi didn't care very much. The Hollywood Historama, the West Coast Theatre in San Bernardino, *Arsenic and Old Lace* in St. Louis, and the Silver Slipper in Las Vegas: all of these came in the space of something like four months. And so returning to Los Angeles in April 1954 meant just a little rest before other work, other jewelled Sivas.

That Lugosi's career was checkered with roles that didn't happen is hardly surprising; projects fall through, scheduling conflicts occur, and other actors get cast. Too many to count, too many to remember. Lugosi was supposed to be *Doctor X* at Warner Brothers in 1932, costarring with Loretta Young and Warren William; none of them ended up in the film.[73] He was going to play the title role in a 1935 British remake of *The Cabinet of Dr. Caligari*, for which Ramon Novarro was also being considered.[74] He was nearly *The Electric Man* at Universal that same year.[75] He almost became *The Hunchback of Notre Dame* in 1939 at RKO, after having already been considered for the same at Universal years earlier.[76] Republic wanted

Contemplating the future or remembering the past?

him for *King of the Zombies* in 1941; Alexander Paal wanted him for *Murder Village* in 1942.[77] And Monogram planned *The Gold Bug* for him in 1944.[78]

Some of these came *so* close to happening, too. Unless he hadn't caught a bad case of the flu, Lugosi would have certainly appeared in *The House of a Thousand Candles* (1935).[79] And, Warner Brothers bought *The Doctor's Secret* just for Lugosi in 1939, a tale that would "resemble *Dracula*."[80] Lya Lys was all set to costar with him in the Anthony Caldewey story. But more revisions on the script by Lee Katz meant less resemblance to *Dracula*.[81] And it meant that for whatever reason, instead of Lugosi, Lys costarred with Humphrey Bogart in the retitled *The Return of Doctor X* (1939).

Short of *Frankenstein* (1931), though, in the 1950s Lugosi likely didn't worry too much about old horror stories that didn't get filmed or didn't end him featuring him. Perhaps he remembered with regret that in 1935 German theater director Max Reinhardt specifically wanted him for Mephistopheles in a planned Hollywood film version of Goethe's *Faust* in color; if Reinhardt had gotten his way, Greta Garbo would have been Marguerite and Fredric March would have been Faust. But it never happened. Such is life, the life of an actor.

Aside from *The Six Arms of Siva*, there were a handful of other possibilities, and surely one or more would come through. In late February, the *Las Vegas Sun* wrote that Lugosi would "costar with Leo Gorcey in a Bowery Boys pic, with Bela getting equal billing with Gorcey. It's now a question of moola."[82] The *LA Times* repeated the same in early March, but *The Bowery Boys Meet the Monsters* (1954) ended up featuring John Dehner instead.[83] The moola question didn't get a good answer.

The curiosity of these projects from late 1953 and through 1954 is not so much in that they didn't happen, but in the backstory of *who* was trying to make *what* happen. Officially Lugosi's agent for most or possibly all of 1954 was Lou Sherrell of the Herdan-Sherrell agency; Sherrell was also Dolores Fuller's agent at the time. But on the sideline was Alex Gordon trying to develop projects, as well as Ed Wood. Who knew what and when did they know it?

In his later years, Gordon claimed that "*Any*thing Lugosi did with Eddie Wood, he did through me, because Lugosi had known me so many years and he trusted me completely. And he mistrusted everybody out here because he'd had several so-called agents who sold him down the river."[84] But Wood once claimed that:

> [Lugosi and I] sat in the bar at the Harvey one night and he said to me, "I didn't like you. I didn't like you at all; you're no good. But now I think I like you better than Alex Gordon."[85]

Though Gordon and Wood had lived together, were friends, and were trying to work on projects together, perhaps there was some resentment too. Or jealousy over the Lugosi friendship. Maybe mutual, maybe one-sided.

What is certain is that when Gordon turned down Lugosi's offer to share an apartment in early 1954, Lugosi asked Wood to try and intervene on his behalf or at least determine why Gordon had made his decision. Wood answered Lugosi by saying that he asked Gordon, but "the question was evaded. I suggest we don't get into any arguments about that because the horror picture deal seems to be set."[86]

And whatever Gordon believed about being Wood's sole conduit to Lugosi, Wood was definitely trying to work with Lugosi individually. He sent a letter to ten comic book companies trying to interest them in "talking a deal for a Bela Lugosi comic."[87] Wood also tried to get the rights to produce a new version of *Dracula–The Vampire Play* from Samuel French. In his letter to them, he wrote that he was "Mr. Bela Lugosi's manager."[88] Sherrell was the agent, but by 1954 Wood was the manager, or at least calling himself that.

He also had plans for several Lugosi film projects that year that didn't involve Gordon or Sherrell. In one letter, he told Lugosi about:

> a man I've known for seven years a man named Frank Winkler, in regards to your doing a picture for him. He was an agent several years back when I went to Seattle to promote fights, wrestling, and ice skating. He is now back and has about decided to do a picture. So I'm looking into this now to see what there is to offer.
>
> Also you must stay on real friendly terms with Ron Ormond. He has been my very close friend for a long time, many years, and he is putting a few pictures in my hands to do. One thing—he likes you very much, and I'm almost sure we can swing one of his pictures your way this year.
>
> We've come a long way since our performance in San Bernardino on New Year's Eve. Our luck's changed.[89]

The Winkler film never seems to have been mentioned again. And the Ormond project wasn't either, though Lugosi did write a brief foreword to Ormond's 1954 book *Your Career in Hollywood*.[90]

Stay on their good side, just in case. Just in case something breaks. Shortly thereafter, in March 1954, Wood told Lugosi that:

> I have definitely set a picture for you which will go within the next sixty days. Now I haven't mentioned anything to Lou Sherrell or Alex, so I

suggest you do not. There is no sense cutting anyone in who has not worked in bringing it about.

Also—a friend of mine—one of the fellows who has put some money into my last picture—and got all his money back from the sale—has given me—or rather okayed to me—$1,000 to promote the [new] picture, not get started on it. I suggest I take this cash, you and I form some sort of an agreement and own the picture together. Of course this fellow would have to be cut in too. But the one thing I have always told you—you should own a piece of one of your pictures since they always make good money. And we can arrange it that way this time along with a sizeable amount of immediate cash.[91]

Don't tell Lou or Alex. After all, Wood was a manager. "Now Bela I haven't let you down yet," he also said in March. "I'm strictly on your side, because I know you will do right by me when the time comes, if I need a favor."[92]

Sometimes, of course, one or the other had to be told some news. In April, Wood was trying to cook up a possible Lugosi radio show called *The Terror*. He sent Lugosi one script with the promise twelve more would follow. "Since it is radio, the scripts will be read, so you will not have to worry about memorizing them—just be familiar with them."[93] And in his letter, Wood mentioned he'd be happy to meet with Sherrell.

And conversely, Wood and Alex Gordon tried to get some projects off the ground without Sherrell. These were the film scripts that they had tried to get produced since 1952. *The Atomic Monster*, the Karloff-Lugosi film *Doctor Voodoo*, and *The Vampire's Tomb*. A possible deal for *The Vampire's Tomb* was the reason that Wood told Lugosi to drop the whole matter of Gordon not wanting to share an apartment with him.

March 1954, Gordon was discussing the script with Allied Artists, who decided to rename the film *The Vampire*. They also wanted Ford Beebe to direct; among his many credits were the Lugosi serial *The Phantom Creeps* (1939) and the Lugosi film *Night Monster* (1942). "Not a word of this has been mentioned to your agent," Wood told Lugosi, meaning Sherrell. "If he has to be

March 12, 1954

Dear Mr. Mazzeo:

It is with the deepest regret that I have not written in answer to your letter before - but my schedule has been so tightened in the last few months, what with my personal appearances in San Bernardino, California, (Jonathan Brewster in "Arsnic & Old Lace") at the Empress in St. Louis, and presently in my fourth week of an eight week stand at the Silver Slipper in Las Vegas, Nevada. Plus studying for two new pictures and studying all the lines and jokes for the play and the new night club routine, (enclosed please find a momentum from the Las Vegas Sun.)

In regards to the publication of "Dracula" with the original pictures from the movie - at the moment I do not know where it is obtainable, however if you were to check with some of the second hand stores you might run across it - stills from the picture may be purchased from many of the shops selling stills - there are two or three such places in New York.

By the way, my next film will be "BRIDE OF THE VAMPIRE" to go before the cameras sometime immediately after the completion of my work here at the Silver Slipper. May I also say your characature's on your letters are quite good. Do you do this sort of thing professionally? You should.

I am always happy to hear from a real fan...

Sincerely

BL/ss

BELA LUGOSI

Mr. Mazzeo:

As Mr. Lugosi's Producer I wish to express my deepest thanks for being a devoted fan - Why do not the others in your group write Mr. Lugosi. An actors work is always much better when he knows his fans enjoy his performance.

EDWARD D. WOOD JR.

EDWjr/ss

In the Spring of 1954, Ed Wood began to help Lugosi with all kinds of responsibilities. Here he types a letter to a Lugosi fan, and–as "Mr. Lugosi's producer"–adds his own note at the end.

wrung in on the deal, first you and I should talk as to what he is to know and what he is not to know."[94]

Later that same month, Gordon met at length with Beebe and Harold Mirisch at Allied Artists, a company that had grown out of the remains of Monogram. "This is very important to all of us," Wood wrote to Lugosi. The topic of discussion may well have included the ill-fated Lugosi appearance in *The Bowery Boys Meet the Monsters*, the Karloff-Lugosi project *Doctor Voodoo*, as well as *The Vampire/The Vampire's Tomb*. The meeting didn't include Wood, but he told Lugosi that it went late into the evening of March 20.[95] At some point during mid-to-late March, it seems likely that *The Bride of the Vampire* was mentioned as another possible title for *The Vampire's Tomb*.[96]

Continued talks with Allied Artists meant that, even though financier Eliot Hyman had okayed the projects, studio boss Steve Broidy demanded another writer needed to get involved. He didn't care for either *Doctor Voodoo* or *The Vampire's Tomb*. And he also didn't like Ford Beebe's script *House of Terror*, originally meant to costar Bela Lugosi and Lon Chaney, or even Beebe's script for Boris Karloff, *Curse of the Undead*.[97]

Gordon quickly turned to Sam Arkoff's brother-in-law Lou Rusoff to write a new script, one for Lugosi, Lon Chaney, and Boris Karloff. Rusoff, who later wrote scripts for such films as *It Conquered the World* (1956) and *Ghost of Dragstrip Hollow* (1959), came up with *House of Horror*.[98] But the Allied Artists deal fell apart completely, with Gordon later saying that the studio was in trouble and couldn't come up with their part of the financing.[99] No more meetings. No movies. No nothing.

As the summer of 1954 approached, photographer Don English kept snapping picture after picture for the Las Vegas News Bureau. More neon, more stars. Showgirls showing skin at the Silver Slipper. Plenty to photograph, because Vegas was going to end up spending eight million dollars hiring 4,300 performers that year. All to lure in the more than 9.5 million visitors to the city throughout 1954.[100] And every one of the gamblers were hoping to hit the jackpot. As adventurer Dan Mellody learned, "Old Siva's got a bellyful of jewels." It's just a matter of getting to them.

CHAPTER NINE

The Power of Suggestion

Gerald Schnitzer was a man who understood stories. Maybe he never understood how the studios in Hollywood worked, but he did understand stories. He grew up in the Bronx and attended Dartmouth, planning all the time to be a writer.[1] Pretty soon, though, he realized that he was more interested in building naratives out of images instead of words.

Once Schnitzer arrived in California, he made money from both skills. He dreamed up the idea and script for the Lugosi film *Bowery at Midnight* in 1942, and that same year worked on the outlandish story that become Lugosi's *The Corpse Vanishes*. Schnitzer also made money from being an assistant director on films like *Black Dragons* (1942), another of those Lugosi B-movies. He even did some writing for a few films starring the East Side Kids (later the Bowery Boys).[2]

As time went on, Schnitzer spent more and more time making his own movies, very short films that didn't require any dialogue. Tiny bits with, say, a postman walking down a sidewalk, finding a hopscotch board, and then sneaking a go at it after glancing around to see if anyone was watching. And that was it, the whole movie. A short film that captured a brief, authentic moment about America and Americans.

During the Eisenhower era and the age of the TV, Schnitzer found a new life thanks to his short little films. Working for Kensinger Jones, Schnitzer channeled his economy of storytelling time into television commercials. No longer would an actor have to just stand up in front of a camera and bark about a product. With ads like those Schnitzer created for GM, a short visual story could be told in fleeting seconds, stories that would sell products. The author of *Bowery at Midnight* had found a new career in TV.[3]

Schnitzer's success was partially the result of mathematics. In 1946, only about 44,000 television sets had been sold in the US. By 1954, the number had exploded to a point that fifty percent of US homes had TVs.[4] Half of America could turn on the box and tune in to the hit programs and the advertising that supported them. It was a TV decade, an era that gave so many opportunities to writers and directors and producers.

Many actors and actresses found new careers in TV as well, like Lucille Ball and Jackie Gleason. For those who didn't rely completely on television, it still gave them a steady supply of work. This was true for actors like Boris Karloff and Peter Lorre. But not everyone was so lucky. The likes of radio star Fred Allen, for exam-

Maila "Vampira" Nurmi in a photograph taken by Edward D. Wood, Jr. *(Courtesy of Dennis Phelps)*

ple, who just didn't find a receptive audience once he made the move to TV.[5]

And this was increasingly true of Bela Lugosi. The TV appearances he had made hadn't created much buzz. Talks of his own show in 1952 had gone nowhere. Then in 1953 when he appeared on *You Asked For it*, he claimed he would star in *Dr. Acula*, a program to be written and directed by Ed Wood and produced by Ted Allan. In it, Lugosi would play a kind of investigator into supernatural goings-on. Several months later, in January 1954, Hedda Hopper's column claimed that Lugosi and actor Sonny Tufts would "costar in the same picture, *Oui Oui Paree*, and in a TV series, *Robinson Crusoe on Mars*."[6] But none of these projects got off the ground; Lugosi never had his own television show.[7] By 1954, even his number of guest appearances was dwindling.

Sometime in May or early June of 1954, though, Lugosi did get an important chance. It was the only TV opportunity he got the entire year, and in a way it was the best opportunity he ever had. A phone call came, likely to Lou Sherrell, that Red Skelton wanted Lugosi for an episode of his comedy show. Skelton's program was popular, and the viewing audience was enormous. It was bigger than *You Asked For It* or *Spade Cooley* had in 1953. Thanks to the increase in the number of homes with TVs, the Skelton show in 1954 had a much bigger audience than the *Texaco Star Theatre* with Milton Berle had when Lugosi guested on it in 1949.

The episode's gimmick was to collect the horror stars together for Skelton's final show of the season. Lon Chaney Jr. and Peter Lorre's agents also got phone calls. Perhaps Karloff's did as well, but he wasn't booked for the show. Skelton's lineup was Lugosi, Lorre, and Chaney. But when the day of the show came, one name towered above the others in the *LA Times*. Skelton had "grabbed one of television's newest sensations" to appear as well: Maila Nurmi, known to late-night TV watchers as Vampira.[8]

Then married to a TV writer named Dean Reisner, Maila Nurmi had previously been a bell-hop and a hat-check girl.[9] By May 1954, Vampira was on the air every Saturday night at KABC, quickly moving from a midnight spot to 11PM.[10] She was the original horror host of television, a vision of Charles Addams' cartoon character Morticia, and an echo of Carroll Borland's Luna in the film *Mark of the Vampire*

Bela Lugosi and Vampira on the set of *The Red Skelton Show* in June 1954.
(Courtesy of Getty Images, Inc.)

(1935): large chest, skinny waist, and shaking hips in a low-cut dress. She was the darker side of the ideal fifties woman, sporting black hair, black fingernails, and a black costume. Vampira was sexy and she was funny and she was an immediate hit in Southern California.

She ran for "night mayor" of Hollywood with a platform of "dead issues."[11] She sent out pictures of herself reclining voluptuously in a coffin with the slogan, "My bier is a dry bier!"[12] On a personal appearance in San Francisco, she presented a gift of LA smog.[13] The *LA Times* had dubbed Vampira the city's "current sensation" the very day before she was on Skelton's program, and a *Life* magazine photo spread came out that same week.[14] A few days later, columnist Louella Parsons was writing about several movie deals in the works.[15]

Dick Sheffield actually spotted Vampira around the time of the Skelton appearance, when she was at the height of her fame. A chauffeur was driving her up and down Hollywood Boulevard in a 1932 Packard touring car with no top. She was in the middle of the backseat dressed in full costume and makeup, holding a bumbershoot umbrella to shade her from the sun. She stared straight ahead, not making eye contact with anyone. But Dick and everybody else turned to look at her, the new horror star, the first horror star of television, a sensation that had happened almost overnight.

So when the group of four horror stars appeared on Skelton's show on June 15, 1954, Lugosi and Lon Chaney Jr. received only brief mention in the *LA Times;* Peter Lorre not at all. The spotlight of attention was on Vampira, and of course Red Skelton himself. Maila "Vampira" Nurmi recalled:

> Bela played a mad scientist, and I was in a rollaway drawer. Skelton pulled me out by the feet. We did several other little bits. At the time, Johnny Carson was the gag writer, and he was pitching jokes at me during the rehearsal.
>
> I remember when Bela took me out by the arm and walked me out after the show was over, because it was a live audience. He walked me to the stage front. We just drifted forward like royalty. He was in great form.[16]

Great form at times, perhaps, but Nurmi also added that during the show Lugosi had encountered a problem or two with his lines.

Lugosi's friend Alex Gordon, who was with him that night, also remarked on these troubles:

> Bela was worried about the show because he knew that Red did not stick to the script but adlibbed most of the show. ... Red treated him well, but he did use adlibs which almost threw Bela. The comedian managed to fill in so well that the audience never knew. However, it was an unhappy experience for Bela.[17]

He later amplified on this memory, saying Lugosi had a "very rough time" because Skelton didn't throw him his cues.[18] Lugosi proved his skills at improvisation at the Silver Slipper earlier that year, but in that instance he had performance after performance to get adjusted to Hank Henry and the others.

For Skelton's program, Lugosi would have gotten little in the way of rehearsals and was crowded into a cast with three other horror performers and a famous comedian. Allegedly Ed Wood helped Lugosi with his dialogue, but even if true, it may not have had an impact on the outcome. Dick watched the program at home, and it seemed to come off okay. No problems, none noticeable anyway. The only thing Dick thought was that Lugosi just didn't have much to do, what with all the others on the show. The biggest TV audience Lugosi ever had, and he wasn't able to take advantage of it. And it

Planning future projects. Standing beside Lugosi is Dolores Fuller; seated at the table is Ed Wood.

became the last time he appeared on a nationally-televised program.

What then? No more guesting on TV that year, let alone his own show. No calls from the studios. That Bowery Boys film had gone ahead without him. All the activity of late 1953 and early 1954 was increasingly in the past. In the summer and autumn of 1954, opportunities were fewer and fewer.

The talk he did hear was largely from Ed Wood. If Wood is to be believed, he spoke to Lugosi in the middle of the night around this same time. Arriving at Lugosi's apartment at about 3AM, Wood found the actor wielding a revolver and threatening to commit suicide. Even threatening to take Wood with him, until Wood calmed him down.[19]

After all, they had work to do together. That the Allied Artists deal fell apart that spring, well, the hell with them. Wood decided to forge ahead on his own. He'd do it without them, produce and direct one of those scripts that he still owned. Not *Doctor Voodoo*, likely because it had roles for two horror stars. No, of the scripts he had, Wood chose one particularly suited to Lugosi. He'd revive *The Vampire's Tomb*.

A page from the script for *The Vampire's Tomb*.

The Vampire's Tomb: it echoes through horror film history as the most famous film that Ed Wood and Lugosi *didn't* make. So often mentioned, but what really would it have been? Alex Gordon once remembered that the story would have had Lugosi playing a famous actor who:

> invites a group of friends to his house in the country for a weekend. Mysterious murders, apparently caused by a vampire, begin to occur, and there are visions of a beautiful girl, clad in an angora nightgown (Wood's trademark), wandering through the gardens of the estate. Eventually it is revealed that the killings are not due to the activities of the undead but the daughter of a famous actress ruined by the actor.[20]

Gordon added that along with Lugosi, the cast would have included Helen Gilbert, Richard Denning, Raymond Hatton, Jack Mulhall, and Jack Perrin.[21] But all of this was likely part of the Allied Artists plan, or even dates back before 1954.

On another occasion, Gordon also remembered that, "Eddie decided to rework *The Vampire's Tomb* script."[22] When that happened is uncertain, but Wood definite-

Lugosi and Tor Johnson in a still from
Bride of the Atom/Monster (1955).

ly tried to gear up for production in the summer of 1954. By the end of July, the *LA Times* announced that Wood's script would go into production as soon as August. Costarring with Lugosi would be Loretta King, who had just scored in the play *Sabrina Fair* at the Biltmore.[23]

Just a few days later, the same newspaper claimed that Dolores Fuller had "considered the lead," but instead took a smaller "sexy type" role because of its "dramatic opportunities."[24] This was in addition to Wood casting Richard Powers (aka Tom Keene) for the male lead and Frank Yaconelli as a "comic killer."[25] Another cast list appeared in *Variety* on August 4, listing Lugosi, King, and Fuller. Lyle Talbot and Hazel Franklyn were also "signed."[26]

And then there was also the fact that Wood announced his hope to cast Vampira.[27] After all, the TV sensation was a hotter property that summer than any of the old film stars like Lugosi or Chaney. She later remembered feeling indignance that–at a moment when she was entertaining major studio offers and hosting a hit TV show–Ed Wood was touting her name as someone he was trying to cast.[28] But on August 27, 1954, the *LA Times* claimed Wood had indeed signed her to a contract to appear in *The Vampire's Tomb*.[29] A mistake? Maybe, but the newspaper repeated the same claim four days later.[30]

Lugosi was also supposed to star in "six more features" for Wood, the *LA Times* wrote. A half dozen. One was a "spooky western," a script that Wood planned to shoot in Sedona, Arizona. The western was "as yet untitled," but presumably it was just *The Phantom Ghoul* script awaiting a fresh, new title.[31] Wood wasn't prepared to let go of it yet, any more than he was *The Vampire's Tomb*. And why should he? Newspaper accounts suggest he was *Making Things Happen*. After all, *The Vampire's Tomb* began production on August 27, 1954.[32]

But it wasn't with the storyline that Gordon recounted; it was something that emerged after the rewrites. Or, the script changes may actually have been back to where Wood began, before Gordon's involvement. The surviving copy does feature a page with all the character names typed, next to which are the handwritten actor names like Loretta King and Richard Powers and Hazel Franklyn—the cast Wood announced in the summer of 1954, save for one. Instead of Vampira, the name "Devila" is written down, suggesting perhaps a replacement actor name of Wood's own creation devised after Vampira refused to appear.

Equally curious is that typed on the the title page is "Registered 1951 – Screen Writer's Guild." Had Wood written this version in 1951 and simply pulled it back out in 1954, after discarding any other changes/ideas like those Alex Gordon mentioned in his plot synopsis? Or perhaps changes *were* made in the script and he just kept the same title page rather than retype it?

It's difficult to tell, but given the handwritten actor names it seems very likely that the surviving script was the draft Wood had in mind to use in the summer of 1954. It begins at the site of:

> A once proud mansion, now old and gloomy, near ruin. The grass surrounding the semi-circle driveway is high and burned brown by the long hours of the sun's scorching heat without proper care. The drive is directly in front of the large wooden front door of the two-story mansion. A private cemetery can be seen off to the far left and a long winding lake beyond that. There are trees, vines, and brush intermingled among the grave stones of the cemetery. The night is very dark with heavy rain clouds in the sky. However the mansion is streaked in light as lightning suddenly flashes across the sky followed by deep, rolling thunder claps. It is at this time, during one of the lightning flashes, that a giant bat flies into view — hovers in the sky a moment — then heads in a streak towards the old house.

Inside are six siblings: Flinch, Judson, Bobbie, Boris, Diana, and Barbara. Along with them are the husbands of the two women, Frank and Lake, as well as a maid and housekeeper. All the heirs together on the night before the reading of wealthy Aunt Lucille's will, all except Lucille's long-lost sister Helen. And the one road to the mansion is washed out.

A male and female vampire begin making appearances near the home, with the female vampire hovering over Barbara in her bedroom. And she resembles Aunt Lucille. Then a scream rings out from the cemetery, and near a cliff all that is left of Flinch is his hat. Fear grips the family, some of whom bear an awful secret. All of them except Barbara and Lake murdered Lucille for her money; even the housekeeper Emma was involved. The plot thickens.

They haven't been caught in part because Boris, an attorney, reported Lucille's passing. Judson, a doctor, recorded the cause of death. And Frank is an undertaker. All very convenient, very tidy. Except the rash of continued vampire sightings that night provokes a necessary visit to Lucille's tomb, where the lock is broken. Entering they find a well-preserved body in the coffin, and they are quickly interrupted by a new presence. The caped male figure introduces himself as Dr. Acula, and he proposes to help them:

> DR. ACULA
> In this quick diagnosis – I would say – in a sense – she lives – Yet in a sense – she does not – She is one of the undead – a vampire...
> BORIS
> Oh, good John, Jacob and Harry. Vampires...What next? Vampires exist only in the minds of writers, small children, and crazy old wives tales...
> DR. ACULA
> That is like saying, there is no – *Satan*.
> *Dr. Acula motions to the coffin but his words seem to infer much more...*
> DR. ACULA
> ...The *proof* is there before your eyes.
> The torn dress – and the hem – It is muddy and wet — It has recently been worn in weather such as this...

> *(indicates outside)*
> Notice the bright redness to the lips... It appears this young lady has
> returned to our world as a vampire...
> BORIS
> I'll go along with the gag... What about Flinch? Was he murdered by a
> vampire?
> JUDSON
> No...
> DR. ACULA
> Who-so-ever is bitten by the vampire, himself becomes a vampire...
> JUDSON
> I know the legend...

Dr. Acula offers to drive a stake through Lucille's heart as the others leave the crypt,
but instead he tosses the stake aside. Perhaps he is protecting a fellow vampire?
When he rejoins the others, they invite him to stay at the mansion. Their return to
the house quickly means more encounters with Lucille, one that even leaves the
housekeeper dead. They can't leave, because of the impassible road. And there is no
phone in the house.

Soon Boris is killed, then Frank, and then Judson. It was Flinch, apparently trying to increase his cut of the fortune. He faked his earlier dissappearance. But then
he sees Lucille rise up from her coffin, and he accidentally falls over a nearby cliff.

In all the chaos, Dr. Acula has overheard the particulars of Lucille's murder by
arsenic poisoning. With the plot exposed, he is able to reveal his own identity as a
private detective. And helping him is Lucille's sister Helen, pretending to be her
vampire skulking around the mansion.

> DR. ACULA
> From that point it simply became the power of suggestion. Lucille's
> coffin was switched for the one presently here – and along with my own
> electrically charged cape – and a good illusion...
> *(indicates Helen)*
> ...We were successful...
> Clever – am I not?
> *(smiles)*

The power of suggestion. Wood's script was certainly crafted to take advantage of
Lugosi's persona, and was presumably similar to what Wood intended for the
unmade TV series *Dr. Acula*. An investigator into the supernatural whose name and
persona smack of Count Dracula.

Dick read the script at Lugosi's apartment and thought it was far better than the
other Wood scripts that Lugosi had sitting around. It had a better role for Lugosi,
allowing him to be more like a vampire, instead of just another mad scientist. The
script featured decent dialogue and a fairly strong understanding of three-act
Hollywood story structure.

Dick was right on every count and believed it would make for a good movie.
And perhaps he was right because to a degree *The Vampire's Tomb* had been made
before. Twice, actually, both times by director Tod Browning. First, it was the silent
film *London After Midnight* (1927) with Lon Chaney Sr., in which a detective pre-
tends to be a vampire in order to solve a murder case. Then Browning split the
detective and fake vampire into two separate roles for *Mark of the Vampire* (1935),
with Lionel Barrymore as the former character and Lugosi as the latter.

In creating the part of Dr. Acula, Wood simply reverted to Browning's original telling of the story. The detective and fake vampire would again be the same character. To add a new dimension to the story, Wood co-opted the basic "old dark house" formula that pervaded the US stage and screen in the 1920s and 1930s. Instead of an individual murderer like Browning used, Wood had several operating in collusion. All gathered for the reading of a will, trapped in an old mansion with bad weather raging outside.

Wood's script had begun production on August 27, 1954— at least that's what the *Los Angeles Times* said four days later on August 31. But in reality of

An unknown journalist, Lugosi, Paul Marco, and Dolores Fuller at Marco's West Hollywood home in December 1954.

course, it hadn't, it hadn't at all. Perhaps some preproduction work was occurring on those days, and perhaps some of the contracts were signed. But there was no shooting; there was no actual production work at all, mainly because there was no money.

How could false accounts like the August 31 *Los Angeles Times* column have gotten printed? Edwin Schallert, the columnist who wrote notices like the one printed on August 31, had been a supporter of Lugosi's during the thirties and forties, and was likely happy to print these small items about Wood's films. Lugosi had long maintained strong relations with a number of journalists in the Hollywood area, ranging from Jimmie Fidler to Erskine Johnson.[33]

But that Wood announced overly-optimistic or even outright false information to the *LA Times* and others seems clear. Why would he do this? The power of suggestion. It's difficult to say for sure, but it is highly possible he was planting some stories in the media to give the appearance of activity to potential investors and distributors.

By September 9, 1954, an industry trade claimed Wood was on an airplane to San Francisco to clinch a deal for funding.[34] The start date had been pushed to October 1. Another effort. But once again, nothing happened. The day came and went, and the cameras didn't crank through a single foot of film. Instead, in late October, a new round of industry trade notices spoke about a different project Wood was directing, *Bride of the Atom.*

The sudden shift in emphasis from *The Vampire's Tomb* to *Bride of the Atom* is difficult to understand, especially given the fact that both film ideas had existed since 1952 or even earlier. The *Bride of the Atom* script had apparently undergone revisions since the time Alex Gordon first tried to produce it in 1952 as *The Atomic Monster.* Presumably Wood made major changes to the script. He also was the person who re-titled it, perhaps as a result of reading articles in 1953 about the bride of an "atom spy."[35] But as with everything else regarding Gordon and Wood–and really anything

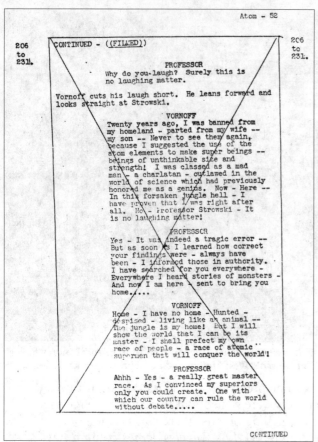

Lugosi's famous speech as Vornoff.
From the *Bride of the Atom* script.

to do with Wood at all—the history of what happened is cloudy, uncertain, and elusive.

In 1963, Gordon recalled "an independent producer rewrote my *Atomic Monster* script and made a very low budget picture vaguely based on it called *Bride of the Monster* [aka *Bride of the Atom*]."[36] But a few decades later, his memory suggested he was a more active participant. "With my script needing some revisions in order to get Bela Lugosi to do it and to set it up, I got Eddie involved to help 'polish' the script."[37] Gordon added that "[Lugosi] and I worked together on the sequence where he was talking about having no home–his big speech, which is credited to Eddie Wood but was actually written by myself, with Lugosi's input."[38]

But Dolores Fuller believed, "I'm ... not certain that [Gordon] made any significant contribution to *Bride of the Monster*."[39] Wood himself once said that he "wrote every line in it," giving Gordon a credit because Gordon had given him the "idea."[40] On a different occasion, though, Wood took credit for the idea as well, saying, "I even keep a pencil and pad beside my bed at night because many a dream turns out to be a good plot. That's where *Bride of the Monster* came from, although it was first called *Bride of the Atom*."[41] Dreams or nightmares? Wood or Gordon? Whatever the answers, *Bride of the Atom* was now the script of choice. No more *Vampire's Tomb*, at least for the moment.

Wood was set to shoot in late October, with Loretta King signed for the lead female role Janet Lawson, leaving Dolores Fuller the tiny part of Margie. There was George Becwar as Professor Strowski and Harvey B. Dunn as Captain Robbins. And Bud Osborne and Don Nagel from Wood's *Jail Bait* (1954) were both back.

As it turned out, the second-billed star under Lugosi was popular wrestler Tor Johnson, the "Super Swedish Angel" of the ring. Cast as Vornoff's hulking assistant Lobo, Johnson had been in films since 1934; by the time of *Bride of the Atom,* he had appeared in some 25 movies, two of which had cast him as the Super Swedish Angel.[42] But to the degree Johnson was famous, it was thanks to his wrestling career. Television broadcasts had made him a name, and in 1952 he even appeared outside the ring on a TV show with the likes of Milton Berle, Harpo Marx, and Dinah Shore.[43] As for the *Bride of the Atom* shoot, Wood recalled later, "Tor's legs were getting worse all the time. It was hard for him to work. He liked to work for me."[44]

And then there was Paul Marco as the bumbling and frightened "Kelton the

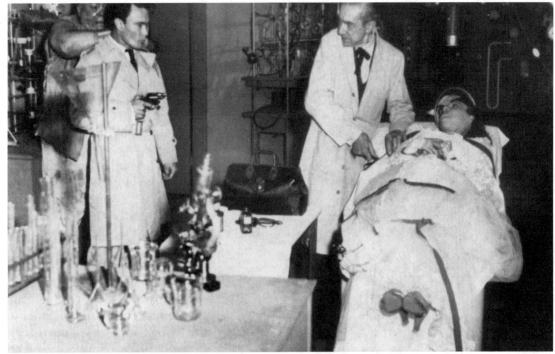

Vornoff's laboratory in *Bride of the Atom*.
From left to right: Tor Johnson, Tony McCoy, Lugosi, and Loretta King.

Cop." Though unknown to moviegoers, Marco was a major fixture in the LA social scene during the early-to-mid fifties. LA columnists like James Copp regularly mentioned him and his parties above the Sunset Strip, where the guests ranged from Liberace to actor Peter Coe.[45] In late 1954, Copp even mentioned Marco's nose job, which he may have gotten for his role in *Bride of the Atom*.[46]

As for Lugosi, well, he was the star. In *The Tragedy of Man*, Madách's Adam asks "Why dost thou treat thine art so scurvily? Dost thou enjoy what thou art forced to play?" For Ed Wood, Lugosi played Dr. Eric Vornoff, mad scientist. Alex Gordon later said that Lugosi, "thought it was going to be much, much more than it turned out to be. But being the old pro that he was, he did the best he could."[47] By contrast, Dick thought Lugosi didn't pay too much attention to the quality of Wood's scripts. To the extent he did, Lugosi didn't see them as being much different from the kinds of things he had done time after time at Monogram. That he was making money and had the chance to act: that was what made him happy.

Did Wood exploit Lugosi? Though Dick had just met Wood at the time *Bride of the Atom* began, he noticed fairly quickly that—however friendly they seemed towards one another—both had something the other needed. As for Wood, he later remembered that he "paid [Lugosi] more in *Bride* than he got for *Dracula*. Sure he needed the money, but don't we all." [48] He had signed Lugosi to a contract that paid $750 a day, but claimed Lugosi feigned sickness to the Screen Actors Guild in order to get an increase to $1,000 a day.[49]

For better or worse, Lugosi was in the cast, and Wood's "Catacomb Productions" began production on October 26, 1954 at the Ted Allan Studios.[50] By November 1, the *Hollywood Reporter* said *Bride of the Atom* had been in production for six days. But they also mentioned the production had been shut down for

Shooting *Bride of the Atom* in March 1955. Standing from left to right are Tony McCoy, Tor Johnson, William C. Thompson, and an unknown woman. Squatting in front are Ed Wood (left) and Don Nagel (right). *(Courtesy of Dennis Phelps)*

a couple of days because of the "construction of sets."[51] They also announced the film had a new executive producer, Lyman C. Abbott, and wrote that only two days of actual filming had occurred.[52]

Only two days of filming, and Dick was there alongside Lugosi for both. The Ted Allan Studios in Hollywood at Yucca and Argyle, a nondescript building and a fairly minimal interior. Wood shot the scene with Lugosi and Becwar that takes place in the living room of the old "Willow's Place." Watching all the preparation, Dick was struck by the fact that a secret panel in the living room set fell open accidentally of its own accord. And then the cameras rolled.

Confronted by Professor Strowski, Dr. Vornoff gives his biggest speech in the film. Paul Marco had cue cards ready, but Lugosi allegedly did not need them. He powerfully recited the dialogue, making only one minor mistake: "Here–in this forsaken jungle hell–I have proven that I was all right!" Examining the script, the line actually ended with "I have proven that I was right after all!"

With the exception of that small change in wording, Paul Marco remembered that Lugosi got the speech down in a single take. After he finished, the room was dead quiet until some applause broke out among the cast and crew.[53] Dick was there too, but he was more struck by how tired and ill Lugosi appeared. At that point, they had known each other for 18 months. A year and a half, and yet Lugosi looked as if he had aged several years since their first meeting.[54]

As far as shooting goes, Dick didn't get to see any more. By November 4, 1954, *Bride of the Atom* was "suspended" for several days because the Ted Allan Studios was "undergoing a remodeling job" and Wood planned to move the production to KTTV. At least that was the story the *Hollywood Reporter* ran.[55] According to *Variety* on the same day, the move was necessitated by a "change of management" at the Ted Allan Studios.[56]

It's difficult to tell what if anything was shot at KTTV. Looking at the film, Vornoff's laboratory certainly has the appearance of being built on a small television stage. Stones painted on the background wall are noticeable in some measure because they remain in sharp focus, where a shallow depth of field would have made them seem more out-of-focus and more realistic. Perhaps the painter(s) expected something other than the high-key lighting from above.

But it's the camerawork in the laboratory set that seems most evocative of a TV program, not that that means necessarily it was shot at KTTV; after all, Wood claimed the lab scenes were shot at Sunset Studios.[57] The camera moves a fair bit, with slow shot lengths that pan the room back and forth rather than cutting inward to other images. The camera pushes into the set at times, but it follows Lugosi rather than being in control of the composition. Far different than the more well-composed but static William C. Thompson cinematography, which suggests that it may well have been footage shot by the other cameraman, Ted Allan. [58]

Whatever Wood shot at KTTV, though, was probably minimal. The entire production shut down again, this time because George Becwar had made a complaint to the Screen Actors Guild.[59] Union trouble meant a delay and a delay meant that whatever initial funding source Wood had–whether Lyman C. Abbott or someone else–dried up. All of this happened presumably before the middle of November.

At the same time, Wood was able to get Phillip K. Scheuer to announce on November 10 that he had just signed Loretta King for *Bride of the Atom* and *The Vampire's Tomb*.[60] On November 12, the *Hollywood Reporter* announced that *The Vampire's Tomb* would go into production right after *Bride of the Atom* finished. And then one day later, columnist Erskine Johnson mentioned *Bride of the Atom* in his syndicated column.[61] A far cry from the reality of his SAG troubles, the newspapers reports seem to be another example of Wood's tactic. Get some press, which in turn can get some investors.

But new funding took nearly four months. It wasn't until March 11, 1955 that the *Hollywood Reporter* announced that Wood had a new backer in Tony McCoy, the actor.[62] In reality, it was apparently his father Donald who had the dollars to get the film finished, money made from a thriving meat packing plant. Whether McCoy was already cast by the time his dad signed the check is hard to tell. Certainly oral histories generally suggest that the money got him the role as the young male lead, Lieutenant Dick Craig.[63] At the same time, it's hard to believe that Wood hadn't cast such a key role when he originally began shooting. Regardless, McCoy had been part of the LA theater scene, having appeared in a production of *Doctor in Spite of Himself* in January 1954.[64] Before that, he had gotten a positive review for a role in Cocteau's *The Infernal Machine*.[65]

Whatever the exact sequence of events, though, Wood proceeded to shoot the remaining scenes with McCoy, King, and the others. And of course there was that prop octopus. That most famous of film octopi, first seen in Republic's *Wake of the Red Witch* (1948) with John Wayne. Wood rented it. Or he borrowed it. Or he just plain stole it. And he didn't pick up the mechanism that operated it. Or it didn't work. Wood then dragged its motionless tentacles to Griffith Park for a location shoot in mid-March 1955; his crew dammed up a little stream to give it a home. That was at night (or was it in the daytime with Wood just shooting day-for-night?) This story was told and retold, ad infinitum. A cinematic tale for the ages, really; possibly the greatest anecdote of independent filmmaking history.

Was Lugosi in the water when Vornoff wrestled with the octopus? Viewing the film makes extremely clear it was a double, just as a double had been used for the lab scene where Vornoff struggles with Lobo. Paul Marco confirmed that Lugosi was in Griffith Park at the shoot, but not in the water.[66] Loretta King also remembered someone doubling for him.[67] But who was the stuntman? Anyhow, Wood claimed that he

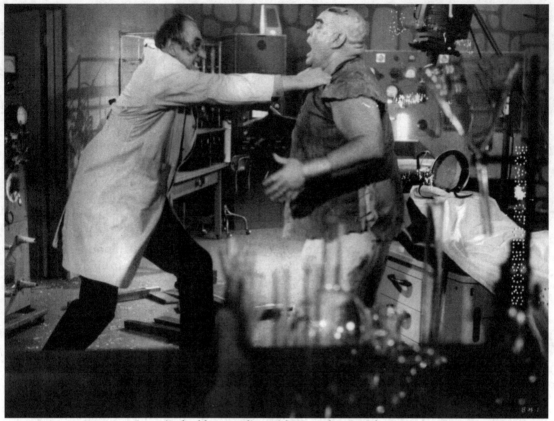
Lugosi's double struggling with Tor Johnson's character.

got into the cold water himself with someone named Sgt. Sullivan, just to help make its tentacles look like they were moving.[68] But he also claimed Lugosi got in as well, having to drink a bottle of Jack Daniels afterwards to warm back up.[69] The beauty of the story is largely that it never seems to be told the same way twice. Even the flourish of Jack Daniels becomes a debate; Lugosi was generally a Scotch drinker.[70]

Along with the crazy production anecdotes, the finished film ended up spawning its own legend. One of the worst ever made. A Golden Turkey. Nonsense of that type. Is it a bad film? For most viewers and critics, the answer would certainly be yes. it's definitely plagued by several problems. Acting varies greatly from the professional work of Lugosi, Becwar, Dunn, and Ann Wilner to the theatrical overplaying of McCoy and King and Fuller. And every one of them struggles with the poor dialogue.

Continuity problems mean that the front door of the Willow's Place as seen from the outside of the house is clearly a different door than the one that opens into the interior set. When secretary Tillie (Ann Wilner) is seen in over-the-shoulder shots, a pencil juts out of her hair, just over her ear; when the film cuts to show her face, though, Tillie's pencil is noticeably absent. But even more distracting than these continuity goofs is the shadow of a boomed microphone that appears above Lugosi's head in the one of the laboratory scenes.

But bad acting, continuity problems, and microphone shadows surface in so many films, including some that are highly regarded. Those aren't at all the only reasons that *Bride of the Atom* seems to be the lowest budget horror movie of Lugosi's career. It's also, shots of an alligator and the night sky illuminated by lightning; stock footage, in other words, and in a heavier dose than any of his other horror films. Throughout the film, there are also all-too-minimal angle changes that cut uncomfortably. These are at their worst when McCoy puts on a coat in an outdoor scene and the images jump cut in and out. And once again, that horrible camerawork in the lab scene appears so much more amateurish than any seen in Lugosi's prior films.

At the same time, the fractured production schedule and tiny budget didn't keep some nice touches from emerging.[71] Thompson's footage sometimes shows very credible visual composition and some genuinely thoughtful lighting. For example, actors are generally backlit to instill a sense of depth. At the police station, particularly in Captain Robbins's office, Thompson labored even more on interesting background shadows representing things like Venetian blinds.

Bad, good, or indifferent is after all in the eye of the beholder. Thumbs go up; others go down. These judgments generally aren't that helpful to anyone other than the very people who translate them into so many stars out of four. What can be said of *Bride of the Atom* is that at times critics have been factually incorrect in their descriptions of the film. For example, various writers have claimed Lugosi flubbed a line about Lobo being as gentle as a "kitchen," when audibly it's clear he said the intended word "kitten."[72] It's as if the golden turkey has to be dressed with inaccuracies to make it seem all the more bad, all the more ridiculous.

Ridiculous or not, *Bride of the Atom* seems to be a prime example of the weird and rather porous world of Ed Wood's films. He never made sequels per se, but instead created a kind of postmodernist cinematic landscape where some of his same characters appear in film after film. Lobo and Kelton the Cop, for example.[73] Or vague allusions to one movie plot inside of another.[74] Even Wood movie posters show up inside of one of his films.[75]

That *Bride of the Atom* is a part of this world is clear only in retrospect, of course. It came before these other films that share some of its characters or plot devices. When *Bride of the Atom* was made, it was its own film. Perhaps Wood was using some actors he had worked with on *Jail Bait* or *Glen or Glenda*, as well as William C. Thompson on camera. But there is little within *Bride of the Atom* to connect it to Wood's prior stories.[76]

Like Dr. Acula and *The Vampire's Tomb*, *Bride of the Atom* didn't herald Wood's future as much as it explored Lugosi's cinematic past. His first speaking role in a talking film was in *Prisoners* in 1929; a quarter of a century later his last speaking role in film was in *Bride of the Atom*. It was as Dr. Eric Vornoff, whose name and "homeland" implied an Eastern European, even Russian background of the type he had played so many times in film and on stage.[77]

Bride of the Atom acts as something of a chronicle of Lugosi's history in the horror film, an omnibus of scenes and ideas that evoke both the major films and low-budget movies. For example, Vornoff hypnotizes Janet Lawton (Loretta King) with his arched hand held in front of her face; his fingers writhe before her eyes in punctuated movements. The gesture is from the Dracula of New Haven, of Broadway, of Browning's film, of vaudeville and stage revivals, and of *Abbott and Costello Meet Frankenstein*.

The emphasis on Lugosi's eyes in extreme close-ups revisits their importance in *Dracula*. It invokes their predominance among his physical features at being the site of horror. They mark low-budget films like *Voodoo Man* (1944), where he hypnotizes Stella Saunders (Louise Currie). And they stare out from major studio efforts like *The Raven* (1935), where Mary Burns (Inez Courtney) eerily pronounces that

Lugosi's Dr. Vollin character is crazed: "It's no use, Geoffrey ... *Look at his eyes!*"

And those extreme close-ups of his eyes in *Bride of the Atom*, Lugosi's final independent horror movie, bring to mind similar shots in *White Zombie* (1932), Lugosi first independent horror movie. Wood consciously drew on that film for inspiration, recounting that the "hand bit" where Vornoff clasps both of his hands together came from *White Zombie*.[78] Through that motion, Vornoff controls Janet from afar, causing her to enter his laboratory clothed in a wedding dress that echoes images of Madeline (Madge Bellamy) in *White Zombie*.

But more than anything else, Vornoff exemplifies the kind of mad scientists that Lugosi played so many times. His attempt to take over the world harkens back to everything from *Phantom Creeps* (1939) to *Mother Riley Meets the Vampire* (1952). And some story elements recall the Gerald Schnitzer stories, ranging from the secret panels that had been seen in, say, *Bowery at Midnight*, to the oafish assistant Angel (Frank Moran) in *The Corpse Vanishes*. Like Angel, Lobo develops an affection for the young heroine and is beaten by Lugosi's mad scientist character.

"He tampered in God's domain," Captain Robbins says in the film's closing moments. Trying to create a new form of life in the laboratory with an assistant at his side. Vornoff is yet another version of Henry Frankenstein, the role that Lugosi never got to play, but strangely did play time after time. Mad scientists cast in the mold of James Whale's *Frankenstein*, going under other names in other, lesser films. The relentless echo of all that went wrong in 1931.

And thus it's somehow fitting that Wood's film also brings to mind Robert Florey and *Murders in the Rue Morgue*. Janet is to be the "bride of the atom," just as Camille (Sidney Fox) was to be the "bride of science." In *Rue Morgue*, Dr. Mirakle's ape appears in the two forms: authentic animal footage and shots of a man in a costume, splintering the onscreen presence of the same creature into two distinct forms. However inadvertently, *Bride of the Atom* parallels that aesthetic precisely, as Vornoff's octopus emerges both as a movie prop and as an actual sea creature in stock footage.

That *Bride of the Atom* was renamed *Bride of the Monster* before its release then seems somehow remarkably appropriate. The film's brief use of the words "atom" and "atomic supermen," as well as the inexplicable appearance of a mushroom cloud at the film's climax, hardly meant the storyline was modern by fifties standards. No, in the end *Bride of the Monster* hadn't really become a science fiction film for the Eisenhower era. It was something out of the past, and its final title more accurately reflects that fact.

And so Lugosi's last speaking role in the film industry was behind him, and so was his career in national television. But many of Lugosi's earlier movies were still playing on late night TV. Some played on Vampira's KABC program, and others were broadcast over other stations throughout the US.[79] Those old horror stories Gerald Schnitzer wrote with were among them.[80] Over and over again, sometimes as the final broadcast of the evening. The scratchy old prints would end, and then, well, nothing. Just a silent test pattern.

CHAPTER TEN

The Lightning

In March 1955, Bela Lugosi would hardly have been able to think of himself as a man without friends. He had ongoing relationships with Alex Gordon and Ed Wood, and had become very friendly with Tor Johnson, Dolores Fuller, and Paul Marco. Paul even threw a 1954 Christmas party in Lugosi's honor, with Lugosi exclaiming "I feel at home!" when he saw Paul's specially-designed black Christmas tree.[1]

And of course Lugosi had become close with Dick Sheffield and Dick's pals Mike Spencer and David Katzman. That was in addition to Lugosi getting to know literary agent Forrest J Ackerman, who helped Lugosi with his errands on more than one occasion. Ackerman could drive, and of course Lugosi had never learned how. Knowing he was financially strapped, Ackerman even sent Lugosi money as a 1954 Christmas present.[2]

There were also the Ormonds, film and entertainment entrepreneurs. During 1953, Lugosi had become increasingly friendly with Ron and June. He had met the couple first through Ackerman and again through Wood. Though they didn't end up making a planned film together, Lugosi spent a fair amount of time with them, once going to dinner at their house wearing his Dracula cape. Their relationship grew to the point that Lugosi even became the godfather of Ron and June's son Tim.[3]

Then sometime during 1954 Lugosi became pals with "Cowboy" Dallas Turner, a singer who recorded over 300 songs during his long career. An unlikely friendship? Perhaps, though Lugosi had been friendly with western movie star Buck Jones during the early 1930s.[4] Turner first saw Lugosi by chance at a restaurant on Vine Street, where the two happened to be seated near one another at lunchtime.[5] Turner recognized him immediately; Lugosi was one of his favorite movie stars. Then the two began bumping into each other over and over again at an area drug store. Acquaintance led to friendship, and they started eating lunch together at a buffet-style restaurant in Hollywood.[6]

Of course Lugosi still had so many, many other companions from the years and decades gone by. Friends like Hungarian violinist Duci de Kerekjarto, his wife Marie, and his daughter Rose. Lugosi even stayed with them once briefly when he was between apartments, and they continued to be close friends even after Duci and Marie divorced. To young Rose, Lugosi was forever "Uncle Bela."[7]

Sometime near the end of 1954 or early 1955, though, Lugosi visited Marie's home to speak with her mother, Meta Wittrock. Whether planned or impromptu, Lugosi proposed marriage to Meta that afternoon. Having known him for so many

Ed Wood and Bela Lugosi at Paul Marco's 1954 Christmas party that featured a black tree in Lugosi's honor.

years, Meta laughed a bit as if she was supposed to laugh at that moment, as if Lugosi was only joking. She knew it was coming from the fact Lillian was gone, and that Lugosi was speaking out of loneliness. Lonely, in spite of so many friends new and old.[8] Not feeling well, either, and losing weight.

Lugosi was getting old and frail; his friends knew that. But then on April 22, 1955, many of them learned something new about him. Front-page stories in all the newspapers, talking about how Lugosi was addicted to narcotics and how he had gone to a hospital looking for help. Dick Sheffield read the article in the *LA Times* before going to school that morning, and he was shocked. So were Mike and Katzman. People across the US, the world really, were surprised as well. Even some newspapers in Hungary ran the story.[9]

That night, Lugosi's addiction made the evening news on television. Stalwart Lugosi fan Philip R. Evans remembered, "It almost had to have been KTLA that I saw. It wasn't that Lugosi was interviewed, just photos with the voiceover of the newspaper man. More than anything I recall he was just skin and bones. But I remember seeing him smiling in some of those pictures they showed, as well as images of needle marks."[10]

There were a few people who wouldn't have been surprised, though. Dr. Bill Neff of the "Madhouse of Mystery" had known this news by the end of 1947; he found Lugosi erratic, and learned at the time that it was from drug use.[11] Director Ted Post saw Lillian injecting a needle into Lugosi's arm backstage during a 1948 performance of *Dracula*.[12] Actor Joseph Campanella claimed he learned about Lugosi's narcotics when they were working together on a 1949 episode of the television show *Suspense*.[13] Herman Cohen noticed needles in Lugosi's dressing room while making *Bela Lugosi Meets a Brooklyn Gorilla* (1952).[14] And then Emile O. Schmidt saw marks on Lugosi's arms during the St. Louis rehearsals for *Arsenic and Old Lace* in January 1954.[15]

June Ormond found out at about the same time as Schmidt did. She and Ron offered to take Lugosi on a live tour of movie theatres; they had recently been successful doing just that with the Three Stooges. Good money and steady work. But Lugosi knew that weeks and weeks on the road quickly moving from one town to the next meant potential difficulty in obtaining drugs. He told June about his situation, using pantomimed motions to mimic the act of making an injection. He also said without explanation that Ed Wood helped him obtain drugs in the LA area. No tour happened; June wasn't willing to help continue his addiction, and she certainly wasn't pleased that Ed Wood was.[16]

Wood had of course been responsible for Lugosi's only paid acting job in 1955, in *Bride of the Atom*. During a nighttime shoot on that film in March at Griffith Park, Lugosi asked Paul Marco to take him to his apartment; he told Wood he had to go home for medicine, and he wanted Marco to drive him. Marco later remembered:

> Once we got to his apartment, Bela signalled for me to sit down on an old love seat. And he told me, "You aren't going to like seeing this, Paul. It's not very nice to watch." But I told him, "Bela, please do whatever you need to do."
>
> Then Bela began this dramatic ritual where he pulled back the drapes of a walk-in closet, kind of a small room. And I saw a sink, a table, and a hat rack. He took an apron off of it, and put it on. Then he rolled up his sleeves, washed his hands in the sink, [and] wiped them dry. Then came the hypodermic needle.
>
> This was all extremely strange, a really heartbreaking ceremony. But then he just turned off the light, smiled at me, and said something like "Now I'm ready to go back to work."[17]

Was Paul telling the truth when he later spoke about this event? He and Tor Johnson were probably the only two of Wood's collaborators to actually become friends with Lugosi, so it is conceivable Lugosi trusted him. Given the timing, which was immediately before he sought medical help, Lugosi may have also grown less discreet at that point than he had been in previous months or years. Marco—who grew weary of people asking about Lugosi's drug use in his later years–was one of many people to have seen or known something of Lugosi's drug use.[18]

Of course most people didn't know about Lugosi's drug use, but after it became public knowledge, it raised a number of questions. Director Robert Wise later wondered if Lugosi's illness while working on *The Body Snatcher* (1945) was due to drugs.[19] And then there were various cancellations. In 1947, for example, Lugosi called off a live appearance in Waukesha, Wisconsin; a local newspaper claimed that the cause was a "recurrent attack of illness."[20] And then as 1950 came to an end, Lugosi cancelled a large number of live spook show appearances on the Eastern Seaboard, also due to illness.[21] Were any of these situations due to either drugs or the physical pains that led to his using them?

It's difficult to know, but it certainly seems as if Lugosi had reached a critical moment in March 1955. After he finished his last scenes for *Bride of the Atom*, Lugosi used the check from Wood to pay his rent. It was at that point that he also saw a doctor, presumably for another prescription. Lugosi later remembered that the doctor said:

27 Dec 54

Dear Friend Béla

I hoped to be able to send you $5 for Christmas, but when the time came I simply did not have the money. For one thing, our car chose just that inopportune time to require $110's worth of repairs. (At least the money went to another Hungarian!--our garageman, Mr Paulee.) But Santa Claus gave me a little cash on the 25th, and so, better late than never, I should like to share some of it with you.

I am not a rich man, but I have most of the small things of life I would like. Until I could afford to have the tape recorder of my dreams or a movie projector or a trip to Scandinavia or a color TV, between my spending $5 to enjoy myself for an evening at the Moulin Rouge or offering it to you as a Yuletime present, it gives me much more pleasure to make you the gift, small as I regret that it is. The much greater wish goes with it that your health will improve and your affairs will prosper in 1955.

With kindest personal thoughts...

Letter from Forrest J Ackerman to Bela Lugosi dated December 27, 1954.

> "Look Mr. Lugosi," he said. You either give this stuff up or…"
>   I never let him finish the sentence. "I've got to have it," I screamed. "I've just got to have it."
>   The doctor grabbed me by the shoulders. "You may die in six months," he told me. "How long do you think your body can take this abuse?"[22]

The doctor also suggested that Lugosi should go into a hospital, which he did. Perhaps he took the advice because he believed the doctor's warning. Perhaps it was because he couldn't get another prescription. Perhaps it was also for financial reasons.

The only other reason Lugosi ever gave for choosing that moment to enter a hospital was that his "limbs had become just rings of muscle. When I could no longer find a place to inject, that was the end."[23] To turn to a hospital meant turning to the Motion Picture Relief Fund, into which he had paid money for year after year in Hollywood during the thirties and forties.

> They sent me first to the Kimball Sanitarium for four weeks, but it cost them $30 a day so they didn't want to continue, and the doctor told me that on account of my age … that those four weeks are not enough for me.[24]

Towards the end of his stay, he said he was weaned to just a "dummy shot," just the bare needle with no liquid. After that, he said he started getting "panicky."[25] Panicky and no more help from the Relief Fund, who said he hadn't appeared in a union film within five years.[26] And that meant that they couldn't help him any more than they already had.

The irony of course was that Lugosi had actually signed *two* union contracts during the previous five years. The first was for *Bela Lugosi Meets a Brooklyn Gorilla*, a film for which he reinstated his Screen Actors Guild membership just days before shooting began.[27] And then he had signed a union contract for *Bride of the Atom* in the fall of 1954.[28] So why weren't these film credits good enough?

It's difficult to know for sure. In March 1955, *Bride of the Atom* was not yet released, and had also experienced union problems; either or both of those factors may have kept it from being seen as legitimate. But *Meets a Brooklyn Gorilla* had been in release for over two years, so what really was the problem? Perhaps it had something to do with the fact Lugosi hadn't been a Screen Actor's Guild member from November 1950 to May 1952. That

Smoking a cigar while talking to reporters at the Los Angeles County General Hospital on April 22, 1955.

meant that by the time he sought help, Lugosi had only been reinstated for two years and ten months; at that moment, he hadn't been working as a union member for five consecutive years.[29]

Regardless of the reason, though, Lugosi had to leave the Kimball. They suggested that he try the Los Angeles County General Hospital, where he might be able to get treatment without having to pay for it. Though he had at first asked his old pal Willi Szittja, it was another old friend, Manly P. Hall, who ended up driving went him to the hospital. Hall had also recently sent Lugosi food during his financial troubles.[30]

When Lugosi appeared at the County Hospital on April 21, the attendants at first believed that he was a "crank" who was attempting to "masquerade as the famous actor."[31] At that point, Lugosi weighed only something like 125 pounds, far from the 180 he weighed at the peak of his career.[32] Along with being generally skeptical that they were looking at the famous actor, the staff may have also been puzzled by how different he looked from his onscreen appearances.

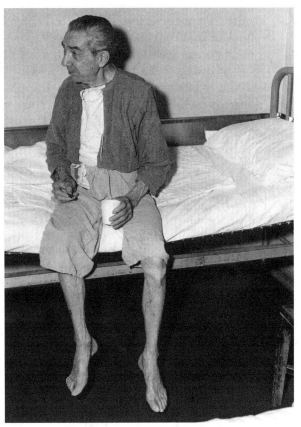

The "ghost of a ghost," according to journalist Henry Sutherland. Lugosi at the Los Angeles County General Hospital in April 1955.
(Courtesy David Wentink)

After arriving, Lugosi spoke to a mental-hygiene counselor and said that he began using narcotics in 1935.[33] "I need help in overcoming the drug habit," he admitted.[34] One early newspaper article claimed the hospital said that Lugosi wasn't technically an addict, but that judgment wasn't ever repeated in the press.[35] As for Lugosi, well, he quickly signed papers claiming he *was* addicted, a necessary move to get the long-term help he was after.[36]

And Lugosi was happy with the immediate care the County Hospital offered. He said:

> I was afraid to come here [to the psychopathic ward] because of the insanity associated with this place. For my mind is all right. It is only my body that is sick. But here I found the most pleasant disappointment. I thought I was to be just a number, but I am getting all of the breaks to bring me back to life.[37]

Lugosi also expressed deep gratitude towards Dr. James McGinnis, head of the psychopathic ward.[38]

Newspaper journalists quickly descended on the hospital of course. On April 21, 1955, Lugosi "shunned" all visitors and reporters, but the next day he spoke to them from a hospital bed while smoking a cigar and nursing a cup of coffee.[39] Frank Laro of the *LA Times*, Henry Sutherland of the *LA Herald Examiner*, and Roby Heard of the *LA Mirror-News*. Representatives of the Associated Press and the

United Press too. He tearfully told them his shocking story, and they were equally shocked by his appearance.

Photographers snapped photo after photo, with the images later causing Henry Sutherland to write that Lugosi looked like the "ghost of a ghost" as his "emaciated" body sat on a hospital cot, his "pipe-stem legs" and "bare feet" dangling towards the ground.[40] As for the *LA Times*, their photo caption dubbed him an "ex-actor."[41]

What did Lugosi tell all those journalists as the camera bulbs flashed over and over again? He told them that he had used drugs for twenty years. Two decades of pain and two decades of drug use to cope with it. It all began because of "shooting pains" in his sciatica nerve, a pain that felt like "lightning."[42] He said:

> I started using morphine under [a] doctor's care. I knew after a time it was getting out of control. Seventeen years ago, on a trip to England, I heard of a new drug, less harmful than morphine. It was called methadone. I smuggled a big box of it back home. I guess I brought about a pound. Ever since, I used that or Demerol. I just took the drugs. I didn't eat. I got sicker and sicker.
>
> There was one period, a few years ago, when I quit. My wife Lillian, who divorced me in 1953, got me to quit. She gave me the shots. And she weaned me. Finally I got only the bare needle. A fake shot, that's all. I was done with it.
>
> Then she left me. She took our son. He was my flesh. I went back on the drugs. My heart was broken.[43]

Thus was the basic story that he gave to the public. And he added that over the years he had spent "thousands and thousands" of dollars to stop the lightning, or at least to blunt it.[44]

Roby Heard at the *Mirror-News* got a few more details from him, like the fact he took barbiturates to help him sleep, something doctors confirmed.[45] Lugosi also claimed that some of the methadone he took was in capsule form. And Henry Sutherland quoted him as saying that once he switched to methadone, he "injected two cubic centimeters every two hours," and also injected the same amount of Demerol and ingested some barbiturates before going to bed.[46]

Did Lugosi get some things wrong when he spun his story? Well, there's no doubt that he told the tale differently as time went on. In April, he said that he started taking morphine injections in 1935.[47] Later, though, he would say he began injections at the age of 56, which would have meant roughly 1938, or even 1944, given that he regularly claimed 1888 was his year of birth.[48] In April, he also implied that he had taken morphine for at least three years, maybe more.[49] Subsequently, he said that he

Visited on April 25, 1955 at the County General Hospital by his *Bride of the Atom* costars, Loretta King and Tony McCoy.

only took morphine for "the first half year or year, until Demerol was discovered."[50]

Lugosi likely didn't get methadone in England in 1939, which he basically claimed on April 22 as well.[51] Though the drug had been synthesized in Germany in 1937, it wasn't in any widespread usage until during and after World War II. But then there's the question if Lugosi really said that he had gotten methadone "seventeen years" earlier. A different newspaper claimed he had brought back the box of methadone "seven years ago" when he was appearing in a stage revival of *Dracula*.[52] Neither would be correct because the stage revival happened in 1951, but at least one of these errors—seven years versus seventeen—had to be a reporter's.

As time went on, other aspects of Lugosi's story changed as well. Under oath in late 1955, he decreased the addiction period from twenty years:

> I started about 16 years ago. ... I started first with one shot every 2 or 3 weeks. Then I increased it to once a week and so on and finally after 14 or 15 years, no, about 12 years, I don't know exactly, unfortunately, my wife divorced me, and then I increased the amount to such an amount, such a number, so that later, before I started my withdrawal, I took between 6 and 8 shots a day, and, naturally, it took away my capacity to memorize lines. So, I didn't accept for the last two or three years any jobs because I felt like couldn't make good.[53]

Of course this statement also seems problematic. Even if drug use affected his ability to deliver lines, potentially even causing his problems on the *Red Skelton Show* in 1954, Lugosi had indeed worked in a variety of capacities during the "last two or three years."

Then of course there were things that Lugosi was careful not to say to those first reporters. In April 1955, *Time* magazine ran a story talking about how some writers and artists derived pleasure from drug use.[54] But when Lugosi spoke that same month, he never mentioned the escapist euphoria he felt. Only later would he admit that drugs, "put me so much in a good state of feeling that I used it later myself even if I didn't have pain."[55] By 1956, he even admitted that they gave him an "edge," a nice feeling of elation" that helped him to "escape from [his] unhappy reality."[56]

Conversely, there were aspects of his story that never changed and that he repeatedly talked about. Lugosi was consistent, even adamant, in discussing how he obtained narcotics. "When one doctor refused to give it to me, I saw another," he said. "When he, in turn, became wary, I consulted a third physician."[57] Over and over again, he would make clear that he always got drugs from doctors and never from the black market.[58]

Who noticed what changed and what stayed the same in his stories? Perhaps not many people, but one was his ex-wife Lillian. Aside from her anger that Lugosi essentially blamed her for his addiction, Lillian was out-

A section of the Metropolitan State Hospital as photographed some two months before Lugosi's arrival.

Lugosi at the Metropolitan State Hospital pointing to the script of *The Ghoul Goes West*.

raged by what she saw as a pack of lies. In her version, Lugosi hadn't used narcotics for twenty years, but only for about twelve, beginning in World War II, and the usage had hit a peak when he was in England in 1951. True, he had leg pains during the second half of the 1930s, but at that point he took no medication. Instead, she claimed that he drank asparagus juice for natural pain relief.[59]

On many key points, though, Lugosi and Lillian weren't that far apart in recounting what happened. Leg pains meant Lugosi was prescribed morphine and then Demerol. He obtained methadone in England, and then Lillian weaned him to a point that he wasn't using any drugs.

Once she left him, he went back to narcotics with a usage that far exceeded any during their marriage. Both of them also alluded to the psychosomatic component of his drug use.[60]

So the big difference in their accounts was really timing. How long had he been using drugs, and how long had he actually been *addicted* to them? Perhaps Lugosi spoke of a twenty-years to add more drama to his story. Perhaps, as Lillian said, during some of the earlier years Lugosi made only a minor use of drugs for infrequent pains.[61]

But all of this becomes confused when examining Lillian's own memories, such as her claim that she gave Lugosi an injection in May 1944 in Denver, Colorado, when in fact they were nowhere near Denver that month.[62] Or that she said as of April 1955 that Lugosi had only been using Demerol for two years. Of course the two were already separated by April 1953, so it's questionable how much she would have known about his Demerol use that year.[63] These small questions–combined with minor journalistic errors and Lugosi's own very inconsistent retellings of the story–make building a precise timeline of his drug use difficult, if not impossible.

Lillian's other major problem with Lugosi's story also had to do with timing, in particular his choice of April 21, 1955 as the day to appear at the County Hospital. That day was very definitely Lillian's birthday, a fact Lugosi must have realized.[64] Perhaps he planned the event for that day to get her attention, even to exact a kind of revenge; that certainly seems to have been Lillian's belief.[65]

If it was a kind of statement to her, it may have come as a result of romantic rumors about Lillian and Brian Donlevy. Lillian was a single woman in 1955, of course. But nonetheless, famed gossip columnist Louella O. Parsons still found it odd when she saw Lillian with someone else. On March 25, 1955, her syndicated column reported that "a strange huddlesome at the Huddle Restaurant were Brian Donlevy with Bela Lugosi's ex, Lily Lugosi."[66] Lugosi was increasingly aware that Lillian was gone for good.

But given his quiet admittance to the Kimball in March, it also seems like that Lugosi was genuinely in need of immediate medical help. And certainly doctors at the County Hospital believed that on April 21, Lugosi was even too ill to go to a court hearing that would determine whether he would receive treatment at the state's

Advertisement from the *Hollywood Citizen-News* for the preview of *Bride of the Atom*.

expense.[67] They let him stay overnight for a hearing in which the judge actually came to the hospital.[68] One doctor even told the press that if Lugosi had waited more than a few more weeks to seek out help, it could have been fatal.[69]

After all, Lugosi was definitely abusing drugs regularly after the 1953 divorce from Lillian, and it wasn't just a few of his friends who knew. By 1954, the FBI was aware of it as well. During his show at the Silver Slipper, Lugosi had approached a Las Vegas doctor for drugs. Knowing he was a "heavy user of narcotics, the doctor turned him down and promptly told the Clark County Sheriff's Office about Lugosi's visit. They in turn told the FBI."[70]

So Lugosi's choice of going to the County Hospital on that particular day may well have been planned. But there was also the fact that he genuinely had a problem; he had to get help that month. And in April, the help he needed was financial as well as medical. Thus the hearing to determine his eligibility for state assistance.

Judge Wallace L. Ware presided. If he committed Lugosi, he still had to determine where he should go; the two main options were the state hospitals in Norwalk and Camarillo.[71] The hearing seems to have been brief, with Ware telling Lugosi:

> The court wants to commend you for this very courageous act of yours. It is commendable that you have come forward voluntarily to cure your addiction to the use of drugs. After all, you are only 72 years of age. And it will be wonderful to get well and live the rest of your life as you should.[72]

Ware then ordered Lugosi to be under the care of the Metropolitan State Hospital in Norwalk for a "minimum of three months and a maximum of two years."[73] Lugosi's reply: "God bless you, judge."[74]

The County Hospital then kept him for a number of days before transferring him to Norwalk. They told the press that they were waiting for his physical condition to improve, which buttresses again the idea that he was in particularly bad shape that month.[75] He later described the withdrawals he suffered there:

> I cannot describe the tortures I underwent. My body grew hot, then cold. I tried to eat the bed sheets, my pajamas. My heart beat madly. Then it seemed to stop. Every joint in my body ached.[76]

Perhaps Lugosi remembered his old film *The Rejected Woman* from 1924, a movie that starred Alma Rubens, a silent film actress whose drug abuse destroyed her life and career. Her addiction had made big news from the late twenties until her death just before *Dracula* (1931) opened.[77] But then again, Lugosi's mind and body were probably racked with too much horror to remember such trivia.

Attending the "Bela Lugosi Testimonial Benefit." From left to right are Ed Wood, Maila "Vampira" Nurmi, Paul Marco, and actress Meg Randall. *(Courtesy of David Wentink)*

While he was awaiting the transfer, though, Lugosi did have some guests at the County Hospital. On April 25, it was the cast and crew from *Bride of the Atom*. Ed Wood, Tony McCoy, Tor Johnson, Loretta King, Don Nagel, and others. The *LA Examiner* was there to snap a photo of McCoy giving Lugosi a new script for his next film, which "producer McCoy" claimed he was postponing until Lugosi was released.[78] The movie was *The Ghoul Goes West*, and the script—with perhaps some minor changes—was nothing more than *The Phantom Ghoul*, which Wood had already given to Lugosi in 1953. And Wood even still had the photos of Lugosi and Dolores Fuller from the Hollywood Historama to circulate as publicity stills for the film.[79]

McCoy also announced that *Bride of the Atom* was going to have a premiere in May 1955 "with all the trimmings, arc lights and all." Money raised from it would go into a trust fund for Lugosi. "You will draw from it weekly," McCoy said. Lugosi told McCoy and the entire group that their visit was "so heart-warming. Such a miracle, I cannot believe it. To know that people have such faith in me is better than medicine. I will not let them down."[80] He also told Loretta King that he was looking forward to getting "unhooked."[81]

All the journalists and the photographers crowded in again to get the news, of course. The Lugosi story had worked well that week, from the announcement of his drug addiction to coverage of the judge's decision and finally plans for a film comeback. Almost a three-act play, really: tragedy, redemption, and salvation. Frank Laro of the *LA Times* even won an award for his work on the Lugosi story.[82]

But the story was quickly Old News, at least for the moment, and the news cycle cycled on. Everything from US-China disputes over Formosa to the Justice Department's anti-trust lawsuit against Hilton Hotels.[83] And just days later, there were even two drug-related stories involving other movie stars. On April 26, headlines announced that Susan Hayward was rushed to the hospital after an overdose of pills in an apparent suicide attempt.[84] A couple of days after that, Diana Barrymore collapsed from taking too many sleeping pills.[85]

As for Lugosi, well, he had more a few more guests wanting to see him, but no cameraman was with them. On April 26, immigration agents arrived at the County Hospital to interview Lugosi about his possible Communist affiliations. In dealing once again with this old problem, Lugosi denied party membership or any sympathy for the Communists. He also told them that he was affiliated with the Hungarian-American Council for Democracy as a figurehead, that at the time he was their president he was "an alcoholic and did not care what he did."[86] Presumably they had a newfound interest in him because of his newfound publicity. And so that discomforting interview was his send-off to the coming days and weeks and months into the unknown awaiting him at the Metropolitan State Hospital.

Noteworthy Metropolitan inmates around that time included Humphrey Bogart's first wife.[87] There was also respected elementary school principal Clarence McGinn, who made news when he was placed under observation in 1954 to determine if he was a "sex psychopath."[88] And then there was the sad case of Gordon and Diane Clark, a young couple

With two unknown children during his stay at Metropolitan.
(Courtesy of Bill Chase)

addicted to narcotics who spent three months at Norwalk in the autumn of 1954. The press announced that they were "cured," with the two giving credit to their religious faith. But less than ninety days after their release from Metropolitan, a judge sentenced them to jail time for going back to the drugs.[89]

When Lugosi was driven to Metropolitan sometime near the end of April, it would have been a fairly short drive, probably less than an hour. And then he would have he glimpsed what a 1955 newspaper account dubbed "a city within a city":

> It is a quiet and beautiful city, with its matchless green lawns, its rows of palm trees threading along the narrow footpaths and winding roads, which connect the attractive English-style buildings.
> There are no walls, no gates, no guards. It looks more like a typical English college campus. But there is an eerie and unnatural calmness over the city.
> A man sits on a bench looking down at his hands, his lips moving but his voice imperceptible–he believes he has committed a horrible crime for which he is being punished. A woman walks down a path, singing happily and speaking to each passerby, confident that everyone recognizes her as the famous historical personage she thinks she is.[90]

When Lugosi arrived, this "city" contained about 2,500 patients, ranging from "paranoiacs, manic depressives, schizophrenics, alcoholics, drug addicts, [and] sexual psychopaths."[91]

Though the hospital had existed since 1916, its name change from the Norwalk State Hospital to the Metropolitan came in 1952 after area residents complained it bore the name of their community.[92] By 1955, it contained 34 wards contained in 20 two-story buildings over an area of 360 acres. Dr. Robert Wyers headed the staff of 640 people, ranging from 525 medical personnel to chaplains like the Reverend Myles Renear.[93]

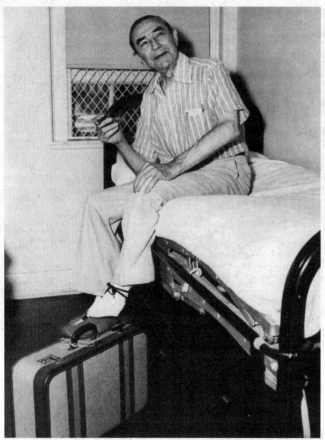

With his bag packed, Lugosi prepares to leave Metropolitan on August 5, 1955. *(Courtesy of Dennis Phelps)*

In 1955, the "city" also featured athletic fields and a "little store" where patients could buy personal items. There was a dance band formed by a group of musical patients. There was even a "farm and a dairy, all part of the industrial therapy provided for the patients."[94] But when Lugosi arrived that spring, the attempt at serenity would have been interrupted by workers constructing an enormous new building that was set to double their number of beds.[95]

Around the same time, Metropolitan touted its use of modern and humane medical care. But the institution was plagued with a number of problems. Some of them were common to the time period, such as an overuse of electro-shock therapy. Other difficulties came out of a lack of resources. Leilani McCandless, a Metro nurse in the 1950s, remembered that patients were segregated by gender, but not by much else. Drug addicts might be housed in the same ward with the mentally ill and sexual psychopaths, for example.[96] The lack of space in closed wards meant some violent patients were able to move about freely, even escaping with relative ease.[97] Others ran into the oncoming traffic of the street to commit suicide.[98]

And McCandless wasn't the only one to notice these problems. As a young man, John Browne spent three months at Metro during the summer of 1955 to study psychiatric nursing. While he was there, Browne saw a variety of disturbing practices. He witnessed a doctor performing spinal taps without observing sterile techniques or even wearing gloves. He saw several patients who seemed to be getting better during those months, but whose pleas to their doctors fell on deaf ears. And he learned that patients sent to the closed wards were probably stuck there for life.[99]

Hardly a perfect place. Once admitted, Lugosi was under the care of Clinical Director John Mitchell, with his personal physician being Dr. Nicholas Langer, a fellow Hungarian. Later, Lugosi mentioned that Langer "remembered me when I was the big cheese of the National Theater in Budapest, something like John Barrymore."[100] Despite their shared heritage, Lugosi said that during his first days and weeks at Metro he believed Langer "was sadistic because he wouldn't give me any kind of medicine. He just put his foot down."[101]

As for Langer, years later he recalled Lugosi's recovery at the hospital. He found Lugosi initially unstable in their talks, reasoning that both stress and alcohol had played a major role in his lightning pains and subsequent addiction. Langer put Lugosi on a regimen of proper food and vitamins, with only a limited amount of Demerol and paraldehyde. During Lugosi's first days at the hospital, Langer said Lugosi went through a horrible experience, moaning that he just wanted to die or crying that he was insane.[102] More withdrawals, more pain.

During his first month, Lugosi stayed in the acute admitting ward, where he would have worn only hospital dress. Hospital staff shaved him each day using straight razors, because patients weren't allowed sharp objects. He also would have been bathed by hospital staff. That's how he first met John Browne:

> Mr. L. was one of my patients, and he seemed to enjoy talking to me. He was a soft-spoken elderly gentleman. He was almost shy. He talked to me about drugs.
>
> One day he said, "I received most of my drugs from my doctors. I have taken narcotics for many years. Drugs are expensive even when you get them by prescription at the druggist. It was only when I could not afford them that I suffered. Recently, when I was not able to afford drugs, the suffering became too much for me, and I had myself committed to this state hospital here in Norwalk."[103]

And of course Lugosi regaled Browne with stories of his stage successes in Europe, all of which in his opinion came to a resounding end with *Dracula*, and with horror films.

Horror films like *Bride of the Atom*, which was still awaiting the premiere that Tony McCoy promised. Ed Wood was able to get the Hollywood Paramount to book the film for a May 11 screening after *The End of the Affair* (1955) with Deborah Kerr.[104] Newspaper ads called it a "Major Studio Preview" and mentioned the "Bela Lugosi Testimonial Fund."[105] *Variety* added that any money raised would be handled by Price-Waterhouse.[106]

Before the screening, Wood also coordinated a "Testimonial Benefit" cocktail party at the Gardens Restaurant in faraway Burbank. The host was Dolores Fuller, and the speakers included Wood and Lugosi's son, Bela Jr. Dick Sheffield went as well, tossing what little money he had into a hat that Wood passed around. And newspapers announced that Maila "Vampira" Nurmi would appear with escort Paul Marco, who was also with actress Meg Randall.[107]

"There is a famous photograph of about ten of us and that was practically it [as far as attendance]," Vampira once remembered. "Nobody else showed." The most exciting news of the evening, she remembered, was the announcement of a $100 check from Frank Sinatra.[108] And as for the screening, Paul Marco remembered that Wood tried with no success to sell blocks of seats. Almost everyone seemed to turn him down, including Universal Studios.[109] The *Oakland Tribune* soon wrote "receipts were pitifully low."[110] No arc lights, and hardly any money.

In the small audience that night were Lugosi's friend Alex Gordon and attorney Sam Arkoff of American-International Pictures. The idea was to get Arkoff excited about *The Ghoul Goes West*. Gordon later recalled that he "did not react unfavorably to Eddie's effort, considering the budget problems."[111] But Arkoff had worries about getting involved in a film with Lugosi. Given his health problems, insurance on Lugosi "seemed impossible."[112] Rather than get Lugosi more work, all the publicity over his drug use might actually have made him less employable than ever before.

What did Wood tell the hospitalized Lugosi about all of this? Likely he didn't men-

Getting a kiss from student nurse Susie Michael as he leaves
Metropolitan on August 5, 1955.

tion Arkoff's worries, and likely he didn't mention the *Variety* review of *Bride of the Atom* that claimed, "Lugosi's histrionics are reduced to the ridiculous through over-direction."[113] Instead, he kept talking up *The Ghoul Goes West*, which he was hoping would costar Lugosi with cowboy Gene Autry.[114]

But in May, Lugosi's thoughts may have been on his immediate present as much as anything else. Sometime around the end of the month, Lugosi would have moved to another ward, which was likely decorated in cheerful colors and adorned with paintings created by inmates.[115] By that time, when Lugosi complained of pain, Langer allowed nurses to give him placebo tablets.[116]

In his new room, Lugosi would have been able to wear his own clothes, though not with a belt or shoe strings. He could have eaten in his room or in his ward's dining area. He could have played cards and checkers in his ward's day-room, or spent time anywhere on the hospital grounds. He could have socialized with Whittier College students that came to Metro on Wednesday evenings, or with Red Cross volunteers at twice-monthly parties.[117] He could have even left the grounds briefly with Red Cross volunteers who took patients on designated drives once a week.[118]

Whether or not he availed himself of any of these chances to socialize is unknown, but later he did talk about some of the patients he met: "I was incarcerated with these addicts who got their narcotics on the black market, you know, for $50 or $100 a day. They told me all about the details of these things."[119] But he wasn't just incarcerated with drug addicts. He also recalled that, "They have no money, no finances to make segregation between narcotic addicts and alcoholics, and [the] mentally ill. So all these categories are mixed up."[120]

Everyone mixed together. Doctor James Johnson, who spent time at Metro for clinical training, later recalled that much of the treatment during those years would have been custodial, with the "main goal of the staff to avoid a *Cuckoo's Nest* situation and violence. The best we could offer was regular group therapy."[121] His new ward might have been nicer in some ways, but he hardly got specialized treatment.

Lugosi could receive visitors, but it's hard to know whether many people came to visit him. Presumably people like Willi Szittja, Manly Hall, Béla Loosz, and Ed Wood dropped by.[122] At least one movie fan who had never previously met him went to Metro as well.[123] But Dick and his friends didn't. They were so taken aback by all that had happened. Proud of his efforts to get off of drugs, but unaware that he would have even been able to receive guests.

More than anything else, Lugosi likely spent a great deal of his time with books from the hospital's "well-stocked library" headed by volunteer Dorothy Haas. Along with their own holdings, they tried to cater to requests for various books, magazines, and newspapers.[124] John Browne once remembered that the patient's life was "boring," and so Lugosi might well have tried to indulge his love for reading. Aside from anything else, he was certainly reading and rereading the script to *The Ghoul Goes West*.

He read letter after letter that arrived for him at the hospital. They came from all over the US. From Egypt and from South Africa. From France and Turkey. Even from "behind the Iron Curtain." [125] One letter after another, and almost all of them from strangers. Lugosi even took a phone call from an Air Force Lieutenant stationed in Japan who told Lugosi how courageous he was.[126]

He also took pride in telling John Browne that he was getting mail from a woman he didn't know. She wished him well, and in at least one communication allegedly asked him to marry her.[127] The woman signed the letters "A Dash of Hope," and described how she had been a fan of his since the original release of the 1931 *Dracula*. On at least one occasion, she also spoke about the fact her own father had been a narcotics addict.[128] Lugosi later claimed that each day he "waited for her letter of encouragement. It was the only thing that sustained me."[129]

As July 1955 came to a close, Lugosi was reaching the end of the mandatory 90-day stay. Newspapers picked up on his story again when the hospital announced that a board of physicians would examine his situation. Journalists reported that he had gained twenty pounds, that he was feeling much better, and that he would likely be released.[130] That expectation was strong enough that before the examination a news reporter filmed footage of Lugosi outside of a hospital building shaking the hands of several nurses and doctors as if he was already released and saying goodbye. The footage shows him looking remarkably healthier than he had in April.

Wearing a short-sleeve shirt and holding his trademark cigar, Lugosi also spoke to the reporter, saying, "I became a new man, a new lease on life. I'm cured." Rather than simply construct a Q&A narrative out of his redemption, though, the reporter badgered him about the past, bringing up Lugosi's divorce from Lillian and his alcoholism, which Lugosi claimed to have kicked three years earlier. The reporter also expended a lot of effort talking about drugs on the black market, even though Lugosi made clear he always got what he needed from doctors.[131]

At his August 2, 1955 hearing, Lugosi found a more receptive audience than he had with the reporter, and he "passed with flying colors."[132] Dr. Langer told the press, "he has shown remarkable improvement physically, emotionally, and mentally," adding the caveat that "only time will tell if he is completely cured."[133] The news media circulated the story, a tale that Lugosi called the "greatest thing that ever happened" to him.[134] At the time of his release, when one reporter asked his age, Lugosi said with a "twinkle" that he was 63. "After all, Jack Benny is only 39."[135]

But he told John Browne something he didn't tell the press: "I am feeling much better now, but I can't leave until I get somebody to take responsibility for me. I'm broke."[136] The solution was that he would stay with Béla Loosz until getting a new apartment with the limited funds raised by the *Bride of the Atom* benefit.[137] Loosz was there to greet him on August 5 when he was released, and so was Lillian.[138]

As Lugosi left Metropolitan, he left a chapter in his life that he later called a "world of darkness."[139] It was the dawn of a new day. He was planning a comeback with *The Ghoul Goes West*, which was set to begin production on August 20.[140] He took the script with him when he left the hospital, telling one reporter, "I get to play an undertaker! That's turning the tables. Three months ago, some of my friends thought I was ready for one."[141]

And he took the letters from "Hope." The entire experience had taught Lugosi that he had many more friends than he ever knew. But Hope seemed somehow different than the others.

CHAPTER ELEVEN

Repeat Performance

Digging up a grave is no easy task, that's for sure. It requires a kind of grim determination combined with a lot of elbow grease. After all, excavating six feet of dirt is a slow, gruelling process, especially if there hasn't been any recent rainfall. But finally the shovel hits wood: that's the sound of success.

Dick was awfully proud of what he and a pal took home from the graveyard that night in 1955. He scrubbed it with bleach as hard as he could, and then polished the gold tooth still firmly lodged in its mouth. Pretty good looking, as far as unearthed skulls go.

By then, Dick and his buddies were in high school. He went to Hollywood High, Katzman attended Los Angeles High, and Mike enrolled at Fairfax. Instead of splintering the old Lugosi group, though, that just made things grow. Through Mike, Dick and Katzman met Bob Shomer and Jimmy Haines. And Dick introduced the others to his new Hollywood High pals Steve Buscaino, Carl Armstrong, and Tony Bass. Teenagers all.[1]

Of course, the new, post-war middle class had meant a new kind of US teenager. By the mid-fifties, they were 13 million strong: rebels without causes. James Dean led the way with rock and roll providing the background music. The average teen had a weekly income of $10.55, and he or she was spending it on everything from portable record players and afternoons at the malt shop to admission at drive-in theatres that were spreading across the country like wildfire.[2]

For Dick's ever-larger group of friends, that also meant continuing to explore the unknown, the bizarre. He and Katzman made gunpowder and went searching for fossilized shark's teeth. He and Mike caught live wrestling matches thanks to free tickets from Tor Johnson; that was in between investigating things like *The Ocean of Theosophy*.[3] And of course the whole group regularly watched *Criswell Predicts* on television, featuring LA's most famous psychic. By 1955, Criswell had become popular enough that Mae West even recorded a song about him.[4]

High school also meant driver's licenses. Hell on wheels. Getting in gear for wild trips, like the time they took off for Vegas, only to get thrown out of the Silver Slipper.[5] Or hot-rodding to football games dressed as mobsters with violin cases in hand.[6] Or dragging Hollywood Boulevard, tooling around in a Model T Ford that Dick was restoring.[7] Dick's growing interest in old automobiles meant that he became pals with Bob Figge, who had graduated from high school something like ten years earlier. He was an expert at scavenging around for rare antique cars.[8]

One evening Dick got smashed on some of his stepfather's Four Roses Whiskey before the group hit the road. His buddy Carleton Savell remembered:

> It was late and we were hungry, so we stopped for food. Dick was so drunk that he couldn't find his mouth, and so he ended up with ketchup all over his face from trying to eat French fries.
>
> Then we pulled up next to some girls on Hollywood Boulevard. We tried to pick up girls a lot, but this time he was so drunk that he blurted out "You want some Dickin? Because I'm Dick."[9]

Fun times. Crazy times. Even romantic times, like when Dick met his high school sweetheart Barbara Woods. "Siamese twins joined at the mouth," Katzman said.

Then there were the Hadians, who sported club jackets with a vampire logo.[10] It started as a small gang at Hollywood High, mainly Dick, Buscaino, Savell, and a few others. Over time the club grew, complete with a silly initiation ceremony. Hopeful candidates had to street bark tickets to the Hollywood Bowl made out of toilet paper squares.

Even more insane was the time when Dick threw one of LA's biggest teen parties. He schemed up the shindig just after his family moved to a three-story home on Manola Way. Katzman remembered:

> They passed out something like 750 invitations to anyone and everyone. They left some of them on car windshields in Hollywood. They invited the whole world. Well, that evening there were cars like you couldn't believe. At least a block in every direction, parked on both sides of the road. The rock and roll band that was supposed to play couldn't even get to the house. Things got really crazy, and eventually eleven squad cars showed up, with the police trying to get everyone to go home. Dick's stepfather was in a state of shock. It was a madhouse.[11]

Richard "Dick" Sheffield (left) and Norm Fist (right) with their hero, Bela Lugosi.

A madhouse featuring a special guest of honor: Dick's purloined skull was on special display that night.

But more than anything else, the cornerstone of Dick's interests remained Bela Lugosi. His life, his stories, and his films. After all, Dick's biggest high school row with his stepfather Lewis wasn't over girls or booze. No, it happened when Lewis tore Dick's Lugosi movie posters off of the ceiling; his collection had grown too big for the wall space in his room.

Of course Dick hadn't heard from Lugosi since March 1955, what with those months in the hospital. But he kept up with all the newspaper reports about Lugosi's drug use, his treatment, his release. And then there was the "Dash of Hope" that reporters described in August 1955. A Dash of Hope: she was the woman Lugosi had told John Browne about, the woman who wrote to him regularly at Metropolitan Hospital.

Once released, Lugosi decided that it was time to write her back. He didn't know her last name, or whether "Hope" was really even her first name. But he had the return address on the envelopes she used. So in early August, 1955 he finally sat down to type a letter from his new home, Béla Loosz's apartment. It read:

> My dear "Hope"
>   Received all your letters but was in no condition to reply – I just returned home, but I don't feel too "hot," yet....
>   I also received the share of your Christmas gift – and I thank you....Will you please give me a ring....[12]

Hope quickly phoned him, remembering years later that, when she called him for the first time, "he invited me over to see him. I think it was just a foregone conclusion [that we would marry]. He saw a sucker and I was it."[13]

But that remark speaks more out of the bitterness Hope developed in the months and years to come. In August 1955, she felt very differently, saying at the time:

> There was of course the fact I was a fan of [Lugosi's] while I was a little girl. But, then when he got in trouble I felt he was such a stray sheep. I think no one can ever accuse me of being a gold digger. [Lugosi] doesn't have a dime and no one but me wants him. If he doesn't want to work that is all right with me. I have a job. He needs help, and I think I can give it to him.[14]

As for Lugosi, well, he said he was "curious about [Hope's] angle," adding "I have no money, my youth is gone, and I am a sick man." So why would she really want to be with him?[15] But then he realized that they spoke the "same language," and that she had "sophistication and education."[16]

Who really was this woman who so quickly became the focus of Lugosi's life? Born in Johnstown, Pennsylvania in 1919, Hope Lininger lived through a difficult and challenging childhood. "A variety of stepfathers, no brothers, and I lived alone most

of the time," she said.[17] But then there was Lugosi. "He was so good-looking and spooky," Hope said of seeing Lugosi in *Dracula* (1931) when she was twelve years old. And she also thought that because Lugosi was the horror man, she wouldn't have as much competition for his affections from other girls her age. Bewitched, bothered, and bewildered.[18]

From that point forward, it seems as if Hope tried to get closer and closer to Lugosi.[19] She saw him in several stage performances, sitting in the same auditorium with the man who had enthralled her in 1931. Then she moved to California and went to work at RKO as a continuity writer. The relocation meant more opportunities to see Lugosi onstage, and it even meant the chance to see him on the set of RKO's *The Body Snatcher* (1945).[20]

And she had also corresponded with him. "I wrote fan letters, of course, and yes I kept the answers," Hope added. "He answered me."[21] By

Dick's friend David Katzman.

Dick and Norm Fist clowning around.

1955, though, Lugosi had either forgotten those old letters or had left them for someone else to answer on his behalf. He believed her first letters were those she mailed to Metropolitan, something that touched him all the more.[22]

When they finally met in person, Lugosi told her, "If I did not think that you would turn me down, I would propose." She encouraged him to give it a try, and then she quickly said "yes."[23] When they obtained their marriage license on August 24, 1955, Lugosi told the press, "Where there's life, there's Hope."[24] But of course Hope had aged three years in mere minutes. Lugosi encouraged her to claim that she was 39 on the marriage certificate, thinking the gulf of time that separated their ages would sound much wider if she listed her real age of 36.[25]

Lugosi's old friend Manly P. Hall agreed to have the wedding at his home; he would also perform the ceremony himself.[26] Everything was happening fast, so fast that Lugosi briefly had second thoughts. Hope remembered that it was her good friends:

> Pat and Jim [Delaney] that took him to the wedding. My good friend Pat was a big Irish woman, and she settled him right down [when Lugosi said he had changed his mind about marrying me]. Boy, he curled in his ears.
>
> She said Jim couldn't stop laughing...he thought it was the funniest thing [that Lugosi was trying to back out]. [Lugosi] was probably being coy, but maybe he did have a change of feeling. But with Pat, it was "No, no, no. Get dressed."

So he put on a blue double-breasted suit accented with a white carnation. Elsewhere, Hope dressed in a green and pink dress with a matching hat.[27]

When Lugosi arrived at Hall's home, he saw more of Hope's friends, ranging from police officer Afton Farnsworth to Phyllis and Dale Buffington, both of whom worked for RKO.[28] Outside of Manly Hall and Bela Jr., Lugosi invited few guests to the ceremony. Paul Marco recalled that he and Ed Wood were among the select group:

> Ed says, "Bela's going to get married. And we're invited." We were going, just the two of us. It was all quickly done. Los Feliz used to have all Japanese florists around. And I said, "Ed, we didn't buy a present or anything. Stop the car," I said. "I'm going to go up there and buy some flowers." I talked to them, and said I wanted something for a wedding, something big.
>
> "Open the door, open the door" [I said at Manly Hall's home]. I got in with all these flowers. And when we opened the door, [a lady there said] "Hey wonderful, all the flowers. We didn't have time to buy any." She put them in a big vase in front of the fireplace, the mantel. And they said this was just what they needed for an altar.[29]

Marco also noticed the extreme discrepancy between the small number of guests and the large group of photojournalists. "All around the room you could see cameras," he said. "There must have been fifty of them."[30]

And then, sometime after 8PM on August 24, camera bulbs flashed as Hall married the two against Marco's flowers and the backdrop of his own home. Chinese devil dog statues protected the wedding flora from both sides, with Asian tapestries and Egyptian relics decorating the rest of the room.[31] Bela Jr. was Lugosi's best man, and Pat Delaney was Hope's matron of honor. As the smell of incense filled the room, Hope and Lugosi spoke their vows. Hall prompted Lugosi through the ceremony; the actor's nervousness soon caused him to stumble through the line, "With all my worldly goods, I thee endow."[32]

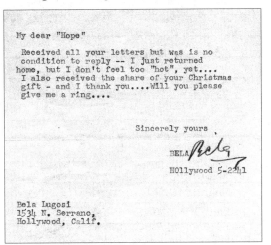

More cameras flashed as everyone applauded the newly-married couple. Then they cut the wedding cake and poured the champagne before heading to their new apartment on Harold Way for a reception.[33] Paul Marco remembered:

> So [Ed Wood and I] took Hope and Bela, taking them to their apartment. We stopped on Western Avenue at an Italian store with salami and everything. "We've gotta go in there," Lugosi said. He was happy, and everybody knew him when he came in. I want this and that, salami and provolone cheese and wine. Lots of kidding about the wedding and man talk. And we walked out with the biggest bag of everything. "This is on us," they said
>
> And we got back in the convertible. And we go about four or five blocks to their new apartment. They were just moving in. There must have been fifteen people there to greet him. So we made it in the door. And he said, "Just a minute." It was dark, really dark. One little lamp in the kitchen. And on the floor a big trunk [that he had used for many years when he travelled]. And Hope moved all the chairs around that trunk, and we all had an Italian feast around it. Nothing fancy, but, you know, it was nice.[34]

Marco also recalled that Lugosi was so very happy, acting "like he was 39 years old."[35]

There were still wedding gifts to receive and open, including a double chafing dish from Saks Fifth Avenue courtesy of Frank Sinatra. And even later, a short honeymoon. "Ed Wood drove us to Big Bear Lake," Hope recalled. "A wedding trip, something like that."[36]

Above: **Lugosi's letter to Hope Lininger from August 1955.** *(Courtesy of Dennis Phelps)*
Below: **Kissing Hope after obtaining their marriage license in Santa Monica.**

Lugosi and Hope are married by Manly P. Hall (right).

Dick gave the newlyweds a week or two before calling. He was eager to see Lugosi, to find out how he was doing. Hope answered the phone and quickly invited him and his pals to the apartment. Given the months that had gone by since they had last seen each other, Dick could scarcely have realized that he was about to become far closer to Lugosi than ever before, that he would start seeing Lugosi a few times a week.

Lugosi loved the whole gang, of course. He kidded Figge about how fast he talked, "like a machine gun."[37] He ate hamburgers outside of the Harold Way apartment with Buscanio.[38] He tried to convince Carl Armstrong to talk to Bela Jr. about the importance of education, changing the subject after learning Carl had dropped out of high school.[39] He let Shomer borrow his tuxedo and cape for a 1955 Halloween party; thanks to that, Shomer nabbed the first place award for his costume.[49] And of course Dick borrowed Lugosi's cape as well. As Katzman filmed home movies, Dick wore it while holding his infamous skull.[41]

When Lugosi was in a good mood, the Hadians got him out of his apartment. Along with Mike and Katzman, this meant Bob Shomer, Bob Figge, Carl Armstrong, and Jimmy Haines. At times it was as simple as visiting Dick or one of the others in their own homes. Mike remembered:

> I had a very neurotic cocker spaniel named Bucky. He devoured just about anyone who would come into the house. He was very mistrustful of people. There were only two people that I can remember that it was just the opposite. One was my music instructor. The other was Bela. Bucky would come over panting. Bela would give him a little push, and Bucky would roll on his back and want more.[42]

Charm enough to soothe the savage beast; Lugosi had a definite knack with animals.

Then there were times out on the town, like when Dick convinced Lugosi to go to Blum's Ice Cream Parlor in Beverly Hills. Lugosi wasn't a fan of ice cream, but he was in rare form as they enjoyed the night air and then the eyes of customers who instantly recognized him. One of them was TV sensation Danny Thomas, who shook Lugosi's hand while explaining how much he loved Lugosi's work. Lugosi happily signed an autograph for Thomas, unaware that he was a big name actor.[43]

And those meals at Lugosi's favorite Hungarian restaurant on Sunset. They went several times, the whole gang. Over and over the host escorted the group inside, asking Lugosi "Where do you want to sit?" And his response was always the same: "Where do I always sit? Front row center!"[44] Then Lugosi joked, he told stories, he drank red wine, and he smoked his cheap Italian cigars.

In a way, going to that restaurant tapped into Lugosi's past, his happier days. That was a thread that ran through many of Dick's trips with Lugosi. For example, Lugosi once took a notion to visit his old Hollywood homes with Hope, Dick, and Dick's mother Ruth. They went to his house on Westshire, and the earthquake-proof home

on Outpost Drove. And of course, he showed them his beloved house on Whipple in North Hollywood. Lugosi knocked on the door of each, charming the current homeowners and then giving tours for Dick and company. He even pointed out where he had fallen down a staircase drunk so many years before.[45]

Another trip down memory lane happened when Katzman drove Lugosi, Hope, Mike, and Dick to Lake Elsinore. It was where Lugosi and Lillian had bought a number of lots after the war. They travelled there so Lugosi could pick up some of his old things out of a home on one of the lots. Scrapbooks, some of which Lugosi gave to Dick. Katzman stayed in the car the whole time, watching a motorcyclist get stuck trying to cross a dry lakebed.[46] Inside, Hope felt pretty unhappy, meeting Lugosi's ex-father-in-law Stephen Arch, a man she immediately disliked.[47] Exploring Lugosi's past meant colliding with his ex-family.

Of course there were the movies, the kind

Above: **Lugosi and Hope with their marriage license.** *(Courtesy of Dennis Phelps)*
Below: **Lugosi and Hope's apartment on Harold Way.**

that Lugosi *used to make*. When Dick learned that the Carmel Museum Theatre was opening in November 1955 to screen old silent films, he arranged for Lugosi to get on the guest list. Dick had heard about the Carmel's owner, film collector Charles Tarbox, and he had once even played the old Wurlitzer still in the theater's auditorium.[48] So when the night came, Dick drove Lugosi and Hope to the gala opening, which was attended by the likes of Bert Wheeler, Groucho Marx, and Jack Oakie.[49]

It was one of the best evenings Dick ever shared with Lugosi, who was sober, charming, and in a wonderful mood. He introduced Dick to a variety of stars that night; he also helped Dick meet Mrs. Edward Van Sloan, wife of the man who had played Van Helsing in *Dracula* onstage and in the 1931 film. There was the prophet Criswell as Master of Ceremonies and Mack Sennett as the honored guest.[50] Lugosi even enjoyed watching the evening's film, *Tillie's Punctured Romance* (1914) with Charlie Chaplin and Mabel Normand.

That went over much better than the time when Dick, Mike, and Hope took Lugosi to see *Moby Dick* (1956) at the Hollywood's Pantages Theatre. "He was bored stiff," Hope remembered. "I don't think he really understood it."[51] Whatever it was, Dick and his group quickly learned that what Lugosi preferred was watching his own films.

Like the time when Mike Spencer rented a 16mm projector and a print of *Abbott and Costello Meet Frankenstein* (1948) for his sixteenth birthday party. Dick

Top: An advertisement for the RKO Hillstreet in the *Los Angeles Times* of January 7, 1956. Lugosi, Hope, Dick, Mike Spencer, and Bob Shomer attended the screening of *The Vanishing Body*.
Bottom: Bela Jr., Hope, Lugosi, and an unknown individual circa 1956.

and all the others were there for cake while Lugosi as Dracula lit up the screen. Bela Lugosi, himself, was their special guest. "He had never seen the film before," Mike remembered. "While it was running, he would occasionally make some funny remarks, including joking about how good looking he had been."[52]

Then, in January 1956, Dick, Mike, Shomer, and Hope took Lugosi to the RKO Hillstreet in downtown Los Angeles. A theatre was reviving a few of his old films, including *The Black Cat* (1934) under its reissue title *The Vanishing Body*.[53] Mike recalled:

We sat in the balcony that time, maybe because he was smoking cigars. He was sitting there with his long, lanky legs over the seat in front of him as his body slinked down in the chair. Again he said, "Goddammit, what a good looking bastard I was!" And then some kid a few rows away said, "Shut up!" Then this kid turned around and looks and saw it was Bela. And he was scared to death.[54]

An advertisement for the opening of the Carmel Museum Theatre as published in the *Los Angeles Times* on November 3, 1955.

Shomer added that Lugosi had to help calm the young man down a bit; after all, it isn't every day that a kid sees Dracula in the flesh.[55]

That same month, Dick and friends took Lugosi to see *Bride of the Atom*, now rechristened *Bride of the Monster*, at the RKO Pantages.[56] It was playing the bottom end of a double bill with *Ransom!* (1956) starring Glenn Ford and Donna Reed. Flashing their Bela Lugosi Fan Club cards and introducing the theatre manager to Lugosi, the group quickly got free tickets. Carl Armstrong remembered how amused they all were during intermission when a little child spotted the real Lugosi and started screaming "Mommy! Mommy! Look... *it's him*!"[57]

More often though, Lugosi stayed at home, and so Dick and his pals held a movie night at the Harold Way apartment. His old films, on late night TV. Lugosi regularly remarked on "what a good looking bastard" he had been, and gave other occasional commentary. Of one old actress, Lugosi joked with Bob Shomer, "She would have had a better career if she'd had a better brassiere."[58]

Movies and acting were Lugosi's life, of course, so it was no wonder he enjoyed taking a peek at some of his older work sitting around a faithful group of admirers. And of course he told them how hopeful he was to get back in front of the cameras; he didn't want his film career to be something that was purely past tense. So grabbing an old Kodak one day, Katzman shot a few minutes of home movies with Lugosi holding his cigar as he sat near Dick, Mike, and Hope.[59]

Lugosi loved those moments, smiling as each frame of footage clicked through the camera's gate. But what he really had in mind were feature films and an elusive comeback. That was where Dick and Mike tried to help out, writing a treatment for a story called *Repeat Performance*:

> Mr. Lugosi plays the part of a poor retired actor of horror films, whose wife has suddenly taken ill with a rare brain disease and desperately needs an operation which is financially beyond his reach.
>
> This impels him to visit four of his old producers who had long given up making horror films. He begs them to put him into a new horror film, but they each tell him that the trend for horror films is over and that the public wants bloodcurdling murders.
>
> Unable to have the operation, his wife dies. After weeks of suffering over his wife's death, he swears to get revenge, blaming the four producers for her death. He carefully plans the death of each and, one by one, he murders them in a gruesome manner similar to the way he was killed in many of his horror films.[60]

They showed it to Lugosi after Mike typed it up on an old Underwood. In some ways, it spoke to the way that Lugosi had been treated by the Hollywood system.

Lugosi enjoyed it quite a bit, later ringing Dick and Mike to have them stop by the apartment. "There is Lugosi sitting in this one chair, and this other guy sitting in another chair, and they were both drinking beer," Mike Spencer remembered. Lugosi told Mike, "This is Eddie Wood. Eddie would like to make [*Repeat Performance*] into a film." Mike said he would be delighted to give the story to Wood, free of charge. "No, no, he wants to buy it," Lugosi said. "He'll pay you a dollar."[61] One buck, just enough to make things legal.

Well, anything to get Lugosi back on the screen.

CHAPTER TWELVE

You Cannot Receive with a Tight Fist

B oth of Dick's hands were full when he carried his easel, oil paints, and canvas into the Lugosi apartment on Harold Way. Lugosi's life was trudging forward day by day, but Dick wanted to capture a single moment from it that could last forever.

It had actually been quite a few years since Lugosi sat for a portrait artist. He patiently kept still underneath one of his two Dracula capes as Dick made brush stroke after brush stroke. Later Dick finished the painting in Mike Spencer's back-yard under the tutelage of Mike's mother Ethel. Given that he used an old photograph as a model, the result looked closer to the Lugosi of the 1930s than of the 1950s. It recalled and preserved his entire history in the horror film.

Lugosi loved the painting, telling Dick it was his favorite of the many portraits that had been painted of him. But by the spring of 1956, he had other plans in mind for preserving his history. "A New York publisher is urging [Lugosi] to write his memoirs," columnist Jimmie Fidler wrote in March of that year.[1] He didn't need all that much urging, really. Just Dick by his side to help him get everything down on paper.[2]

This wasn't the first time Lugosi thought about penning an autobiography. When his career slowed down after World War II, Lugosi started to write a book about his experiences as an actor. He even told a journalist that he was jotting down stories in between shooting scenes for *Scared to Death* (1947).[3] But apparently he never got around to compiling the notes into book form.

Of course Lugosi had always worked hard at preserving his life through photographs. Scrapbook after scrapbook, along with a filing cabinet brimming with 8x10s. At times he told Dick and his friends stories of his past glory. Mike Spencer recalled:

> When we would hang out with him, he'd suddenly remember something about the making of one of his films. But he was quiet a lot of the time. When he did tell stories, he would turn to you slowly, and speak *so slowly*.[4]

But all of that was informal conversation. Now Lugosi wanted to get everything written down and published.

So day after day, night after night, Dick sat beside Lugosi in the spring of 1956, taking notes while he recalled the events of his life. Occasionally Lugosi would stop to drink some warm beer or to smoke one of his beloved "El Ropo-El Stinko" Italian cigars. Some of what he told Dick was probably riddled with half-truths and errors of omission. In the end, Lugosi may have been at his best when rewriting the past.

What could he have told Dick during those sessions? He might have claimed, as he had in years past, that he was a direct descendant of Hungarian nobility and that he was a graduate of Oxford.[5] Or perhaps at that late of an age he no longer felt the need to impress others with fictional tales of his family or of his education.

Perhaps he spoke about his birthplace of Lugos, Hungary, a beautiful town with a river flowing right through its heart. He was born there under the name Béla Ferenc Dezsö Blaskó on October 20, 1882 to István Blaskó and Paula Vojnits. Lugosi had three siblings, two brothers and a sister. That was in addition to his godparents Ferenc Bayer and Vilma Küszer; Bayer had once served as vice-mayor of Lugos.[6] And father István? Well, he was known as a wonderful baker, operating his own bakery on a little street that intersected with Kirschengasse.[7] Later he became a banker by virtue of his involvement with cooperative "Volksbank."[8]

At the time of Lugosi's birth, his parents lived at Number 6 Kirschengasse, which was right next to the Roman Catholic church that his family attended.[9] It was also on the Hungarian/German side of the river, with Romanians populating the other part of town. As a young child, Lugosi would have encountered people from all of those backgrounds, as well as some of the Serbians who lived in Lugos. That would have been particularly possible at the marketplace, where people from every background congregated. A mix of cultures, and also a mix of time periods. Peasants brought crops to the marketplace in the same way as they had for centuries, but on nearby streets stores sold the latest fashions in Viennese furniture.[10]

At an early age, Lugosi likely heard about Vlad the Impaler, Prince of Wallachia and the real Dracula of world history. What he heard would probably have been stories of Vlad's war victories. Living in what was the German side of Lugos, he may have even heard about Vlad's cruelty. Either way, he wouldn't have connected the Prince of Wallachia with vampires.[11]

Above: **Dick Sheffield's painting of Bela Lugosi.**
Below: **Lugosi in his Harold Way apartment circa 1956.**

But he did hear a great many ghost stories from "peasant maids who talked by the hour of … evil spirits and the undead."[12] The area surrounding Lugos was rife with tales of restless spirits. The dead walked, which caused those in the Banat region to perform ritual exhumations to help them rest in peace. Pre-Christian traditions still surviving, still in place, and likely discussed regularly at the town marketplace.[13]

Lugosi also had an early exposure to romance. He claimed he made his first money at age seven, looking after a young lady's little dog while she and her sweetheart necked on a park bench. *The Film Daily* later wrote, "All he remembers is that the dog seemed unusually strong and kept tugging at the leash and that the kisses were rather lengthy affairs."[14]

And then of course there was school. Lugosi's family paid for him to attend, but his only achievement academically seems to have been in music.[15] Why he bridled at formal education is unknown. Perhaps he was already interested in acting. Or perhaps his schoolwork was affected by an unhappy home life.

After clashes with his father, Lugosi left his hometown around 1894 or 1895, spending the next few years in towns like Resita working various jobs: a miner, a riveter, and a machinist's apprentice.[16] Then he found his widowed mother and sister in the town of Szabadka in 1897. That led to work on a railroad and a failed attempt to finish his education. And then–at long last–he became a part of the chorus for a local theatre production.[17]

His earliest recorded appearance came in Hatseg in 1902. It was a production of Herczeg's *Ocskay brigadéros*, in which he appeared under the name Béla Blaskó. By the next day, he appeared in the play *Házasodjunk* under the name "Béla Lugosi."[18] The new stage name, which literally means "originating from Lugos," tied him to the geography of his birthplace. But at the same time it shed his family name, signalling a new beginning. Years later, in 1917, he even applied for an official change of name from Blaskó, having settled on

Above: **Historic postcard shows the Blaskó home where Lugosi lived as a child, Number Six Kirschengasse, immediately left of the Roman Catholic church where he was baptized.**
Below: **A modern image of the Blaskó home beside the Roman Catholic church.** *(Courtesy of Petrina Calabalic)*

spelling his new name "Lugosi" rather than "Lugossi," "Lugosy" or "Lugossy."[19]

By late 1903, he joined an acting company in Temesvár, a beautiful city whose population dwarfed that of Lugos. It was there that Lugosi became a regularly working actor. He took to the stage in such plays as *Az ember trajédiája* (*The Tragedy of Man*), *Bánk bán*, *Bob herczeg*, and *Trilby*.[20] He even sang in seven performances of Wagner's *Tannhäuser*.[21] And then, when the season ended in 1904, he toured in the provinces of what is modern-day Romania and Hungary.

Perhaps Lugosi's first major triumph with audiences came when he spent 1908-1909 with a theatrical troupe in Debreczen. Out of the darkness of the provinces into the light of an important city. That meant working with such renowned Hungarian actors as Gyula Gal and Sandor Góth.[22] It meant Lugosi receiving top-billing—perhaps for the first time—in such roles as Armand Duval in Dumas's *Kaméliás hölgy*.[23] And it meant Lugosi taking on the lead role of Adam in *Az ember trajédiája*.[24] As he was leaving, Lugosi was awarded a plaque and a group of silk ribbons to commemorate his successes.[25]

But nothing could compare with Szeged. A center of education and the arts, the beautiful city was one of the most modern in Hungary, having been rebuilt after a flood in 1879. Lugosi became a key member of their repertory group for the 1910-1911 season. His debut performance came in a September 2, 1910 production of *Romeo and Juliet*. One critic claimed:

> The company has a new amorous hero actor with Bela Lugosy. As an introduction, what role could be more suitable than the role of the love-torn Romeo. The performance was put on stage with the old, dingy scenery and an even dingier director vision, showing everything but sense and thoughtfulness.[26]

Lugosi then went on to hone his talent in such favorite plays as *Az obsitos*, *Bilincsek*, *A sasfiok*, *Othello*, and *Richard III*.[27] He reappeared in plays from his Temesvár days like *Trilby and Bánk bán*. And he reprised his Debreczen role of Duval in *Kaméliás hölgy*.[28] The theatre gave him top-billing in

Above: An advertisement for the "Lugoser Volksbank" where Lugosi's father worked.
Below: Lugosi on the cover of Szeged's *Szinházi Ujság* for October 30, 1910.

Sárga liliom and even put his name above the title when he played Max in *Anatol*.[29] That was in addition to a repeat performance as Romeo on October 9, 1910.[30] Well over 100 performances in total.[31]

Certainly Lugosi was still perfecting his art. A local theatre publication claimed that in *Amihez minden asszony ért,* "His speech is still too rushed and unarticulated."[32] Much the same was said of his performance as Count Vronsky in *Anna Karenina*.[33] And yet they noticed his passion and his ability to connect with an audience. One theatre writer claimed:

> Bela Lugosy is a 20th century actor. He is human and in love when playing a man in love. He is wild and unbridled, and his heart nearly breaks when, as Romeo, sees his Juliet dying. His speech is sincere and when he says something common, the words do not remain in our ears. But when he presents the great conflicts of human life, he seizes the strings of our hearts and does not let go until they break.[34]

A different critic, noting his "obvious development," wrote quite prophetically "it is likely that the period of his more meaningful achievements is yet to come.[35]

Above: **Lugosi during his Szeged days.** *(Courtesy of Kristin Dewey) Below:* **Lugosi (right) in an unknown Budapest stage performance.** *(Courtesy of the Országos Széchényi Könyvtár)*

Above: Lugosi as Jesus Christ in a 1916 Passion play in Debreczen. *Below:* Lugosi (seated, with shoe) in a portrait from a Hungarian stage play. *(Courtesy of David Wentink)*

But whatever had come before and whatever would come later, Lugosi's time in Szeged must be seen as crucial. The audiences loved him. The women loved him. And Lugosi loved the stage, performing important roles in play after play. It was the bridge between the learning of stagecraft and the creating of important art.

It was also the bridge to Budapest. Even before the Szeged season ended, Lugosi had been offered work there. The Paris of the East beckoned. Sophistication and prestige in a city that thrived on café culture. Writers, artists, actors, and so many others practically lived in those cafes that had a ready supply of food, conversation, and about anything else a person might want.[36]

After appearing at the Hungarian Theatre and the Royal Theatre, Lugosi debuted at the famed Nemzeti Szinház (National Theatre). Play after play during 1913 and 1914 before he went into army service. After his discharge and a brief appearance as Jesus in a *Passion* play in Debreczen, Lugosi returned to the National Theatre from 1916 to early 1919.

That Lugosi was affiliated with the National Theatre for such a long period of time suggests he was among the best actors in Hungary. But an examination of his stageography reveals that he wasn't generally getting particularly large or important roles. To the degree he did, they came near the end of his tenure there, as when he played Tybalt in *Romeo and Juliet* or when he returned to his old role of Duval in *Kaméliás hölgy*.[37] When he later recalled his stage successes in Hungary, it seems he compacted time and place, mentioning the National Theatre while naming roles that he had in Szeged or even earlier.[38]

The fact he did play some very tiny roles on the Budapest stage was something he didn't always want to remember. At a party in the US, composer Gabriel Von

Wayditch saw Lugosi and reminded him of a play for which he conducted the orchestra and Lugosi appeared briefly as a supernumerary, carrying a spear. Lugosi allegedly refused to admit that it had happened, that he had played such a minor part, and forever severed their relationship.[39]

While still acting at the National Theatre, Lugosi began to work in the Hungarian film industry during 1917-1918. Was it an opportunity for larger parts than he received at the National Theatre? Or a way to increase his salary the year that he married? Perhaps both. At any rate, a survey of Lugosi's early filmography finds fascinating films like *Az ezredes* (1918) and *99* (1918), both being directed by Mihály Kertész (Michael Curtiz) for the Phönix company. *99* even teamed Lugosi with Gyula Gal, Mihály Várkonyi (Victor Varconi), and Lajos Réthey, who had played Svengali to Lugosi's Gecko fifteen years earlier in Temesvár.

But Lugosi's work for Alfréd Deésy at the Star company received much more attention at the time. Unlike Phönix, Star was a major studio whose facilities on the outskirts of Budapest were made up of some ten buildings.[40] Lugosi appeared in eight films and one short subject at Star, all of which billed him as Arisztid Olt. Again his choice of pseudonym played off of geography, as Olt is the name of a river that lies to the east of his hometown.

The idea was to make him sound less Hungarian, thus helping to sell Star films in other countries. But it isn't difficult to imagine that some viewers in Budapest and Szeged recognized him. Whatever his onscreen name, though, Hungarian critics responded well to Lugosi's film acting. One wrote that for *Tavaszi Vihar* (1917), he "presented the role of the husband artfully and with dramatic depth."[41] Another said of *Az élet királya* (1918), "The role of Lord Watton was played by Arisztid Olt with an artfulness of the highest quality."[42] From the beginning his face, his physique, and his acting style seemed to fit the cinema.

Above: Lugosi (left) wears a mask in Star's 1917 film *Álarcosbál* (*The Masked Ball*) as a man approaches from behind with a knife. *Below:* Another image of Lugosi in *Álarcosbál*.

Above: **Lugosi (right) as Chingachgook in *Lederstrumpf* (1920). (Courtesy of David Wentink)** *Below:* **Lugosi (right) as a gang leader in the German film *Nat Pinkerton im Kampf* (1920).**

But Lugosi fled Hungary in 1919, its peak year of silent film production; had he been able to remain, he may well have continued making movies there.[43] At any rate, he first landed in Vienna, where he found little or no work. With America already in his mind as a final destination, Lugosi moved on to Berlin. His Star films had been released in Germany, so some producers might have known his work.[44] And he already spoke German, probably dating back to his early life in Lugos.

The Berlin of 1919 must have fascinated Lugosi. It was the dawn of Weimar Republic; political philosophies clashed as inflation went out of control. The moral codes of the city burst at the seams, exposing all manner of depravity.[45] Sex was seemingly on display everywhere, including in a film industry that lived without censorship until May 1920.[46] And then of course there was *The Cabinet of Dr. Caligari* (1920) and Expressionist cinema, topics of conversation for everyone working in the movies.[47]

It's unknown whether Lugosi did any live theatre in Berlin, but he did find work at a number of film companies between 1919-1920. Collectively, the roles he had show a fair amount of diversity, ranging from a sheik to a gang leader to a professor. A butler in F.W. Murnau's *Schrecken*, an adaptation of *Dr. Jekyll and Mr. Hyde*. Even as the Native American Chingachgook in an adaptation of Cooper's *Leatherstocking* tales.

Equally diverse were the responses that critics gave him. *Film-Kurier* said of his work in *Hypnose* (1919), "Lugosi is a welcome new face and makes a strong impression. He definitely has talent, but he's got to avoid facial exaggeration."[48] *Lichtbild-Bühne* went even further while discussing his work in *Der Tanz auf dem Vulkan* (1920), saying "Lugosi shouldn't try such 'gymnastics' with his eyes. It is a pity when the artistic effect of a good film is compromised by the inadequacies of individual players."[49] By contrast, *Film-Kurier* believed he "excels in figure and makeup" for his role in *Wildtöter und Chingachgook*.[50]

Good reviews or bad, though, Lugosi left Berlin. Why he chose late 1920 as the moment to leave is difficult to understand. Perhaps he believed he had saved enough money. Perhaps he had increased fears over the value of the money in his possession, what with ongoing Weimar currency troubles. Or perhaps he decided to go after some love affair ended.

Unable to find much work in New York City after his arrival in the US, Lugosi began to mount a series of his own Hungarian-language productions.

Above: **Lugosi in the 1920 German film *Die Teufelsanbeter* (*The Devil Worshippers*)** *(Courtesy of David Wentink)*
Below: **Lugosi appears on the cover of the January 1, 1922 issue New York's *Szinházi Ujság*.**

For example, he was both director and star of *Törvény* and Molnár's *Liliom*, staging both in September 1921. Then came Bíró's *Sárga liliom* in January 1922. Of that performance, the *Szinhazi Ujság* wrote:

> The New York public wanted to enjoy Lugosi's art, and the most suitable way to make this possible was for him to have a play put on stage there.
>
> The joint committee of the associations has taken up the awesome task of presenting the play out of respect for the artist and has already contacted the Hungarians of Bridgeport, Trenton, Philadelphia and New Brunswick to organize a theatre performance presenting Lugosi's art at each of these locations. The cultural event of the New Year's performance will open a new period in the life of theatre performances of the Hungarian America.[51]

In the weeks that followed, Lugosi directed and starred in *Gettó* in February 1922, and then *A demarkacio szinmu* and *Az ember tragédiája* in April 1922.[52]

Lugosi's first opportunity to act in an English-language production came in *The Red Poppy*, a tale of romance in the Parisian underworld. Henry Baron staged the play in Greenwich Village during December 1922.[53] After it opened, Alexander Woollcott of the *New York Herald* wrote, "So much is effected by silent clutches, occasional tangos, and long panting stillness broken only by the thud of someone being knocked to the floor or the resounding impact of [a] loving fist on [a] loving jaw." As for Lugosi, Woollcott said, "He is indeed the most mysterious Spaniard we have ever encountered in the theatre."[54]

Not everyone felt the same, though. Percy Hammond at the *New York Tribune* wrote, "A tall, sallow, lugubrious and earnest person, with luscious eyes and an accent, he strove last night to please. But we thought him least likely of all the other criminals present to inspire desperate behavior in this or any other naughty princess."[55] Kenneth MacGowan at the *New York Globe* added, "His figure is admirable, but his voice seemed rather empty last night."[56]

His entry into English-speaking theatre wasn't a complete break with the past, of course. Lugosi became involved in at least one German-language play at Columbia University's German Club, Georg Kaiser's *Die Sorina*.[57] In November 1923, the press announced that Lugosi would be a German-language "coach," but by the time it opened he had become its director.[58] The actors were culled from Barnard College and the Columbia University School of Journalism. Three evening performances and a matinee. And after the Friday night show, a dance featuring the Erwin K. Guttman orchestra.[59]

Even as late as 1925, Lugosi continued to be involved in Hungarian-language stage shows. He directed and starred in a New York version of *Forradalmi nász* in

Above: **Lugosi as Fernando in** *The Red Poppy* **(1922).** *(Courtesy of David Wentink)*
Left: **Portrait of Lugosi by Goldberg as published in** *Theatre Magazine* **of May 1923.**

Lugosi in a 1920s stage play. *(Courtesy of David Wentink)*

February of that year.[60] A few months later, Lugosi appeared in *Ady-est*, an evening of Hungarian poetry readings.[61]

That was all in addition to his staying heavily involved with the Hungarian community of New York. Likely he met his Hungarian friend Duci de Kerekjarto in this period; Kerekjarto was performing violin concerts in New York in the early twenties.[62] And Lugosi certainly relied on his own name to establish some financial credit. In 1924, the Feszek Club even filed a mechanics' lien against him for the $142.70 he owed them.[63] He also frequented Hungarian establishments in the city. A reporter for the *New York Herald Tribune* wrote:

When Mr. Lugosi came from his dressing room [during the production of *Arabesque*], he said he hadn't eaten or slept for forty-eight hours, so we drove across town with him to a Hungarian restaurant on Eighty-second Street and Second Avenue, where they have noodles and chicken paprika, and a gypsy band, and thus may one minister to his spiritual and physical needs at the same time.[64]

The journalist added that Lugosi, despite his stage persona, "looks [offstage] like a prosperous banker or the president of a railroad."[65]

For his Broadway debut, Lugosi was an Arabian sheik in *Arabesque* (1925).[66] That same year, he was the Russian admirer of a married woman in *Open House*.[67] And then he was a bandit in *The Devil in the Cheese* in 1926.[68] These three Broadway plays built on the image he began in *The Red Poppy*. Always a foreigner, oscillating between lover or villain or both. To be sure, he had done the same as a "sleek Don Juanish [Spanish] butler" in a Chicago production of *The Werewolf* in 1924.[69]

And he quickly made his way into a handful of film productions, generally playing heavies. A foreign spy who wants to blow up the Panama Canal in *The Silent Command* (1923); "A new screen villain and a convincing one," *The Film Daily* declared.[70] A Frenchman in *The Rejected Woman*.[71] A philanderer in *The Midnight Girl* (1925); the *Moving Picture World* dubbed it an "exceptionally satisfactory performance."[72] A Russian spy in *Daughters Who Pay* (1925).[73] Even for his tiny part in *The Veiled Woman* (1928), Lugosi was a "menace" to women.[74]

Above: **He Who Gets Slapped** (1924) with Lon Chaney Sr. (center). This is one of two photos that Dick Sheffield saw inside one of Lugosi's personal scrapbooks. Could the clown on the left be Lugosi? *Below:* Lugosi and Lia Tora in *The Veiled Woman* (1928).

Perhaps the only exceptions were two roles as clowns. One came in the short film *Punchinello* (1926) with Duncan Renaldo, and the other might have been in the feature film *He Who Gets Slapped* (1924) with Lon Chaney Sr. While combing through one of Lugosi's own scrapbooks, Dick came across two separate photos from the film that showed Lugosi in clown makeup; one of them even had Lugosi standing next to Chaney Sr. If he was in the film, it would represent the first

Lugosi as Dracula in the 1940s, after years of playing the vampire. Location unknown.
(Courtesy of David Wentink)

footage of him shot in Hollywood.[75]

Another milestone came in *Prisoners* (1929), a First National feature based on the novel by Hungarian writer Ferenc Molnar. It was the first time Lugosi's face and voice were united onscreen.[76] The movie was actually a hybrid production containing mostly silent scenes combined with some synchronized dialogue at the story's climax.[77] After that came Tod Browning's "ALL-TALKING MYSTERY THRILLER," *The Thirteenth Chair* (1929) at MGM.

Firmly ensconced in the sound era, Lugosi then appeared in the "Fox Six," a half-dozen fascinating movies produced by the Fox Film Corporation. Their storylines gave him a much wider variety of roles than he had gotten from the English-speaking stage or from his US silent films. And they represented Lugosi's final chance to establish a persona in Hollywood that wasn't dependent on horror.

For example, he was a kind and sympathetic plastic surgeon in the drama *Such Men Are Dangerous* (1930). A shady nightclub owner in *Wild Company* (1930), a tale of reckless youth. A colorful, womanizing marabout in the French Foreign Legion story of *Renegades* (1930). An enthusiastic opera impresario in *Oh, for a Man* (1930). And then Prince Hassan of the Mediterranean, who jealously guards his harem in the comedy *Women of All Nations* (1931).

The final film in this group was another French Foreign Legion story, *The Devil's in Love*. Produced in 1933, it is chronologically an outlier from the others to be sure. But it fits neatly with the core group not just because it was made by Fox, but because it gave Lugosi another small, nonhorror role. Unlike the other five films, Lugosi didn't even receive billing in *The Devil's in Love*. But it may well be his best acting of the six, as he gives a vigorous performance as a military prosecutor in a tense, well-edited trial scene marked by some very moody lighting.

Above: Hypnotizing Van Helsing (Maury Hill) in a July 1948 summer stock version of *Dracula* in Reading, Pennsylvania. *Below:* Advertisement for Lugosi's July 1950 production of *Dracula* in Burlington, Vermont.

In the end, though, the Fox films couldn't overpower *Dracula*. First there was the stage play. In 1927 and 1928 and 1929 and 1930. So many performances, beginning in New Haven and then onto Broadway and then the West Coast. Again he was a foreigner, a heavy, and a lover. In those ways, the character was similar to Lugosi's previous New York stage roles. But in other ways, *Dracula* was unique.

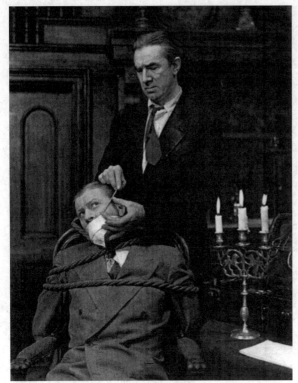

Above: **Lugosi as Jonathan Brewster and Jack Whiting as Mortimer Brewster in a 1944 roadshow version of** *Arsenic and Old Lace.*
Below: **Relaxing on the beach, possibly during the Hawaii shoot of** *The Black Camel* **(1931).**

While starring in an Oakland, California version of the show in 1930, Lugosi claimed:

> It is a peculiar role in many respects. When you see the play, Dracula seems to be constantly on the stage. A casual glance would indicate that he speaks as many lines as Hamlet. Yet, as a matter of fact, the number of "sides" is small.
>
> But if Dracula is not particularly chatty, he presents other difficulties. I find that it requires time and meditation to catch the mood of the character; each performance must be approached with some care.[78]

Backstage, of course, his meditation had to contend with all kinds of noise. After all, when they weren't performing, other members of the cast had to supply the sounds of howling wolves.[79]

Even with the character's peculiarities, perhaps Lugosi saw in Dracula something of Fernando from *The Red Poppy*. A kind of animal-like passion. He did speak at length to one reporter about what he called "Dracula Kiss," the "kiss of the villains."[80] Sensual, but still evil. After starring in the 1931 film version of *Dracula*, Lugosi claimed:

> Women wrote me letters. Ah, what letters women wrote me! Young girls. Women from seventeen to thirty. Letters of a horrible hunger. Asking me if I cared only for maidens' blood. Asking me if I had done the play because I was in reality that sort of Thing. And through these letters, couched in terms of shuddering, transparent fear, there ran the hideous note of—hope. They hoped that I was Dracula. They hoped that my love was the love of Dracula.[81]

The love of Dracula. The Dracula Kiss. After all, even Universal publicity tagged the film version as "The Story of the Strangest Passion the World Has Ever Known."

Lugosi's fan mail from women included Margaret Sylvester of Denver, Colorado, who mailed him a letter adorned with her own artwork of him:

> Keep up your good work, and remember, if you hold feminine hearts, treat the ladies rough. They enjoy it, so do we. Of course, I mean for you to act cavemanish only during the filming of your pictures.

> I wonder if you have ever been in the embarrassing situation of having a perfectly unknown young lady throw her arms about your neck and sob praises down in the region of your collar. This may remain unanswered as the answer would probably be as embarrassing as the question, if not more so.

She ended the letter by suggesting that the first crowds to see his next film would be "fortunate indeed."[82]

Another female Lugosi fan shared her praise with the *Chicago Daily Tribune* in the summer of 1932:

> With the exception of one, I haven't missed one of Lugosi's pictures, and can say by now that he is the "finishing touch" to mystery plays. But why always make a villain of him? Why not a hero? It is not pleasant seeing his plays usually end in death for him–a stake through his heart or killed by a gorilla!
>
> Am hoping to see him in a romance soon where the audience is for him, wishing him victory, instead of against him, wishing him–death.[83]

This was the kind of letter that Lugosi would have particularly enjoyed. A female fan who loved him in *Dracula*, but who yearned to see him in other kinds of roles.

Of course letters weren't the only things that the post office delivered to Lugosi's home. In 1935, a woman sent Lugosi a dozen pieces of jewelry, allegedly as an advance payment for him to help her find a husband. Presumably she had Lugosi himself in mind. But when Lugosi took the diamonds to an expert, he quickly learned that they were made of glass.[84]

Ever picturing himself as a romantic figure, Lugosi did help spark a love affair between Hollywood actors Dennis O'Keefe and Steffi Duna. O'Keefe wanted to reach Duna's heart by sending her romantic telegrams in Hungarian; Lugosi provided the translations from English, which then baffled the local telegraphers.[85]

To the bulk of the world, though, Lugosi's Dracula became known not for his kiss, but for his bite. For example, publicity man Andrew J. Sharick once recalled the hard work that went into promoting *Dracula* when it opened in Cleveland in 1931:

Above: **Publicity portrait of Lugosi from the 1930s.**
Below: **Lugosi (far right, back row) at an unknown social gathering from the early thirties.**

We sold that picture with all the horror we could put on it. We had an ambulance in front of the theatre. We had the house full of girls in hospital uniforms, and signs saying: "See the Doctor–Nurses in Attendance." In the papers we ran ads made to look like tombstones, daring people to see the picture and warning those with weak hearts to see their doctors first. We hired women to faint. The funny thing was, we got as many real ones as plants. People lined up in the lobby could see the limp bodies of the patrons being carried out. Pretty soon they were fainting themselves.[86]

All the horror that could be put on it. Audience members fainting, not swooning. And so Lugosi became a horror star, the first real horror movie star of the talkie era. From there, Dick already knew most of what happened.

Particular horror movies? A lot of them Lugosi didn't even recall. The title role in *Dracula* (1931) was his favorite, followed by Ygor in *Son of Frankenstein* (1939). *Black Friday* (1940) was another one that he remembered. That was the one where the studio and press claimed he had been hypnotized. Of course, he hadn't been. Not at all.

It was true that Universal had a real nurse on hand.[87] But the hypnotist was Lugosi's longtime friend Manly P. Hall, and so they faked the hypnotism for the sake of the studio's cameras. Among his other pursuits, Hall had been the founder of the Philosophical Research Society, lecturing for years on the occult.[88] Shortly after *Black Friday*, the press reported that Hall had arranged for Lugosi to speak at an astrologers' convention in San Francisco; Lugosi allegedly ended up declining because the stars weren't right for him to travel.[89]

Were stories like that one true? Probably not, but they fed into Lugosi's unbreakable link with horror. In 1939, for example, a journalist claimed, "Bela Lugosi is building a little theatre [in his basement] patterned after Paris' Grand Guignol. Only Bela is going them one better. He is having trick seats and other startling gadgets installed where the audience sits."[90]

Another news story alleged that a press agent installed a "ghostly sound machine" in the hills behind Lugosi's home. The idea was to "build up Lugosi's reputation as a monster." Wailing in the darkness of night, the siren scared the

Above: Lugosi with wife Lillian (right) and secretary Valeria Miller (left) at court during the trial of Mano Glucksman.
Below: Lugosi (center) at a masquerade party in the 1930s.

neighborhood, but sent a restless Lugosi packing to a hotel.[91]

"People approach me somewhat fearfully," he admitted in 1944. "Girls running elevators have been known to stay home when I visited certain towns."[92] And then there was the time that a tourist noticeably pulled her children close to her side when she spotted Lugosi at the Hollywood Roosevelt.[93]

Of course, that wasn't always the case, though. Quite a few children loved Lugosi, and not always because of his horror films. Walter Winchell once spotted Lugosi buying an ice cream cone for a little girl who dropped one she already had. Tears quickly turned into dimples and a bright smile.[94] Hardly the actions of a real-life Dracula.

But to keep working, Lugosi at times embraced the vampire image, even to the degree of becoming protective of his famous capes. For a 1948 produc-

Receiving a 1936 plaque commemorating his honorary presidency of the Los Angeles Soccer League.

tion of *Dracula* in Reading, Pennsylvania, he spoke to George Snell of the Green Hills Theatre. Snell remembered him saying:

> "George, the cape I wear is very sentimental to me since it is the original I wore in the motion picture and ever since. Not to demean your theatre security, but it would be a tragedy if something happened to it during the night. I would greatly appreciate it if you could take it to your home in West Reading each night, and, of course, return it for the next performance."
>
> My response without hesitancy, "It would be a pleasure and no trouble at all."
>
> So after the opening night's performance concluded when we all departed the theatre and went our way, I arrived at my garage (about a city block away from my home) and removed the cape from the car and a question arose. How to treat this huge cape without getting it wrinkled? Aha! Wear it on my shoulders. One problem: Bela was over 6 feet tall, and I was 5'8 and a half. So, I hiked the bottom up so it wouldn't drag the sidewalk, and walked up the street. Since it was after midnight and our upper crust neighbors were in bed, no one observed this strange spectacle.[95]

That same week, Lugosi kissed Snell's wife Dottie on the cheek. "Gee, thanks Bela for not drawing blood," Snell quipped, causing Lugosi to laugh out loud.[96]

Even though Lugosi knew that his livelihood was dependent on "drawing blood," he never really understood the intricacies of the Hollywood studio system. For example, at the height of his fame in 1931, Lugosi made a successful screen test for a film project that was never made. Studio executives applauded his acting in the test, but then mystified Lugosi by asking if he would read the same lines again in the same way while wearing a different colored suit. He didn't understand why that would make any difference, and their request left him somewhat bewildered.[97]

What else could Lugosi and Dick talk about for the book? Well, there was his personal life during the California years. In a 1932 interview, he had claimed to be a "lone wolf," shunning the social scene in Hollywood.[98] That was generally true, that he didn't go in for Hollywood parties. But it wasn't that he avoided all contact with other movie stars.

For example, he did attend a 1931 reception along with more than 200 guests that ranged from Constance Bennett and Mary Astor to Gus Arnheim and Roland Young.[99] In 1932, he went to a gathering held by a group of Russians that included Michael Visaroff, an actor who appeared in *Dracula* (1931) and *Mark of the Vampire* (1935).[100] In 1936, he made it to a party for Carl Laemmle that was also attended by Buster Crabbe, Buck Jones, Irving Thalberg, and many others.[101] In 1940, he appeared at the opening of The Hurricane, an "aloha"-style nightclub; Betty Grable, Harry Richman, and Milton Berle were also there.[102] And in 1941, he and Lillian attended a reception whose other guests included Suzanne Kaaren and Sidney Blackmer.[103]

All of that aside, though, he spent much more time with his friends in the Hungarian community of Los Angeles. Pianist Ervin Nyiregyházi, writer Melchior Lengyel, violinist Duci de Kerekjarto, and others, sometimes at Lugosi's own home for long evenings of conversation and music and Hungarian food.[104] So many important Hungarian figures visited him as well, from director Michael Curtiz to composer Béla Bartók. That was in addition to dining out; in his heyday, he once left a $200 tip at a restaurant in Hollywood.[105]

Above: An image from the loose adaptation of Lugosi's life story in *Shock SuspenStories*. From their Oct.-Nov. 1954 issue.
Below: Lugosi at the Harold Way apartment in 1956 with two unknown interviewers. Could these be the men who took Dick Sheffield's notes with the intention of finishing Lugosi's autobiography?

And then there were different Hungarian events and causes. In 1932, Lugosi participated in an international broadcast linking the Americas, Europe, and Japan as part of a celebration for the Olympic Games; he spoke in Hungarian on the widely-publicized program.[106] Seven years later, he officially opened the Press Day Festival of Southern California Hungarians.[107] And then in 1947, he acted in *Continental Varieties,* a live benefit in New York that tried to raise money for "needy Budapest actors and artists."[108]

He also became very friendly with Hungarian athletes in California. For example, Lugosi put up the guarantee for Sándor Szabo when he fought Vincent Lopez in a major Olympic-style wrestling match in 1935.[109] More notably, he organized and managed a Hungarian soccer team near the beginning of 1935; by October of the same year, Lugosi was President of a Los Angeles soccer league made up of eight teams.[110] And the "Bela Lugosi Cup" continued to be offered through at least 1943.[111] He even sponsored a "Bela Lugosi Junior Cup" and a team of Magyar youngsters.[112]

Fellow countrymen meant a great deal to him. All of his friends did. That was why Lugosi was particularly sad, for example, when an old pal of his named Mano Glucksman forged Lugosi's signature on a check for 100 pounds at a British bank. Lugosi and Lillian had to testify in court against Glucksman, with Lugosi bemoaning the fact that "If he wanted money, I would have lent it to him."[113]

With one of his beloved dogs in the 1930s.

Along with his many friends, there were also Lugosi's beloved dogs. In 1931, he had a Great Dane named Goulash.[114] Then a prize-winning German Shepherd name Bodri; that was the one that somebody tried to poison with strychnine in 1935.[115] Bodri, along with Kadves and Hectorn, was caught up in more trouble in 1938. Lugosi didn't have licenses for the trio, and one of them jumped over his fence and attacked Spanky McFarland's father. A neighborhood petition circulated to have the dogs destroyed, something Lugosi avoided by obtaining the proper licenses and increasing the height of his fence.[116]

He had six Malamutes in the late thirties that he really loved. When times were tough, Lugosi grudgingly decided to sell them. He just couldn't afford the amount of food they ate each day. But only three hours after signing a Universal Studios contract for *Son of Frankenstein* (1939), Lugosi had bought them back at a premium price.[117]

What else? Well, Lugosi enjoyed gardening during his peak of stardom; once he even grew a particularly rare and special variety of dahlia.[118] He became very interested in sculpting in the 1930s.[119] He collected stamps in the 1940s.[120] He used to enjoy gooseberries and milk in the morning, as well as drenching breakfast foods in honey.[121] And he loved old Hungarian proverbs, his favorite being "You cannot receive with a tight fist."[122]

Other thoughts? Lugosi thought he was the "world's biggest ham," quickly adding that Dick was the second biggest.[123] More than anything else, he was surprised a bit by how things had turned out. That his career had featured so many ups and downs. Thinking about so many of those old memories made his eyes well with tears. As Adam in Madách's *The Tragedy of Man* proclaims:

> Oh, why did I not perish on the heights,
> Where I was conscious of my strength and soul,
> Instead of being forced to listen here
> To my own epitaph.

His own epitaph. Strange to think, but some two thirds of his life were over by the time that he became known for horror. After that, he'd hardly be known for anything else.

After just a few weeks, Lugosi called Dick, asking him to rush over with all the notes about his life and career. Two writers were at the apartment, promising to use them as the basis for a book. The duo parted with handshakes and smiles and promises. But in the end they never wrote anything and never returned the notes.[124]

Instead of a book, the most notable Lugosi biography in the 1950s was likely a fictionalized story in *Shock SuspenStories*, an EC comic of the type that caused such a furor with moral groups. In it, a fictional horror movie star named Bela Kardiff appears at a testimonial dinner given by the key players in his career: an agent, a cameraman, and some studio personnel. As they eat, he recounts the story of his career in Hollywood:

> "After *Dracula* opened, my name became synonymous with horror and
> mayhem and death. ... Oh, I don't deny that I was financially rewarded for
> this self-degradation. [But eventually] the public was tired of horror pic-
> tures. I was a has-been... a faded star. The era was over.
> I slipped down... down. I slept in cheap hotels. I ate in cheap restaurants.[125]

As he reaches the end of his tale, Bela Kardiff admits that–since he could never escape the horror stereotype—he has decided to accept it. And so he put strychnine in all their champagne glasses, which quickly kills everyone else at the table.

CHAPTER THIRTEEN

Going It Alone

Near the beginning of September 1955, Dick Sheffield tagged along with Lugosi when he wanted to buy a new walking stick. Lugosi had aches and pains, but he didn't need a cane to walk. It was really to help him look elegant for a trip to New York later that same month. A US Senate Subcommittee wanted to hear what Lugosi had to say about narcotics abuse and illegal drug trafficking in the US.[1]

Senator Price Daniel of Texas was chair of the committee, which interviewed scores of doctors, law enforcement agents, and former drug addicts. He was distressed at the growing number of US addicts and hoped to find a way to eliminate illegal drug sales by increasing penalties for drug pushers. Daniel even recommended the death penalty for smugglers and dealers "who commit murder on the installment plan."[2]

It was Daniel who asked Lugosi to appear before the committee, telling the actor:

> I do not believe there is another American who can so dramatically present the dangers of narcotic drugs. I believe your testimony would cause scores of other addicts to seek treatment and also would re-emphasize to the medical profession the great responsibility it has in administering narcotic drugs.[3]

The latter point was presumably what Daniel wanted Lugosi to address, since Lugosi had always made clear that he never bought drugs on the black market.

Hearings in New York and Washington had to go on without Lugosi, though. In the end, he wasn't really up to making the cross-country journey; there was also the fact he couldn't legally leave California while still under the jurisdiction of a state hospital.[4] So Daniel continued gathering testimony from a number of other witnesses, including a dope peddler who was arrested immediately after being dismissed by his committee.[5] In October, though, Daniel decided to hold more hearings in California, largely because the state ranked first in drug-related arrests.[6] And that meant he rescheduled Lugosi to testify the following month.[7]

Along with talking about his career and how he started using drugs, Lugosi told the committee that he beat his addiction with "God's help," believing that mandatory treatment for addicts should focus on "the spiritual" as well as the medical. But he spent even more time worrying about the youth of America, so susceptible to drug peddlers:

Lugosi and the walking stick he bought to take to the Price Daniel hearing. *(Courtesy of Dennis Phelps)*

They have to realize the danger of being approached by people who for money want to sell, regardless of whether they use it or not, just to make a business, sell them marihuana, heroin, or morphine or opium or whatever, because they are selfish people, greedy people, who want nothing else but money, and they tell them the most wonderful fairy tales and stories about how wonderful they are going to feel. So they should be prepared for all these, whether they come dressed as angels, knowing that they are the real devils; they are the most dangerous people in the world. They are the murderers of our civilization and of our country.[8]

That final comment equating drug peddlers and murderers was quickly reprinted in newspapers across the country.[9]

Later, Lugosi would say that he started a "one-man crusade to induce young addicts to submit to treatment. I preach one message: Addiction is filled with misery and torture. Only through work and faith can you achieve lasting satisfaction and self-fulfillment in life."[10] Was his limited "crusade" waged for publicity purposes? Perhaps in part, but at the same time there isn't any reason to doubt Lugosi's sincerity or dedication.

As part of his campaign, Lugosi appeared on at least two television programs to discuss his personal battle with drugs. Bob Burns remembered one that was broadcast over KNXT, either in late 1955 or early 1956:

It was an evening show, as I recall, and it was live. KNXT was where I was working at the time; I was in the mail department. The makeup man, Grant Wilson, said to me "Bela Lugosi's comin' in tonight," and I said "What?" He said, "Yeah. You might wanna stick around."

So I sat in there [backstage]. Grant didn't put much makeup on him, just kinda powdered him down more than anything else. And I got to talk to him for about twenty minutes while he was being made up. Oh, he looked like death warmed over. He was so thin, but his mood was very bright.

They brought Bela out and they said, "Tell us your story of what happened." And he kinda teared up a little bit; he got pretty emotional. They treated him really nice.[11]

The program's gimmick was to interview only those people who had overcome some horrible problem in life, awarding every one of them a trophy.

Lugosi also appeared on the *Tom Duggan Show* to discuss his battle with drugs sometime during the spring or summer of 1956, but the outcome was

Above: **Lugosi with Senator Price Daniel.**
Below: **Lugosi at the Senate Subcommittee hearing in November 1955.** *(Courtesy of Dennis Phelps)*

very different than the show Bob Burns saw.[12] KTLA in Los Angeles had just given Duggan an hour-long program that year thanks to the notoriety of his controversial broadcasts in Chicago. The LA program was a nightly talk show; Duggan interviewed guests as his sidekick Judith Jones took phone-in questions.[13]

Ed Wood watched Lugosi's appearance, remembering that Duggan "couldn't have cared less" about Lugosi's sincere story of rehabilitation; instead he wanted to sensationalize the horrors of the abuse.[14] Of course, Duggan's flair for controversy inadvertently extended to his own life. Near the time Lugosi was on his show, Duggan's wife showed up at Judith Jones's apartment with a revolver. She fired a bullet into the lock of the door, believing her husband was inside having an affair. That led to her arrest and a firestorm of publicity.[15]

Lugosi's own TV interviews were in addition to *Out of the Darkness*, a CBS documentary film on the Metropolitan Hospital. Shortly after Lugosi's discharge, Albert Wasserman and a camera crew spent over three months covering the life of Metropolitan's patients. The result, complete with narration by Orson Welles, aired in March 1956.[16] Whether or not Lugosi watched the broadcast is unknown; certainly he had seen it all in real life.

Television wasn't the only forum for a discussion of narcotics, of course. In 1955, Frank Sinatra starred in Otto Preminger's film *The Man with the Golden Arm*, playing a card dealer who gets hooked on hard drugs.[17] He signed to do the role while Lugosi was still at Metropolitan, which may have been one reason he had sent Lugosi and Hope a wedding gift.[18] Dick, Mike, and Katzman convinced Lugosi to see the movie, and even persuaded the theatre manager to give him a free ticket.[19] With tears in his eyes, Lugosi later told a reporter:

> The movie made it so easy for the dope victim to get out of it. The youth of this country did not get the impression of what a terrible thing it is. Oh, if only the young people could see me [and learn my story], the result–![20]

Lugosi repeatedly expressed surprise to Dick and Mike that no producer had wanted to bring his tale of drug abuse to the screen.[21]

In *The Man with the Golden Arm*,

Above: Advertisement from the *Los Angeles Times* of December 27, 1955. *Below:* Lugosi with the award he was given on a KNXT television program.

Sinatra's character kicks his drug addiction, but later falls back into the habit. "They say that narcotics addicts never really overcome the habit, that sooner or later they succumb to temptation," Lugosi once said. "That's not true. I am proof of the fact that it is not true... Not once since I left the hospital have I had that awful craving for narcotics."[22] And this truly seems to have been the case, that his time at Metropolitan really did cure him. That chapter in his life really had ended in 1955.

But so many of his other old problems churned onward. Politics, for example. With his habit of regularly reading so many newspapers, he had to have been aware of Communism in Hungary in 1955 and 1956.[23] More important, though, was his own past involvement in politics, which Lugosi continued to suppress. At the Senate subcommittee hearing, for example, he lied to Senator Daniel, claiming that he "left Hungary when Communism came... I didn't like the idea."[24]

Rewriting history was easier than dealing with the problems he was having with his new bride. "It was a difficult year," Hope later said of their time together.[25] Many years earlier, Lugosi claimed that he had learned a lesson after his disastrous marriage to Beatrice Woodruff Weeks.[26] But with Hope, well, he had been far less cautious in marrying her than he had been with any of his four earlier wives. After all, he hardly knew Hope when he proposed, as opposed to the months or years he had known all of his other fiancées.

Top: The married couple: Hope and Bela. *Bottom:* Edward D. Wood Jr.'s wedding to Norma McCarty. Paul Marco and Lugosi are to the left of the wedding cake; McCarty and Wood are to the right of the cake.

Lugosi and Hope in their Harold Way apartment.

To mention problems shouldn't suggest that there weren't happy times together. Nor is it to say that their marriage necessarily worked as a continually disintegrating union. It may have been a good day, then a bad day, and then another good day. Shifts from positive to negative even during the course of a single afternoon or evening.

"He was pretty good; let's face it," Hope later admitted.[27] She appreciated the times when Lugosi revealed his legendary charm. And also his humor, like the times he answered the phone by saying, "This is the morgue." Hope particularly appreciated the moments when he seemed to understand what was on her mind. Moments like the time he insisted on hiring a maid to occasionally clean the apartment; he knew she worked hard at her job before coming home to make his dinner.[28] At times he even felt guilty saddling Hope with his problems.[29]

And there were the times the couple shared with Hope's friends, particularly Pat Delaney, Phyllis Buffington, and Afton Farnsworth. Hope remembered:

> Lugosi liked Pat. She bossed him, and he kinda liked that. She was a bossy old lady, and she'd swear at him. And he liked that; it made him laugh. Phyllis, well, he tolerated her.
> [They] adored him, because he'd come in and kiss their hands. Of course, I won't repeat what he'd say after they'd leave, because that was just a little whiskey talking.[30]

Most of the times he saw Pat and Phyllis were on their frequent visits to the apartment when they played cards with Hope and Dick's mother Ruth; Lugosi didn't join in.

Neither Hope or Lugosi drove. But they did go for occasional walks, with her particularly remembering a time they strolled down Hollywood Boulevard. While passing in front of Grauman's Chinese Theatre, Lugosi spotted a group of tourists admiring the hands and footprints of the stars. He invited all of them to meet a real actor, a living legend. The star-struck group immediately clustered around him for handshakes, autographs, and pictures. It was then that Hope revelled in Lugosi's good mood, and that she saw a bit of his past fame.

She also glimpsed some of his former glory when she went with Lugosi, Dick, and Dick's mother Ruth to look at his old homes. And of course, Dick was at the Harold Way apartment constantly after September 1955; his mother made frequent visits as well. Hope was relieved at how much they could improve Lugosi's mood. Hope and Lugosi also enjoyed attending Ed Wood's wedding to Norma McCarty, and the time they came to dinner at the Lugosi apartment.[31]

At times dinner went very well, whether or not they had guests. Lugosi "was a good eater," Hope said.[32] Occasionally they went to his favorite restaurants, sometimes with other friends. With a smile on her face, Ruth remembered that Lugosi would take them to a Hungarian eatery that literally rolled out a red carpet for him.[33] But as Hope explained:

> Lugosi couldn't do any cooking himself. One day he blew up the eggs and they ended up on the ceiling. I don't know how he managed to do that. So I did the cooking at home. He said he'd have five wives and had hired the best cooks, and I was the best.[34]

Ruth remembered that "Hope would make him leg of lamb, or lamb chops, and that was what he had almost every day. He loved it." [35] And though she couldn't afford the imported sulphur water that Lugosi loved, Hope bought him Sparkletts, water allegedly bottled from artesian wells.[36]

But Hope claimed that their day-to-day life generally featured little contact between them. Occasionally she went to bed early, tired from work, as he continued to read or watch television. More often, though, Lugosi was the one who went to sleep first, with Hope able to spend time alone or play canasta with Pat and Phyllis. If the game included Ruth, Dick and Lugosi would sit together in the living room watching TV. "[Lugosi] seldom talked about anything, really," Hope remembered. "We'd talk a bit, but he would sometimes tell me to mind my own business about certain things."[37]

So what caused their larger problems? There was the fact Lugosi was becoming more religious in his latter years. Part of this was connected to his treatment at Metropolitan, but it was more than just that. Makeup man Harry Thomas found him with rosary beads while they were making *Bride of the Atom*, for example. "I am with my God all the time," Lugosi proclaimed in late 1955.[38] By contrast, Hope remembered:

> I made a very unfortunate remark one time. I got so sick of his eternal religious arguments that I said, "You know, Bela, I don't think I even believe in God." He was furious. He had a memory like an elephant, you know, and he would always throw it up to me. "You don't even believe in God!"[39]

```
(4-8-11)  reopic nic - ....
(7-13) Lawrence Welk Show
9:30—(2-8-9) Star Jubilee
(4-11) Star Theater
(5)  Bela Lugosi Presents
10:00—(4-11) George Gobel Show
(7)  Eddy Arnold Time
(12) Life Begins At 80
```

This was a far cry from what Lugosi originally saw as their shared religious feelings.[40]

Whatever else she did or didn't believe in, Hope certainly dabbled in witchcraft; at different times, Dick Sheffield and his high school friends saw evidence of it on numerous occasions.[41] Hope confided to Dick that she had been able to marry Lugosi thanks to magic. And Mike Spencer recalled that she even "moved in her enormous cat, and Bela was scared to death of the thing."[42]

And then there was Hope's challenging personality. Her obsession with Lugosi the film

Above: TV listing for *Bela Lugosi Presents* in *The Gettysburg Times* of February 10, 1956. *Below:* Lugosi advertising Spooky Foods.

Top: Lugosi as Casimir in *The Black Sleep.*
Bottom: The key cast members of *The Black Sleep* (1956).
Back row: Akim Tamiroff and John Carradine.
Front row: Basil Rathbone, Lugosi, and Lon Chaney Jr.

star was well-known; she told Dick that years before she had hired a detective to follow him around a studio and keep tabs on what he was doing. But living with Lugosi the man twisted her views on the subject. "He was looking for a sucker, and I was it," she claimed, with a good deal of bitterness in her voice.[43] That kind of disappointment must have only fuelled her gruff, difficult side. At one point, for example, she gloated over the fact that Lugosi was scared of her.[44]

That Lugosi found this Hope to be different from the woman who wrote him such sweet letters is clear. He confided in Forrest J Ackerman about their troubles; Ackerman even witnessed the Lugosis fighting in front of his own eyes.[45] And when Lugosi's long time friends Meta Wittrock and Marie Kerekjarto-Staats visited the apartment, they found Hope to be particularly icy and unpleasant. She had gotten "her claws" into him, they thought, and was hardly treating him well.[46]

Of course Lugosi could scarcely have been easy to deal with for a variety of reasons; some of them stemmed from his closely held beliefs about marriage. Hope continued to work, for example, and earned the bulk of the money they had. Certainly it meant that the bills were paid and that they lived with a degree of comfort. But that she was the key earner in their home could hardly have served Lugosi's ego.

Lugosi's own financial wellbeing was of course questionable. Sporadic acting jobs meant sporadic income. He did receive Social Security checks, though, and he still had some assets, particularly some lots that he and Lillian had bought years earlier near Lake Elsinore. A good investment, really. Lugosi had built seven homes in the area in 1947, and had planned to build many more.[47] Whether he did or not is hard to know. At the least, he and Lillian held onto the lots even after their divorce.[48] Perhaps there was income from leases on the land, or perhaps they eventually sold one or more out of the 19 lots they still had when their divorce was finalized.[49]

But money wasn't the only problem that weighed on Lugosi's mind. Suspicion raged within him, just as it had years earlier with wives like Von Montagh, Beatrice, and Lillian. In some ways Lugosi felt this way from the start, telling his nephew Béla Loosz that he had called the FBI to see if Hope had a record on file.[50] During their honeymoon, he accused Ed Wood of fooling around with her.[51] Later, Lugosi thought she might be fooling around with Paul Marco, who was homosexual.[52]

Eventually, he also cast jealous eyes down on Dick Sheffield. Lugosi's heated verbal assault one day caused Hope to leave the apartment in disgust. After an hour of sitting on the floor and holding

Basil Rathbone (left) and Lon Chaney Jr. (right) present Lugosi with a bound copy of the script for *The Black Sleep*.

hands, Dick and Lugosi ended up crying. And then came Lugosi's confession: it wasn't just the same old jealousy he had felt towards Lillian. No, Lugosi knew he was old. And he knew that he physically wasn't the man he had once been, even the man he was at the beginning of his marriage to Hope.[53] Dick took the brunt of his anger and sadness that day, perhaps just because he was nearby.

Of course Lugosi's jealousies had always been one-sided, apparently believing a different standard was at work for men than for women. Though it doesn't seem he actually cheated on Hope, he did look for affection from another woman. Dick's mother Ruth remembered an evening when Lugosi was in her own home. At a point when the two were alone together, he suggested that he could "get a divorce from Hope, so that you and I can get married." But Ruth told Lugosi she couldn't do it. "I laughed and told him he was crazy," she said. "And of course I didn't tell Hope about it."[54]

Added to all of this was Lugosi's drinking. When he left Metropolitan Hospital, he told an interviewer that he had "kicked" the problem three years earlier, presumably meaning 1952 or 1953.[55] At a minimum, he must have been away from alcohol during his three months of treatment. But he was certainly drinking after his release. For awhile, Lugosi was buying liquor at an Italian grocery store on Harold Way, sometimes going in with a friend who also bought booze.[56] And then he increasingly had them make deliveries to the apartment. Store worker Ted Gargano remembered:

> I used to deliver his Scotch every week for six months, a year maybe. It was Black and White Scotch. That was his favorite.
>
> He would call when the wife was at work. I never saw the wife. Each time I used to go, he used to pick a bottle out [of the bag], and the rest he used to hide from the wife. He never called for a delivery when the wife was around. She didn't like him to drink, I guess.[57]

Advertisement for the May 5, 1956 TV premiere of *The Body Snatcher* (1945).

Gargano wasn't alone, though. Dick and Katzman frequently saw Lugosi drinking vast quantities of Scotch, and also knew he concealed it as much as possible from Hope.[58]

In November of 1955, Lugosi claimed he was attending two meetings a week at Alcoholics Anonymous. "It helps me spiritually," he said.[59] Who went with him? He tried to get Forrest Ackerman to attend, but Ackerman turned him down because he wasn't a drinker.[60] So Lugosi went with actor Tor Johnson, but Mike Spencer remembered, "Amazingly, he and Tor would go home from AA and celebrate having gone by drinking all afternoon."[61] And there was also Ed Wood, who once claimed Lugosi actually drank some Scotch during an AA meeting.[62]

As time went on, though, Lugosi went to AA less and less. When he did go, it was increasingly with a friend that he had made there. An unrepentant drinker; Hope was little pleased. She hadn't forgotten the time she went to the Metropolitan Hospital with Lugosi for an appointment:

> We made a trip down to Norwalk, and he talked to [Dr. Nicholas Langer]. They'd sit there and jabber in Hungarian. But that shrink did whisper in my ear that he wasn't there because of drugs as much as he was there because he was an out and out drunk."[63]

Gargano had been right when he said "the wife" didn't want Lugosi to drink. Hope was on something of an unsuccessful mission to get him to stop.

An example of how difficult the overall situation must have been is the occasion when Dick, Mike Spencer, and David Katzman went with Lugosi and Hope to Lake Elsinore. On the way home, Katzman was behind the wheel of his 1947 Dodge Sedan; Lugosi was beside him in the front seat. Hope and Dick were in the backseat, with Mike squeezed between them. Katzman recalled:

> On the way back, we stopped at a restaurant. Bela was drinking heavily. Hope knew, but he was trying to conceal it. He made a grab for the waitress's behind, and Hope scolded him, saying "Bela, behave yourself." And he said, "Oh, shut up."
>
> In the car again, he finished off the bottle and threw it out of the window, which worried me because I was on a learner's permit. Hope made some remark, and Bela said "Oh, shut up" again.
>
> Then he started saying things like "My wife has such a beautiful body. More beautiful than any other woman I've known." And in an absolutely acerbic tone, she said, "Yeah Bela, you tell it," which was followed by Lugosi saying "Oh shut up" again.

Publicity luncheon for *The Black Sleep* at the Tail o' the Cock restaurant in late February 1956. From left to right are: Lugosi, Akim Tamiroff, Tor Johnson, Sally Yarnell, and John Carradine.

He then opened the window to spit, but it wasn't rolled down all the way, so the spit hit the window and drizzled downward. He said, "Look boys, an oyster." And they were laughing themselves sick in the backseat.

He did it again in a few miles, and this time the spit went out the front window but through the back window into the back seat, where it hit Mike. And then everyone back there was yelling, and Bela kept saying "Shut up."

Finally he grogged out completely. And so we had to help Hope get him inside.[64]

Evenings like this must have been trying for Lugosi and Hope, as both of them had ended up far less happy together than they wanted to be.

Booze, jealousy, colliding philosophies. More than enough problems, and soon it wasn't just Lugosi's friends who knew about them. At the beginning of March 1956, Jimmie Fidler wrote in his nationally-syndicated newspaper column:

I hear that [Lugosi] and his bride have absolutely nothing in common, now that he is well and working again—and say his friends, his marital unhappiness is proving to be an added burden in his effort to stay well. It seems a great pity that he should have to face this kind of unhappiness at a late stage in life.[65]

Unhappiness, perhaps some of it self-inflicted on Lugosi's part. And perhaps some of it due to Hope's abrasive personality and predilection towards witchcraft. Whatever the exact details, though, Lugosi was increasingly distraught as time went on, and thanks to Fidler the whole country knew about it.

Of course, the fact that Fidler said Lugosi was "working again" was only some-

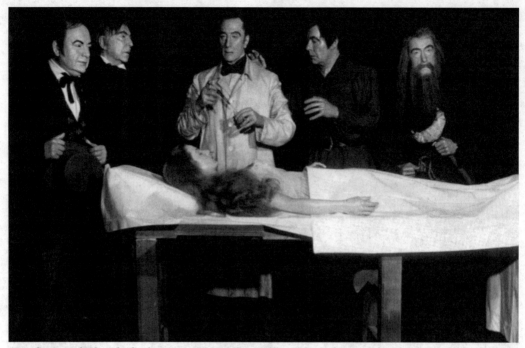

Wax figures of *The Black Sleep* cast. From left to right are wax figures of Akim Tamiroff, Lugosi, Basil Rathbone, Lon Chaney Jr., and John Carradine. On the operating table is the wax figure of Louanna Gardner.

what accurate; his career troubles of recent years were actually mounting. Science fiction still held sway at the box office, just as it had throughout the decade. A 1956 article in the *LA Times* claimed:

> Any horror film that hopes to achieve any self-respect these days must have three elements: A creature–preferably an atomic mutation–a pretty girl and a handsome man.[66]

That formula hardly had room for Lugosi. After all, a review of *Tarantula* (1955) claimed that the mutant insect "evidently intends to make *Dracula* look like a mere kissing bandit."[67]

Except for his on-camera interviews about narcotics, Lugosi wasn't getting any new television offers. But as much as ever, he was on TV thanks to endless repeats of his old B-movies. When a viewer asked a newspaper about the availability of old Boris Karloff movies, a columnist responded that his old Frankenstein films weren't yet available for broadcast. "However, there are a number of Bela Lugosi horror films on tap which should be frightening enough. Of course, you have already seen enough Bela Lugosi films [on TV] to make you wince at the thought."[68] And they kept on coming too. By February 1956, for example, a station in Virginia ran them steadily enough to have a show entitled *Bela Lugosi Presents*.[69]

New opportunities, not revivals of old films. That's what Lugosi needed for his mental health and for his pocketbook. His best job in the latter part of 1955 was a product endorsement for Epicurean Reese of California. He had done that kind of thing before, ranging from KOOL cigarettes to Royal Crown Cola.[70] And in late 1950 he went around "seriously" telling friends that he would be promoting a soft drink called "Dracola."[71] This time, he donned the cape for Halloween promotion of Epicurean's "Spooky Foods Box" that contained alligator soup, rattlesnake meat, fried grasshoppers, and more.[72] Hardly the makings of a comeback.

But with all of his other problems, it does seem that Lugosi believed he could return to the screen, just as he had in 1939 after the British horror film ban. At times when Ted Gargano delivered alcohol, he found Lugosi wearing "the cape of Dracula, and he used to make like the part of Dracula, and he used to tell me, 'I'll be back. I'll be back.'" He was rehearsing, perhaps dialogue for scripts like *The Ghoul Goes West*. But so little was happening in the autumn of 1955. Whether Lugosi even still had Lou Sherrell as an agent after he got out of Metropolitan seems doubtful.[73]

"Nobody remembers me," he complained to Paul Marco. "I want to make a movie and let them know I'm alive."[74] "He thought he was forgotten," Ruth Sheffield remembered, "and that was why he wanted to make another picture."[75] Desperate to get on a film set, and eager to prove that he still had what it took.

His longstanding unhappiness with horror could hardly have mattered when he got a phone call at the beginning of 1956 asking him to appear in a movie called *The Black Sleep*. It was to be an old-style mad doctor film, a direct contrast to the big bugs and space aliens of the fifties. In the midst of so much going wrong, this was a glimmer of hope, at long last.

Planning to include a variety of known horror stars, producers Aubrey Schenck and Howard W. Koch budgeted the new film at $229,000.[76] Their Bel-Air Productions had started with the title and proceeded to have a story written once their distributor, United Artists, gave the go-ahead.[77] Director Reginald Le Borg took over from Allen Miner before shooting began, which likely helped the film; Le Borg's lengthy career was checkered with horror film credits.[78]

By mid-January 1956, Lugosi and John Carradine were added to a cast that already included Basil Rathbone, Lon Chaney Jr., and Peter Lorre.[79] In the end, though, Akim Tamiroff replaced Lorre because of a salary dispute.[80] At some point, Lugosi's pal Tor Johnson was also signed. Of this impressive group, columnist Erskine Johnson claimed "Between 'em, they committed 341 celluloid murders. Not to mention all their scene-stealing larceny."[81] Together they began shooting on February 9, 1956 at the Ziv studios.

But bitterness at times outweighed any happiness from working. "There is Basil playing my part," Lugosi told a reporter. "I used to be the big cheese."[82] "He certain-

ly had some choice words about Rathbone," David Katzman remembered. Some of this may have been ingrained from their history together. They had made personal appearances together at the National Photographic Show in 1951, where Rathbone's name was mentioned before Lugosi's in newspaper publicity.[83] Rathbone also got top billing in 1949 when they worked together on *The Man in the Shadows* radio drama, just as he had when they both appeared in the 1941 film version of *The Black Cat*.[84] And even if Lugosi's role of Ygor had stolen the show in *Son of*

Lon Chaney Jr., John Carradine, and Lugosi dine on Tor Johnson while in San Francisco promoting *The Black Sleep*.

Frankenstein (1939), Rathbone's name came first on all of the publicity.

As for Casimir, the role he played in *The Black Sleep*, Lugosi said: "Now I'm just playing a dumb part. [A servant] who just lets people in and out." In a way, of course, the character Casimir signified the worst feature of Lugosi's Hollywood career: the many horror films that cast him purely for the use of his name value, giving him few scenes and little to do.[85] More than any other particular role, Casimir resembled his work as Joseph in Robert Wise's *The Body Snatcher* (1945), which coincidentally premiered on television in May 1956 as *The Black Sleep* was being readied for theatrical release.[86]

In a way, *The Black Sleep* is somewhat reminiscent of *The Body Snatcher*; Tamiroff's Odo supplies bodies to Rathbone's Dr. Cadman just as Karloff's Cabman Gray had to Henry Daniell's Dr. McFarlane. But *The Black Sleep* is also part of a tradition of Lugosi films like *The Corpse Vanishes (*1942) and *Voodoo Man* (1944), where Lugosi's doctors committed horrible crimes to keep their wives alive.

A key difference was that Casimir was a nonspeaking part. Lugosi told a journalist that "I have no dialogue because I was a bit worried whether I could do justice to the expectations. I'm still recuperating."[87] But that was just Lugosi's pride talking, as Casimir was scripted as a mute character from the beginning. Director Reginald Le Borg claimed that Lugosi came to him "quite often and said, 'Herr Director, please give me some lines.' And I said, 'I cannot do that; your character is a mute.'"[88] And so as Rathbone played Lugosi's mad scientist part, something of a Henry Frankenstein, Lugosi was left to play the kind of mute monster that he had turned down 25 years earlier.

His character wasn't the only nonspeaking role in the group, though. Neither Tor Johnson or Lon Chaney Jr. had dialogue. But this was hardly helpful to Lugosi's mood, which was dour in part because he was drinking; Le Borg knew that some friend of Lugosi's was supplying him with whiskey. That producer Koch noticed Lugosi being "confused," "glazed over," and "not knowing where he was part of the time" was probably due, at least in part, to the alcohol.[89] Aubrey Schenck said much the same, claiming that Lugosi seemed "numb" to everything that was happening.[90]

But at times Lugosi fumed with unhappiness. Among other things, he may well have known that he was paid less than Rathbone, Chaney, and Carradine.[91] At any rate, Rathbone felt Lugosi's resentment strongly enough to send him an apologetic note during the shoot.[92] Worse still was that Lugosi ended up in an argument with Lon Chaney Jr. Le Borg understood that it had roots in the fact that, in Universal's *Son of Dracula* (1943), Chaney Jr. played the lead role instead of Lugosi. That Chaney later picked Lugosi up off the floor meant more trouble; Lugosi hardly appreciated the maneuver, and Le Borg had to intercede.[93] From then on, they basically had to be kept apart.[94]

Aside from Chaney, though, it does seem that the cast tried to placate Lugosi as best they could. And whatever resentment he felt, perhaps much of his behavior came out of the aloof quality he had brought to his work for decades. Costar Louanna Gardner remembered:

> I remember one day when I wanted to go watch some of the film footage; they were showing some of the rushes. And as I started to head over there, I saw Bela just standing alone, doing nothing. So I asked him to go with me. Given his unhappy relations with some of the others, everyone was surprised to see him walk in with me. Later they all congratulated me for involving him, for convincing him to see the rushes.[95]

Gardner was hardly the only one to show him kindness, of course. At some point during the shoot, Rathbone and Chaney Jr. appeared to present him with a leather bound copy of the script. And producer Schenck even claimed that he saw Lugosi's pal Tor Johnson carry him on and off the set when he wasn't feeling well.[96] Perhaps Lugosi's mood improved slightly when he had visitors on the set. Dick and Katzman and Jimmy Haines ditched school to watch him work. Katzman of course marvelled at Dick's outfit: he was decked out in full beatnik attire, from a beret and ascot to a swagger stick and a cigarette holder. Even the guard at the studio gate did a double take at Dick's get-up, which must have appeared even more extreme next to Katzman and Haines' street clothes.

What the trio found when they made it to the set was a Lugosi who felt bad, who wasn't in good shape at all. They knew he was drinking, but there was also the fact he just seemed to have so little energy.[97] Someone on the crew had even placed a Chaise longue just off the set so Lugosi could lie down between takes. And they watched him struggle through a scene where he opens the door for two constables.[98]

Dick visited the set the next day to watch Dr. Ramsay (Herbert Rudley) discover Cadman's monstrous experiments in a cave-like prison. This time his mother Ruth went with him. She was excited at the chance to see Lugosi act, but noticed that "he wasn't feeling well. Between the takes, he told me he was a bit nervous to be back at work."[99]

Near the end of February, Lugosi, Chaney, Carradine, Tamiroff, and other cast members visited the Tail o' the Cock Restaurant as a publicity stunt.[100] "Tired of eating in the commissary" and "too rushed to take off their makeup," was what the group told the journalist Gene Sherman. But Sherman thought the fact they were driven to lunch in a hearse felt a little like "overacting"[101] An old-style horror film sporting an equally old-style publicity gimmick.

Nearly a quarter of a century earlier at the height of his fame, Lugosi had sat for a wax figure crafted by Madame Stubergh. She talked to him for hours, finally throwing wet plaster on his face unexpectedly to catch the right expression.[102] Captured in his famous role as Dracula, when he was the "big cheese." By the time George Bau created wax figures of the *Black Sleep* cast, things had changed so much: his status, his appearance.[103] The fifties were a different era

Above: Tor Johnson, John Carradine, Lon Chaney Jr., and Lugosi menace Phyllis Lauritz of *The Oregonian* newspaper. Taken in Portland on June 7, 1956. *Below:* Lugosi and James B. Leong (in the back row) in a publicity still for *The Devil's Paradise,* as printed in the advance program for the play.

Lugosi at the Los Angeles opening of *The Black Sleep*. Mike Spencer (left) and Dick Sheffield (right) help to keep him standing after the amount of alcohol he drank that night.

altogether; after all, Bau had actually used a lot of plastic to create the figures.[104]

During the whole production, though, Lugosi attracted more interest among journalists than any of his *Black Sleep* costars. Bitterness and booze aside, he told one of them that:

> Even though surrounded by friends [on the set], you've got to go it alone. I keep telling myself I must believe I will make the grade again. If I stop believing even for a minute, I find myself sinking into despair. It's fighting this feeling—a thing that comes to all former drug addicts—that saps up my energy. ... God has been good and given me this second chance, and I'll do my best not to fail.[105]

You've got to go it alone. Friends and family aside, you've got to go it alone.

When the summer of 1956 arrived, his cacophony of problems seemed only to grow more unbearable. Dick saw him on Mother's Day. Drinking and feeling poorly. Tears welled in his eyes when he explained what was wrong. He wasn't with Lillian and Bela Jr. that day. He hadn't heard from them; that he had been remarried for nine months hardly seemed to enter his mind; his interest in Hope was declining.[106]

And then there was his stalled comeback. "Bela Lugosi has returned," proclaimed a United Artists press release.[107] Returned, perhaps, but not to much acclaim. The *Hollywood Reporter* gave him a brief nod for turning in a "good" performance, but that was about it.[108]

No other studios called, and Lugosi's key chance for work was to help promote *The Black Sleep*. As the *Black Sleep* wax figures were sent to New York for a theatre lobby display, plans were announced that Lugosi, Chaney, Carradine, and Tor would tour San Francisco and Portland in person to promote some of the first screenings of the film.[109]

The quartet arrived in the Golden Gate city on June 6, 1956, holding a press luncheon at the S-Palace. The choice of a luncheon event seems well-planned, as photographers there delighted in taking pictures of Tor Johnson's head poking up through a dining table as the main course.[110] The actors don't seem to have made a theatre appearance, though, as they left town on June 7, the very day *The Black Sleep* opened at a local theatre.[111]

But they did stay at a San Francisco hotel on the night of June 6. It seems surprising that Lugosi did not want to visit the members of the famed Hungarian String Quartet in the city, a group led by Zoltán Szekely, a friend of Béla Bartók's.[112] Perhaps he didn't know they were there; perhaps he was just getting too tired to be interested in such things.

Instead, Lugosi spent that evening drinking at the group's hotel. Koch had told press agent Chuck Moses not to let Lugosi out of his sight, but Moses claimed that when he was in the bathroom he heard Lugosi screaming, "I can fly! I can fly." He rushed out to find Lugosi allegedly standing on the window ledge with the window wide open and the wind blowing against his face. He continued to shout "I can fly" over and over again.[113] But whatever feeling of elation that came from alcohol was coupled with other moments of severe depression, a problem that Tor Johnson witnessed on the trip.[114]

And then the group was in Portland on June 7 for another press luncheon, this time at the "Aloha Room" of the Heathman Hotel.[115] Instead of the dinner table gag, Tor and Carradine wielded butcher knives around a female reporter while

Advertisement in the June 27, 1956 *Los Angeles Times* promoting Vampira
and Tor Johnson's live appearances for *The Black Sleep*.

Lugosi arched his hypnotic fingers in her direction.[116] Lugosi also recalled a "wealth
of theatrical lore" for the press before going onstage at the local Paramount Theatre
screening the film.[117] "He made a favorable impression on those who saw him," one
journalist wrote. "[But] Bela became very emotional in telling his story [about nar-
cotics] on the stage and fainted. He had to be brought back to Los Angeles."[118] That
was the night of June 7 or the morning of June 8.

That incident leads into a little play called *The Devil's Paradise*, a tale of two
girls who narrowly escape being recruited to sell narcotics. A third girl, who sells
her soul to the devil, isn't so lucky; the thin storyline was apparently fleshed out
with musical performances. [119] James B. Leong, who had appeared with Lugosi two
decades earlier in the serial *Shadow of Chinatown* (1936), produced and directed.
"He was kind of like an Ed Wood," Leong's son once remembered. "Always trying
to put together little shows."[120]

Leong starred Lugosi as an international drug peddler, planning for him to greet
audiences at the end of each performance.[121] The rest of the cast included the 1910
bantamweight champion Kid Mitchell, as well as a number of young performers like
Marilyn Zack, who was already working on TV while still attending San Fernando
High.[122]

A program was prepared for the show, with a key surviving copy having been
stamped and mailed to columnist Hedda Hopper. It was actually meant for use
before the show, being really more of a sales brochure. A hopeful audience member
had to fill it out and send it back with their money. So it was likely prepared in May
before Lugosi's UA tour, and distributed in late May and/or very early June; any
later probably wouldn't have given enough turn around time for the mail. It lists
two evening performances at the Troupers Green Room in Hollywood on June 8
and June 9, with an additional matinee on June 9.[123]

But it's a very open question as to whether *The Devil's Paradise* was actually
staged. Lugosi couldn't have been back in LA till June 8, and that was on the heels
of allegedly collapsing in Portland the day before. Did he cancel after his collapse?
Perhaps. In fact, he could have cancelled even earlier when United Artists booked
him for the tour to San Francisco and Portland. And then there's also the chance
that Leong's tactic of sending out the program to generate mail-in ticket sales may
not have yielded enough interest to stage the play.

Regardless of whether the play occurred, it seems likely that Lugosi didn't
appear. Neither Hope nor Dick recalled him doing the show, though they both knew
about his UA tour and his collapsing in Portland.[124] That's in addition to actress
Evelyn Bunn–who was listed on *The Devil's Paradise* program–claiming she never
performed in it.[125] Actress Sally Jones said the same, as did the family of the late

Lugosi in front of Tor Johnson's home in footage Ed Wood shot in the summer of 1956.

Howard Amacker.[126] And of course no newspaper advertisement or review appeared, not even in the most likely candidate, the *Hollywood Citizen-News*.[127] In the end, *The Devil's Paradise* may have only existed in the form of a rehearsal or two that resulted in photos for the program.

Whatever the case, sometime between mid-June and July, Lugosi apparently appeared before a movie camera for the last time. Some footage shot by Ed Wood, with Paul Marco later claiming that it was for "a picture called *The Vampire's Tomb*."[128] But that doesn't seem to be the case, unless Wood was recycling the old title with a new story in mind, as the images he shot of Lugosi bear no similarity to any part of the existing *Vampire's Tomb* script.

Wood once remembered, "Lugosi was ill and needed some cash. I gave him $1000 and we shot a day at a cemetery that was being excavated. I wrote the film around the scene."[129] But on another occasion, he said that he only had "$800 promotion money" for the entire graveyard shoot.[130] Either way, Tor Johnson's son Karl and Wood's pal Carl Anthony went along to help with the film equipment. They also gave Wood a hand in moving around some gravemarkers to make the location more picturesque.[131]

Dick tagged along, too. Spent the day watching Wood run camera, though Wood later bemoaned the fact that someone else acted as cinematographer and had "used bad film."[132] Anyhow, before too long, Dick stuffed a few of the wooden cemetery crosses into the car as mementos. And while he and Lugosi stood by, Wood threw a hubcap into the air and filmed it, presumably as a test.[133] No, this wasn't *The Vampire's Tomb* of years before; Wood already had science fiction in mind for his next film.

Of course, the sequences that Dick watched that day weren't really even scenes. One image had Lugosi amongst a group of mourners at a funeral. The others had him skulking around the cemetery in his Dracula cape. And that was it for the day's shoot. At some point Wood filmed *other* footage of Lugosi coming out of Tor Johnson's home. Grief-stricken, his character stops to pick a fragile little flower that he then drops to the ground.

And then there's the fact that Lugosi looks a little different in the cemetery footage than in the footage at Johnson's home, as if he was a little thinner. Frail, even. That–along with Dick only seeing the cemetery footage being shot–suggests the images were shot on two different days. A third reason to suspect this may have been the case is that the quality of the film appears less muddy in the footage at Johnson's home.[134]

One would presume that the cemetery footage came closest to the time of Lugosi's death, given how old and ill he appears. But in reality, it may have been shot months earlier. A small item in the *Los Angeles Times* of November 27, 1955 claims:

> Patrons at Johnny Davis' Cameo Room were, to say the least, startled the other evening when Mr. Bela Lugosi came in for a snack. He'd been on location in a Hollywood cemetery and hadn't bothered to get out of makeup.[135]

Though from an earlier date than expected, the description sounds very much like Wood's cemetery shoot. And so the Wood shoot of June-July 1956 was likely when they filmed at Tor Johnson's home. At any rate, Wood had his Lugosi footage in the can, even though it wouldn't be seen until after Lugosi's death.

That wasn't the case with *The Black Sleep* of course. Near the end of June 1956, it finally opened in Los Angeles. United Artists booked it for eighteen theatres, ranging from drive-ins to some of the more important old "hardtop" movie palaces.[136] It was featured as the lead film on a double bill with *The Creeping Unknown* starring Brian Donlevy, the actor whom the press had linked romantically with Lugosi's former wife Lillian in 1955.[137]

Newspaper ads promoted four theatres screening the film, all of which would see opening day visits by Vampira and Tor Johnson. None of the screenings really functioned as a major premiere; producer Koch remembered it being little more than "just a regular opening."[138] After all, Rathbone, Chaney, Tamiroff, Carradine–none of them were scheduled to appear at any theatre. But for Lugosi, who was wasn't receiving any new studio offers, it was an important evening.

Dick cooked up a wonderful idea. Lugosi would attend the New Fox Theatre when Tor and Vampira were scheduled to appear. Dick and Mike Spencer arranged to take him in their pal Dick Nedwick's 1941 Cadillac; to add to the grandeur, Nedwick drove them in a borrowed chauffeur's uniform. Drinking on the way, Lugosi was in excellent spirits. It would be his last big night, even if he didn't realize it. And the more he drank, the happier he got.

"We had to keep a cap on him," Mike remembered. "He was going to sing [in front of everyone]." Soon the two of them were on either side of Lugosi, helping to keep him from falling down. He was drunk, and his eyesight suffered even more due to the fact he wouldn't wear his glasses in public. Forrest Ackerman quickly joined their group, and just as quickly realized Lugosi had been drinking.

Then came the amazing moment when Vampira arrived, which meant the television crew arrived as well. Lights and camera meant action; they wanted to interview Lugosi. "Boys, point me in the right direction," he asked, with Ackerman telling him to take about six steps forward to get into the perfect position. His back straightened and his mind sobered. His charm and his poise were again at his command as he appeared on camera for the last time.[139]

No more calls came for film appearances or stage shows. These were the reasons that many years earlier Lugosi had expressed hopes that his son would not go into show business. And it was the reason that he spoke to Jimmy Haines, whose father was an actor:

> One evening he spoke to me very lucid and candidly and looking into my eyes saying, in his almost Dracula sounding voice, "Don't go into show business. Don't go into show business." With that voice still echoing in my head I didn't pursue my father's vocation and went directly into civil service, leaving all thoughts of Hollywood and nightclubs behind me.[140]

That Lugosi was a compelling speaker on this of all subjects seems easy to believe.

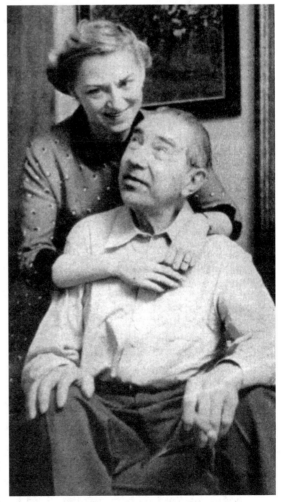

His studio bio for *The Black Sleep* had him referring repeatedly to what he had described for years: the "Dracula curse."[141]

Even though he wasn't working in July 1956, he was likely still reading his beloved newspapers. It was that month that President Eisenhower signed the "new anti-narcotics bill," which had been drafted by the US House and Senate. Testimony gathered by Price Daniel's subcommittee had been key in crafting the legislation, which imposed tougher penalties on dope peddlers. After all, the health of the nation was at risk.[142] As Lugosi told *Parade* magazine that summer, "Dope brings only misery."[143]

Of course Lugosi's own health was a problem those final months, and it was getting worse throughout the summer of 1956. He was feeling worse and worse, and he was too ill to make it to Dick's high school graduation. Donning their caps and gowns, Dick and Steve Buscaino attended without him in an old 1919 Model T Ford, driving in reverse gear down Hollywood Boulevard after the ceremony.[144]

Certainly Lugosi consulted a doctor, but wasn't at all happy with the treatment he was getting; "He's no good," Lugosi confided to Ruth. And then there was the time Lugosi phoned Mike Spencer:

> One Sunday afternoon he calls, and my father says, "It's him." "Who?" And he repeated, "*It's him.*"
>
> "Mike. I need medicine. Where's

Lugosi and Hope in their Harold Way apartment. Published in *Parade* magazine just four days before Lugosi's death in August 1956, but photographed perhaps some weeks earlier.

Dick?" "I don't know, Bela. I'm coming over."

So we went to the pharmacist, and he got this stuff that you could smell right through the bottle. It wasn't formaldehyde, but it was of the same family. It was in a small bottle, and he just poured it down. At the time I thought it was like embalming fluid, but he took it, because without it he would get the tremors.

That was in addition to nightly doses of paregoric, which had taken the place of Enzypan tablets to help his digestion.[145]

"I think he was just wearing out, that's all," Hope remembered.[146] Seeing him nearly every day, Hope wasn't even as aware of the gradual changes as visitors who saw him infrequently. Sometime near the end, for example, Jimmy Haines visited the apartment with Dick and couldn't believe how much worse Lugosi had become since February of the same year:

> He had deteriorated so much that he was hardly ambulatory, and he seemed to be in a kind of mental stupor. My heart went out to him. The last impression I have of Bela is when I helped him off the floor when he was unable to stand. That was my last visit. [147]

Lugosi still had the cane he had bought with Dick in September 1955. What he had bought as an accent to his attire was fast becoming a necessity.

None of this kept him from drinking, though. Making a delivery shortly before Lugosi's death, Ted Gargano recalled:

> I went in, and he was really in bad shape. He grabbed a bottle of Scotch from the bag in my hands, and he took the top off, and he drank, drank, drank almost half of the bottle. In one sip. Almost like water.[148]

After all, Lugosi was home each day, day after day in July and August. Still no phone calls for work.[149] Even though *The Black Sleep* was doing great business throughout the summer.[150]

Sometime during those final weeks he woke from a deep sleep and made his way into the living room. Hope found him confused and hardly awake, sitting in the dark. He told her that Karloff was waiting for him. Boris Karloff, in the middle of the night.[151] Perhaps he had just seen Karloff on *Frankie Laine Time* at the beginning of August.[152] Or perhaps it was a nightmare borne out of his ingrained unhappiness with the man whose career had overshadowed his own, a man whose career was still forging ahead.

All of these problems–the changes wrought by the fifties, his fading career, his feelings about Boris Karloff, his alcoholism, and his poor health–they were all things Lugosi couldn't gain control over. Problems that wouldn't go away. During his final days, he quietly told Ruth, "It's too late. It's too late."[153] Lugosi wasn't specific as to the meaning of the phrase, but perhaps he knew that he was waging a losing war.

"[Death] is the only thing that really frightens me," Lugosi said. "The calendar turns, and eventually you have to go."[154] He repeated this fear to Hope on more than one occasion. Even in August 1956.[155] As Adam in Madách's *Tragedy of Man* questions, "Beauty in death? One contradicts the other."

A losing war, but there was one battle he thought he had to win, and that he could. In August, Dick walked in to find Lugosi chatting with his son, whose career choice at age seventeen was law. A couple of attorneys were there as well. [156] Dick inadvertently learned the subject of their conversation; Lugosi wanted to file divorce proceedings against Hope. Five wives, and now five divorces. If he had cried on

Mother's Day being away from his beloved son, Lugosi was now going to be able to unite with him for the purpose of ending his marriage to Hope. A far cry from the happy photograph of the couple published in *Parade* magazine that same month.[157]

Only days later, Lugosi called Dick for help. It wasn't legal advice that he needed; it was physical help. "He'd call Dick, and Dick would go down and put five-gallon water containers [in Lugosi's water dispenser]," Ruth remembered. "He changed it many times."[158] Dick helped Lugosi so many times over their three-year friendship. They had become so very close, a hip fifties teenager and an aging horror film actor. Everything from women and politics to drugs and the movies had plagued Lugosi's last years, much of his life really. But Dick had brought some happiness.

This time, though, it was some hours before Dick could get to the Harold Way apartment. Lugosi finally answered the door; he explained that a neighbor had already helped with the jug of water. Lugosi looked ill and unhappy. He was in his underwear, and had apparently been sleeping. Maybe drinking too. And so Dick helped him back into bed, closing the door behind him.[159]

He was the last person to see him alive. Lugosi died later that same day. Thursday, August 16, 1956.

AFTERWORD

Hope Lininger Lugosi came in during the early evening of August 16, 1956, and saw Lugosi lying on their bed:

> He looked like he was having a nap. Shall I wake him now or put the food on first? And I thought, I'll put the food on first, so I went to the kitchen. And then I thought, no, I'll wake him up first. And I went in there. He hadn't been dead very long. A very short time, because he was nice and warm, and I petted him all over and nothing moved, so I thought, I guess he's dead. What else would he be?
>
> So I called the neighbor, but she wouldn't come in, because she was a good Buddhist or something; she didn't want to see any dead people. So I called the landlord who lived above us. And he came down and said, "Yeah I think he is [dead], so we'll call the police."[1]

They also called an ambulance.[2] And then Hope tried to find as many of Lugosi's liquor bottles as she could to throw them out before anyone arrived.[3]

After doctors examined Lugosi's body, they determined that he had died around 6:45PM. The cause of death was a coronary occlusion with a myocardial, a heart attack. The autopsy revealed that fibrosis had been a contributing factor.[4] At the time of his death, Lugosi was 73 years old, and weighed 140 pounds.[5]

For years a story circulated that Lugosi was clutching an Ed Wood script entitled *The Final Curtain* at the time of his death. That was how Hope found him, the story went: a kind of fitting conclusion to Bela Lugosi's life. But in the end this may have been little more than a story that Ed Wood concocted.[6] The script might have been in Lugosi's apartment, but Hope later bristled at the idea that it was on the bed with him when she discovered he was dead.[7] Perhaps this makes for even a more fitting end, a created memory of the type that journalists like Gladys Hall had invented so many times in Lugosi's Hollywood past.

More than worrying about any script, Hope devoted the rest of her time that night to getting on the phone, calling the home of Lillian Arch. Bela Lugosi Jr. recalled, "I believe it was Hope Lugosi who told me that my father had died. And I just handed the phone to my mother, because I was very upset about it. It was a long time before I could get over the immediate grief."[8] After that, Hope phoned Dick Sheffield's home, leaving a message with Ruth, who later had to tell him that his friend was gone. Then Hope made an announcement to the press, claiming that she and Lugosi had been "very happy together," something of a necessary lie.[9]

As Lugosi's body was removed from the apartment, it left the bedroom, where his old nude painting of Clara Bow hung above the bed. It passed by some of his old film costumes in the closet, and his collection of theatre photographs filed in an old cabinet. It passed by a few scrapbooks that covered his movie career. And finally, it passed by that enormous portrait of Lugosi in a Prince Albert-style costume that stared down from its place on the wall of the living room. Mementos of a long life and career.

257

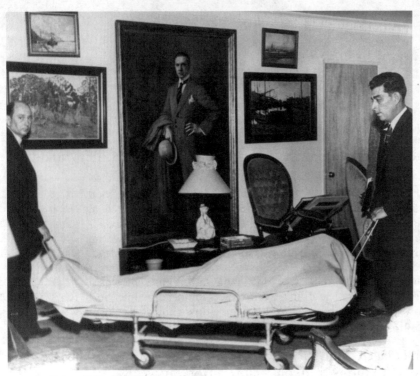

Lugosi's body being removed from the Harold Way apartment.

Eventually, Hope decided to give some of Lugosi's things to Forrest Ackerman, but the bulk of everything went to Dick. That cane that Lugosi had bought months earlier; the monocle he used in *Dracula* (1931); the Dracula ring that Lugosi had borrowed from Universal but never returned.[10] So many scrapbooks and photographs. Even one of Lugosi's two Dracula capes.

Lugosi would forever remain with the other Dracula cape, which Hope delivered to the Utter-McKinley Mortuary on the morning of August 17, 1956. "It was the decision of my mother [Lillian] and I that he would be buried in his cape," Bela Lugosi Jr. recalled.[11] After all, newspapers quickly announced that it had been Lugosi's wish; he had finally accepted the "Dracula curse."[12] And when Dick learned all of this, he persuaded Hope to send over Lugosi's full dress tuxedo and Dracula medallion as well. "I thought he should go out in full style," Dick said.[13]

Hope agreed with him, and she also "insisted" that the mortuary schedule his funeral on Saturday, August 18, so that her friends could more easily attend. But otherwise she didn't do any of the planning or interfere with his other family. "[The funeral] was mainly handled by his ex-wife [Lillian] and son and his former sister-in-law. I had very little to do [with it]."[14]

Their choice of Utter-McKinley was due in large part to the fact that Marie Kerekjarto's second husband Ralph Staats worked there as the Vice-President.[15] And over the years, Utter-McKinley handled a variety of Hollywood funerals; only three weeks earlier, they had buried the publisher of the *Hollywood Citizen-News*.[16] In years past, they had buried silent film stars Bonnie Earle and Albert Austin, comedian Skeets Gallagher, and Broadway star Frankie Bailey.[17] Even Harry Walker Soursby, who had played Renfield in a 1929 tour of *Dracula* with Bela Lugosi.[18]

And it was *Dracula* that Dick went to see on the night of August 17, accompanied by David Katzman. Lugosi was lying in state, complete with vampire wardrobe. Katzman took several pictures, including one with Dick beside the casket.[19] Then Dick stared at his friend, tucking some of Lugosi's beloved "El Ropo, El Stinko" cigars inside his jacket pocket.

Lugosi's funeral at 2:30PM the next day certainly made headlines across the

A publicity still that Ed Wood circulated with *Grave Robbers from Outer Space*
(later *Plan 9 From Outer Space* (1959).

Hope on a trip she made to the Hollywood Memorial Cemetery with Dick Sheffield immediately after Lugosi's death. She had hoped Lugosi could be buried there.

country, even if the *Los Angeles Times* claimed that it attracted "few notables."[20] Who showed up? Close to 140 people.[21] And to be fair, the *LA Times* was correct. Only a few of Lugosi's friends from the movie business were present. Hungarian film directors Steve Szekely and Zoltán Korda, a man who had written some of Lugosi's first film reviews in 1918.[22] And then there was Scott Beal, the assistant director of *Murders in the Rue Morgue* (1932) and *Dracula* (1931).

There was a much larger contingent from Lugosi's final films. Ed Wood, along with wife Kathy and former wife Norma E. McCarty. Producer George Weiss of *Glen or Glenda* (1953). Tor Johnson and his wife. Paul Marco, Conrad Brooks, and Loretta King. Even George Becwar, who had caused union troubles on the set of *Bride of the Monster* (1955).[23]

The biggest group were old friends like *Californiai Magyarság* publisher Zoltán Szabados, and Dr. Manly Hall, the man who had officiated at Lugosi's wedding to Hope. There was Meta Wittrock and her granddaughter Rose Marie. And cowboy singer Dallas E. Turner, who sat thinking about how he should have followed up on Lugosi's invitation to visit the Harold Way apartment.[24] A number of Dick's friends attended as well: Mike Spencer, Forrest Ackerman, David Katzman, and David Oyler.

As for Hope, well, she didn't sit in the special room reserved for the family; instead, she sat in the main chamber with everyone else. Her long-time friends Pat Delaney, Afton Farnsworth, and Phyllis Buffington were at her side as tears rolled down her face. Lillian Arch was also crying; Dallas Turner looked back to see Bela Jr. going from woman to woman in the family room, admirably trying to comfort all of them.

Once the ceremony began, Lugosi's close friend Duci de Kerekjarto played

Hungarian dirges on the violin. "Morbid, morose sounds," Mike Spencer recalled. "It was awesome, really."[25] Then the Reverend Joseph Vaughn gave a eulogy, which contrasted Lugosi the kindly actor with Lugosi the onscreen villain.[26] But the fact he hadn't really known Lugosi meant that some of his discussion drifted into descriptions of things like Lugosi being bounced on his father's knee.[27] A journalist present was more taken by a short tribute from Ralph Staats; he quietly said, "There never was a broken-down actor in Hollywood who couldn't get a ten or twenty from [Lugosi] when he had it."[28]

More music, and then the group began to pass in front of the open casket. That was when Tor Johnson's cries grew louder and louder; as he finally made it to the body, he broke down completely.[29] Hope realized then that the funeral had become an event that would have pleased Lugosi. His friends grieving. A widow, an ex-wife, and a bevy of

Above: **Two photographs taken by David Katzman of Lugosi at rest. Katzman's photographs have been printed innumerable times around the world, and yet he has never been given credit for them.**
Below: **Dick with Lugosi at rest. Taken the night before the funeral by David Katzman.**

old mistresses. All present as Hungarian music sent a chill through the air. And everything illuminated by an unending stream of photographers' flash bulbs.[30]

Then the casket was carried outside to the hearse, with Hope following close behind. Zoltán Korda and Ed Wood were pallbearers. Dick was as well, though as he neared the Utter-McKinley doorway, he and Mike Spencer were pushed aside by Don Marlowe, who had years earlier been one of Lugosi's agents.[31] Marlowe–who placed an advertisement in *Variety* that week as a memorial to Lugosi–had seemingly shoved them out of the way to become a pallbearer himself. Camera bulbs were still flashing, and Marlowe wanted to be in the pictures. A curious irony, really, given that Lugosi believed agents had caused many of his career problems.[32]

The engine of the hearse started and the procession began. Dick remembered what Lugosi had said in May, 1956. His old friend Louis Calhern died that month and was interred at the Hollywood Memorial Cemetery; Lugosi thought he might want to be buried there as well.[33] But in the end, Lillian's choice was Holy Cross in Culver City, mainly because it was a Catholic cemetery.[34] And so car after car left Utter-McKinley, and all of them followed the hearse down Lugosi's beloved Hollywood Boulevard.[35] Lugosi's headstone would read "Beloved Father," signifying his bond with the son he loved so very much.

A page from the "Friend's Register" book from Lugosi's funeral. Among the names are Lugosi's friends Marie and Ralph Staats, Lugosi's *Bride of the Monster* costar George Becwar, Dick (Frank Richard Sheffield), Mike Spencer, David Oyler, Edward D. Wood Jr., Conrad Brooks, and Paul Marco.

Later Dick remembered that the first time he had ever seen Lugosi was during the actor's first scene in *Abbott and Costello Meet Frankenstein* (1948). A coffin lid creaked open, and inside was Lugosi in his Dracula cape. At the funeral that day, Dick saw Lugosi the man for the last time; the two images were much the same. This time, though, the coffin lid closed. And soon it was time to go home.

It had been an unpleasant few days, a time that deserved a happy ending. So Dick rounded up as many of his pals as he could, booking a memorial dinner for Lugosi at a Hungarian restaurant, the one on Sunset that Lugosi had loved so much. Some of the fellas who knew Bela best were there, like Mike and Katzman. And even some who had only met him once or twice, like Steve Buscaino. Ten or twelve of them altogether at a long banquet table, complete with a blood-red tablecloth. They traded stories, they ate dishes brimming with paprika, and they raised a somber toast to the dearly departed to the strains of Hungarian music.[36]

A few more weeks passed, and then Dick heard about the Bela Lugosi estate. After all was said and done, Lugosi's assets totalled about $2,900 at the time of his death. That included his remaining share of lots at Lake Elsinore, as well as about $1,000 in cash. Though his 1954

Above: Pallbearer's carry Lugosi's coffin from the Utter-McKinley mortuary to the hearse that would take it to Holy Cross Cemetery. By the time this photo was snapped, Lugosi's old agent Don Marlowe (back left) had pushed Dick out of the way to get in the picture, thus becoming an unofficial pallbearer. *Right:* The "THANK YOU" that Mike Spencer and Richard Sheffield received for being pallbeares. *(Courtesy of Mike Spencer)*

The honor which you conferred upon

Bela Lugosi

by acting as a Pallbearer helped immeasurably to make the memorial services perfect. Please accept our deepest appreciation.

UTTER-McKINLEY MORTUARIES

YOU HAVE JUST SEEN
"Grave Robbers from Outer Space"
IN YOUR OPINION WAS THE PICTURE?

☐ EXCELLENT   ☐ GOOD   ☐ FAIR   ☐ POOR
PERFORMANCES BY PLAYERS ☐ EXCELLENT ☐ GOOD ☐ FAIR

WHAT SCENE DID YOU LIKE MOST?_____

OTHER COMMENT
_____
_____

AGE____   ☐ MALE   ☐ FEMALE
CARLTON THEATRE — FRIDAY, MARCH 15th, 1957

Above: Lugosi in footage that W262ood cut into *Grave Robbers from Outer Space* (later *Plan 9 from Outer Space*).
Below: From the 1957 preview of Wood's *Grave Robbers from Outer Space*.

Last Will and Testament left everything to his son (short of two lots at Elsinore that went to Béla Loosz), California law meant that everything was divided between Hope and Bela Jr.[37] Dick also learned that Lillian had paid for the plot and headstone at Holy Cross, and that Hope paid for the casket and the cost of the funeral service.[38]

Dick continued going to the Harold Way apartment occasionally to see Hope. Not too long after Lugosi's death, he and Katzman went over to play a game of canasta. Hope told them that she had found more of Lugosi's hidden liquor bottles. She came across them while searching the apartment for several thousand dollars that she believed Lugosi had hidden as well. Katzman thought to himself that she would never find a dime, that Lugosi had probably spent all of the money on alcohol.[39]

Of course Dick at times dwelled on the fact that Lugosi was gone. He and Mike Spencer talked about the fact that if Lugosi had lasted just two more months, he might have become energized by the Hungarian revolution, that it might have galvanized him into a longer life. There was even a little joke printed in a newspaper that November: "I hear Bela Lugosi died," with the rejoinder "Don't worry, he'll be back."[40]

Strangely enough, the joke wasn't too far wrong. Dick and Hope attended the LA premiere of Ed Wood's *Grave Robbers from Outer Space* at the Carlton Theatre in March 1957.[41] Lugosi's final film, screened before its eventual title change to *Plan 9 from Outer Space*. Of course it wasn't really Lugosi's last movie at all; Lugosi likely had never even heard of it. Wood merely edited those clips of Lugosi that he had shot in 1955 and 1956 into a story starring Gregory Walcott and a friend of Wood's named Dudley Manlove. In 1956, Manlove attended Lugosi's funeral; now, after Lugosi's death, they were something on the order of costars.[42] Costars in the kind of 1950s science fiction movie that had helped end Lugosi's horror movie career. Dick and Hope were hardly impressed.

After all, things just weren't the same. By 1957, Dick was working on a degree at the LA City College, and his old gang of friends were increasingly scattered. Some of them moved. Mike Spencer had enrolled at a different university than Dick, and David Katzman went into welding. Life was growing more serious, more complicated for all of them.

For Dick, well, a wedding was right around the corner, and then a move to Mexico. He ended up giving Lugosi's Dracula cape to Bela Lugosi Jr. And he sold some of his other Lugosi memorabilia to Forrest Ackerman. It was a new stage in his life. A lot of change and a lot of responsibility. But none of that meant his interest in Bela Lugosi lessened. No, he still held onto quite a few of Lugosi's personal effects. And he certainly held onto his memories.

After all, when he married his beloved Maria Padilla, Lugosi was kind of there with him. Dick showed up at the ceremony dressed in the pants and vest that Lugosi had worn in *The Raven* (1935).

Dick weds his beloved Maria Padilla. He is wearing trousers that
originally belonged to Bela Lugosi.

Filmography

The following filmography is the most complete and accurate catalog of Lugosi's feature film, serial, and fictional short subject appearances ever compiled.[1] They are listed in chronological order and divided into three categories that denote their country of origin: Hungary, Germany, and the United States and England.

Four "new" Lugosi films appear in this filmography, one being the Hungarian silent comedy short *A régiséggyujto* (1918); three different articles in Hungarian trade publications confirm Lugosi's appearance in it.[2]

The other three are all German silent features, including *Der Sklavenhalter von Kansas-City* (1920) and *Ihre Hoheit die Tänzerin* (1922).[3] German censorship records for *Der Skalvenhalter* and *Ihre Hoheit* make clear that Lugosi definitely did appear in them. And then there is *Das ganze Sein ist flammend Leid* (1920), a four-act feature based upon a novel by Gustav (*The Golem*) Meyrink, for which a 1920 critical review mentioning Lugosi exists.[4]

At the same time, other alleged Lugosi films do not appear in this filmography.[5] For example, ads in Hungarian trade publications announced Lugosi would star in the title role of Star Film's *Casanova* (1917). But in the released film, Alfréd Deésy played Casanova; Lugosi wasn't listed in the cast. It now seems clear that he did not appear in the finished version.[6]

Also, this filmography does not contain *Lulu* (Phönix, 1918), which was included in the filmography of Robert Cremer's *Lugosi: The Man Behind the Cape* (New York: Henry Regnery, 1976). Lugosi did not appear in this movie; perhaps Cremer confused it with *Lili* (1918), a Star film that did feature Lugosi.[7]

Then there is a bevy of questionable German silent films. For example, Lugosi was announced as an actor in three films for Eichberg's 1919-1920 season: *Jettatore*, *Sünden der Eltern*, and *Nonne und Tänzerin*.[8] And the film trade *Lichtbild-Bühne* claimed he would appear in Ustad's *Auf den Trümmern des Paradieses* (1920).[9] Shortly thereafter, they also said he would appear with Herta Hedin and Eduard Eysenek in Luna Film's *Die Silbermine* (1920).[10] But a careful examination of period cast listings and censorship records for these films suggests that his appearance in any of them is highly doubtful. In fact, it doesn't seem that *Die Silbermine* was even produced.[11]

The US film *He Who Gets Slapped* (MGM, 1924) is another questionable Lugosi movie. In Lugosi's own scrapbook, Richard Sheffield saw a photograph from that movie showing Lugosi as a clown alongside star Lon Chaney Sr. He also saw a second photograph of a large group of clowns, one of which looked like Lugosi. But Lugosi's name does not appear in any materials from 1924. And of course Lugosi appearing in a publicity photo with Chaney does not necessarily mean he appeared in the running time of the released film.[12]

Finally, the British film *Lock Up Your Daughters* (New Realm, 1959) presents another mystery. A British trade publication review claimed Lugosi hosted this collection of clips from his earlier films, a point also made separately by a viewer of the film in the early 1960s. But attempts to confirm this have failed.[13]

The films that are listed below have been checked and double-checked for accuracy against existing copyright records, censorship records, and available film trade publications.[14] The Hungarian and German entries are listed by their release dates; any variances from previous filmographies are intentional and should be seen as corrections.[15] The US entries have been ordered according to the dates on which the films were copyrighted.[16]

HUNGARY

Leoni leo (*Leoni Leo*)[17]
Star, 1917
Lugosi played Leoni Leo.
NOTE: Lugosi was billed under the pseudonym Arisztid Olt. Exact release date unknown.

A régiséggyujto (*The Antiquarian*)
Star, 1917
Lugosi's role is unknown.
NOTE: Fictional short subject (640 meters). Lugosi was billed under the pseudonym

Advertisement from *Mozgófénykép Hiradó*
of April 21, 1918.

Arisztid Olt. Exact release date unknown.

Lili (*Lili*)
Star, 1917
Lugosi played Plinchard and Tábornok.
NOTE: Lugosi was billed under the pseudonym Arisztid Olt. First screening occurred at the Uraniá in Budapest sometime during the week of October 21-28, 1917.

Álarcosbál (*The Masked Ball*)
Star Film, 1917
Lugosi played René.
NOTE: Lugosi was billed under the pseudonym Arisztid Olt. As with *Lili*, the first screening *Álarcosbál* occurred at the Uraniá in Budapest sometime during the week of October 21-28, 1917.

Az élet királya (*The King of Life*)[18]
Star, 1917
Lugosi played Lord Harry Watton.
NOTE: Lugosi was billed under the pseudonym Arisztid Olt. The Hungarian film trade publications also referred to this movie as *Dorian Gray* and *Dorian Gray Arcképe*. First screening occurred at the Uránia in Budapest on October 23, 1917.

Nászdal (*The Wedding Song*)
Star, 1918
Lugosi played Paul Bertram
NOTE: Lugosi was billed under the pseudonym Arisztid Olt. First screening on February 27, 1918 at the Corso in Budapest.

Tavaszi vihar (*Spring Tempest*)
Star, 1918
Lugosi played Renner

Lugosi in a scene from *Az élet királya* (1917)

NOTE: Lugosi was billed under the pseudonym Arisztid Olt. First screening on February 28, 1918 at the Corso in Budapest.

99 (99)
Phönix, 1918
Lugosi's role is unknown.
NOTE: First screening on September 12, 1918 at the Royal-Apolló in Budapest.

Küzdelem a létért (*The Struggle for Life*)
Star, 1918
Lugosi played Pál Orlay
NOTE: Lugosi was billed under the pseudonym Arisztid Olt. First screening on July 16, 1918 at the Mozgókép-Otthon in Budapest. The film was also advertised and discussed in Hungarian trade publications as *A Leopárd* (*The Leopard*).[19]

Az ezredes (*The Colonel*)
Phönix, 1918
Lugosi played the Colonel.
NOTE: First screening occurred on December 30, 1918 at the Omnia in Budapest.

GERMANY

Hypnose (*Hypnosis*)
Eichberg Film, 1919
Lugosi played Professor Mors.
NOTE: Filmographies generally list this film *Sklaven fremden Willens* (or a mis-spelling thereof), which was another of its titles. However, in the German trade publications the most commonly-used title was *Hypnose*. [20]

Der Tanz auf dem Vulkan
(*The Dance on the Volcano*)
Eichberg, 1920
Lugosi played Andre Fleurot.
NOTE: Released in two parts, *Sybil Joung* (*Sybil Young*) and *Der Tod des Großfürsten* (*Death of the Grand Duke*). In the US, the film was retitled *Daughter of the Night*.

Die Frau im Delphin
(*The Woman in the Dolphin*)[21]
Gaci Film, 1920
Lugosi played Tom Bill.

Schrecken (*The Terror*)
Lipow, 1920
Lugosi played a butler.
NOTE: Film historians generally list this movie as *Der Januskopf* (*The Head of Janus*). But German trade publications in 1920 more commonly used the title *Schrecken*.[22]

Advertisement for *Schrecken* featuring artwork and photo of Conrad Veidt.
As printed in *Lichtbild-Bühne* 21 (1920).

Lugosi in a scene from an unknown Hungarian or German film.

Johann Hopkins III (*John Hopkins the Third*)
Dua, 1920
Lugosi played a cowboy.

Der Sklavenhalter von Kansas-City
(*The Slaveholder of Kansas City*)
Dua, 1920
Lugosi played George Corvin.

Nat Pinkerton im Kampf
(*Nat Pinkerton in Combat*)
Dua, 1920

Advertisement for Eichberg films with Lugosi.

Lugosi played a gang leader.
NOTE: Released in two parts. The second part was screened in 1921.

Das ganze Sein ist flammend Leid
(*The Whole of Being is a Flaming Misery*)
Münchener Lichtspielkunst AG, 1920
Lugosi's role is unknown.

Die Teufelsanbeter (*The Devil Worshippers*)
Ustad, 1920
Lugosi's role is unknown.

Der Fluch der Menschheit (*The Curse of Man*)
Eichberg, 1920
Lugosi played Mälzer.
NOTE: Released in two parts, *Die Tochter der Arbeit* (*The Daughter of Labor*) and *Im Rausche der Milliarden* (*Intoxicated by Billions*).

Lederstrumpf (*Leatherstocking*)
Luna Film, 1920
Lugosi played Chingachgook.
NOTE: *Lederstrumpf* appeared in two parts, *Der Letzte Mohikaner* (*Last of the Mohicans*) and *Wildtöter und Chingachgook* (*The Deerslayer and Chingachgook*).[23]

Die Todeskarawane (*The Caravan of Death*)
Ustad Film, 1920
Lugosi played a sheik.

Ihre Hoheit die Tänzerin
(*Her Highness, the Dancer*)
Eichberg, 1922
Lugosi's role is unknown.
NOTE: Due to censorship problems, this film was not released.

UNITED STATES AND ENGLAND[24]

The Silent Command
Fox, 1923
Lugosi played Benedict Hisston.

The Rejected Woman
Distinctive Pictures, 1924
Lugosi played Jean Gagnon.

Daughters Who Pay
Banner Productions, 1925
Lugosi played Serge Oumanski.

The Midnight Girl
Chadwick Pictures, 1925
Lugosi played Nicholas Harmon.

Punchinello
Famous Lovers, 1926
Lugosi played Pierrot
NOTE: Fictional short subject. Reissued as *The Mask*.

How to Handle Women
Universal Studios, 1928
Lugosi played a bodyguard.

The Last Performance
Universal, 1928
Lugosi did not appear on-camera in this film; he dubbed actor Conrad Veidt's lines into Hungarian for Hungarian distribution.

The Veiled Woman
Fox, 1928
Lugosi played a suitor to Nanon.

Prisoners
First National, 1929
Lugosi played Brottos.
NOTE: *Prisoners* was simultaneously Lugosi's last silent film and first talkie. A hybrid pro-

Lugosi in a scene from *Prisoners* (1929).
(Courtesy of Bill Chase)

duction, ten percent of *Prisoners* featured recorded dialogue, whereas the bulk of the film used intertitles.

The Thirteenth Chair
MGM, 1929
Lugosi played Inspector Delzante.

Such Men Are Dangerous
Fox, 1930
Lugosi played Dr. Goodman.

The King of Jazz
Universal, 1930
Lugosi appeared as a kind of Hungarian-language host in a version prepared for distribution in Hungary.

Wild Company
Fox, 1930
Lugosi played Felix Brown.

Renegades
Fox, 1930
Lugosi played the Marabout.

Viennese Nights
Warner Brothers, 1930
Lugosi played an ambassador.

Oh, for a Man
Fox, 1930
Lugosi played Frescatti.

Dracula
Universal, 1931
Lugosi played Count Dracula.

Fifty Million Frenchmen
Warner Brothers, 1931
Lugosi played a magician.

Lugosi in *John Hopkins III* (1920).
(Courtesy of Bill Chase)

Women of All Nations
Fox, 1931
Lugosi played Prince Hassan.

The Black Camel
Fox, 1931
Lugosi played Tarneverro.

Broadminded
First National, 1931
Lugosi played Pancho.

Murders in the Rue Morgue
Universal, 1932
Lugosi played Dr. Mirakle.

White Zombie
Amusement Securities Corporation, 1932
Lugosi played Murder Legendre.
NOTE: Released by United Artists.

Chandu the Magician
Fox, 1932
Lugosi played Roxor.

Island of Lost Souls
Paramount, 1933
Lugosi played the Sayer of the Law.

The Death Kiss
World Wide Pictures, 1933
Lugosi played Joseph Steiner.

Hollywood on Parade, No. A8
Paramount Publix Corp, 1933
Lugosi played a wax figure of "Bela Lugosi as Dracula."
NOTE: Fictional short subject.

Night of Terror
Columbia Pictures, 1933
Lugosi played Degar.

International House
Paramount, 1933
Lugosi played General Petronovich.

The Devil's in Love
Fox, 1933
Lugosi played a military prosecutor.

The Whispering Shadow
Mascot, 1933
Lugosi played Professor Adam Strang.
NOTE: This was a 12-chapter serial.[25]

The Black Cat
Universal, 1934
Lugosi played Dr. Vitus Werdegast.

Gift of Gab
Universal, 1934
Lugosi played an Apache.

An still from *He Who Gets Slapped* (1924); Lon Chaney stands pointing in the front of the image. Could Lugosi be seated on the front row, second from the left?

The Hollywood Movie Parade
Educational Films Corp of America, 1934
Lugosi's role is unknown.
NOTE: Fictional short subject.

Return of Chandu
Principal, 1934
Lugosi played Chandu
NOTE: This was a 12-chapter serial, which was also released as two different feature films, *Return of Chandu* (1934) and *Chandu on the Magic Island* (1935).[26]

Best Man Wins
Columbia, 1935
Lugosi played Dr. Boehm.

The Mysterious Mr. Wong
Monogram, 1935
Lugosi played Mr. Wong.

Mark of the Vampire
MGM, 1935
Lugosi played Count Mora.

The Raven
Universal, 1935
Lugosi played Dr. Richard Vollin.

Murder by Television
Imperial-Cameo, 1935
Lugosi played Arthur Perry and Professor Houghland's Assistant.

The Mystery of the Mary Celeste
Hammer, 1935
Lugosi played Anton Lorenzen.
NOTE: Filmed in England. Released in the US as *Phantom Ship*.

The Invisible Ray
Universal, 1936
Lugosi played Dr. Felix Benet.

Postal Inspector
Universal, 1936
Lugosi played Benez.

Shadow of Chinatown
Victory, 1936
Lugosi played Victor Poten.
NOTE: This was a 15-chapter serial, which was cut into a feature circa 1936.[27]

SOS Coast Guard
Republic Pictures, 1937
Lugosi played Boroff.
NOTE: This was a 12-chapter serial, which was cut into a feature-length release in 1942.

Son of Frankenstein
Universal, 1939
Lugosi played Ygor.

Advertisement for *The Thirteenth Chair* (1929) from the *Los Angeles Times* of October 31, 1929.

The Gorilla
Twentieth Century-Fox, 1939
Lugosi played Peters.[28]

The Phantom Creeps
Universal, 1939
Lugosi played Dr. Alex Zorka.
NOTE: This was a 12-chapter serial, which was cut into a feature-length release some years later, likely for early television.

Ninotchka
MGM, 1939
Lugosi played Commissar Razinin.

The Dark Eyes of London
An Argyle British Production, 1939
Lugosi played Dr. Orloff (who masquerades as John Dearborn).
NOTE: Filmed in England. Released in the US as *The Human Monster*.

The Saint's Double Trouble
RKO Radio Pictures, 1940
Lugosi played Partner.

Black Friday
Universal, 1940
Lugosi played Eric Marnay.

You'll Find Out
RKO, 1940
Lugosi played Prince Saliano.

The Devil Bat
Producers Releasing Corporation (PRC), 1940
Lugosi played Dr. Paul Carruthers.

Invisible Ghost
Monogram, 1941
Lugosi played Dr. Charles Kessler.

The Black Cat
Universal, 1941
Lugosi played Eduardo.

Spooks Run Wild
Monogram, 1941
Lugosi played Nardo.

The Wolf Man
Universal, 1941
Lugosi played Bela.

Above: Lugosi shakes the hand of Paul Whiteman in a publicity still for the Hungarian version of *The King of Jazz* (1930). *Below:* Myrna Loy and Lugosi in a scene from *Renegades* (1930).

Black Dragons
Monogram, 1942
Lugosi played Dr. Melcher/Colomb.

The Ghost of Frankenstein
Universal, 1942
Lugosi played Ygor.

The Corpse Vanishes
Monogram, 1942
Lugosi played Dr. Lorenz.

Bowery at Midnight
Monogram, 1942
Lugosi played Professor Brenner
(whose alias is Karl Wagner).

Night Monster
Universal, 1942
Lugosi played Rolf.

Frankenstein Meets the Wolf Man
Universal, 1943
Lugosi played the Frankenstein monster.

The Ape Man
Monogram, 1943
Lugosi played Dr. James Brewster.

Ghosts on the Loose
Monogram, 1943
Lugosi played Emil.

The Return of the Vampire
Columbia, 1943
Lugosi played Armand Tesla.

Voodoo Man
Monogram, 1944
Lugosi played Dr. Richard Marlowe.

Return of the Ape Man
Monogram, 1944
Lugosi played Professor Dexter.

One Body Too Many
Paramount, 1944
Lugosi played Merkel.

The Body Snatcher
RKO, 1945
Lugosi played Joseph.

Above: Theatre lobby display promoting *White Zombie* (1932). *(Courtesy of Dennis Phelps)*
Below: Advertisement pasted in Lugosi's own scrapbook, now owned by Dennis Phelps.

Zombies on Broadway
RKO, 1945
Lugosi played Professor Richard Renault.

Genius at Work
RKO, 1946
Lugosi played Stone.

Scared to Death
Screen Guild Productions, 1947
Lugosi played Leonide.

Abbott and Costello Meet Frankenstein
Universal, 1948
Lugosi played Count Dracula.

Mother Riley Meets the Vampire
Renown Pictures, 1952
Lugosi played Von Housen.
NOTE: Filmed in England. Released in the US as *Vampire Over London* and *My Son, the Vampire*.

Bela Lugosi Meets a Brooklyn Gorilla
Realart Pictures, 1952
Lugosi played Dr. Zabor.

Glen or Glenda
Screen Classics Release, 1953
Lugosi played a "Scientist."
Also known as *I Changed My Sex, I Led 2 Lives*, and *He or She?*

Bride of the Monster
Banner Productions Release, 1955
Lugosi played Dr. Eric Vornoff.[29]
NOTE: Originally screened in 1955 as *Bride of the Atom*.

The Black Sleep
United Artists, 1956
Lugosi played Casimir.

Plan 9 from Outer Space
DCA, 1959
Lugosi played the Ghoul Man.[30]
NOTE: Originally screened in 1957 as *Grave Robbers from Outer Space*.

Above: Lugosi takes a break during the filming of *Mark of the Vampire* (1935). *Below:* Lugosi has lunch at the Tail O'the Cock restaurant with the cast and crew of *The Black Sleep* in late February 1956. On the left are Lon Chaney and Tor Johnson. At the head of the table is John Carradine.

CHAPTER ONE FOOTNOTES

[1] "Laura La Plante at the Roger Sherman." *New Haven Journal-Courier* 17 Sept. 1927: 13.

[2] Scarborough, Dorothy. *The Supernatural in Modern English Fiction.* New York: G. P. Putnam's Sons, 1917.

[3] The character names here are no mistake. In the 1927 play, Mina has become Dracula's victim by the time Act One begins, and during the rest of the play Dracula pursues Lucy. The 1931 film, on the other hand, features Dracula first taking Lucy as a victim, and then pursuing Mina.

[4] "*Dracula*, a Play of Intense Moments." *New Haven Journal-Courier* 19 Sept. 1927: 12.

[5] Articles on Stoker's *Dracula* appeared in the US as early as 1897, as in "Fresh Literary Notes." *Chicago Daily Tribune* 15 July 1897. Paul Murray's *From the Shadow of Dracula: A Life of Bram Stoker* (Jonathan Cape, 2004) claims Doubleday told Stoker's widow that the novel had never been out of print in the US from 1899 until their conversation in 1931 (p. 165).

[6] "*Dracula*, A Play of Intense Moments," p. 12.

[7] *Ibid.*, p. 12. [Here I believe the author intends the use of the word "denouncement" (as in "to proclaim"), rather than the similarly-spelled word "denoument."]

[8] The play ran four performances at Hartford, Connecticut's Parson's Theatre between September 22-24, 1927. Then the company moved on to give two performances at the Lyceum in New London, Connecticut on September 26-27, and two performances at the Stamford Theatre in Stamford, Connecticut on September 28-29, 1927. It then opened at the Fulton Theatre on Broadway on October 5, 1927.

[9] "Our Own Broadway and for Diversion." *Stamford Advocate* (Stamford, CT) 29 Sept. 1927.

[10] In chronicling Lugosi's appearances in *Dracula–The Vampire Play* on the website www.cultmoviespress.com (accessed on February 20, 2006) Lugosi scholar Frank J. Dello Stritto counts the number of Broadway performances between the show's opening on October 5, 1927 and its closing on May 19, 1928. He suggests Lugosi appeared as *Dracula* in the three-act play 261 times during its Broadway run. This website is the latest in a series of sources that have used this number; I myself certainly took it as accurate for many years, as in my *Lugosi* (McFarland, 1997). But I have discovered that the official number of performances given in the *New York Times* was 282 ("The Final Reckoning." *New York Times* 3 June 1928: X1). In neither case do these numbers suggest the very real possibility that Lugosi may have missed a performance due to illness or some other reason. Though we don't know who it was, there must have been an understudy. That issue aside, I cannot now tell as to whether either tabulation includes the three "holiday matinees" listed in the *New York Times* (25 Dec. 1927: X2), the special Actor's Fund performance of *Dracula* with Lugosi given on April 13, 1928 ("Actor's Fund Matinees Begin Today." *New York Times* 30 Mar 1928: 32; "Other Events." *New York Times* 8 Apr. 1928: X1.), or the radio performance over WJZ as cited in the text. It might well make sense not to include the radio performance, as it was an abbreviated version performed in New Jersey. Regardless, there remains still a 21-show discrepancy between the two counts.

[11] "A Mystery Play Took to the Road." *New York Times* 2 Mar. 1930: 118.

[12] Woollcott, Alexander. "The Stage." *New York World* 6 Oct. 1927.

[13] "Brooklyn Station Ends Iowa Squeal." *New York Times* 22 Mar. 1928: 28. [Along with Lugosi–whose name was misspelled "Lugosa" in the *New York Times* coverage of the WJZ broadcast–the radio cast included Terrence Neill, Dorothy Peterson, and Edward Van Sloan. The broadcast occurred at 3:30PM EST. In addition to the initial announcement, the broadcast listed in the "Today on the Radio" column in the *New York Times* on March 30, 1928: 30.]

[14] See, for example, "Takes Steps to Curb WJZ Radio Station." *New York Times* 17 Feb. 1926: 31.

[15] Even during the 1930s, *Dracula* was generally given credit for starting the horror film cycle. See, for example, "Thoughts on Horror Era, Renaissance, and Miss Ulric" (*Washington Post* 21 Feb. 1932), "Universal–Master of Mystery" (*Universal Weekly* 2 Feb. 1935), and "Vampires, Monsters, Horrors!" (*New York Times* 1 Mar. 1936).

[16] At least one critic at the time (Soanes, Wood. *Oakland Tribune* 11 Feb. 1933: 8) did notice what he believed was a near-remake of Lugosi's *Dracula* in *The Mummy* (1932). A dead figure brought back to life who wreaks havoc in pursuit of a woman; to be sure, a few similarities do exist between the two films. For some viewers, the fact that John L. Balderston–who is credited as an author of *Dracula–The Vampire Play* with Hamilton Deane–worked on Universal's script for *The Mummy* further buttresses the argument that *The Mummy* is a remake of *Dracula*. My contention remains that the Mummy character operates out the love he has felt for a woman over centuries of time. By contrast, Dracula, in the Lugosi play and film, shows no love for anything but his own well-being. It is blood-lust that drives him to Lucy and Mina. In the 1931 film, he might stop to reflect verbally on how glorious it might be to be "really dead," but that seems mere rhetoric. Dracula tries to protect his undead life to the end of the film.

[17] Other films where Larry Talbot tried to end his supernatural curse would include *Frankenstein Meets the Wolf Man* (1943), *House of Frankenstein* (1944), and *House of*

(Courtesy of Lynn Naron)

Dracula (1945).

[18] Sometimes the count was given higher. The syndicated "News of Comment of Stage and Screen" [*Fitchburg, Sentinel* (Fitchburg, MA) 13 Apr. 1935] claimed that Lugosi "played in 1122 performances before the play's lure waned." That count, especially coming in 1935, seems to be an overestimate.

Then, at the time Lugosi appeared in *Abbott and Costello Meet Frankenstein* (1948), the article "Bela Lugosi Has Been Dracula 5000 Times" appeared in various newspapers, such as *The Advocate* (Newark, Ohio) 25 Aug. 1948. That count also seems easy to dismiss in terms of historical accuracy.

But it is very possible Lugosi appeared as Dracula around 1000 times during his entire career. Dello Stritto's aforementioned count of Lugosi's portrayals in *Dracula–The Vampire Play* on the website www.cultmoviespress.com brings the count to 818. He admits his count cannot be definitive, as there are likely undiscovered summer stock productions in which Lugosi appeared in between 1946-52. As mentioned earlier, the Broadway count is somewhat in question as well; even if 261 performances was the correct number, we still have no way at this time of proving Lugosi appeared at every performance, rather than an understudy.

More importantly, though, is that Dello Stritto's count by his own choice does not include any vaudeville or live appearances Lugosi made in Dracula attire. In vaudeville, Lugosi often performed excerpts from the play. There are almost certainly many undiscovered vaudeville performances of Lugosi as Dracula, and some that are catalogued were actually much higher profile appearances than later productions of the full, three-act play. For example, in 1933, he played at Loew's State in New York to great publicity in a condensed version that caused much more media attention than, say, numerous of his British appearances in 1951. The line between the vaudeville condensations and the full play seems further blurred when we take into account that Lugosi's 1943 tour in the "full play" was actually streamlined for length (see, for example, the *Indiana Evening Gazette* of 11 June 1943).

If Dello Stritto's count can be seen as a rough estimate of the three-act versions of the play, however, it is not at all difficult to believe that all of Lugosi's vaudeville performances and live appearances as Dracula push the entire number of times he appeared in the role to around the 1000 mark.

[19] Mosby, Aline. "Chill-Maker Lugosi Fears Child Star." *New York Daily News* 10 Sept. 1952.

[20] Weber had earlier worked with Lugosi in a summer stock performance of *Dracula* in Litchfield, Connecticut during the first week of September 1947.

[21] Lugosi spoke about this question with reporter Jack Mangan on a television interview for *The Ship's Reporter* in December 1951.

[22] Nagle, James J. "News of the Advertising and Marketing Fields." *New York Times* 7 Sept. 1952: F11.

[23] See, for example, Gary D. Rhodes' "The Horror Film Crisis of 1932." *Monsters from the Vault* Summer 2003. Issue 16.

[24] Schallert, Edwin. "Hollywood Growls at NRA 'Censorship.'" *Los Angeles Times* 3 Dec. 1933: A1.

[25] Blumer, Herbert. *Movies and Conduct.* New York: MacMillan, 1933: 23.

[26] Robinson, William J., M.D. "Concerning Horror Films." *New York Times* 28 July 1935: X2.

[27] Shaffer, Rosiland. "Children Like Sophisticated Movie Fare." *Chicago Daily Tribune* 9 Aug. 1936: D13.

[28] The key resource on the British horror film ban is Tom Johnson's excellent study *Censored Screams* (Jefferson, NC: McFarland, 1997).

[29] Sullivan, Ed. "Looking at Hollywood." *Chicago Daily Tribune* 10 Jan. 1939.

[30] The most extended study of the 1938 horror revival is Gary D. Rhodes' essay "A Hunger for Horror: The 1938 Revival of a Genre," published in two-parts in the magazine *Scarlet Street* (issue 26 of 1997 and issue 27 of 1998).

[31] Smith, H. Allen. "Bela Lugosi Can Imagine No Horror Quite So Bad as Having a Horror That Runs Out on You." *New York World-Telegram* 17 Oct. 1939.

[32] Hopper, Hedda. "Hedda Hopper's Hollywood." *Los Angeles Times* 23 Jan. 1939.

[33] "Mothers in Drive for Better Films." *New York Times* 18 Nov. 1939. [These mothers were not only against horror films, but also movie serials and "crime pictures."]

[34] "Movies Criticized as Ignoring Young." *New York Times* 5 Oct. 1941: 51.

[35] "Are Movies Good or Bad for Them?" *New York Times* 30 Mar. 1941: SM8.

[36] "Horror Movies Studied as Source of Delinquency." *Washington Post* 18 Oct. 1944: 7.

[37] "Plaster in a Movie House Showers Down as a Horror Film Unfolds on the Screen." *New York Times* 14 Feb. 1946: 37.

[38] An excellent resource on the changing box-office receipts during World War II, 1946, and the rest of the decade can be found in Thomas Schatz's *Boom or Bust: American Cinema in the 1940s.* History of the American Cinema, Volume 6. Los Angeles: Univ. of Calif. Press, 1999.

[39] Siodmak, Curt. "In Defense of the Ghouls." *The Screen Writer* Feb 1946: 1-6.

[40] "Camp Horror Films Are Exhibited Here." *New York Times* 2 May 1945: 3.

[41] Harrington, Curtis. "Ghoulies and Ghosties." *The Quarterly of Film, Radio, and Television.* Winter 1952: 191-202.

[42] "Film Deals in Horror." *Los Angeles Times* 15 Dec. 1951: 8.

[43] The key resource on Lugosi's British tour of *Dracula –The Vampire Play* in 1951 is Frank Dello Stritto and Andi Brook's *Vampire Over London: Bela Lugosi in Britain* (Cult Movies Press, 2001). Dello Stritto and Brooks proved that the tour last longer had been previously thought. The question is whether the added length was a positive, meaning that it gave Lugosi work, or whether it was a negative, meaning that a bad production had such a long life.

[44] Gordon, Richard. Letter to Gary D. Rhodes. 20 Aug. 1986. [In this letter, Gordon claimed, "the British management had great difficulty in raising the money for the production and was counting so strongly on Bela's name to carry the show that they had skimped horribly on practically every other aspect of the tour."]

[45] The Pathe newsreel was the *'Sunday Pictorial' Garden Party* section of *Seein' Stars.* June 21, 1951. Burt Lancaster, Bette Davis, and Anna Neagle appear in the same segment. As for the children waiting to see Lugosi outside the stage door of Belfast, see McIlwaine, Eddie. "Did 'Dracula' Bela Lugosi Appear on Stage in Belfast?" *Belfast Telegraph* 2 Apr. 1999.

[46] Gordon, letter to Rhodes.

[47] Winchell, Walter. "Walter Winchell...in New York." *Washington Post* 20 Apr. 1951: B13.

[48] Berg, Louis. "Hollywood Discovers MARS." *Los Angeles Times* 14 Sept. 1952: 18.

[49] "*Suspense.*" *The Billboard* 22 Oct. 1949: 10.

[50] In "Tele Follow-up Comment" on 5 Oct. 1949, *Variety* wrote a review of that *Texaco Star Theatre* saying, "A hoke-horror bit with Bela Lugosi with a surprise ending in which Olsen & Johnson, plus a midget, came out of a mummy case, provided a good deal of yocks...."

[51] Berle's comment followed Lugosi flubbing the words "Otchi Chornya" (sometimes spelled "Ochi Chornya") after Berle said the phrase correctly. The reference is to the Russian song of the same name (meaning "Dark Eyes"). This tune became a pop song in the US, recorded by everyone from Louis Armstrong to Chet Atkins; it also featured prominently in the 1945 film *Wonder Man* with Danny Kaye. Arthur Lennig's *The Immortal Count: The Life and Films of Bela Lugosi* (Univ. Press of KY, 2003) spells "Otchi Chornya" phonetically ("Chi-Chonya") and incorrectly suggests it was an "old vaudevillian line" (p. 370). To the degree it would have ever even been said in vaudeville, it would have been a reference to this song.

[52] "Programs on the Air." *New York Times* 27 Jan. 1950: 33. [Lugosi appeared on *Versatile Varieties* at 9PM EST on January 27, 1950.]

[53] *Syracuse Herald-American* 22 Jan. 1950. [Lugosi appeared on January 22, 1950; the other guest was Lisa Kirk. Arlene Francis acted as host, subbing that night for Ilke Chase.]

[54] "Leading Events Today." *New York Times* 21 May 1950: X9. [Lugosi appeared on *Starlit Time* at 7PM EST over station WABD on May 21, 1950.]

[55] "On Television." *New York Times* 2 Oct. 1950: 31. [Lugosi appeared on Winchell's WNBT show on October 2, 1950 at 8PM EST. The newspaper also referred to this program as the *Paul Winchell and Jerry Mahoney Show*. Other guests included Patrica Bright and Jimmy Blaine.]

[56] Paul, Adrian. "Last Night's TV." *Sunday Graphic* (London) 15 Apr. 1951. [Lugosi appeared on Chester's program on the evening of April 14, 1951. Other guests included Tessie O'Shea and Joan Gilbert. Paul's column joked, "(Lugosi's) attempt to 'strangle' Joan Gilbert ... is somewhat outside the scope of reasonable criticism."]

[57] "On Television." *New York Times* 28 Dec. 1950: 31. [Lillian appeared on the program at 1PM EST on December 28, 1950.]

[58] Ames, Walter. "Movie Writer Likes Video, Film War to Weather; Bela Lugosi Fails 'Candid' Stunt." *Los Angeles Times* 7 Aug. 1950: 22. [*Candid Microphone* was first heard on radio in 1947, reviewed then in *Variety* on 2 July 1947. Unfortunately for my own earlier book *Lugosi* (McFarland, 1997), I took the word of an alleged radio show "historian" about the date of Lugosi's appearance, for which I was told 1947 . That was in error. As this *Los Angeles Times* item makes clear, Lugosi was on the show in 1950, not 1947.]

[59] "Broastcasts: Horror Man in New Air Crime Series." *Dallas Morning News* 17 Feb. 1951.

[60] Bailey, Clay. "Theater-of-the-Air." *Dallas Morning News* 30 Jan. 1951. [Lugosi guest-starred on the Crocker program on January 29, 1951.]

[61] Johnson, Erskine. "Lugosi Will Haunt TV." *Dixon Evening Telegraph* (Dixon, Illinois) 28 Jan. 1952.

[62] Boyle, Hal. "Boyle's Column." *The Kerrville Times* (Kerrville, Texas) 27 May 1952.

[63] *Bela Lugosi Meets a Brooklyn Gorilla* would also eventually be screened under the title *The Boys From Brooklyn*.

[64] Associate Producer of *Bela Lugosi Meets a Brooklyn Gorilla* Herman Cohen noticed the professional friendship between Lugosi and Beaudine during the shoot, as he later noted to interviewer Tom Weaver ("Bela in Hell! Herman Cohen on *Bela Lugosi Meets a Brooklyn Gorilla.*" *Classic Images* Oct. 2001. Issue 316). Beaudine had earlier directed Lugosi in *The Ape Man* (1943), *Ghosts on the Loose* (1943), and *Voodoo Man* (1944).

[65] Graham, Sheila. "Hollywood in Person." *Dallas Morning News* 1952 July 25: 10.

[66] *Ibid.*, p. 10.

[67] "*Untamed Women* Has Novel Plot." *Los Angeles Times* 7 Oct. 1952: B6.

[68] "Fantasy, Scary Comedy Bracketed on Program." *Los Angeles Times* 9 Oct. 1952: B8. [An example of a negative critical response to this film came in *Variety* on 10 Sept. 1952. Their critic wrote that the film

was "destined for a quick demise," with a plot that was "hinged together on a slim yarn that never builds in yocks or in horror."]

[69] Nisbet, Fairfax. "Today's Chatterbox." *Dallas Morning News* 12 Sept. 1952: III, 8.

[70] Taylor, May A. "For the Diagramless Fans." *New York Times* 7 Sept. 1952.

[71] Advertisement. *New York Times* 8 Mar. 1949: 30.

[72] Advertisement. *Chicago Daily Tribune* 18 Dec. 1949: H3.

[73] "Horror Bill Due." *Los Angeles Times* 15 Dec. 1950: 31.

[74] "Horror Films Due Friday." *Dallas Morning News* 11 July 1951.

[75] An advertisement for *The Corpse Vanishes* in Washington D.C. can be found on 29 June 1950 in the *Washington Post*. An ad for *The Devil Bat* in the same city can be found in the 10 Jan. 1952 issue of the *Washington Post*.

[76] Advertisement. *The Coschocton Tribune* (Coschocton, Ohio) 29 Oct. 1949.

[77] Among others, they played the Rialto Theater in Dallas in the spring of 1952 ("Double Bill Horror Films for Rialto." *Dallas Morning News* 29 Apr. 1952: 9), Chicago in June of 1952 ("Loop Movie Schedule." *Chicago Daily Tribune* 1 June 1952: G3), and Washington D.C. in September (Advertisement. *Washington Post* 18 Sept. 1952: 33).

[78] "Horror Program to be Reissued." *Los Angeles Times* 21 May 1952: B6.

[79] "Broder Will Reissue Ball, Arnaz Pictures." *Los Angeles Times* 6 Oct. 1952: B9.

[80] Advertisements. *Washington Post* 19 Sept. 1950: B8.

[81] "On Television." *New York Times* 17 Jan. 1951: 44. [The Bartholomew-introduced screening occurred on WPIX at 7:15PM EST on January 17, 1951.]

[82] *The Death Kiss* was broadcast over KHJ in Los Angeles on March 16, 1952 ("TV Movie Highlights." *Los Angeles Times* 16 Mar. 1952: IV6). *The Mysterious Mr. Wong* played on New York's WJZ on September 6, 1952 ("On Television." *New York Times* 6 Sept. 1952: 23.) *Return of the Ape Man* played on January 16, 1952 over New York's WPIX ("On Television." *New York Times* 16 Jan 1952: 32). *Scared to Death* played on January 23, 1952 over WCBS in New York

("On Television." *New York Times* 23 Jan. 1952: 34). *Scared to Death* also played over New York's WCBS on October 9, 1952 ("On Television." *New York Times* 9 Oct. 1952: 46), and over Los Angeles' KTLA on May 18, 1952 ("TV Movie Highlights." *Los Angeles Times* 18 May 1952).

[83] Advertisement. *Washington Post* 2 Jan. 1952.

[84] On December 8, 1949, WBAD in New York broadcast *The Death Kiss* ("Programs on the Air." *New York Times* 8 Dec. 1949: 66). In 1951, audiences also saw *The Mysterious Mr. Wong* on March 6, 1951 on New York's WPIX ("On Television." *New York Times* 6 Mar. 1951: 36). *Return of the Ape Man* had been broadcast on WPIX in New York on November 17, 1951 ("On Television." *New York Times* 17 Nov. 1951: 14). *Scared to Death* was also broadcast that year, on October 2, 1951 over NBC, as noted in "Today's Television Programs" in the *Washington Post* 2 Oct. 1951: B11. *Phantom Ship* had been broadcast over WOR on October 11, 1950 ("On Television." *New York Times* 11 Oct. 1950: 66); on September 28, 1950, KTTV in Los Angeles also broadcast the film ("Thursday Television." *Los Angeles Times* 28 Sept. 1950: 26.) *White Zombie* had been broadcast over WJZ on September 11, 1950 with host Frank Albertson, as noted in the *New York Times* 11 Sept. 1950: 34). *Shadow of Chinatown* in its feature-length form (it had originally been a 15-chapter serial in 1936) was broadcast over WPIX on July 7, 1950 ("On Television." *New York Times* 7 July 1950: 40); during the summer of 1951, the serial version of *Shadow of Chinatown* was seen over KECA in Los Angeles one chapter each week. *The Devil Bat* had been broadcast over WPIX on August 14, 1949 ("On Television." *New York Times* 14 Aug. 1949: X8), and again over WABD on November 17, 1949 ("Programs on the Air." *New York Times* 17 Nov. 1949: 58). *The Corpse Vanishes* had been broadcast over WABD on June 7, 1950 ("On Television." *New York Times* 7 June 1950: 58), as well as Los Angeles' KECA on February 4, 1951 (Untitled. *Los Angeles Times* 4 Feb. 1951: B6). *The Ape Man* was seen in Los Angeles over KTLA on August 16, 1950 ("Television This Week." *Los Angeles Times* 13 Aug. 1950: B6). It is important to note that this is only a partial catalogue of television broadcasts; its concentration on New

York and Los Angeles is due to their being the anchor television markets. However, as examples from Washington D.C. and Dallas, Texas in the text should already suggest, broadcasts on Lugosi films were not at all limited to New York and Los Angeles.

85 Copp, James. "Skylarking." *Los Angeles Times* 26 July 1952: B3.

86 Gordon, Alex. "My Favorite Vampire." *Fantastic Monsters* 1963. Vol. 2, Issue 5: 26.

87 "In Hollywood." *The Independent Record* (Helena, Montana) 10 Oct. 1952. [This particular column added, "Gordon's also planning *Doctor Voodoo*, *The Vampire's Tomb*, and *The Zombie's Curse*." But it is clear that the key project he was trying to push was *The Atomic Monster*.]

88 Schallert, Edwin. "*Atomic Monster* Will Star Lugosi; New Paris Dancer Found by Kelly." *Los Angeles Times* 15 Sept. 1952: B9.

89 Gordon, p. 46.

90 Arkoff, Sam, with Richard Trubo. *Flying Through Hollywood by the Seat of My Pants*. New York: Carol, 1992: 23-24. [Curiously, in an interview with Gordon published as "Alex Gordon Meets a Brooklyn Gorilla" in the October 2001 *Classic Images* (Issue 316), Gordon remembered that the incident with Broder over the title *The Atomic Monster* occurred before *Bela Lugosi Meets a Brooklyn Gorilla* was shot. But it seems his memory was likely mistaken, as the sources of the time clearly show that *Brooklyn Gorilla* shot in May 1952, whereas discussion of Gordon and Broder jointly working on *The Atomic Monster* was printed some months afterwards in September of 1952.]

CHAPTER TWO FOOTNOTES

1 Dick, Bernard F. *Radical Innocence: A Critical Study Of The Hollywood Ten*. Lexington, KY: University Press of KY, 1989.

2 Bela Lugosi file. US Immigration and Naturalization Service.

3 *Communist Activities Among Aliens and National Groups. Hearings before the Subcommittee on Immigration and Naturalization of the Committee on the Judiciary of the United States Senate. Eighty-First Congress. First Session on S.1832, a Bill to Amend the Immigration Act of 16 Oct. 1918, as Amended*. Washington: Government Printing Office, 1950: 591.

4 *Ibid*., p. 858-859 and 886.

5 *Ibid*., p. 834-835.

6 Cremer, Robert. *Lugosi: The Man Behind the Cape*. New York: Henry Regnery, 1976: 48.

7 See Miklós Molnár's *A Concise History of Hungary*. Cambridge, MA: Cambridge Univ. Press, 2001.

8 Cremer, p. 56.

9 Rhodes, Gary D. Interview with David Katzman. 14 June 2005.

10 Molnár, *A Concise History of Hungary*.

11 *Ibid*.

12 *Ibid*.

13 Lugosi, Bela. "The Founding of Our Union." *Szineszek Lapja* 15 May 1919. [Translation by Elemer Szasz.]

14 "Professional Movements" lists nine members of the Union of Theatre Employees. Lugosi's name appears first, which is not a result of alphabetical ordering.

15 Lugosi, "The Founding of Our Union." [See Chapter 12 for an examination of Lugosi's successes in Szeged.]

16 Kaas, Baron Albert and Fedor De Lazarovics. *Bolshevism in Hungary: The Béla Kun Period*. London: Grant Richards, 1931.

17 "Lugosi Béla Feladata." *Szinházi Élet* 30 Mar. 1919: 20. [Translation by Elemer Szasz.]

18 *Ibid*., p. 20.

19 Lugosi has been referred to as "secretary" in Cremer (p. 69), a word that suggests he was merely

Lugosi circa 1908-1910.

administrative personnel. While the word "secretary" is an apt English translation of the name of Lugosi's post, it does not convey the importance of the position, unless thought of in the same way as, say, "Secretary of State."

[20] Rhodes, Gary D. Interview with Noémi Saly. 24 May 2006.

[21] Lenin posed this question to László Rudas. Qtd. in *Szabad Nep* 21 Jan. 1949.

[22] *Népsava* 7 Mar. 1919.

[23] Lugosi, "The Founding of Our Union."

[24] Kaas, p. 147

[25] Abstract from the order of the District Captaincy of the Red Army on 14th of May, current year. No. 18, Clothing Confiscation. Signed by Bela Lugosi. 22 May 1919. [Translated by Elemer Szasz.]

[26] Kaas, p. 131.

[27] *Ibid.*, p. 107.

[28] Molnár, *A Concise History of Hungary.*

[29] Sziklay, Andor. Letter to Gary D. Rhodes. 30 July 1994.

[30] Cremer, p. 68.

[31] See Dello Stritto, Frank and Gary D. Rhodes. "Strange Cargo: Bela Lugosi's Maiden Voyage to America." *Cult Movies* 28. 1999: 80-81.

[32] Molnár, *A Concise History of Hungary.*

[33] Dello Stritto and Rhodes, "Strange Cargo."

[34] *Ibid.*

[35] *Inspector's Interrogation During Primary Alien Inspection.* Immigration Services. Ellis Island, New York. 23 Mar. 1921.

[36] *Ibid.*

[37] Cremer, p. 84.

[38] Shirley, Lillian. "Afraid of Himself." *Modern Screen* Mar. 1931: 106, 61.

[39] "Notes on the Passing Show." *Dallas Morning News* 9 Mar. 1931.

[40] Advertisement. *Motion Picture News* 30 Aug. 1919: 1746. [The Kun images appeared in *Kinograms* No. 59, distributed by World Pictures.]

[41] "*Daughters Who Pay.*" *The Film Daily* 10 May 1925.

[42] "Béla Kun." *Oakland Tribune* 1 Aug. 1927.

[43] "Béla Kun Admits Reds Aim to End Hungary Regime." *Chicago Daily Tribune* 29 Apr. 1928.

[44] "Károlyi a Man Without Friend, His People Say: Held Traitor, Communists His Only Backers." *Chicago Daily Tribune* 15 Apr. 1925.

[45] "Hungarian Art Angers Károlyi; Claims Slander." *Chicago Daily Tribune* 13 Oct. 1929.

[46] "Károlyis Given Right to Enter US for a Visit." *Chicago Daily Tribune* 29 Oct. 1929.

[47] Károlyi, Michael. *Faith Without Illusion.* Trans. by Catherine Károlyi. London: Jonathan Cape, 1956: 245.

[48] Harrison, Paul. "In Hollywood." *Wisconsin Rapids Daily Tribune* (Wisconsin Rapids, WI) 28 Feb. 1936.

[49] "Biography of Bela Lugosi (appearing in Paramount's *One Body Too Many*)." Paramount Studios press release, 1944. [The name Simonton appears on this two-page bio; perhaps he/she was the author.]

[50] Bela Lugosi file. US Immigration and Naturalization Service.

[51] "Bela Lugosi, Actor, Now Anxious for Citizenship." *Circleville Herald* (Circleville, OH) 21 July 1931.

[52] *Inspector's Interrogation.* Bela Lugosi's file at the Immigration and Naturalization Service.

[53] "Actor Cuts Ties of Two Nations." *Los Angeles Times* 27 July 1931.

[54] "Opportunities Offered Here." *Los Angeles Times* 1 Dec. 1929.

[55] Thomas, Dan. "Hollywood Panic Stricken at Possibility of Congress Placing Ban on Foreign Stars." *The Sheboygan Press* (Sheboygan, WI) 29 Feb. 1932.

[56] *Ibid.* Also, "Many Favorites of Screen Fans May Be Barred by New Law." *Reno Evening Gazette* (Reno, NV) 19 Mar. 1932.

[57] "Noted Players from Abroad." *New York Times* 19 Jan. 1933: 11.

[58] "Movie Aliens Under Scrutiny of Doak's Agent." *Chicago Daily Tribune* 19 Jan. 1933: 6.

[59] "Actor Shows Citizenship." *Los Angeles Times* 25 Jan. 1933: A8.

[60] Lugosi, Bela. *Screen Actors' Guild, Inc. Application for Class A Membership.* July 1933. [By July 3, 1933, SAG Secretary Ken Thomson sent Lugosi a letter accepting his July-dated application.]

[61] Yaros, Valerie, SAG Archivist. Letter to Gary D. Rhodes. 10 June 1998. [The Masquer's Club was an all-male actor's social club in Hollywood; its female counterpart was The Dominos. As for Waycoff enlisting Lugosi, they had appeared together in *Murders in the Rue Morgue* (1932) and a stage version of *Dracula* held in Portland

during May 1932. In the Guild's early days, a new membership often occurred when an existing member lobbied fellow actors to join; Waycoff is the most likely candidate for having brought Lugosi into the fold.]

[62] "Frolic of Film Stars Open Tomorrow." *Los Angeles Evening Herald Express* 17 May 1934. Also, "Frolic of Film Stars in Final Shows Today." *Los Angeles Examiner* 20 May 1934.

[63] This newsreel clip of Karloff and Lugosi appeared in *Screen Snapshots* 11, released in 1934; they perform a parody of their chess game in *The Black Cat* (1934), which Karloff claims is to decide who will lead the Film Star Frolic parade. Appearing elsewhere in this same newsreel were then-SAG President Eddie Cantor, SAG member James Cagney, and Pat O'Brien, who performed at the Film Star Frolic. It is likely that the footage in this newsreel was shot immediately before or during the Frolic.

[64] See Sheldon, Isabel. "All Filmland Mobilizing for Screen Actors' Party." *Los Angeles Times* 16 Feb. 1936: D10. Also, Davies, Reine. "Hollywood Parade." *Los Angeles Examiner* 1 Feb. 1936. [The distance between dates on these articles is not in error; the *Examiner* article was an advance discussion of the mid-February SAG event.]

[65] Lugosi, Bela. Letter to Kenneth Thomson, SAG Secretary. 3 July 1934.

[66] Minutes of SAG meetings that Lugosi attended from August 1934 through February 1936 show a great deal of flux in the advisory board membership. During that period, Lugosi's fellow advisory board members included Lee Tracy, Genevieve Tobin, Dorothy Peterson, Lyle Talbot, Charles Starrett, Jean Muir, Francis Lederer, Hugh Herbert, and numerous others. Lugosi either had a longer term of office than most of his fellow advisory board members, or he was more diligent than others at attending SAG meetings.

[67] Lugosi, Bela. Telegram to Kenneth Thompson (*sic*). 28 Feb. 1935. Sent at 4:14AM PST. [This communication was to do with the plight of film extras, in which Lugosi was lobbying Thomson for his support and vote.]

[68] Lugosi's interest in actors working freelance for various studios, rather than being under contract, can be seen in Lugosi, Bela.

Letter to Kenneth Thomson. 26 Feb. 1938. Also, Thomson, Kenneth. Letter to Bela Lugosi. 17 Mar. 1938. Also, Lugosi, Bela. Letter to Kenneth Thomson. 25 Mar. 1938.

[69] Lugosi, Bela. Letter to Kenneth Thomson. 25 Mar. 1935.

[70] Lugosi, Bela. Letter to Kenneth Thomson. 23 June 1938.

[71] Lugosi, Bela. Completed form on union memberships for SAG. Received by SAG on 4 Nov. 1939.

[72] Bordages, Asa. "Being Horrible Is a Good Business to Bela Lugosi, But He Enjoyed Being Lovable in New British Role." *New York World Telegram* 28 Aug. 1935: 15.

[73] Ottanelli, Fraser M. *The Communist Party of the United States: From the Depression to World War II*. Newark, NJ: Rutgers Univ. Press, 1991.

[74] Brinkley, Alan. *Voices of Protest: Huey Long, Father Coughlin, and the Great Depression*. New York: Vintage, 1983.

[75] Leuchtenburg, William E. *Franklin D. Roosevelt and the New Deal*. New York: Harper Perennial, 1963.

[76] Lugosi, Bela. "Bela Lugosi, Star of *Dracula*, in Person." *Boston Globe* 4 May 1943.

[77] Whitney, Dwight. "The World of Drama–Bela Lugosi." *San Francisco Chronicle, The World Sunday Supplement* 8 Nov. 1943.

[78] Fidler, Jimmie. "Fidler in Hollywood." *Nevada State Journal* (Reno, NV) 25 Oct. 1942.

[79] "Monogram Trailers to Use Bond Slogan." *Dallas Morning News* 4 Mar. 1942.

[80] "Chatterbox." *Dallas Morning News* 9 Sept. 1943. Also, "Piccadilly Arcade to Reopen." *New York Times* 14 Feb. 1943: X13.

[81] Photo Caption. *Los Angeles Times* 22 May 1944.

[82] "Patriotic Tunes Will Highlight Barn Dance." *Lima News* (Lima, OH) 20 May 1944. [They played the song for Lugosi during the episode that aired on 20 May 1944 at 10PM EST.]

[83] "Lugosi, 'Horror' Actor, 'Gentleman' for Visit to Vet." *The Post-Standard* (Syracuse, NY) 10 July 1949: 29.

[84] Hopper, Hedda. *Los Angeles Times* 14 Jan. 1940.

[85] Hopper, Hedda. "Cinema Fans Urged to Protest Any Signs of Un-Americanism Left in Hollywood." *Los Angeles Times* 24 Nov. 1940: 3.

[86] *Ibid.*, p. 3.

[87] "Memorandum: Hungarian Politics in the United States." Foreign Nationalities Brach, Office of Strategic Services. US Government, 1942.

[88] Lyons, Leonard. "Heard in New York." *Dallas Morning News* 9 July 1943.

[89] Dreisziger, N.F. "Émigré Artists and Wartime Politics, 1939-1945. *Hungarian Studies Review*. No. 1-2, Spring-Fall, 1995: 52.

[90] *Ibid.*, p. 54.

[91] Várdy, Ágnes Huszár and Steven Béla Várdy. "Treaty of Trianon and the Hungarian-Americans." *Eurasian Studies Yearbook*. Bloomington, Indiana: Eurolingua, 1997: 132.

[92] The HACD adopted these aims on June 27, 1943, at their national conference. They were written into the "Declaration and Guide to Policy and Action of the Hungarian -American Council for Democracy."

[93] For a major study on this topic, see Várdy, Steven Bela. "Hungarian National Consciousness and the Question of Dual and Multiple Identity." *Hungarian Studies Review*. No. 1-2, Spring-Fall 1993: 53-70.

[94] Várdy and Várdy, p. 133.

[95] Dreisziger, p. 44.

[96] "Memorandum Digest, Confidential: Free Hungary Movement," OSS. [Dr. Mozés Simon supplied this view of Lugosi's leadership.]

[97] "Dies Called Publicity Seeker in Oral Blast by Dickstein." *Los Angeles Times* 29 Nov. 1940.

[98] "International Group Maps Germany Future." *Los Angeles Times* 26 Nov. 1942.

[99] Infod, CNY. "Memorandum Digest, Confidential: Free Hungary Movement." Office of Strategic Services (OSS). 8 Mar. 1944. [The OSS believed that *Hungarian Future (Magyar Jovo)* was owned by Arthur Reich, who was a "registered Communist in the 1936 elections."]

[100] *Ibid.*

[101] Dreisziger, p. 54.

[102] Lugosi, Bela. Telegram to Michael

Lugosi's house on Whipple in North Hollywood, the location of a major HACD event.

Károlyi. 2 Feb 1944. [HACD branches included Bridgeport, NJ, Hollywood, San Francisco, Canada, and some Latin American countries; this was in addition to offices in Chicago and New York.]

[103] The HACD compiled a page of typed "Opinions" that included positive statements about them from US Senators Claude Pepper, Sheridan Downey, Harold H. Burton, Joseph H. Ball, and Joseph Barnes. It also included a positive quotation from an undated editorial in the *Chicago Sun*. [A copy of "Opinions" exists in the Robert W. Kenny papers at the Bancroft Library, University of California-Berkeley.]

[104] Dreisziger, p. 53.

[105] "Group Formed to Save "Jews from Blood Bath." *Los Angeles Times* 20 Aug. 1944. [The mass meeting was held on August 28, 1944 at the Philharmonic Auditorium in Los Angeles.]

[106] "Russia Seeks Truce with Miklós Body." *New York Times* 26 Dec. 1944: 5.

[107] See, for example, Simon, Dr. Mózes. Letters to Edward A. Cahill, Associate Director of the Unitarian Service Committee. 8 Aug. 1945; 14 Aug. 1945; 31 Aug. 1945; and 27 Sept. 1945.

[108] Whitney, "The World of Drama–Bela Lugosi."

[109] Here I am thinking of Lugosi's exchanges with Károlyi, Jászi, and with Clare Boothe Luce. All are cited in these notes.

[110] "Memorandum Digest, Confidential: Free Hungary Movement," OSS. [Dr. Mózes Simon spoke these words about Lugosi's leadership.]

[111] Lugosi, telegram to Károlyi.

[112] This information appears in Lugosi's file at the Immigration and Naturalization Service. Also, Lugosi spoke of his discussions with OWI Director Elmer Davis in a 29 June 1943 letter to Oscar Jászi.

[113] Lengyel, Melchior, Stephen Arch, Michael Curtiz, and Nicholas Bela. Telegram to Robert W. Kenny. 3 Mar. 1944.

[114] Lugosi appeared on William S. Gailmore's radio talk show on 23 Apr. 1944.

[115] "Memorandum Digest, Confidential: Free Hungary Movement," OSS.

[116] Károlyi, Michael. Letter to Bela Lugosi. 26 June 1943.

[117] *Ibid.*

[118] Károlyi, Michael. Telegram to Mózes Simon. 27 July 1943.

[119] *Ibid.*

[120] Várdy, Steven Béla. "Hungarian Americans During World War II: Their Role in Defending Hungary's Interests." *Ideology, Politics, and Diplomacy in East Central Europe*. Ed. by M.B.B. Biskupski. Rochester, NY: Univ. of Rochester Press, 2003: 134.

[121] "Memorandum Digest, Confidential: Free Hungary Movement," OSS.

[122] "Memorandum Digest, Confidential: Free Hungary Movement," OSS.

[123] Vámbéry, Rustem. Letter to Mózes Simon. 14 Aug. 1943.

[124] Dreisziger, p. 54.

[125] Jászi, Oscar. Letter to Bela Lugosi. Undated, circa Summer 1943.

[126] Lugosi, Bela. Letter to Oscar Jászi. 21 July 1943.

[127] Dreisziger, p. 55.

[128] *Ibid.*, p. 54

[129] Jászi, letter to Lugosi.

[130] Várdy, "Hungarian Americans During World War II," p. 134. [Várdy refers to Károlyi as an "outright Stalin worshipper."]

[131] "Memorandum Digest, Confidential: Free Hungary Movement," OSS.

[132] *Ibid.*

[133] *Ibid.*

[134] *Ibid.*

[135] Advertisement. *Washington Post* 16 Apr. 1944: B6.

[136] A reprint of the poster for that mass meeting can be found in Rhodes, *Lugosi*, p. 58.

[137] *Communist Activities Among Aliens and National Groups*, p. 858. [In his "Lugosi in Politics" (in Rhodes, *Lugosi*) Frank J. Dello Stritto implies that Takaró–whom he vaguely refers to as "a Protestant minister"–wasn't a Communist. But repeated allegations suggested otherwise. Along with *Communist Activities*, see "Memorandum Digest, Confidential: Free Hungary Movement," OSS.]

[138] "Hungarian Council Unit Formed Here." *Los Angeles Times* 20 Dec. 1943: AI.

[139] "Hungarians to Hold Red Cross Benefit." *Los Angeles Times* 19 Mar. 1942: 26.

[140] "Hungarian Council Unit Formed Here," p. AI.

[141] Data in Bela's Lugosi's file at the US Immigration and Naturalization Service, supplied by the FBI on 2 Dec. 1947.

[142] Dreisziger, p. 52.

[143] All of this data stems from a page in Lugosi's FBI file signed by R.B. Hood, SAC and titled "L A 200-10364."

[144] Hoover, J. Edgar. Letter to the Special Agent in Charge. FBI Field office, Los Angeles. 5 Sept. 1944. [Copy exists in Lugosi's FBI file.]

[145] This article and supplementary information exists in Lugosi's FBI file.

[146] Both Lugosi's FBI file and his files at the Immigration and Naturalization Service's central office (C-34487-26) and Los Angeles district office (246-P-33491) include evidence of shared information. For example, Immigration wrote to the FBI requesting and/or offering information on Lugosi in November 1947, August 1948, September 1948, and approximately March 1949.

[147] This quotation from the Immigration and Naturalization Service appears in an FBI letter dated 21 March 1949. The letter is part of Lugosi's FBI file.

[148] This information appears in the Lugosi file of the Immigration and Naturalization Service, dated 2 Dec. 1947.

[149] *Communist Activities Among Aliens and National Groups*, p. 835. [The article was printed in the 28 Jan. 1949 issue of the *Magyarok Varsarnapja*; the Budapest article to which it referred was published in the December issue of the *Budapest Kisujág*.]

[150] *Ibid.*, p. 835.

[151] Manly, Chesly. "Truman Relief Board Hit for Favoring Reds." *Chicago Daily Tribune* 28 Apr. 1946: 8.

[152] "Groups Called Disloyal." *New York Times* 5 Dec. 1947: 18. Also, "Attorney General Lists 3 Sets of Organizations." *Washington Post* 5 Dec. 194-7: 1.

[153] Moore, William. "Tells How Reds Used Girls to Lure Gis in War." *Chicago Daily Tribune* 21 Dec. 1949: 3.

[154] Várdy, "Hungarian Americans During World War II," p. 125.

[155] Belmont, A. H. Office Memorandum to Mr. Ladd. 20 Dec. 1950. [Contained in Lugosi's FBI file. In response to

Congressman Howell, the FBI stated that, given the confidential nature of their files, they were unable to furnish him with any information.]

[156] Bela Lugosi file. US Immigration and Naturalization Service.

[157] Cremer, p. 210. [The Hungarian name of *California Hungarians* was the *Californiai Magyarság*.]

[158] Lugosi, Bela. Letter to Congresswoman Clare Boothe Luce. 27 July 1945.

[159] See, for example, Simon, Dr. Mózes. Letter to Edward A. Cahill. 27 Sept. 1945. [Granted, the stationery featuring his name could have been in use after he left, but Lugosi's own letter to Luce still proves his presidency of the HACD was longer than he admitted.]

[160] "Hungarians to Celebrate Restoration of Republic." *Chicago Daily Tribune* 1 Feb. 1947: 10.

[161] Lugosi, Bela. Letter to John S. Wood, Chairman. 19 Jan. 1951. [The full text of this letter appears in Rhodes, *Lugosi*, p. 298.

[162] Sziklay, Andor. *Magyar Lábnyomok*. Liberty Media, 1988: 151.]

[163] *Ibid.*, p. 153. [Translation by Elemer Szasz.]

[164] Várdy, "Hungarian Americans During World War II," p. 131.

[165] "Marxists Prepare May Day Events." Los Angeles Times 29 Apr. 1952: 26.

[166] "Daughter of Former US Envoy Clearly Identified as Red Spy." *Syracuse Herald-Journal* 19 Aug. 1957: 19.

[167] Bela Lugosi file. US Immigration and Naturalization Service.

[168] Fried, Albert. *Communism in America: A History in Documents*. New York: Columbia University Press, 1997: 108.

[169] Agreement between the William Morris Agency and Bela Lugosi. 10 Nov. 1949.

[170] "Names Listed by Writer in Probe on Film Reds." *Los Angeles Times* 20 Sept. 1951: 8.

[171] Data in Bela Lugosi's file at the US Immigration and Naturalization Service.

288

Lugosi and unknown friends in a publicity still.

[1] "Gladys Hall, 86; Writer for Film-Fan Magazines." *New York Times* 22 Sept. 1977: 28.

[2] "Gladys Hall." *Motion Picture Classic* July 1923. [An example of Hall's poetry would be her "Rudolph Valentino: In Memoriam." *Motion Picture Classic* Sept. 1927.

[3] Hopper, Hedda. "Hedda Hopper's Hollywood." *Los Angeles Times* 8 Oct. 1941: 12.

[4] Qtd. in "Gladys Hall, 86," p. 28.

[5] These five occasions were presumably for each of the four articles she wrote (or transcribed, in the case of "Memos of a Madman.") about Lugosi, with the fifth being the 1930 dinner that she and Lugosi attended. But it is possible that she did not meet Lugosi face-to-face for each of the four articles she wrote.

[6] "Film Publicists Dinner." *Los Angeles Times* 23 Feb. 1930.

[7] Along with Hall's four articles, the fan magazine pieces on Lugosi include: "Is He the Second Chaney?" (*Silver Screen* Jan. 1931); "Afraid of Himself" (Shirley, Lillian. *Modern Screen* Mar. 1931); "Master of Horrors" (Sinclair, John. *Silver Screen* Jan. 1932); "Exposing Our Screen Villains" (Howe, Hal. *Screen Book Magazine* Apr. 1932); "Meet the Vampire" (Barry, Barbara. *The New Movie Magazine* Jan. 1933); "The Philosophy of Bela Lugosi–The Horror Man of Hollywood" (Mitchell, Helen. *To You! Magazine* May 1935); "Horror Men Talk About Horror" (*Modern Screen* Jan. 1940); and "The House that Horror Built" (Barnett, Hoyt. *Hollywood Magazine* July 1942). Though the date and publication is unknown, part of another fan magazine article has surfaced as well: a story entitled "Big Bad Bela" by Joe Mackey.

[8] Hall, Gladys. "The Feminine Love of Horror." *Motion Picture Classic* Jan. 1931.

[9] Carroll, Harrison. *Los Angeles Evening Herald Examiner* 11 Feb. 1935.

[10] "This Rialto and Others." *Dallas Morning News* 6 July 1935.

[11] Hall, Gladys. "True Hollywood Ghost Stories II: The Case of the Man Who Dares Not Fall Asleep." *Motion Picture* Aug. 1929.

[12] Hall, Gladys. "Do You Believe This Story?" *Modern Screen* June 1935.

[13] Lugosi, Bela, as told to Gladys Hall. "Memos of a Madman!" *Silver Screen* July 1941.

[14] *Ibid.*

[15] Chrisman, J. Eugene. "Masters of Horror." *Modern Screen* Apr. 1932.

[16] Rhodes, Gary D. Interview with Noémi Saly. 24 May 2006.

[17] "Stars at Sword Points, All in Fun." *Dallas Morning News* 26 Mar. 1932. [In the mid-fifties, Lugosi repeated his claim of having fought duels to Bob Shomer. (Rhodes, Gary D. *Lugosi: Hollywood's Dracula.* Documentary Film. Spinning Our Wheels, 1997.)]

[18] Rhodes, interview with Saly.

[19] All information on Ilona Szmik and her family comes from Noémi Saly, Ilona's granddaughter.

[20] Rhodes, interview with Saly.

[21] Chrisman, p. 83.

[22] Cremer, Robert. *Lugosi: The Man Behind the Cape.* New York: Henry Regnery, 1976.

[23] Rhodes, interview with Saly.

[24] *Ibid.*

[25] Cremer (p. 76) reprints a love letter that Lugosi wrote to Napierska.

[26] An example of how mysterious Ilona Von Montagh [whose name was sometimes spelled "Montag" in the Hungarian press, and "Montagh" in the US and Germany] has been would be the fact that Arthur Lennig's book *The Immortal Count: The Life and Films of Bela Lugosi* (Lexington, KY: Univ. Press of Kentucky, 2003) makes only an extremely brief reference to Von Montagh (p. 43), so brief in fact that she—who was, after all, one of Lugosi's wives—does not even get listed in the book's index.

[27] Ship Manifest for the *Manchuria.* 6 Jan. 1921. Courtesy of the Statue of Liberty-Ellis Island Foundation, Inc.

[28] She played the role of Sári Petráss in *Polish Blood/Legeyelvér.* See "Ilona Montag." *Szinházi Élet.* 12 Aug. 1917: 5.

[29] Her two Hungarian films were *Házasság a Lipótvárosban* (1916) and *A Grófnó Betörói* (1916).

[30] "Ilona Montag [sic]." *Szinházi Élet.* 13 Apr. 1919.

[31] Numerous items on Von Montagh

```
~~~~~~~~~~~~~~~~~~~~~~~~~~~~~~~~~~~~~~~~
   ! ! ! ALL STAR CAST ! ! !
            L I L I O M
     az amerikai magyar szinpadon!
  Molnár. Ferenc világhirü darabjá-
  nak szereposztása:

  Liliom .............. Lugosi Béla
  Juli ................ Montagh Ilona
  Mari ............... Váradi Juliska
  Muskátné ........... Thury Ilona
  Ficsur ............. Horváth Lajos
  Hordár ............. Erdélyi Emil
  Hollenderné ........ Kenesseyné
  Hollender fia ..... Nyikos Zsigmond
  Lujza, Juli lánya..... Winton Klári
  Dr. Reich, öngyilkos...... — —
  Kádár öngyilkos .... Darvas Károly
  1. csendör .......... Tóth István
  2. csendör .......... Nagy Lajos
  Főkapitány az égben.. Hegedüs Lajos
  Ajtónálló az égben......... Pataky
  1. rendőr az égben....... Hatvary
  2. rendőr az égben....... — —
  Linz, pénztáros...... Szalay Gyula
    Népség, katonaság a ligetben: a
  többiek, nem kivéve Fülöp Ilonát sem,
  akinek a fantáziájában az első elő-
  adást lejátszották.
    Második előadás: az állandó ma-
  gyar szinházban, New Yorkban, ha a
  szinház és müvészetkedvelő magyar-
  ság is ugy akarja!
```

The cast list for Lugosi's production of Molnár's *Liliom* with Ilona Von Montagh, as printed in the September 15, 1921 issue of the *Szinházi Ujság*.

appear in the *Szinházi Élet* during 1917-1919. These include 12 Aug. 1917, 30 Mar. 1919, 6 Apr. 1919, and 7 Sept. 1919.

[32] Her German film *Juck Und Schlau* (1920) was directed by E. Waldmann and also starred Anna Müeller-Lincke and Hans Laskus. See the announcement in *Lichtbild-Bühne* July 1920. No. 28, p. 19.

[33] "Ilona Montag [sic]," p. 5.

[34] Ship Manifest for the *Manchuria*.

[35] "Operetta at Irving Place." *New York Times* 17 Oct. 1911: 11.

[36] "Julius Kessler, 85; Long a Distiller." *New York Times* 11 Dec. 1940: 27. [An example of Kessler's philanthropic work

close to the time that Von Montagh came to the US would be his involvement in a million-dollar drive to help suffering children in Hungary. See "Plan Found to Save Starving Children." *New York Times* 30 Sept. 1919: 16.]

[37] "$7,500 Willed by Word of Mouth." *New York Times* 1 June 1921: 27.

[38] "Wild Wooing Tactics of a Temperamental Adonis." *Indianapolis Star, The Sunday Star Magazine Section* 28 Dec. 1924.

[39] Cremer, p. 86.

[40] This performance was given at Rákószi Hall in Bridgeport on September 8, 1921. For more information, see *Küföldi Magyarság* 1 Oct. 1921.

[41] See the cast list and notes in *Szinházi Ujság* (New York) 15 Sept. 1921: 21.

[42] Cremer, p. 86. [The exact date of their marriage was September 7, 1921.]

[43] "Wild Wooing Tactics."

[44] Hopper, Hedda. "Bogey Men-About-Town." *Washington Post* 14 Jan. 1940.

[45] "Wild Wooing Tactics."

[46] See *Szinházi Ujság* (New York) 15 Mar. 1922: 24.

[47] Ilona Lugosi, Plaintiff, against Bela Lugosi, Defendant. *Interlocutory Judgment on Default with Provision for Becoming Final Judgment*. Supreme Court, New York County. 11 Nov. 1924.

[48] "Wild Wooing Tactics" does feature at least one or two definite inaccuracies, such as the claim that Von Montagh was born in Budapest, when in fact she was not.

[49] Hanifin, Ada. "Dracula Found Out; Secret of Lugosi Revealed." *San Francisco Examiner* 28 July 1929.

[50] Cremer, p. 88.

[51] "Wild Wooing Tactics."

[52] *Ibid.*

[53] *Ibid.*

[54] Mefford, Arthur. "Lugosi Wins Heart of Clara Bow, Says Second Wife, Seeking Divorce." *The Daily Mirror* (New York) 5 Nov. 1929. [Some of the same stories in Mefford had earlier appeared in Walter Winchell's syndicated newspaper column on 14 Oct. 1929.]

[55] Ilona Lugosi, Plaintiff, *Interlocutory Judgment*.

[56] Hall, "The Feminine Love of Horror," p. 33, 86.

[57] Oakie, Jack. *Jack Oakie's Double Takes*. Portland, OR: Strawberry Hill, 1980.

[58] "Marion Schilling." In Goldrup, Jim and Tom. *Feature Players: The Stories Behind the Faces.* Vol. 3. Ben Lomond, CA, 1986: 271.

[59] Whitaker, Alma. "Flamboyant Clara Bow Now Emerges as Lady." *Los Angeles Times* 25 Sept. 1932.

[60] Cremer, p. 110-111.

[61] Stenn, David. *Clara Bow: Runnin' Wild.* New York: Doubleday, 1988: 143.

[62] "C.P. Weeks, Bay City Architect, Expires." *Los Angeles Times* 26 May 1928: 3.

[63] *Ibid.*, p. 3.

[64] See "C.P. Weeks," p. 3. Also, see Woods, Virginia. "Society." *Los Angeles Times* 1 Sept. 1920: H2.

[65] "New York Divorcee Bride of San Francisco Man Day after Decree is Final." *San Francisco Chronicle* 31 Jan. 1923.

[66] "Comdr. Woodruff Dies of Influenza." *Washington Post* 14 Jan. 1929: 14.

[67] "John S. Woodruff Dies in Washington." *New York Times* 14 Jan. 1929: 19.

[68] *Ibid.*, p. 19.

[69] "Hungarian Stage Star Weds Widow of S.F. Architect." *San Francisco Examiner* 28 July 1929. [Lugosi and Weeks married on July 26, 1929.]

[70] Details on these plays, their casts, credits, and critical reviews can be found in Rhodes, Gary D. *Lugosi.* Jefferson, NC: McFarland, 1997.

[71] "Mrs. Weeks to Wed Bela Lugosi Today." *San Francisco Examiner* 27 July 1929. Also, "Charles Peter Weeks, S.F. Architect, Found Dead." *San Francisco Chronicle* 25 Mar. 1928. Also, Rhodes, Gary D. Interview with Ruth Sheffield 17 Mar. 1996. [Lugosi told Ruth and Dick Sheffield about having all the rooms on the top floor of the hotel.]

[72] Hopper, p. 12. Also, Mefford, "Lugosi Wins Heart of Clara Bow." [Lennig (p. 498) suggests that there is no reason to believe the Lugosi-Weeks marriage was as short as four days. His reasoning is based on the fact that Weeks said Lugosi had furniture installed during that time. Lennig does not believe this was possible, given that the first day of their marriage Lugosi gave a matinee and evening performance in the play *Dracula.* But that ignores the fact that an understudy could have performed the after-

One of the few photos of Lugosi that Szmik kept after their divorce. *(Courtesy of Noémi Saly)*

noon matinee (quite possible, actually, given his wedding). Or that Lugosi, who surely knew his lines in *Dracula* well by 1929, could not have gone to a furniture store before or after the matinee. Or that Lugosi told someone else to go to a furniture store on his behalf, describing in advance the kind of furniture he wanted. Or that Weeks was mistaken about the furniture. Or that Weeks didn't even speak those words. Too many variables exist to place any trust in Lennig's argument.]

[73] Cremer, Robert. *Lugosi: The Man Behind the Cape.* New York: Henry Regnery, 1976.

[74] Sheffield, Richard. Letter to Gary D. Rhodes. 27 June 1989.

[75] "*Dracula* Star Divorced Here." *Reno Evening Gazette* (Reno, NV) 9 Dec. 1929.

[76] Mefford, "Lugosi Wins Heart of Clara Bow."

[77] *Ibid.*

[78] *Ibid.*

[79] Denbo, Doris. "Bela Lugosi Hails Chance at 'Straight' Film Roles." *Hollywood Citizen-News* 4 Dec. 1929.

[80] Sinclair, John. "Master of Horrors!" *Silver Screen* Jan. 1932.

[81] Sheffield, Richard. Email to Gary D. Rhodes. 16 June 2006.

[82] "Deaths." *New York Times* 24 May 1931: N9. [This obituary includes text requesting that papers in New Jersey, Boston, and Washington D.C. copy and reprint it. Curiously, it does not mention San Francisco or Los Angeles.] Also, Sheffield,

email to Rhodes. [Lugosi told Sheffield in the 1950s that he regretted not staying married to Weeks, as he would have become wealthy at the time of her death.]

[83] Mank, Greg. "A Very Lonely Soul: A Tribute to Helen Chandler." *Monsters from the Vault*. Vol 10: Issue 19, 2004: 29

[84] Hopper, p. 12.

[85] Barry, Barbara. "Meet the Vampire." *The New Movie Magazine* Jan 1933: 68.

[86] Barry, p. 68. [Barry refers to Bow as the "Brooklyn Bonfire."]

[87] Sziklay, Andor. Letter to Gary D. Rhodes. 30 July 1994.

[88] Sinclair, p. 70.

[89] *Ibid.*, p. 70.

[90] Cremer, p. 136.

[91] Morin, Relman. *Los Angeles Record* 28 Aug. 1931.

[92] In "Bela Lugosi Weds in Vegas," (*Reno Evening Gazette* [Reno, Nevada] 1 Feb. 1933), Mimi Arch claimed that Lugosi and Lillian had been "keeping company for two years," which would mean that they were together from before the February 1931 release of the film *Dracula*. Cremer (p. 127) mentions Lugosi's hopes to have taken Lillian with him to Hawaii for the production of *The Black Camel* (1931). That film finished shooting in March 1931 (*Variety* 1 Apr. 1931).

Ilona Szmik and Imre Francsek, her second husband, at Lido in 1924. *(Courtesy Noémi Saly)*

[93] Cremer, p. 137.

[94] Arch's name and post at the Hungarian-American Council for Democracy arises in several surviving documents. These include the HACD's telegram to California Attorney General Robert W. Kenny 2 Mar. 1944.

[95] Cremer, p. 132-133. [In *The Immortal Count*, Lennig mentions a rumor that Lugosi may have had an affair with Lenore Ulric (p. 49). But he noticeably offers no citation at all for this claim.]

[96] "Bela Lugosi Elopes and Weds." 1 Feb. 1933.

[97] That Stephen Arch owned and operated a Hungarian restaurant in the early 1930s is noted in Martin, Edwin. "Cinemania." *Hollywood Citizen-News* 3 Apr. 1933. Also, his involvement with the Magyar Athletic Club is mentioned in "Bela Lugosi Weds in Vegas." *Reno Evening Gazette* 1 Feb. 1933.

[98] "Bela Lugosi Sued for Rent." 6 Feb. 1933.

[99] Thirer, Irene. "Bela 'Dracula' Lugosi a Regular Fellow—Pokes Fun at Jinx." *New York Daily News* 3 July 1935.

[100] Hall, "Memos," p. 52, 88.

[101] Cremer, p. 138.

[102] Heffernan, Harold. "Those Film Villains Mild Souls at Home." *Dallas Morning News* 23 Jan. 1939.

[103] The best and most exhaustive account of Lugosi and Lillian's marriage remains Cremer.

[104] See "2 Held As Shoplifters." *New York Times* 22 June 1935: 18. Also, "Actress and Companion Jailed in Dress Theft." *Los Angeles Times* 21 June 1935: 1.

[105] "Business Records." *New York Times* 16 Oct. 1935. [Von Montagh and her roommate Irene Humphrey together owed $725.80 to the Manufacturer's Trust Company."]

[106] "Irene Humphrey to Wed." *New York Times* 22 Dec. 1935: N4. [As for Von Montagh's unknown fate, it has been presumed that she returned to Europe at some point. In his file from the Immigration Bureau in the US Department of Justice, Lugosi himself claimed she returned to Hungary. But he said that in 1931, and clearly the shoplifting situation happened in New York in 1935. So either Lugosi was mistaken (perhaps due to her telling him that she planned to go to Hungary), or Von Montagh left for Hungary at some point and

then returned again to New York. The latter seems unlikely, but it's certainly possible. Another question is whether she returned to Europe *after* the shoplifting event, because that event seems to be the last trace of her in the US. Perhaps, but no evidence seems to exist either way.]

[107] Fidler, Jimmie. "Jimmie Fidler in Hollywood." *Los Angeles Times* 13 June 1939: A9.

[108] Fidler, Jimmie. "Jimmie Fidler in Hollywood." *Nevada State Journal* (Reno, NV) 16 July 1939.

[109] "Bela Lugosi Son Fetes Birthday." *Los Angeles Times* 14 Jan. 1940.

[110] Hopper, Hedda. "Hedda Hopper's Hollywood." *Los Angeles Times* 14 Jan. 1940: C3.

[111] Sullivan, Ed. "Looking at Hollywood." *Chicago Daily Tribune* 1 Nov. 1937. [Edwin Martin had announced the upcoming birth even before Sullivan in his "Cinemania" column. *Hollywood Citizen-News* 26 Oct. 1937.]

[112] Fidler, Jimmie. "Jimmie Fidler in Hollywood." *Los Angeles Times* 16 Aug. 1941

[113] Fidler, Jimmie. "Jimmie Fidler in Hollywood." *Los Angeles Times* 22 Sept. 1941. [Could this situation be what Lillian vaguely alluded to in 1943 when she said, "The storks are gentle, too. They nest atop our house and only fly into the faces of those Bela dislikes"—?(Finn, Elsie. "Menace with Cold Feet–That's Bela Lugosi." *Philadelphia Record* 19 May 1943.)]

[114] This is made clear in the file on Lillian's suit (D264947) at the Los Angeles County Clerk's Office.

[115] "Bela Lugosis Reconciled." *Los Angeles Times* 29 Oct. 1944: A8. [If this article is correct, Lillian left him in February or March 1944. At the end of January, they were together as he began touring in *Arsenic and Old Lace*. Apparently, after a short time on the tour, she returned to California as he soldiered on in the play.]

[116] See "Bela Lugosi Sued by Wife." *Los Angeles Examiner* 18 Aug. 1944. Also, the file on Lillian's divorce suit (D264947) at the Los Angeles County Clerk's Office.

[117] "Bela Lugosis Reconciled," p. A8.

[118] *Ibid.*, p. A8.

[119] Fidler, Jimmie. "Jimmie Fidler in Hollywood." *Joplin Globe* (Joplin, MO) 19

From the late forties.

Apr. 1946.

[120] "Lugosi Divorce Suit Dismissed." *Los Angeles Times* 10 Mar. 1945: A1.

[121] *Ibid.*, p. AI.

[122] Cremer, p 28.

[123] Lugosi, Bela, as told to Lloyd Shearer. "How I Beat the Curse of Dope Addiction." *Parade* 12 Aug. 1956.

[124] Rhodes, Gary D. Interview with Forrest Ackerman. 11 June 1989. [Ackerman met the woman who claimed that Lugosi was her father.]

[125] Weaver, Tom. *Poverty Row Horrors! Monogram, PRC and Republic Horror Films of the Forties.* Jefferson, NC: McFarland, 1993: 23.

[126] Rhodes, Gary D. Interview with David Durston. 18 Mar. 1996. [This incident occurred when Lugosi and Durston were starring in a stage version of *Dracula* at the Phipps Auditorium in Denver during July 8-13, 1948.]

[127] Rhodes, Gary D. *Lugosi: Hollywood's Dracula.* Documentary Film. Spinning Our Wheels, 1997.

[128] Reverend Géza Takaró's involvement in the Hungarian-American Council for Democracy is noted in a letter from the Council's Executive Secretary Dr. Mozes Simon to Edward A. Cahill of the Unitarian Service Committee, dated 14 Aug. 1945. The content of the letter suggests Takaró was serving as chairman of an HADC committee that was soliciting donations for "long suffering Hungarian youth who are now in Paris."

[129] Rhodes, interview with Saly.

[130] Mosby, Aline. "Chill-Maker Lugosi Fears Child Star." *New York Daily News* 10 Sept. 1952.

[131] Cremer (p. 214) mentions that Lillian left Lugosi in March 1953. But given the exact date of the suicide story, it seems that it must have been late February 1953.

[132] Cremer (p. 214-215) reprints two of Lugosi's letters to Lillian, including his 12 Mar. 1953 to her that is quoted here.

[133] "Dracula Laughs Off 'Suicide' Report." *Los Angeles Herald and Express* 26 Feb. 1953.

[134] *Ibid.*

[135] "Wife Again Asks Lugosi Divorce." *Los Angeles Examiner* 3 June 1953. Also "Bela Lugosi Accused of Cruelty in Divorce Suit." *Los Angeles Times* 3 June 1953. [Presumably newspapers got the May 1 separation date came from information filed by Lillian's attorney. See File D452510. 1953.]

[136] Lugosi had appeared earlier after he received the summons to appear on 29 June 1953. But even at that stage he appeared a day late, on 30 June 1953. See File D452510.

[137] "Divorces Jealous Dracula." *Los Angeles Herald Express* 17 July 1953.

[138] *Ibid.*

[139] In an interview with Greg Mank, Lillian said she began to work as a secretary circa 1952. She seems to have continued in this capacity for many years.

[139] *Ibid.*

[140] "Lugosi Terror, Wife Claims-Gets Divorce." *Los Angeles Daily News* 19 July 1953.

[141] *Lillian A. Lugosi vs. Bela Lugosi*, D-152810. In The Superior Court of the State of California in and for the County of Los Angeles." 17 July 1953.

[142] *Ibid.*

[143] "Gladys Hall, 86," p. 28.

[144] Hall, "The Feminine Love of Horror," p. 33.

Advertisement published in the
Santa Barbara Daily on December 31, 1953.

1 See, for example, Whitney, Dwight. "The World of Drama–Bela Lugosi." *San Francisco Chronicle. The World Sunday Supplement* 8 Aug. 1943. Also, "'Dracula' a Relief from Real-life Horror." *Boston Globe* 9 May 1943.

2 Weiss's *Test-Tube Babies* (1948) featured a storyline about artificial insemination, and *The Devil's Sleep* (1949) covered the narcotics racket.

3 "Former GI Transformed Into Lovely Woman in Long Series of Treatments." *Los Angeles Times* 1 Dec. 1952.

4 "Man-Turned-Woman Deluged by Show Offers." *Los Angeles Times* 7 Dec. 1952: 43. [That Jorgensen was thinking about writing a book appears in "May Write Book, Says Man Changed to Woman." *Los Angeles Times* 2 Dec. 1952: 8.]

5 "Man Turned Into Woman Coming Home." *Los Angeles Times* 12 Feb. 1953: 24.

6 "Christine Jorgensen Due Here Tuesday for Show." *Los Angeles Times* 29 Apr. 1953: 11. [Weiss wasn't the only person to capitalize on the Jorgensen story without having Jorgensen's involvement. In 1953, Louis Farrakhan–later the head of the Nation of Islam–recorded a song entitled "Is She Is, or Is She Ain't." The tune, one of several Farrakhan sang on records in 1953-54, was a calypso number that featured lyrics about "this modern surgery" that "changed him from he to she."]

7 These must have been the production times for the film, not only because of press items like the Wood Soanes article in the *Oakland Tribune* (cited later in footnote 22), but due to Lugosi's personal life. His wife Lillian was still with him when his footage for *Glen or Glenda* was shot; at some point in the latter part of February she left him.

8 Thomas, Harry. Interview with Gary D. Rhodes. 15 Mar. 1996.

9 Weaver, Tom, Debbie Rochon, the Phantom of the Movies, and Peter Schmideg. "Alex Gordon on Ed Wood and *Ed Wood. Cult Movies* 22. 1997: 44.

10 Wood, Edward D., Jr. Response to "Questionnaire" sent to him by Fred Olen Ray. Undated.

11 Cremer, Robert. *Lugosi: The Man Behind the Cape.* New York: Henry Regnery, 1976: 212.

12 Fuller, Dolores. *A Fuller Life: Hollywood, Ed Wood, and Me.* Unpublished at the time of writing.

13 Cremer, p. 212.

14 Grey, Rudolph. *Nightmare of Ecstasy: The Life and Art of Edward D. Wood, Jr.* Los Angeles: Feral House, 1992: 39. [Grey's book remains the key work on Wood.]

15 Thomas, Harry. Interview with Gary D. Rhodes. 5 June 1996.

16 Grey, p. 42.

17 Brooks, Conrad. "Edward D. Wood, Jr.: The Story Must Be Told." *Cult Movies/Videosonic Arts* 3. 1991: 30.

18 Sheffield, Richard. Email to Gary D. Rhodes. 5 Feb. 2006.

19 Grey's *Nightmare of Ecstasy* builds its expert account of Wood's life and career out of oral histories that exemplify these kinds of contradictions.

20 *Ibid.*, p. 42.

21 Grey, Rudolph. "Umberto Scali Lives!!!: The Timothy Farrell Interview." *Psychotronic.* Issue 14, Winter 1992/1993.

22 Weiss, George to Aline Mosby. Qtd. in Soanes, Wood. "Lend an Ear, Broadway Hit, Scheduled Under Hale Aegis." *Oakland Tribune* 25 Feb. 1952: 23.

23 *Ibid.*, p. 23.

24 Grey, p. 46.

25 Advertisement. *Oakland Tribune* 30 Nov. 1957: B5.

26 "At the Theaters." *Lima News* (Lima, OH) 15 June 1958: B6.

27 For the most exhaustive examination of the exploitation film genre, see Eric Schaefer's *"Bold! Daring! Shocking! True!": A History of Exploitation Films, 1919-1959.* Durham, NC: Duke University Press, 1999. Also very valuable is Brett Wood and Felicia Feaster's *Forbidden Fruit: The Golden Age of the Exploitation Film.* Baltimore, MD: Midnight Marquee, 1999.

28 Brooks, p. 30

29 Of the two groups, Universal remains particularly curious in that at times in the 1920s and the early 1930s (whether *The Phantom of the Opera* in 1925 or *All Quiet on the Western Front* in 1930), it mounted prestige productions ("Super-Productions") on very high level.

30 Numerous important books have investi-

gated the studio system, such as Thomas Schatz's *The Genius of the System* (New York: Pantheon, 1988), which includes particularly valuable information about Universal's place within the system of the "Big Five" and "Little Three." Also of great value is Tino Balio's *Grand Design: Hollywood as a Modern Business Enterprise, 1930-1939* (Berkeley: University of California, 1993), which offers a very helpful examination not only of the production side of the major studios, but also their distribution techniques and theatre ownership.

[31] Additional relevant data on these numbers would include the fact that of his ten Fox films, only one (*The Gorilla* of 1939) was released under the studio name 20th Century Fox. Also, two of his Warner Brothers films were released under the company name First National; however, both of them (*Prisoners* in 1929 and *Broadminded* in 1931) were produced and released after Warner Brothers bought First National in September 1928, a move that was largely about improving WB's prestige. See Sperling, Cass Warner and Cork Millner, with Jack Warner Jr. *Hollywood Be Thy Name: The Warner Brothers Story*. Rocklin, CA: Prima Publishing, 1994: 147. Lastly, it should be added that Lugosi didn't work for United Artists until *The Black Sleep* in 1956; UA had distributed his 1932 film *White Zombie*, but they didn't produce it.

[32] The 19 films at Universal deserve some explanation. Lugosi acted in 16 feature films for the studio, as well as one serial (*The Phantom Creeps* in 1939, which was later trimmed heavily into a feature). Thus, 17 films. He also dubbed Conrad Veidt's character in *The Last Performance* (1928) for release in Hungary, and appeared onscreen as a host for the Hungarian release of *The King of Jazz* (1930). Hence, 19 films. [Film counts in this chapter do include Lugosi's five serials, such as *The Phantom Creeps* in this tabulation of the Universals. At the same time, they are not counted twice in those instances like *The Phantom Creeps* when a serial and a feature were released; this is also true for *The Return of Chandu* (1934), a serial for which two feature films emerged. Also, none of this is to suggest that feature-length and serials were the same thing; they certainly were not. But they both represent film projects Lugosi made at studios like Universal or independents like Republic.]

[33] Lange, Johnny. Interview with Gary D. Rhodes. 6 Sept. 2005. [In addition to his role

as a musical director, Lange–who gave this interview at the age of 100–wrote some music for the Lugosi films *Spooks Run Wild* (1941) and *Black Dragons* (1942) with his partner Lew Porter.]

[34] The studio Imperial-Cameo is also known as Imperial. Interestingly, while the name Imperial-Cameo appears on publicity materials for Lugosi's *Murder By Television* (1935), the onscreen credits simply say "Imperial."

[35] Lugosi made a 1935 film for Monogram called *The Mysterious Mr. Wong* (1935), and then, after the studio reorganized, he made another nine films for them in the 1940s.

[36] Fidler, Jimmie. "Jimmie Fidler in Hollywood." *Los Angeles Times* 26 Jan. 1942.

[37] This count includes Lugosi's 16 poverty row films made after his success in *Dracula* (starting with *White Zombie* in 1932) to *Bela Lugosi Meets a Brooklyn Gorilla* in 1952. It also includes his four poverty row serials (all of which except *The Whispering Shadow* of 1933 were also trimmed heavily to release as feature films). As for the trio of low-budget British films, they are *The Mystery of the Mary Celeste* (1935), *The Dark Eyes of London* (1939), and *Mother Riley Meets the Vampire* (1952). As for *Mary Celeste*, the initial knowledge that it was made by Hammer evokes an idea of a successful company, but the noted "Hammer Film Productions, Ltd." was not founded until 1949. In 1935, the company was certainly close to some US poverty-row companies. And *Mary Celeste* essentially became a poverty-row horror in the US, thanks to its distribution as *The Phantom Ship* by Guaranteed Pictures Corporation, Ltd. The same could be said of *The Dark Eyes of London*, distributed in 1940 in the US as *The Human Monster* by Monogram.

[38] The exceptions included: *The Death Kiss* (1932), which gave him third billing under David Manners and Adrienne Ames; *SOS Coast Guard* (1937), which in both its serial and feature form gave him second billing under Ralph Byrd; and *Mother Riley Meets the Vampire* (1952), which gave him second billing under Arthur Lucan. [The discussion of Lugosi's screen billing in this chapter refers to original releases. Occasionally, billing changed in reissues, if not necessarily onscreen than in publicity materials. Some lobby cards for a

reissue of *The Black Cat* (1934) as *The Vanishing Body* (1947) even billed Lugosi over Boris Karloff. An even wider variance in billing is revealed by looking at individual city newspaper reviews, which often gave Lugosi better billing than he received onscreen.]

[39] The four films were: *Dracula* (1931) and *Night Monster* (1942) at Universal, and *Night of Terror* (1933) and *The Return of the Vampire* (1943) at Columbia.

[40] The key book on the poverty-row horror films of the 1930s remains George E. Turner and Michael H. Price's *Forgotten Horrors* (San Diego: A.S. Barnes, 1979; revised and released under the title *Forgotten Horrors: The Definitive Edition* by Baltimore, MD: Midnight Marquee, 1999). As for the same kinds of films from the 1940s, the key book on the subject is Tom Weaver's *Poverty Row Horrors! Monogram, PRC and Republic Horror Films of the Forties* (Jefferson, NC: McFarland, 1993).

[41] "Tragedy-Comedy Tradition Safe with Bela Lugosi." *Los Angeles Times* 6 Sept. 1943. Also, Kirkley, Donald. "The Theater—*Arsenic and Old Lace*." *Baltimore Sun* 27 Feb. 1944.

[42] For more information on *White Zombie*, see Gary D. Rhodes's *White Zombie: Anatomy of a Horror Film* (Jefferson, NC: McFarland, 2002).

[43] Rhodes, Gary D. Interview with Harry Thomas. 15 Mar. 1996. [Thomas claimed that Lugosi watched *Glen or Glenda*.]

[44] Wood, Ed. Letter to Bela Lugosi. 20 July 1953. Copy in the Forrest J Ackerman collection as of 1985. [If Alex Gordon remembered correctly, he introduced Wood and Lugosi sometime in the second half of 1952.]

[45] Wood, Edward D., Jr. *The Phantom Ghoul*. Original Story and Screenplay. 1953.

[46] Wood, Edward D., Jr.. Letter to Bela Lugosi. 20 July 1953. [*The Hidden Face* became *Jail Bait* (1954), with Herbert Rawlinson playing the role intended for Lugosi. Why Lugosi didn't end up appearing in that film is unclear.]

[47] Fuller, *A Fuller Life*.

[48] The *Players Directory Bulletin* for November 1953 shows Herdan-Sherrell as being Lugosi's agency at that time.

[49] Manners, Dorothy. "Enchanted Cup Next Tyrone Power Picture." *The Chronicle Telegram* (Elyria, OH) 4 Dec. 1953.

[50] "Hollywood Historama Exhibit Viewed By 8,000." *Los Angeles Times* 30 Nov. 1953: 4.

[51] "Hollywood's Historama to Open Friday." *The Valley News* (Van Nuys, CA) 19 Nov. 1953.

[52] Sherman, Gene. "Cityside with Gene Sherman." *Los Angeles Times* 6 Dec. 1953.

[53] "Hollywood Historama," p. 4.

[54] Fuller, *A Fuller Life*.

[55] Wood, Edward D., Jr. *Hollywood Rat Race*. New York: Four Walls Eight Windows, 1998: 95-96.

[56] These shows are detailed in Gary Rhodes's *Lugosi* (Jefferson, NC: McFarland, 1997).

[57] "'Night of 1000 Stars' Huge Program Ready." *Los Angeles Times* 28 June 1936.

[58] Wood, p. 96-97.

[59] A thorough investigation of San Bernardino newspapers like the *San Bernardino Daily* and the *San Bernardino Evening Telegram* resulted in no mention of the West Coast Theatre event outside of paid advertisements.

[60] The five films were (in order): *At Sword's Point* (1952), *When the Daltons Rode* (1940), *Pagan Love Song* (1950), *Arabian Nights* (1942), and *In the Navy* (1941).

[61] See Rhodes, *Lugosi* (p.188-200) for a lengthy list of Lugosi's live appearances.

[62] Advertisement. *Los Angeles Times* 17 Apr. 1931. Also, "Stars Invited to Durbin Film Preview." *Los Angeles Times* 22 Sept. 1940.

[63] Advertisement. *Los Angeles Times* 30 Jan. 1932: A7. Also, "Stars Cast for Benefit." *Los Angeles Times* 20 Jan. 1935: 19. Also, "May Robson Volunteers to Help Benefit Show." *Los Angeles Times* 16 Jan. 1936: A2.

[64] "The Stamp Collector's Review: Coast Clubs Meeting in Hollywood." *Oakland Tribune* 4 Feb. 1940. Also, "Mystery Writers Eat, Too." *Indiana Evening Gazette* (Indiana, PA) 21 Apr. 1950.

[65] "Hungarians to Parade in Celebration Sunday." *Los Angeles Times* 24 June 1936. Also, "Hungarians Dance at Press Festival." *Los Angeles Times* 11 Sept. 1939.

[66] Cremer, p. 221.

[67] Fuller, *A Fuller Life*.

[68] Lugosi, Bela. Foreword to Ron Ormond's book *Your Career in Hollywood*. Hollywood: Screen Guild Press, 1954.

Above: Lugosi visits a film set circa 1930. *Below*: Lugosi on another film set in the 1930s.

[1] Thomas, Bob. "Celebrity Service Locates the Stars." *Bismarck Tribune* (Bismarck, North Dakota) 25 Sept. 1952.

[2] Unless noted otherwise, biographical information and details in this chapter stem from literally dozens of conversations, letters, and emails between Richard Sheffield and Gary D. Rhodes over a twenty-year period.

[3] Like Dick, Joe Dassin was born in 1938. The two lost touch in the early fifties when the HUAC hearings caused the Dassins moved to France. Some time later, Joe became a popular singer in France with such recordings as "Bip Bip" and "L'Eté Indien."

[4] Buder, Leonard. "Vicarious Thrills Sought by Youth." *New York Times* 19 Sept. 1948: E9.

[5] Spencer, Michael. Email to Richard Sheffield. 19 June 2000.

[6] Heyn, Howard C. "Hollywood Property Men Reap Varied Harvest From War Surplus." *The Hartford Courant* 4 Apr. 1948: SM7.

[7] This improvised "feel" is largely that. Examining the shooting script (Riley, Philip J., ed. *Abbott and Costello Meet Frankenstein: The Original Shooting Script.* Absecon, NJ: MagicImage Filmbooks, 1990), the finished film does not feature many derivations from the written word. As far as Costello's character referring to Bud Abbott by his real name, that happens in a flurry of words when Costello is beating on a secret door in a basement area of the castle.

[8] No photos from Lugosi's stage portrayals show him using the cape in this way, and apparently no costars, directors, or audience members have ever remembered that he did.

[9] Rhodes, Gary D. Interview with David Katzman. 13 Mar. 1996.

[10] Spencer, Michael. Interview with Gary D. Rhodes. 15 Apr. 1996.

[11] Advertisement. *Los Angeles Times* 16 Apr. 1953. [Stars advertised to appear during the "Premathon" included Gracie Allen, William Bendix, Walter Brennan, George Burns, Eddie Cantor, Hoagy Carmichael, Chuck Connors, Broderick Crawford, Tony Curtis, Irene Dunne, Judy Garland, Merv Griffin, Edmund Gwenn, Sterling Hayden, Jean Hersholt, Charlton Heston, Paulette Goddard, Rock Hudson, Janet Leigh, Dean Martin, Merle Oberon, Pat O'Brien, Ginger Rogers, Robert Stack, and Jane Wyman, among many others.]

[12] "Movie Closeup." *Chicago Daily Tribune* 29 Feb. 1940.

[13] Gordon, Alex. "My Favorite Vampire." *Fantastic Monsters.* Volume 2, Issue 5. 1963.

[14] *Ibid.*

[15] In the 1941 show, which was called "One Night of Horror" in Chicago during May 2-8, *The Billboard* (10 May 1941) wrote, "a man in a gorilla outfit marches in and out of the stage and aisles for no good reason." Lugosi performed the act again, perhaps with some modifications, as "Mirth and Horror" in Fort Wayne, Indiana on May 10 and 11, 1941.

In late 1950 and early 1951, Lugosi's "Horror and Magic Stage Show" featured a gorilla as well. Many years later, an actor named Charles Stanley told Lugosi biographer Richard Bojarski that he was inside the suit for those appearances.

[16] Clips from the newsreel appear in Gary D. Rhodes's documentary film *Lugosi: Hollywood's Dracula* (Spinning Our Wheels, 1997). The original newsreel, which also included images of John Foster Dulles in Paris at a NATO meeting, was recorded as negative number 36618 and as issue number PSN 74 C-1A-1B-1C. [Important in this sentence is the word "mainstream." Certainly *Glen or Glenda* was playing a small number

A still photograph Lugosi kept in his own collection. From the 1930s.

of third-rate theaters in 1953 and 1954.]

[17] Rhodes, Gary D. Interview with Forrest J Ackerman. 8 July 1989.

[18] *Ibid.*

[19] At times the broadcast date of this program has been given as 9 Aug. 1953. However, that date represents the East Coast rebroadcast. See, for example, the *Washington Post* of 9 Aug. 1953.

[20] Was Lugosi happy to be making money on *You Asked for It*, or happy because he was paying off a debt? Allegedly, Lugosi owed money to Hollywood's Magic Castle, founded by Milt Larsen. Larsen was also a producer of *You Asked for It*; the show's host Art Baker was married to Larsen's mother. According to the rumor, Lugosi's appearance on the program was to clear his debt to Larsen. [Windley, Charles. Email to Gary D. Rhodes. 18 May 2006.]

[21] Carroll, Harrison. *Los Angeles Evening Herald Express* 9 Feb 1935.

[22] Lugosi appeared on *Country Fair* on July 31, 1945 over ABC at 10:30PM EST. ["Woman'n Half by Bela Lugosi on Radio Fair." *Dallas Morning News* 31 July 1945.]

[23] Coe, Richard L. "Mena's Sphinx Wasn't the Type for Pascal; Capitol's Spook Show." Washington Post 12 Aug. 1946.

[24] The best history of the US spook shows is Walker, Mark. *Ghostmasters*. Boca Raton, FL: Cool Hand Communications, Inc., 1994.

[25] See "Spook in Person." *Variety* 22 Jan. 1947. Also, see Rhodes, *Lugosi* (p. 193) for more details on the show.

[26] *The Newark Star-Ledger*. 19 Dec. 1947.

[27] Neff's friend Charles Windley mentioned that this trailer did exist. But even if it did, it is still possible the Lugosi clips were simply taken from one of his films and not shot specifically for it. [Windley, Charles. Email to Gary D. Rhodes 24 Oct. 2005.]

[28] Neff's friend Charles Windley mentioned that Neff continued to publicize Lugosi's name even after Lugosi's appearances stopped; he did this by booking a Lugosi film to show onscreen. [Windley, Charles. Email to Gary D. Rhodes. 20 Feb. 2006.]

[29] Blankenhorn, Richard. "The Great Lugosi as Remembered by Alexander the Great." *Famous Monsters of Filmland* 132. Mar. 1932. [Blankenhorn's article refers to Campbell using the stage name of "Alexander Great," rather than "Alexander the Great." Either way, it seems Campbell used this stage name to build on the fame of the nineteenth-century magician Alexander the Great. Also, the name "Loring Campbell" may have been a pseudonym as well, as Campbell claimed to have been from Hungary.]

[30] Walker, 85. [No outside verification of this appearance has turned up. It is possible that Lugosi did not make a live appearance, and that his name appeared in conjunction with the show thanks to Silkini (John Edwin Baker) screening a Lugosi film.]

[31] Windley, Charles. Email to Gary D. Rhodes. 26 Dec. 2005. [Windley mentioned that when he played Hubert's, the management told him that Lugosi had previously appeared there. Much later, he learned that a contract Lugosi had signed with Hubert's manager Charles Lucas turned up in Lucas's papers.]

[32] These details stem from ads found in the *Standard-Star* (New Rochelle, NY) on 29 Dec. 1950 and in the *Camden Courier-Post* (Camden, NJ) on 17 Mar. 1951.

[33] See "Lugosi's Horror Show Set to Hypo Nabe Biz." *Variety* 6 Dec. 1950. Also, see the photo montage with Neff's picture in the *Camden Courier-Post* on 15 Mar. 1951.

[34] Lugosi appeared in Yonkers on 28 Dec, 1950, New Rochelle on 29. Dec. 1950, and then Alden for three shows on 1 Jan. 1951. He then appeared in Patterson on 9 Feb. 1951, and Newark on 19 Feb. 1951.

[35] Windley, Charles. Email to Gary D. Rhodes. 21 Feb. 2006.

Lou Costello, Bobby Barber, Bela Lugosi, and Bud Abbott (from left to right) clowning around during the making of *Abbott and Costello Meet Frankenstein* (1948) in a rare but damaged photograph.

[36] "National Disc Jockey Week Hailed by City." *Los Angeles Times* 27 July 1953: 24.

[37] Actress Shirley Patterson was probably better known as Shawn Smith, appearing under that name in films like *It! The Terror from Beyond Space* (1958).

[38] Ames, Walter. "Lou Costello Collapse Brings Martin, Lewis to Aid on Comedy Hour." *Los Angeles Times* 31 Oct. 1953: A5.

[39] Liner notes. *Spadella! The Essential Spade Cooley.* Sony Compact Disc, 1994.

[40] "What One Monster Could Do." *TV Guide* 14-20 Aug. 1953: A6-A7.

[41] Thomas, "For a Halloween Story, He Went to an Expert."

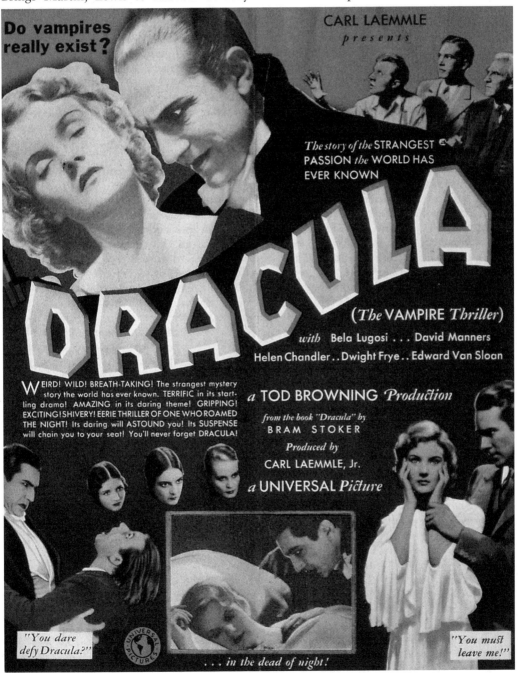

A herald for *Dracula* (1931). *(Courtesy of Lynn Naron)*

CHAPTER SIX FOOTNOTES

[1] Pryour, Thomas M. "U-I Plots Movie About A Vampire." *New York Times* 23 Feb. 1953: 21.

[2] Lugosi had appeared in the following color films: *Viennese Nights* (1930), *Fifty Million Frenchmen* (1931, which survives only in B&W prints), and *Scared to Death* (1947). Mention of the 3-D film *Strange Deception* occurs in "Ink Hampton White For *Dracula* Lead." *The Billboard* 23 April 1949: 54.

[3] For an article on Universal's 1938 reissue, see the syndicated column "Hollywood Speaks" by Robbin Coons in the *Mansfield News-Journal* (Ohio) 7 Dec 1938; the 1938 revival continued into 1939. For mention of the 1947 revival, see A.H. Weiler's "By Way of Report" in the *New York Times* 16 Feb. 1947. And for the 1952 revival, see "Horror Program to Be Reissued" in the *Los Angeles Times* 21 May 1952. The 1952 *Dracula* revival is often mentioned in horror film histories as happening in 1951. It is possible that the reissue started in late 1951, but newspaper ads for a large number cities and towns across the country show that it was playing in their theatres in 1952.

[4] "C. C. C. Chatter." *Garfield County News* (Utah) 26 Jan. 1934.

[5] "I don't know whether I should brag or complain about it, but *Dracula* is the only picture in existence in all of the world which since it is revived, uh, since it was made in 19–I don't know–31, is the only picture which is revived in every city in America every year." Lugosi made these remarks to interviewer Jack Mangan on the *Ship's Reporter* in December 1951.

[6] "[*Dracula* is] the only motion picture which is revived since 1931 every year all over the country in every city." Lugosi made these remarks to Senator Price Daniel and the Senate Subcommittee on Narcotics hearings in Los Angeles held during November 14-16, 1955.

[7] Sheffield, Richard. Letter to Gary D. Rhodes 23 June 1987.

[8] Nye, Myra. "Society of Cinemaland." *Los Angeles Times* 26 Aug. 1928: D21.

[9] Nye, Myra. "Society of Cinemaland." *Los Angeles Times* 26 May 1929: 20.

[10] "Portrait at Theater." *Los Angeles Times* 21 July 1929: 16.

[11] Bolton, Whitney. "Count Dracula, Vampire, Admits He Goes on a Bat Every Night." *New York Times* 9 Oct. 1927.

[12] "Carew [*sic*] Seeks Story." *Los Angeles Times* 29 May 1925: 38.

[13] "Celluloid Svengali Player of So Many Characterizations." *Los Angeles Times* 22 Feb. 1925: 27.

[14] Mayer, Mary. "Midsummer Affords Unbroken List of Attractions." *Los Angeles Times* 22 July 1928: C13.

[15] Soanes, Wood. "Curtain Calls." *Oakland Tribune* 4 July 1930. [This is not to say that some press accounts did not mention Lugosi might play the part. In "Universal Secures Mystery Thriller," the June 21, 1930 *Los Angeles Times* wrote that "we hear that it is entirely likely that Bela Lugosi, who played the role on the stage at the Biltmore, will have the same part, and one cannot imagine anyone else doing it."]

[16] The only other cities in which Lugosi appeared as Dracula before the 1931 film were the Connecticut try-out cities that predated Broadway (New Haven, Hartford, New London, and Stamford) as well as Santa Barbara (1929) and Oakland (1928, 1929, and 1930).

[17] "Dracula!!" *Los Angeles Times* 9 Dec. 1928: L7.

[18] Undated, handwritten questionnaire, presumably submitted to Lugosi by a fan.

[19] That Universal considered Keith and Courtenay is mentioned is "Ian Keith to Play *Dracula*." *Hollywood Filmograph* 13 Sept. 1930

[20] I suggest that Wray may have come the closest to getting the role because his name features most prominently in some 1930 discussions about the role. In particular, see "Wray, the Neck-Biter." *Variety* 21 June 1930. The other actor who seems close to getting the role was Ian Keith; see "Ian Keith to Play *Dracula* for U–Rumored." *The Hollywood Filmograph* 13 Sept. 1930.

[21] "*Dracula* Shows at Pasadena." *Los Angeles Times* 17 Aug. 1930.

[22] "Theatrical Notes." *New York Times* 19 Sept. 1930: 25.

[23] Skal, David J. *Hollywood Gothic: The Tangled Web of Dracula from Novel to Stage to Screen*. New York: W. W. Norton, 1990: 88.

[24] These articles include: "Bela Lugosi." (*Hollywood Filmograph* 9 Aug. 1930); "Bela Lugosi" (*Hollywood Filmograph* 16 Aug. 1930); "Pulling for Him" (*Hollywood Filmograph* 6 Sept. 1930).

[25] Qtd. In "Producers Have Their Eyes on Him." *Hollywood Filmograph* 2 Aug. 1930.

[26] Mok, Michael. "Horror Man at Home." *New York Post* 19 Oct. 1939.

[27] "Bela Lugosi with Universal." *Los Angeles Times* 16 Sept. 1930: A8. This announcement came after mention of Lugosi's screen test in late August, as noted in "Universal Has Made Test of Bela Lugosi for *Dracula* Talkie." *Hollywood Filmograph* 30 Aug. 1930.

[28] "Terror-Film Director Goes Sentimental After Hours." *Los Angeles Times* 1 May 1936: 11.

[29] Rapf, Maurice. Interview with Gary D. Rhodes. Norman, Oklahoma. 1997.

[30] "Universal's Dracula To Have Romance and Thrills." *Exhibitors Herald-World* 4 Oct. 1930: 58.

[31] Advertisement. *Motion Picture Herald* 31 Jan. 1931: 36-37.

[32] Advertisement. *Chicago Daily Tribune* 23 Mar. 1932.

[33] Churchill. "Star Gazer." *Exhibitors Herald-World* 18 Oct. 1930: 52.

[34] For reviews that claimed the film was better than the play, see Norbert Lusk's "*Dracula* Hit on Broadway." *Los Angeles Times* 22 Feb 1931: B9. Also, "Mystery Picture on View at Stanley." *Philadelphia Inquirer* 28 Feb. 1931. For a review that claims it "does not come up to the standard set by the stage production," see Bertrand Calmson's "*Dracula*" in the *Hollywood Filmograph* 9 May 1931: 21.

[35] Among the reviews that give Browning great praise is Richard Watts, Jr.'s "On the Screen" in the *New York Herald-Tribune* 13 Feb. 1931. Also, see "Thrills Abound in Offering at Pantages House" in the *Hollywood Daily-Citizen* 1 May 1931, in which the anonymous critic wrote "Tod Browning has directed the picture wih fine appreciation of its creepy possibilities." Among those that didn't praise Browning is May Tinée's "Awed Stillness Greets Movie About *Dracula*." *Chicago Tribune* 21 Mar. 1931. In it she wrote that "the direction appeared not all it should have been, considering that Tod Browning megaphoned–and I wonder why?"

[36] For a positive review of the camerawork, see "*Dracula*" in *Motion Picture Herald* 3 Jan. 1931. In it, the critic writes "the photography, the settings, and the backgrounds show extreme care." Also see Philip K. Scheuer's "Adventures in *Dracula* Now in Film Form." *Los Angeles Times* 30 Mar. 1931, in which he writes that it is "photographed with an exquisite perception of lights and shadows." For a negative critique, see Sidney Harris's "*Dracula*" in *The Billboard* 21 Feb. 1931. In it, he wrote, "At times the film is faulty in photography and sound recording. Poor work on that end often causes one to strain to get what is flashed and heard onscreen."

[37] In "*Dracula*" in the *Motion Picture Herald* 3 Jan. 1931, a critic wrote: "…the sound effects rank among the unusual in the production of photoplays." Philip K. Sheuer's review in the *Los Angeles Times* claimed, "music, perhaps, would have helped." And Harris in *The Billboard*, as quoted in the previous footnote, remarked on the "faulty" sound recording.

[38] "The New Pictures." *Time* 23 Feb. 1931.

[39] See Gary D. Rhodes and Gregory W. Mank's "A Diary of *Dracula*" in *Midnight Marquee*. Volume 2, Number 1. 2002.

[40] Harris, "*Dracula*." *The Billboard* 21 Feb. 1931.

[41] "*Dracula* Creates Furore Among Picture Fans." *The Bee* (Danville, Virginia) 28 Feb. 1931.

[42] J.T.M. "Eerie Adventures of Vampire Count Make Thrilling Film." *The Times Picayune* (New Orleans) 11 Apr. 1931: 10.

[43] "Power of Screen as Thrill Producer." *The Film Daily* 27 Mar. 1931: 8.

[44] Hall, Mordaunt. "*Dracula* as a Film." 22 Feb. 1931.

[45] Hatcher, Charles M. "Thrilled by *Dracula*." *Motion Picture Classic* June 1931: 6.

[46] He also appeared in two other comedy films of 1931, *Fifty Million Frenchmen* and *Women of All Nations*. These aren't included in the argument because Lugosi worked on *Fifty Million Frenchmen* in 1930, and he signed for *Women of All Nations* in 1931 before *Dracula* was released. Thus, they were not influenced by the success of the film *Dracula*.

[47] The three films were *Murders in the Rue Morgue*, *White Zombie*, and *Chandu the Magician*.

[48] *Bone*. "Play Out of Town." *Variety* 16 Apr. 1947.

[49] Walling, Stratton. Interview with Gary D. Rhodes. 20 Aug. 2005.

[50] *The Devil Also Dreams* is examined at some length in Rhodes, Gary D. *Lugosi*. Jefferson, NC: McFarland, 1997.

[51] "Bela Balks at Blood, Lives for Laughs." *Ottawa Journal* 1 Aug. 1950.

[52] For example, these positive reviews include: "World Premiere Presented of *The Devil Also Dreams* (*Fall River Herald News* 25 July 1950); "*The Devil Also Dreams*." (*Montreal Daily Star* 23 Aug. 1950); and "*The Devil Also Dreams*." (*The Billboard* 3 Sept. 1950).

[53] See, for example, "Bela Lugosi to Produce Here." *Illustrated Daily News* 17 Sept. 1935.

[54] Schallert, Edwin. "Vallee, Kiepura Chosen for *Gala Performance*." *Los Angeles Times* 19 Dec. 1941.

[55] These productions are covered at more length in Rhodes, *Lugosi*.

[56] Original in the Library of Congress. One of the stills on the program is from the film *Scared to Death*, so it presumably dates from either 1946 or likely even later.

[57] That this was a completely separate undertaking seems extremely clear after examining the contract Lugosi signed with Don Marlowe for *The Tell-Tale Heart* tour. It mentions absolutely nothing other than the Poe story.

[58] Hopper, Hedda. "Looking at Hollywood." *Chicago Daily Tribune* 31 Jan. 1948: 13.

[59] Thomas, Bob. "Hollywood News." *Indiana Evening Gazette* (Indiana, PA) 4 Mar. 1948.

[60] "News of Comment of Stage and Screen." *Fitchburg Sentinel* (Fitchburg, MA) 18 Jan. 1936.

[61] Henry Sutherland's column "Hollywood Film Shop" (*Nevada State Journal* 8 Mar. 1936) claimed that when Lugosi was seen with actress Gloria Holden, the star of *Dracula's Daughter*, she introduced him as "my father." And "*Dracula's Daughter* Meets Her 'Dad'" (*Universal Weekly* 7 Mar. 1936: 20) quoted Lugosi as saying, "this is the first time that anyone acquired a vampire daughter by way of the screen!"

[62] Fidler, Jimmie. "Jimmie Fidler in Hollywood." *Los Angeles Times* 10 June 1939.

[63] Schallert, Edwin. "Producer to Hasten Linda Ware's Stardom." *Los Angeles Times* 31 May 1939.

[64] Schallert, Edwin. "Paramount Campaigns for Laurette Taylor." *Los Angeles Times* 11 July 1940.

[65] Schallert, Edwin. "Hutton to Wed Dec. 18; Assigned 'Janie' Lead." *Los Angeles Times* 9 Dec. 1943.

[66] Schallert, Edwin. "Lewis Stone to Play Chief Executive Role." *Los Angeles Times* 12 July 1939.

[67] Schallert, Edwin. "Bela Lugosi Enlisted for *House of Dracula*." *Los Angeles Times* 17 Feb. 1945.

[68] The four Universal Dracula films without Lugosi are: *Dracula's Daughter* (1936), in which Dracula was played by a dummy stand-in; *Son of Dracula* (1943), with Lon Chaney Jr. as Dracula; *House of Frankenstein* (1944), with John Carradine as Dracula; and *House of Dracula* (1945), also with John Carradine as Dracula.

[69] These comments are from Cecilia Ager in the *New York Star*, quoted in "Frankenstein Gets Gold in New York Despite Notices." *Hollywood Reporter* 2 Aug. 1948.

[70] Johnson, Erskine. "Hollywood Notes." *Portland Press Herald* (Portland, Maine) 16 May 1948.

[71] Lyons, Leonard. "The Post's New Yorker." *Washington Post* 12 Mar. 1938.

[72] Fidler, Jimmie. "Jimmie Fidler in Hollywood." *Los Angeles Times* 21 Nov. 1941.

[73] "Repertory Theater Latest Chicago Cultural Attempt." *Dallas Morning News* 15 May 1939. Also, "Notes of the Theater." *Chicago Daily Tribune* 30 Aug. 1942. Also, "Notes of the Theater." *Chicago Daily Tribune* 25 Apr. 1943.

[74] "'Dracula' Lives Again." *Dallas Morning News* 27 Aug. 1942.

[75] *Variety* 4 Feb. 1948.

[76] "Ink Hampton White for *Dracula* Lead." *The Billboard* 23 Apr. 1949: 54.

[77] "London Legit Bits." *Variety* 3 Oct. 1951. [The Australian tour, according to *Variety*, would have occured in 1952.]

[78] See, for example, "Lugosi Gives Weird Drama Tense Touch." *Portland Oregonian* 30 May 1932. Also, "Bela Lugosi Is Splendid in *Dracula*." *Oregon Daily Journal* 30 May 1932.

[79] See, for example, "Bela Lugosi, Film Villain, Playing at Loew's State." *New York Herald-Tribune* 9 Dec. 1933. Also, "New Acts: Bela Lugosi." *Variety* 12 Dec. 1933. Also, "Loew's Fox." *Washington Post* 23 Dec. 1933.

[80] Carmody, Jay. "Lugosi Revives Dracula, in a Manner of Speaking." *The Evening Star* (Washington, DC) 22 June 1943.

[81] A number of these are catalogued in Rhodes, Gary D. *Lugosi*. Jefferson, NC: McFarland, 1997.

[82] The key text on summer stock in the US is also the source of the quoted phrase "American theatrical phenomenon." See LoMonaco, Martha Schmoyer. *Summer Stock! An American Theatrical Phenomenon*. New York: Palgrave Macmillan, 2004.

[83] The Litchfield version of *Dracula* was staged September 2-7, 1947.

[84] The program for *The Devil Also Dreams* from the Famous Artists' Country Playhouse lists Altobell as technical advisor.

[85] Jefferys, Alan. Phone interview with Gary D. Rhodes. 9 Feb. 2006. Also, Email to Gary D. Rhodes. 10 Feb. 2006.

[86] Newirth, Jayne Altobell. Email to Gary D. Rhodes. 5 Apr. 2006.

[87] Bufferd, Esther. "Litchfield Summer Theatre." *The Litchfield Inquirer* 4 Sept. 1947: 4.

[88] Summers, Montague. *The Vampire: His Kith and Kin*. London: Kegan, Paul, Trench, Trubner, and Co., 1928: 337.

[89] Geltzer. "Tod Browning."

[90] Everson, William K. "Horror Films." *Films in Review*. Jan. 1954.

Portrait publicizing Lugosi's association with the Nemzeti Szinház (National Theatre) of Budapest.
(Courtesy of Dennis Phelps)

As Dracula in the 1931 Universal Studios film.

1 Schmidt, Emile O. Interview with Gary D. Rhodes 12 Nov. 2005.

2 Ibid.

3 Ibid.

4 Ibid.

5 Eaton, Fred G. "Humor Survives Flaws in Arsenic's First Night." The Saratogian 7 Aug. 1947.

6 "Lugosi Flits Around Like Phantom." The Saratogian (Saratoga Springs, NY) 7 Aug. 1947. [Information on his television appearance appears in greater detail in "Spa Theater Stars to Shine in Television" in the 7 Aug. 1947 issue of The Saratogian.]

7 Ibid. [The Ripley meeting is described in greater detail in "Shiver-Giver to Trade 'Rip' Tales" in the Albany Times-Union on August 7, 1947.]

8 When I say "maybe" a week in Beverly, Massacussetts, this is not mere jest. The New York Times announced Lugosi would appear in Beverly for a week in Arsenic, placing it in June-July 1947. However, searches at the Beverly Historical Society and Museum have at the time of this writing not yielded any proof of that fact. Also, see Rhodes, Gary D. Lugosi (Jefferson, NC: McFarland, 1997: p. 182) for a description of the New Hope performance.

9 Advertisement. Pottsville Republican (Pottsville, PA) 18 Aug. 1947. [The Deer Lake performance was held at the Deer Lake Theatre near Orwigsburg.]

10 See Rhodes, Lugosi p. 184.

11 Mishkin, Esther. "'Horror King' Heading Cast of Fine Comedy." The Daily Record (Morristown, NJ) 27 July 1949: 8. [The Lakeside version of Arsenic at Lake Hopatcong has not previously been catalogued in Lugosi biographies. It ran from July 26-August 1, 1949. Produced by Grad Boodman and direction by Eddie Hyans, the cast included Elwyn Harvey and Mildred Chandler as the two Brewster aunts, Eddie Hyans as "Uncle Teddy," Robert Healy as Mortimer, and Richard Stevens, owner of the Lakeside, as Lieutenant Rooney.]

12 "Arsenic and Old Lace Proves Potency Again at Green Hills." Reading Eagle 17 Aug. 1949.

13 Snell, George. Letter to Gary D. Rhodes. 7 Apr. 2006.

14 For an indepth look at the original Broadway production starring Boris Karloff, see Rhodes, Gary D. "Arsenic and Old Lace." in Boris Karloff. Ed. by Gary J. and Susan Svehla. Baltimore: Midnight Marquee, 1996.

15 Nisbet, Fairfax. "Broadway Hits in Prospect for Dallas." Dallas Morning News 7 Mar. 1941.

16 "Jimmie Fidler in Hollywood." Los Angeles Times 2 Sept. 1941.

17 Whitney, Dwight. "The World of Drama." San Francisco Chronicle 8 Aug. 1943: 14.

18 Whitney, Dwight. "Arsenic Revived at the Tivoli." San Francisco Chronicle 7 Aug. 1943.

19 "Tragedy-Comedy Tradition Safe with Bela Lugosi." Los Angeles Times 6 Sept. 1943: 14.

20 Ibid., p. 14.

21 Ibid., p. 14.

22 Lugosi was on The Tuesday Program with Walter O'Keefe on 17 Oct. 1939, and then on the Texaco Star Theatre with Ken Murray on 15 Nov. 1939. When he next appeared on the Texaco Star Theatre on 25 Apr. 1943, it was with Fred Allen. See Rhodes, Lugosi (p.202 and 204) for more details.

23 Zolotow, Sam. "Revised 'Sheppey' Due in the Spring." New York Times 14 Jan. 1944.

24 Photo caption. Daily Oklahoman 29 Jan 1944.

25 Daily Oklahoman 29 Jan. 1944.

26 "Dracula's Odd Clothing Taste Horrifies City Shop Operator." Tulsa Tribune 1 Feb. 1944.

27 "Weird Comedy Pleases Crowd." Savannah Morning News 15 Feb 1944: 12. "Audience Likes Play at Academy." Roanoke Times 27 Feb. 1944.

28 Caldwell, Lily May. "Boogieman Bela Lugosi Here–But He Really is a Nice Guy." Birmingham News 5 Feb. 1944.

29 Garber, Mary. "Lugosi, Arsenic and Old Lace Star, Looks Menacing but is Mild-Mannered." Twin City Sentinel (Winston-Salem, North Carolina) 26 Feb. 1944.

30 Marlowe, Don. The Hollywood That Was Fort Worth, TX: Branch Smith, 1974.

31 Johnson, Erskine. "Bogey Man Has Way with Kids." New York World-Telegram 5 June 1952.

[32] Erskine, Anna. "Love Letters for Frankenstein." *Argosy* July 1943: 73.

[33] See Rhodes, *Lugosi*, p. 77. Also, Riley, Philip J. *Frankenstein Meets the Wolf Man.* Universal Filmscripts Series Volume Five. Atlantic City, NJ: Magicimage, 1990. Also, Berman, Scott. "Bela Lugosi as Frankenstein's Monster: The Context and Text of a Performance." *Monsters from the Vault* 22. 2006: 8-16.

[34] The key work on Lon Chaney, Sr. remains Michael F. Blake's *Lon Chaney: The Man Behind the Thousand Faces.* New York: Vestal, 1990.

[35] "Beery in Chaney Roles." *Los Angeles Times* 1 Sept. 1930.

[36] Shaffer, Rosiland. "Copies of Famous Stars Find Hard Sledding in Treading Path of Borrowed Glory in Hollywood." *Chicago Daily Tribune* 19 Oct. 1930: G3.

[37] "Is HE the Second Chaney?" *Silver Screen* Jan. 1931: 51.

[38] *Variety* July 21, 1931.

[39] Wilk, Ralph. "A Little From "Lots." *The Film Daily* 29 Oct. 1930: 8. [The announcement of *The Red Mystery* came about two weeks after an earlier, more general statement that "Young Laemmle, it is learned, has instructed his scenario department to scour the story market for material in which Lugosi can be starred." See "Hollywood Flashes." *The Film Daily* 13 Oct. 1930.]

[40] For an examination of *Dracula*'s 1931 release, see Rhodes, Gary D. and Gregory William Mank. "A Diary of *Dracula*." *Midnight Marquee*. Volume 2, Issue 1. Summer 2002.

[41] "Lugosi Sits High." *Variety* 1 Apr. 1931.

[42] Similar reports showed up in the *Courier-Express* (Buffalo, NY) on 5 Apr. 1931, the *Boston Traveller* on 7 Apr. 1931, and the *New York Daily Mirror* on 7 Apr. 1931.

[43] "U Has Horror Cycle All to Self." *Variety* 8 Apr. 1931.

[44] Miller, Llewellyn. *Los Angeles Record* 13 Apr. 1931.

[45] "Lugosi Signs with 'U' on Long-Term Contract." Hollywood Reporter 20 Apr. 1931.

[46] *Hollywood Filmograph* 16 May 1931

[47] Kingsley, Grace. "Bela Lugosi in It." *Los Angeles Times* 26 May 1931: A11.

[48] "Bela Lugosi Signs." *Los Angeles Evening Examiner* 3 June 1931.

[49] Yeaman, Elizabeth. *Hollywood Daily Citizen* 29 June 1931. [Florey and Lugosi weren't the only key personnel announced to work on *Frankenstein* who didn't once it started production. The article "Carl Laemmle, Jr. in New York, Announces that Two-Thirds of Season's Stories Have Been Purchsed" (*Screen World* 19 June 1931) claimed that *Frankenstein* would be shot by Karl Freund. In the end, Arthur Edeson became the cinematographer.]

[50] *Oakland Tribune* 17 July 1931.

[51] *Variety* 21 July 1931.

[52] Whitaker, Alma. "Superior Intelligence Lurks in Grafted Brain." *Los Angeles Times* 10 June 1932: B11.

[53] The influence of *Frankenstein* on *Rue Morgue* does not mean that I am necessarily suggesting the influence of Whale on Florey. While that may have happened, it seems more likely that for *Rue Morgue* Florey was influenced by his own work in planning for the film *Frankenstein*.

[54] The "mad doctor" films included in this count are: Dr. Mirakle in *Murders in the Rue Morgue* (1932), Dr. Vollin in *The Raven* (1935), Victor Poten in *Shadow of Chinatown* (1936), Dr. Zorka in *The Phantom Creeps* (1939, a serial that was also condensed to a feature film), Dr. Carruthers in *The Devil Bat* (1940), Dr. Melcher in *Black Dragons* (1942), Dr. Lorenz in *The Corpse Vanishes* (1942), Dr. Brewster in *The Ape Man* (1943), Dr. Marlowe in *Voodoo Man* (1944), Professor Dexter in *Return of the Ape Man* (1944), Dr. Renault in *Zombies on Broadway* (1945), Dr. Zabor in *Bela Lugosi Meets a Brooklyn Gorilla* (1952), and Dr. Vornoff in *Bride of the Atom* (1955). I am also including in this count *Mother Riley Meets the Vampire* (1952); despite its title and the Dracula-like attire worn by Lugosi's Von Housen, the character is not only human, but he is a scientist who invents a robot–the first of many who will take over the world. Lugosi also appeared opposite Boris Karloff's Dr. Rukh in *The Invisible Ray* (1936).

[55] Lugosi's appearance as a mad doctor onstage came when he played Dr. Orloff in *Murdered Alive* in 1932. The show opened at the Carthay Circle in LA on April 2, 1932, moved onto a week at San Francisco's

Orpheum by April 22, 1932, and then back to LA in condensed form at the Orpheum for April 30-May 5, 1932. Reviews and a plot summary can be found in Gary D. Rhodes' *Lugosi*.

Lugosi's roles as a mad doctor on radio came on the "Dr. Prescribed Death" episode of *Suspense* (February 2, 1943), "The Thirsty Death" pilot of *Mystery House* (recorded in 1945), and a comedy sketch as "Dr. Bikini" on *Command Performance* (July 16, 1946).

[56] Parsons, Louella O. *Los Angeles Examiner* 15 Feb. 1932.

[57] Coons, Robin. "Will Boris Karloff Take Lon Chaney's Place?" *Hollywood Citizen News* 4 Jan. 1932.

[58] Carroll, Harrison. *Los Angeles Evening Herald Express* 19 Jan. 1932.

[59] Parsons, Louella O. *Los Angeles Times* 25 Jan 1933. [I certainly do not wish to suggest that Karloff was Hollywood's final answer to replacing Chaney. Trade publications continued to mention other names. For example, *Universal Weekly* asked in their November 3, 1934 issue if Henry Hull, the star of their *WereWolf of London* (1935), would be the "second Chaney."]

[60] Babcock, Muriel. "He-Men of Hollywood 'Go Garbo' on Public." *Los Angeles Times* 16 Oct. 1932: B13.

[61] I choose these years as they span from Lugosi's 1930 contract for *Dracula* (released in 1931) through *Abbott and Costello Meet Frankenstein*, his last film with the studio in 1948.

[62] I believe that comes more out of a qualitative desire to force Lugosi into a particular historical narrative where someone or something must be to blame. Usually Karloff and/or Universal get the blame. In an objective and quantitative examination, there just isn't any real proof of that occurring.

[63] Brown, Kelly R. *Florence Lawrence, the Biograph Girl: America's First Movie Star.* Jefferson, NC: McFarland, 1999.

[64] Advertisement. *The Motion Picture Daily* 13 Jan. 1932

[65] "U's Three Buildups." *Variety* 23 Feb. 1932.

[66] "What They Say–Thus Far." *Motion PIcture Herald* 18 June 1932: 9.

[67] "The Ten Biggest Money Makers." *Motion Picture Herald* 6 Aug 1932: 10-11. [The top ten money makers in order were:

Marie Dressler, Janet Gaynor, Joan Crawford, Charles Farrell, Greta Garbo, Will Rogers, Norma Shearer, Wallace Beery, Clark Gable, and Joe. E. Brown.]

[68] "Drama First Choice of Story Types, Vote on Stars Indicates." *Motion Picture Herald* 2 July 1932: 54.

[69] "The Ten Biggest Money Makers of 1932-33." *Motion Picture Herald* 6 Jan 1934: 14-15.

[70] "Biggest Money Making Stars of 1934-35." *Motion Picture Herald* Jan. 1935.

[71] "The Money Making Stars of a Season." *The 1935-36 Motion Picture Almanac.* New York: Quigley, 1936: 94.

[72] Karloff was not immune to this battle either, even if he waged the warfare of Hollywood far more successfully than Lugosi. By the early forties, for example, the Universal publicity machine that advanced Karloff shifted largely to the promotion of a new horror film star, Lon Chaney Jr., lead player in *The Wolf Man* (1941) and a host of other Universal movies during World War II.

[73] Of their eight films, six were for Universal Studios: *The Black Cat* (1934), *Gift of Gab* (1934), *The Raven* (1935), *The Invisible Ray* (1936), *Son of Frankenstein* (1939), and *Black Friday* (1940). The other two films were for RKO: *You'll Find Out* (1940) and *The Body Snatcher* (1945)

[74] Karloff and Lugosi appeared together in two 1934 newsreels. One was *Screen Snapshots* 11, in which they play a game of chess. The other (from March 1934) shows them judging black cats; the winner would appear in the film *The Black Cat*.

On March 13, 1938, Karloff and Lugosi both guest-starred on the radio program *Seein' Stars in Hollywood* (aka *Baker's Broadcast*) with Ozzie and Harriet. The two told stories and sang a duet entitled "We're Horrible, Horrible Men." One radio show listing ("Sunday on the Air." *The Hammond Times* [Hammond, Indiana] 13 Mar. 1938: 7) wrote, "Oz Nelson Presents Feg Murray who in turn presents Boris Karloff and Bela Lugosi, who in turn scare the wits out of Harriet Hilliard." Later, they were together on the radio show *Kay Kyser's Kollege of Musical Knowledge* on 25 Sept. 1940.

[75] When I say their next major outing, I choose the word "major" specifically, as the two did make brief cameo performances in Universal's film *Gift of Gab* in 1934 before

appearing in *The Raven*.

[76] "News and Comment of Stage and Screen." *Fitchburg Sentinel* (Fitchburg MA) 18 Jan. 1936: 5.

[77] Harrison, Paul. "In Hollywood." *Wisconsin Rapids Daily Tribune* (Wisconsin Rapids, WI) 28 Feb. 1936.

[78] Lubin, Arthur. Interview with Gary D. Rhodes. 1987.

[79] The gangster role in *Black Friday* did not garner work for Lugosi in other crime films. However, he did take on a final role as a more traditional criminal in *Genius at Work* (1945).

[80] Wise, Robert. Interview with Gary D. Rhodes in the documentary film *Lugosi: Hollywood's Dracula* (Spinning Our Wheels, 1997).

[81] "Film Flattery Sincere if Imitation Means Anything." *Los Angeles Times* 3 July 1932: B5.

[82] Coons, p. 6.

[83] Leicester, Wagner. "Hollywood Film Shop." *Nevada State Journal* (Reno, NV) 19 Sept. 1935.

[84] Advertisement. *Chicago Daily Tribune* 31 May 1948: A13.

[85] "Karloff and Lugosi to be Tame and Peaceful on Air." *The Lima News* (Lima, OH) 13 Mar. 1938.

[86] "Jimmie Fidler in Hollywood." *The Chronicle-Telegram* (Elyria, OH) 15 Mar. 1939.

[87] "Winchell on Broadway." *Nevada State Journal* (Reno, NV) 29 Nov. 1945.

[88] "Alien Stars to Hail Tree." *Los Angeles Times* 16 Dec. 1932: A10.

[89] "Henry Armetta's Spaghetti Party Merry Affair." *Los Angeles Examiner* 25 Nov. 1934.

[90] "4-A Gambol of Stars to Offer Gala Program."

[91] Hopper, Hedda. "Horror Men of Screen Just Pair of Home-loving Folks, After All." *Los Angeles Times* 14 Jan. 1940: C3.

[92] In Bob Thomas's "For a Halloween Story, He Went to an Expert" (*Los Angeles Mirror* 30 Oct. 1953), Lugosi said he hadn't seen Karloff for "two or three years."

[93] Gordon, Alex and Tom Weaver. DVD audio commentary for *The Haunted Strangler* (1958). Unreleased at the time of this writing.

[94] Chester B. Bahn's syndicated column "Cinema Turning Own Corner With *Dirt* Doomed For Eclipse" (*Syracuse Herald* 6 May 1934) claimed that "Bela Lugosi and Boris Karloff are scheduled for Robert Louis Stevenson's *The Suicide Club* and the latter will likewise be seen in *The Golem*." Mollie Merrick's syndicated column "Kay Francis Looks So Well Hollywood Worries" (*Dallas Morning News* 27 Oct. 1934) wrote "*Edwin Drood*, [Dickens's] unfinished mystery, will have both Karloff and Lugosi in it." The article "*Were Wolf* [sic] *of London* for Karloff and Lugosi" (*Syracuse Herald* 24 June 1934) claimed, "Universal has purchased another vehicle for Boris Karloff and Bela Lugosi. It is the *Were Wolf* [sic] *of London*, an original by Rian James."

[95] See Rhodes, *Lugosi*, p. 221-222.

[96] "Waxman Dickering for Horror Pic Release." *The Hollywood Reporter* 15 Nov. 1938.

[97] Johnson, Erskine. "In Hollywood." *The Independent Record* (Helena, MT) 22 May 1952.

[98] Thirer, Irene. "Bela 'Dracula' Lugosi a Regular Fellow–Pokes Fun at Jinx." *New York Daily News* 3 July 1935.

[99] My thanks to film historian Gregory William Mank for this information about Lillian; Greg interviewed her at length before she died. Also, Snell, letter to Rhodes.

[100] Hopper, Hedda. "Horror Men of Screen Just Pair of Home-loving Folks, After All." *Los Angeles Times* 14 Jan 1940: C3.

[101] Hal Boyle. "Boyle's Column." *The Kerrville Times* 27 May 1952.

[102] Thomas, "For a Halloween Story, He Went to an Expert."

[103] Schmidt, Emile O. Interview with Gary D. Rhodes 12 Nov. 2005.

[104] "*Arsenic* Neat $11,000 For Week in St. Louis."

[105] Kimbrough, Mary. "Bela Lugosi a Gentle Dracula Off-Stage." *St. Louis Post-Dispatch* 21 Jan. 1954: D1.

1 Rhodes, Gary D. Interview with Don English. 22 Feb. 2006.

2 Rhodes, Gary D. Interview with Don English. 17 Nov. 2005.

3 "Longtime Burlesque Comic Sparky Kaye Dies in Vegas." *Nevada State Journal* (Reno, NV) 25 Aug. 1971

4 Wright, Frank. "The Las Vegas I Remember: Interview with Herb McDonald." Nevada State Museum and Historical Society. Undated.

5 Harter, Chuck. Interview with Bill Willard. 12 Feb. 1997.

6 Kilgallen, Dorothy. *Mansfield News Journal* (Mansfield, OH) 16 Feb. 1950.

7 Weitschat, Al. "The Screen in Review." *The Detroit News* 21 Aug. 1948.

8 "Olympia, Miami." *Variety* 9 Sept. 1948.

9 Rhodes, Gary D. Interview with Sammy Petrillo. 5 Dec. 1996.

10 Harter, Interview with Bill Willard.

11 Weaver, Tom, Debbie Rochon, The Phantom of the Movies, and Peter Schmideg. "Alex Gordon on Ed Wood and *Ed Wood*." *Cult Movies* Issue 22. 1997: 47.

12 Wood, Edward D. Jr. *Hollywood Rat Race*. New York: Four Walls Eight Windows, 1998: 104.

13 Cremer, Robert. *Lugosi: The Man Behind the Cape*. New York: Henry Regnery, 1976: 221. [In his book *Hollywood Rat Race*, Wood wrote that "[Lugosi] and I devised a nightclub act for the Silver Slipper in Las Vegas, which played to record-breaking audiences and was held several weeks over its original run" (p. 32).]

14 Fuller, Dolores. *A Fuller Life*. Bear Manor Media, publication pending at the time of this writing.

15 Wood, *Hollywood Rat Race*, p. 104. Also, Wood, Edward D., Jr. Letter to Edwin Schallert. 13 Mar. 1954.

16 Harter, Interview with Bill Willard.

17 Wood, Edward D., Jr. Letter to Bela Lugosi. 11 Mar. 1954. [In referring to an upcoming project, Wood tells Lugosi, "I'll be able to help you (study some lines) as I did before." The "before" is not named, so, while it's possible he is referring to the *Bela Lugosi Revue*, it is also possible he is meaning something else—like the San Bernardino / West Coast Theatre appearance or the film *Glen or Glenda* (1953)—or a combination of those.]

18 Harter, Interview with Willard. Also, Cremer, p. 221-222.

19 Cremer, p. 222.

20 That the show was changed seems evident from comments in Bob Clemens's column "Inside Las Vegas" (*Las Vegas Sun* 25 Feb. 1954); Clemens wrote that "since those changes [which are not described], the *Bela Lugosi Revue* is a show you can again and again for [a] new experience every time."

21 Fuller, *A Fuller Life*. Also, Wood, Edward D., Jr. Letter to Bela Lugosi. 11 Mar. 1954.

22 Fuller, *A Fuller Life*.

23 Wood, Edward D., Jr. Letter to Bela Lugosi 11 Mar. 1954. [Later, in a 24 Mar. 1954 letter, Wood wrote, "First, the bag did arrive—Dolores thanks you very much, she wanted it badly."]

24 "Virginia Dew Now Featured in Stage Show." *Los Angeles Times* 24 July 1948: 9.

25 The standard cost of the Silver Slipper shows at that time was $3,500 a week,

Lugosi in a publicity still from the 1930s.

according to Ed Oncken's "Silver Slipper, Las Vegas." *The Billboard* 7 Nov. 1953. That Lugosi made $1,000 a week is mentioned in Cremer, p. 222. Willard said the same in the Chuck Harter interview; he also claimed that Hank Henry made $750 a week.

[26] Advertisement. *Las Vegas Sun* 27 Feb. 1954.

[27] *Bob*. "Silver Slipper, Las Vegas." *Variety* 10 Mar. 1954.

[28] A surviving copy of the script does show that Willard and Hank Henry wrote it. But *Variety*'s review on March 10, 1954 claimed Willard, Hank Henry, *and* Eddie Fox wrote the show.

[29] Harter, Interview with Willard.

[30] Given the Silver Slipper association, the presumption is that it was specifically Bill Kozloff specifically being parodied, as opposed to his brother Jake Kozloff, who was President of the Last Frontier corporation. Regardless, the joke was simultaneously about the management and film actor Boris Karloff.

[31] The press often spelled Katleman's name as "Katelman." See, for example, "Last Frontier Hotel Officers Being Sued." *Nevada State Journal* (Reno, NV) 4 Sept. 1954. As for the paternity suit, it began in June 1953 in Austin, with another suit filed in September 1953 in New York; the situation became a news item in February 1954. See, for example, "Hush-Hush Paternity Suit Against Las Vegan Held at Austin Fails to Stay Hushed." *Nevada State Journal* 26 Feb. 1954.

[32] See, for example, "Report Uranium Find in Northwest Quebec." *Chicago Daily Tribune* 16 Jan. 1954. Also, "Report Uranium Plan." *Chicago Daily Tribune* 29 Dec. 1953.

[33] "Hang Mau Mau Leader Captured in Ambush." *Chicago Daily Tribune* 19 Feb. 1954.

[34] Clemens, Bob. "Inside Las Vegas." *Las Vegas Sun* 24 Feb. 1954.

[35] Advertisement. *Los Angeles Times* 11 Feb. 1954. Also, see Bob Clemens's "Inside Las Vegas." *Las Vegas Sun* 25 Feb. 1954.

[36] *Bob*, "Silver Slipper, Las Vegas." [This review actually says that Sheehan stripped, then put her clothes back on to distribute the champagne, and then—returning to the stage—stripped once again.]

[37] Harter, Interview with Willard.

[38] Clemens, Bob. "Inside Las Vegas." 25 Feb. 1954.

[39] Oncken, 7 Nov. 1953.

[40] Grant, Gogi. Email to Gary D. Rhodes 22 Apr. 2006.

[41] Harter, Interview with Willard. [Ralph Pearl's article "Vegas Daze and Nights" in the *Las Vegas Sun* on March 31, 1954 did mention that at the 2:30AM show on the previous night there "were plenty of empty seats." This may be in part because the show had reached its next-to-the-last evening, as well as the fact that it was the evening that Lugosi himself didn't appear. Attendance may have been lighter because potential audience members learned he wasn't going to appear that night.]

[42] "Silver Slipper, Las Vegas." *The Billboard* 7 Nov. 1953.

[43] Photo Caption. *Las Vegas Sun* 20 Feb. 1954.

[44] *Las Vegas Sun* 26 Feb. 1954.

[45] *Las Vegas Sun* 28 Feb. 1954.

[46] Photo caption. *Las Vegas Sun* 22 Feb. 1954.

[47] Clemens, Bob. "Inside Las Vegas." *Las Vegas Sun* 16 Feb. 1954.

[48] Devor, Les. "Vegas Vagaries." *Las Vegas Revue-Journal* 21 Feb. 1954.

[49] Wood, Edward D., Jr. Letter to Bela Lugosi. 13 Mar. 1954. [In this letter, Wood responds to the fact that the show was interrupted by stating, "It was a wonderful tribute those people paid, even if it did throw you for a moment to see new faces. But I'm sure you went on as if very little had happened." The latter sentence suggests this "tribute" occurred during the performance.]

[50] *Daily Variety* 23 Mar. 1954.

[51] Wood, 13 Mar. 1954.

[52] Wood, Edward D., Jr. Letter to Bela Lugosi. 21 Mar. 1954

[53] Wood was still writing to Lugosi from Los Angeles as of March 24, so the trip must have taken place after that date.

[54] Fuller, *A Fuller Life*.

[55] Clemens, 16 Feb. 1954.

[56] Clemens, 25 Feb. 1954.

[57] *Bob*, 10 Mar. 1954.

[58] Pearl, 31 Mar. 1954.

[59] Advertisement. *Las Vegas Review-Journal* 31 Mar. 1954.

[60] Harter, Interview with Willard.

[61] Clemens, 25 Feb. 1954.

[62] "Fortune Wasted Away." *Los Angeles Herald Express* 22 Apr. 1955.

[63] A copy of a fan letter exists from "Bela Lugosi" in Hollywood to a "Mr. Mazzeo,"

dated 13 Mar. 1954, at which time Lugosi was still in Vegas. Along with bearing Wood's initials, the letter includes an additional note at the bottom of the page from Wood that says "As Mr. Lugosi's producer, I wish to express my deepest thanks for being a devoted fan – Why do not the others in your group write to Mr. Lugosi? An actor's work is always much better when he knows his fans enjoy his performance."

[64] Wood, 11 Mar. 1954 and 13 Mar. 1954.

[65] Wood, 11 Mar. 1954.

[66] Lugosi, Bela. Letter to the Burke Electric Company. 2 May 1954. [The letter includes Wood's initials as the typist.]

[67] Brown, Walter C. Letter to Bela Lugosi. 5 Dec. 1953. [That Lugosi said these things in his letter to Brown are recounted in Brown's response.]

[68] Schallert, Edwin. "Stanwyck, Mac-Murray Named as Stellar Duo." *Los Angeles Times* 10 June 1939.

[69] Scheuer, Philip K. "Good News Tailored to Rooney and Garland." *Los Angeles Times* 4 Sept. 1939.

[70] Schallert, "Stanwyck."

[71] Brown, 5 Dec. 1953.

[72] *Ibid.*

[73] "All Star Cast to Enact Film." *Los Angeles Times* 18 Jan. 1932.

[74] "Fred Stone's Three Daughters May Appear With Him in *Farmer in Dell*." *Los Angeles Times* 12 Oct. 1935.

[75] Soanes, Wood. "Curtain Calls." *Oakland Tribune* 6 Aug. 1935.

[76] Schallert, Edwin. "Producer to Hasten Linda Ware's Stardom." *Los Angeles Times* 31 May 1939.

[77] See "News and Comment of Stage and Screen." *Fitchburg Sentinel* 25 Jan. 1941. Also, see Edwin Schallert's "Red Skelton Will Play *Mr. Coed* for Metro." *Los Angeles Times* 4 Feb. 1942.

[78] Schallert, Edwin. "Simone Back to French Milieu in *Mlle Fifi*." *Los Angeles Times* 12 Feb. 1944.

[79] "Hollywood Happenings." *Chicago Daily Tribune* 2 Feb. 1936: D12.

[80] Soanes, Wood. "Curtain Calls." *Oakland Tribune* 21 June 1939. Also, Schallert, Edwin. "Oakie Likely Choice for Capra Production." *Los Angeles Times*. 17 Mar. 1939.

[81] Schallert, Edwin. "Huston Wins Big Role in *Light That Failed*." *Los Angeles Times*. 16 June 1939.

[82] *Las Vegas Sun* 27 Feb. 1954.

[83] "Bela Lugosi Will Joust with Bowery Boys." *Los Angeles Times* 2 Mar. 1954.

[84] Weaver, Tom, Debbie Rochon, The Phantom of the Movies, and Peter Schmideg, p. 44.

[85] Wood, Edward D., Jr. Audio recording heard on the DVD of *The Haunted World of Edward D. Wood, Jr.* Chatsworth, CA: Image Entertainment, 1996.

[86] Wood, 11 Mar. 1954. ["Now Alex is back. He came in Saturday. I asked him why he didn't take the apartment with you, but the question was evaded."]

[87] Wood, Edward D., Jr. Letter to Ace Publications, Crestwood Comics, Dell Publications, Fiction House, Lev Gleason Comics, National Comics Publishing, St. John Publishing Company, Toby Press, Inc., and Ziff-Davis Publications. 28 Mar. 1954.

[88] Wood, Edward D. Jr. Letter to Samuel French, Inc. 12 Jan. 1954.

[89] Wood, 11 Mar. 1954.

[90] Ormond, Ron. *Your Career in Hollywood*. Hollywood: Screen Guild Press, 1954.

[91] Wood, 21 Mar. 1954.

[92] Wood, 11 Mar. 1954.

[93] Wood, Edward D., Jr. Letter to Bela Lugosi. 18 Apr. 1954. [A similar example comes in Wood, Edward D., Jr. Letter to Lou Sherrell. 27 Mar. 1954. When Wood couldn't get some newspapers in LA to run stories on the *Bela Lugosi Revue*, he turned to Lou Sherrell at Lugosi's request, saying to Lou that he might "have more of an 'in' somewhere."]

[94] Wood, 11 Mar. 1954.

[95] Wood, 21 Mar. 1954.

[96] The Ed Wood-written "Bela Lugosi" letter to "Mr. Mazzeo" of 12 Mar. 1954 mentions that Lugosi's next film would be "*The Bride of the Vampire*, to go before cameras sometime immediately after the completion of my work here at the Silver Slipper." It seems likely this refers to the Allied Artists production of *The Vampire's Tomb* script, which Wood assumed/hoped would be happening shortly after the *Bela Lugosi Revue* ended.

[97] Gordon, Alex. "Further Memories of Ed Wood, Jr.: Part Two." *Fangoria* Issue 65

[98] Gordon, "Further Memories Part Two," p. 61.

[99] Weaver et al., p. 46.

[100] "Strip Hotels at Las Vegas Spend $8 Million for Stars." *Reno Evening Gazette* (Reno, NV) 24 Apr. 1954.

A 1956 one-sheet for *Bride Of The Monster*.

[1] Halberstam, David. *The Fifties*. New York: Fawcett Columbine, 1993.

[2] Schnitzer scripted *Kid Dynamite* (1943), which starred The East Side Kids. He then wrote scripts for six Bowery Boys films: *Angels' Alley* (1948), *Jinx Money* (1948), *Trouble Makers* (1948), *Fighting Fools* (1949), *Hold That Baby!* (1949), and *Angels in Disguise* (1949). He was also assistant director for three films with the East Side Kids: *Mr. Wise Guy* (1942), *Let's Get Tough* (1942), and *Smart Alecks* (1942).

[3] Halberstam, p. 632-633.

[4] See Albert Abramson's *The History of Television, 1942 to 2000* (Jefferson, NC: McFarland, 2003) for a thorough examination of the growth of television in the postwar period.

[5] Halberstam, p. 183-4.

[6] "Studio Planning Another Film for Ann Blyth, Howard Keel." *Chicago Daily Tribune* 15 Jan. 1954.

[7] Obviously *Robinson Crusoe on Mars* did become a film in 1964, and obviously it did not star Lugosi. But aside from a similar title, what relation, if any, the 1964 film had to this 1954 project is unknown.

[8] "Vampira Guests on Skelton's Horror Show." *Los Angeles Times* 15 June 1954: 24.

[9] Ames, Walter. "Bing to Sub for Injured Son; Richfield Takes Bow for New Refinery." *Los Angeles Times* 28 May 1954.

[10] The earliest mention of Vampira's show in the *Los Angeles Times* is in Walter Ames's "Video Survey Brings Out Interesting Data; Suzan Ball, Hubby Cast for TV." 15 May 1954. Her time change to 11PM was announced in Walter Ames's "Robot Tries Hands on *Juke Box Jury*; Reagan Boasts Elaborate Title." *Los Angeles Times* 29 May 1954.

[11] Ames, Walter. "Martin, Lewis Cancel 1st Comedy Hour Show; Sun Gets Betty Furness." *Los Angeles Times* 1 Sept. 1954.

[12] Sherman, Gene. "Cityside with Gene Sherman." *Los Angeles Times* 30 June 1954.

[13] Ames, Walter. "Rocky-Charles Battle on Radio; Champ to Appear on Sunday Comedy Hour." *Los Angeles Times* 15 Sept. 1954.

[14] Kidson, Dick. "Farmers Market Today." *Los Angeles Times* 14 June 1954.

[15] Parsons, Louella. "Babylon Get a Redhead Queen." *The Washington Post and Times Herald* 21 June 1954.

[16] Wentink, David. Interview with Maila "Vampira" Nurmi. 19 May 2006. [In an 8 May 2006 email to Gary D. Rhodes, Don Miller of the Red Skelton archives confirmed that Carson was a writer for Skelton's program in 1954.]

[17] Gordon, Alex. "My Favorite Vampire." *Fantastic Monsters*. Volume 2, Issue 5. 1963.

[18] Weaver, Tom, Debbie Rochon, The Phantom of the Movies, and Peter Schmideg. "Alex Gordon on Ed Wood and *Ed Wood*." *Cult Movies* Issue 22. 1997: 45.

[19] Cremer (*Lugosi: The Man Behind the Cape*. New York: Henry Regnery, 1976: 217) mentions this story, placing it in late 1953, just before Wood scheduled Lugosi's personal appearance in San Bernardino. Grey (*Nightmare of Ecstasy: The Life and Art of Edward D. Wood, Jr.* Los Angeles: Feral House, 1991: 106-107) includes the same story, though Wood's quotation does not give an indication of when this event happened.

[20] Gordon, Alex. "Further Memories of Ed Wood, Jr.: Part One." *Fangoria*. Issue 64: 61.

[21] Gordon, "Further Memories Part One," p. 61.

[22] Gordon, "Further Memories Part Two," p. 61.

[23] Schallert, Edwin. "Irish Critic Acts Mean *Moby Dick* Mate; *Way We Are* Scans Our Town." *Los Angeles Times* 30 July 1954: B7.

[24] In Brett Wood's film *The Haunted World of Edward D. Wood, Jr.* (Chatsworth, CA: Image Entertainment, 1996), actresses Dolores Fuller and Loretta King spoke about how King came to play the lead role in *Bride of the Atom* and Fuller's subsequent unhappiness at taking on a smaller part. But given the clipping, cited in footnote 23, it seems that Wood's shifting Fuller to a smaller part and giving King the lead role happened in the summer of 1954 with *The Vampire's Tomb*. Either the problems both actresses described occurred as a result of *The Vampires Tomb*, or they were perhaps amplified by the fact that for *Bride of the Atom* Wood was doing the same thing to Fuller for a second time.

[25] Schallert, Edwin. "*River of the Sun*

Will Costar Ford, Grahame; Esmond Set for *Fear*." *Los Angeles Times* 2 Aug. 1954: B9.

[26] *Variety* 4 Aug. 1954.

[27] Schallert, "*River of the Sun*."

[28] In Wentink, interview with Vampira, Maila Nurmi claimed "That's bullshit. I was never [signed]. I wanted to meet [Wood] and beat him up!"

[29] Schallert, Edwin. "Sally Forrest to Have *Happy Holiday*; Burr Joins Law; Wynn in Deal." *Los Angeles Times* 27 Aug. 1954: B7.

[30] Schallert, Edwin. "Zanuck Closes Carol Reed Deal; Bela Lugosi to Do Spooky Western." *Los Angeles Times* 31 Aug. 1954: 17.

[31] *Ibid*.

[32] Schallert, "Sally Forrest to Have *Happy Holiday*."

[33] This seems clear given the enormous amount of coverage people like Fidler and Schallert gave Lugosi even during his hard times.

[34] *The Hollywood Reporter* 9 Sept. 1954.

[35] See, for example, "British Atom Spy Weds Viennese-Born Doctor." *Los Angeles Times* 2 Aug. 1953: 30. The previously-jailed British atom spy Dr. Alan Nunn May had wed Dr. Hildegarde Broda. The press at times called her the "bride of the atom spy." [That Wood retitled the script is mentioned by Alex Gordon in Grey (p. 61).]

[36] Gordon," My Favorite Vampire," p. 46. [Grey quotes Gordon as saying that the script was "completely rewritten" (p. 61).]

[37] Weaver et al, p. 44.

[38] *Ibid*., p. 45.

[39] Fuller, Dolores. Unpublished Autobiography.

[40] Grey, p. 67.

[41] Wood, Edward D., Jr. *Hollywood Rat Race*. New York: Four Walls Eight Windows, 1998: 125.

[42] These two films were *Alias the Champ* (1949) and *The Lemon Drop Kid* (1951)

[43] For information on his TV appearance with Berle, Marx, etc., see "Ships Warned to Beware of Minesweepers." *Los Angeles Times* 5 Oct. 1952: B1.

[44] Wood, Edward D., Jr. Response to "Questionnaire" sent to him by Fred Olen Ray. Undated.

[45] See James Copp's "Skylarking" column (*Los Angeles Times* 20 Jan. 1953: B4) for mention of Liberace being at Marco's

house "above the Strip." Or Copp's "Skylarking" column (*Los Angeles Times* 12 Jan. 1956) for a mention of the party attended by Peter Coe.

[46] Copp, James. "Skylarking." *Los Angeles Times* 19 Dec. 1954: C2. [Copp's mention of Marco's new nose is after some shooting occurred on *Bride of the Atom*, but its possible that Marco wasn't before the cameras until the second phase of shooting in March 1955. Or, there's also the possibility that Marco's nose job had been finished some weeks earlier and it was only in December that he bumped into Copp.]

[47] Weaver et al., p. 45.

[48] Wood, "Questionnaire."

[49] Grey (p. 66) quotes Wood as saying that "McCoy was going crazy" about Lugosi's raise, which means that if this did happen, it was likely after the initial shoots in late October-November when Donald McCoy came aboard as producer.

[50] "Here and There." *The Hollywood Reporter* 25 Oct. 1954.

[51] *The Hollywood Reporter* 1 Nov. 1954.

[52] *The Hollywood Reporter* 2 Nov. 1954. [Wood once claimed he was the sole producer of the film until Donald McCoy arrived as an investor (Grey, p. 63). The specific mention of Lyman C. Abbott (and Don Nagel as Associate Producer) in this 2 Nov. 1954 *Hollywood Reporter* would suggest Wood was incorrect.]

[53] Marco, Paul. Interview with Gary D. Rhodes. 12 June 1988.

[54] Wood later claimed that the only footage he shot in the first "three days" (as opposed to the "two" mentioned in *The Hollywood Reporter*) was for the police station scene, the inside of "The Willow's Place" (Vornoff's house) with Lugosi and Tor Johnson, and "The Willow's Place" on fire (Grey, p. 62).

But in addition to Dick Sheffield's memory, careful viewing of the living room area in "The Willow's Place" shows that all of the footage in it must have been shot at the Ted Allan Studios. Unchanging placement of minor background objects and the like do not at all suggest the set was struck and then reconstructed at a different studio.

[55] *The Hollywood Reporter* 4 Nov. 1954.

[56] "*Bride* Elopes." *Daily Variety* 4 Nov. 1954.

[57] Grey, p. 63.

[58] Another reason this may have been shot at KTTV is the fact that it was the other main set up in the film without Tony McCoy, if in fact he wasn't cast until 1955 in exchange for the Donald McCoy investing in the film. That would suggest no one was cast in the "Lt. Dick Craig" role in the autumn of 1954.

[59] *The Hollywood Reporter* 11 Mar. 1955.

[60] "*Topper* Set to Music; Edward Ashley Returns; Clift and Corey in Race." *Los Angeles Times* 10 Nov. 1954: B9.

[61] Johnson, Erskine. "NSGQs Again Hit Spotlight as Grace Kelly Joins Up." *The Modesto Bee* 13 Nov. 1954: 4. [Johnson wrote, "the movies are topping the scientists with *The* [sic] *Bride of the Atom*, a Bela Lugosi film."]

[62] "New *Bride* Bankroll; Pic to Resume Prod'n." *Variety* 11 Mar. 1955: 3.

[63] A quotation from Wood (Grey, p. 63) suggests this was what happened. Quotations from Henry Bederski and Dennis Rodriguez (Grey, p. 68-69) also claim this was the case.

[64] "Farce Given New 'Hypo' at Gallery."

[65] Von Blon, Katherine. "Cocteau Play Given at Ivar." *Los Angeles Times* 15 Aug. 1953: 10. [McCoy also appeared in Horton Foote's The Chase at the Theater Arts Studio on July 17, 1953. See Katherine Von Blon's "Laguna Will Offer Two New Plays; Other Notes." *Los Angeles Times* 8 July 1953: B9.]

[66] Marco, Paul. Interview with Gary D. Rhodes. 12 June 1988.

[67] King, Loretta. Interview with Gary D. Rhodes. 20 June 1997.

[68] Wood, "Questionnaire."

[69] Grey, p. 67. [John Andrews, who only heard stories about *Bride of the Atom* after the fact, said the same in Grey, p. 67.]

[70] Sheffield, Richard. Email to Gary D. Rhodes. 17 June 2006.

[71] In Wood, "Questionnaire." Wood claimed the final budget for *Bride of the Atom* became $89,000.

[72] Robert Cremer makes this error in his *Lugosi: The Man Behind the Cape* (New York: Henry Regnery, 1976: 22). Numerous other writers have claimed this as well. Even Wood himself referred to it (Grey, p. 66).

[73] Kelton the Cop appears as a character in *Bride of the Monster* (1955), *Night of the Ghouls* (1959), and *Plan 9 From Outer Space* (1959). Lobo appears in *Bride of the Atom/Monster* and *Night of the Ghouls*, as well as in Boris Petroff's *The Unearthly* (1957).

[74] *Night of the Ghouls* clearly invokes events that happened in *Bride of the Monster*. And however vaguely, *Plan 9* suggests the same given the appearance of the "Kelton the Cop" character.

[75] See the film *Sinister Urge* (1961).

[76] Lobo does pick up and fondle an angora beret belonging to Janet Lawson, which brings to mind *Glen or Glenda*. But the allusion is brief and extremely oblique.

[77] Grey quotes Wood as saying that he "wanted [Vornoff's homeland] to be [Russia] without saying its Russia." (p. 63).

[78] Wood, "Questionnaire."

[79] "Saturday Television." *Los Angeles Times* 18 Dec. 1954. [However, contrary to popular belief (and even Ed Wood's memory in *Hollywood Rat Race*. New York: Four Walls Eight Windows, 1998: 93). Vampira never screened *White Zombie* on her show. A week-by-week examination of all of her programs makes this point very clear.]

[80] An LA listing for *Bowery at Midnight* on TV turns up in the *Los Angeles Times* on 10 Sept. 1954. And an LA listing for *The Corpse Vanishes* appears in the *Los Angeles Times* on 30 Apr. 1955.

CHAPTER TEN FOOTNOTES

[1] Rhodes, Gary D. Interview with Paul Marco. 8 June 1987.

[2] Ackerman, Forrest J. Letter to Bela Lugosi 27 Dec. 1954. [In this letter, Ackerman expresses holiday greetings and includes five dollars as a Christmas gift.]

[3] Ormond, Tim. Email to Gary D. Rhodes. 15 Apr. 2006.

[4] See Gary D. Rhodes's *Lugosi*. Jefferson, NC: McFarland, 1997: 11.

[5] The first part of Turner's story–that he spotted Lugosi from a distance in Hollywood–is reminiscent of Lisa Mitchell's memories. She was a young teenager who saw Lugosi several times around Hollywood Boulevard in the mid-1950s. See Mitchell, Lisa. "I Remember Bela." *New West* 7 June 1976: 76-77.

[6] Rhodes, Gary D. Interview with Dallas E. Turner. 20 Feb. 2006.

[7] Rhodes, Gary D. Interview with Rose Marie Kerekjarto. 20 Sept. 2005.

[8] Rhodes, interview with Kerekjarto.

[9] Clippings from 1955 Hungarian newspapers commenting on Lugosi's drug addic-

Lugosi at the Los Angeles County General Hospital on April 22, 1955.

tion found in the Lugosi file at the Vasváry Collection of Szeged's Somogyi Library.

[10] Evans, Philip R. Letter to Gary D. Rhodes. 5 Oct. 1989.

[11] Windley, Charles. Email to Gary D. Rhodes. 21 Oct. 2005.

[12] Weaver, Tom. "Post Mortem: Director Ted Post Dissects Bela Lugosi's Final US Stage Production of *Dracula*." www.monstersfromthevault.com. Accessed 2 Sept. 2006.

[13] Jankiewicz, Pat. "The Lizard's Tale." *Starlog* Oct. 2004: 33.

[14] Weaver, Tom. *Attack of the Movie Monsters*. Jefferson, NC: McFarland, 1994: 49.

[15] Rhodes, Gary D. Interview with Emile O. Schmidt. 12 Nov. 2005.

[16] Ormond, June. Email to Gary D. Rhodes, typed and sent by Tim Ormond. 15 Apr. 2006.

[17] Rhodes, interview with Marco.

[18] Some historians have questioned Marco's claims, but they haven't really given much in the way of any substantive reason as to why, outside of pointing out that Marco was eccentric or in their eyes crazy. The larger question though is whether *all* of these people who remembered Lugosi's drug use were lying. Perhaps that is possible, but Emile O. Schmidt had never been interviewed about Lugosi until 2005. Schmidt even expressed surprise that anyone was interested in Lugosi so many years later. Could he still have lied? Theoretically the answer is of course yes, but he certainly doesn't seem to have a motive for doing so.

[19] Wise, Robert. Interview with Gary D. Rhodes. 17 Mar. 1997.

[20] "Up and Down Broadway in Waukesha." *Waukesha Daily Freeman* (Waukesha, WI) 3 Dec. 1947.

[21] "Bela Lugosi Ill, RKO Tour Off." *New York Post* 3 Jan. 1951.

[22] Lugosi, Bela, as told to Lloyd Shearer. "How I Beat the Curse of Dope Addiction." *Parade* 12 Aug. 1956.

[23] Sutherland, Henry. "Bela Lugosi Tells 20 Yr. Dope Horror." *Los Angeles Herald-Examiner* 22 Apr. 1955.

[24] Lugosi made these remarks to Senator Price Daniel and the Senate Subcommittee on Narcotics at Los Angeles hearings held during November 14-16, 1955.

25 Sutherland, "Bela Lugosi Tells 20 Yr. Dope Horror."

26 *Ibid.*

27 Yaros, Valerie, archivist for the Screen Actors Guild. Letter to Gary D. Rhodes 10 June 1998.

28 *Ibid*

29 *Ibid.*

30 Sutherland, Henry. "Bela Lugosi Tells 20 Yr. Dope Horror."

31 "Lugosi Asks for a Cure." *New York Post* 22 Apr. 1955. Also, "Bela Lugosi Surrenders Self as Narcotic Addict." *Los Angeles Examiner* 22 Apr. 1955.

32 "Lugosi Going to State Hospital for Dope Cure." *Hollywood Citizen-News* 23 Apr. 1955.

33 "Bela Lugosi Admits He's Used Narcotics 20 Years." *Los Angeles Times* 22 Apr. 1955.

34 "Bela Lugosi Surrenders Self as Narcotic Addict."

35 "Bela Lugosi is in Hospital for Help in Use of Drugs." *New York Herald Tribune* 22 Apr. 1955.

36 "Bela Lugosi Admits He's Used Narcotics 20 Years."

37 Sutherland, "Bela Lugosi Tells 20-Yr. Dope Horror."

38 *Ibid.*

39 "Bela Lugosi Tells Long Dope Ordeal." *Los Angeles Times* 23 Apr. 1955.

40 Sutherland, Henry. "Bela Lugosi Tells 20-Yr. Dope Horror." *Los Angeles Herald Examiner* 23 Apr. 1955.

41 "Bela Lugosi Admits He's Used Narcotics 20 Years."

42 Lugosi used the term "lightning-like" to describe pains in his legs in Roby Heard's "Bela Lugosi Describes 20 Years of Shame." *Los Angeles Mirror-News.* 22 Apr. 1955.

43 "Bela Lugosi Tells Long Dope Ordeal."

44 Sutherland, "Bela Lugosi Tells 20-Yr. Dope Horror."

45 Heard, "Bela Lugosi Describes 20 Years of Shame." Also, "Lugosi Asks for a Cure as an Addict." *New York Post* 22 Apr. 1955.

46 Sutherland, "Bela Lugosi Tells 20-Yr. Dope Horror."

47 "Lugosi Going to State Hospital for Dope Cure."

48 Lugosi, "How I Beat the Curse of Dope Addiction."

49 Lugosi told reporters he had used drugs for twenty years. Depending upon the

Another image of Lugosi and the script to *The Ghoul Goes West.*

account, he claimed he started using methadone either seven or seventeen years earlier. Since then, he said he had used it or demerol. The implication is that he used morphine until the moment he began using methadone, which would suggest he used it for at least three years.

50 Lugosi made this remark to Senator Price Daniel and the Senate Subcommittee on Narcotics hearings in Los Angeles held during November 14-16, 1955.

51 If he actually meant that he obtained methadone seventeen years earlier in England, that would put him getting it on his trip there in 1939.

52 Heard, "Bela Lugosi Describes 20 Years of Shame."

53 Lugosi made this claim to Senator Price Daniel and the Senate Subcommittee on Narcotics at Los Angeles hearings held during November 14-16, 1955. He also said the same during an interview filmed on 16mm. 1 Aug. 1955. [This interview is archived at the UCLA-Hearst Archives in Los Angeles.]

[54] "Matters of Mood." *Time* 18 Apr. 1955: 93.

[55] Lugosi, Bela. Interview filmed on 16mm. 1 Aug. 1955. [This interview is archived at the UCLA-Hearst Archives in Los Angeles.]

[56] Lugosi, "How I Beat the Curse."

[57] *Ibid.*

[58] Lugosi made these remarks to Senator Price Daniel and the Senate Subcommittee on Narcotics at Los Angeles hearings held during November 14-16, 1955.

[59] Cremer, Robert. *Lugosi; The Man Behind the Cape.* New York: Henry Regnery, 1976: 18-20.

[60] See Lugosi's "How I Beat the Curse of Dope Addiction" for his quotation "Perhaps it was psychosomatic." Also, see Cremer (p. 23) for Lillian's description of the same.

[61] Cremer, p. 20.

[62] *Ibid.*, p. 21.

[63] *Ibid.*, p. 14.

[64] Examining the Social Security death index makes clear that April 21 was indeed Lillian's birthday.

[65] Cremer, p. 12.

[66] "Bendix Takes Douglas Role in *Caine Mutiny*." *The Lima News* (Lima, OH) 25 Mar. 1955.

[67] "Bela Lugosi Seeks Cure." *New York Times* 23 Apr. 1955.

[68] "Horror of Dope Gets Horror Actor Lugosi." Undated clipping in the Bela Lugosi file at the New York Lincoln Center for the Performing Arts.

[69] Dr. Nicholas Langer makes this comment in Cremer, p. 28.

[70] Office Memorandum, United States Government. 29 Mar. 1954. [Letter contained in Lugosi's FBI file.]

[71] "Bela Lugosi Admits He's Used Narcotics 20 Years."

[72] "Lugosi Is Committed on His Own as Addict." *Los Angeles Daily News* 23 Apr. 1955.

[73] "Lugosi Going to State Hospital for Dope Cure." *Hollywood Citizen-News* 23 Apr. 1955.

[74] Sutherland, "Bela Lugosi Tells 20-Yr. Dope Horror."

[75] Bosquet, Jean. "Film Friends to Help Lugosi in Dope Fight." *Los Angeles Examiner* 25 Apr. 1955.

[76] Lugosi, "Hope I Beat the Curse of Dope Addiction."

[77] See Rhodes, Gary D. and Alexander Webb, eds. *Alma Rubens, Silent Snowbird.* Jefferson, NC: McFarland, 2006.

[78] Bosquet, "Film Friends to Help Lugosi in Dope Fight."

[79] Fuller, Dolores. *A Fuller Life.* Bear Manor Media, publication pending.

[80] "Movie People Make Plans to Assist Lugosi." *Hollywood Citizen-News* 25 Apr. 1955.

[81] Rhodes, Gary D. Interview with Loretta King. 22 Mar. 1997.

[82] For his writing about Lugosi's drug abuse, Laro won an "Honorable Mention" award from Theta Sigma Phi. See "Frank Laro, 53, Veteran *Times* Newsman, Dies." *Los Angeles Times* 23 June 1963.

[83] See, for example, "Chou Renews Threat of Drive on Formosa." *Los Angeles Times* 25 Apr. 1955. Also, "U.S. Files Antitrust Suit Against Hilton Hotels." *Los Angeles Times* 28 Apr. 1955.

[84] "Susan Hayward Found Unconscious in Home." *Los Angeles Times* 26 Apr. 1955.

[85] "Barrymore Girl Collapses; Sleep Pills Blamed." *Los Angeles Times* 28 Apr. 1955.

[86] Bela Lugosi file at the Immigration and Naturalization Service. 28 Apr. 1955.

[87] Cunningham, Ernest W. *The Ultimate Bogart: All the Facts and Fantasies About Humphrey Bogart, the Quintessential Movie Tough Guy.* Riverside, CA: Renaissance Books, 1999.

[88] "Ex-Principal Held Possible Sex Psycho." *Long Beach Press-Telegram* (Long Beach, CA) 31 Jan. 1954.

[89] See "Prayers in Dope Case Win Couple Probation" (*Los Angeles Times* 11 Nov. 1954) and "Two Who Failed to Shake Dope Habit Get 6 Months" (*Los Angeles Times* 22 Jan. 1955).

[90] Chandler, Otis. "Snake-Pit Era Ends for Mentally Ill." *Los Angeles Times* 16 Jan. 1955: B1.

[91] *Ibid.*, p. B1.

[92] "Name Change Proposed for Norwalk Hospital." *Los Angeles Times* 14 Feb. 1952.

[93] Chandler, B1.

[94] *Ibid.*, p. B1.

[95] "Ground Broken at Norwalk Hospital." *Los Angeles Times* 17 Dec. 1954.

[96] McCandless, Leilani. Interview with Gary D. Rhodes 24 Sept. 2005.

[97] An example would be four child molesters who escaped wearing their street clothes

in 1954. See "4 Molesters of Children Flee Hospital." *Los Angeles Times* 25 Apr. 1954.

[98] McCandless, interview with Rhodes.

[99] Browne, John. "Bela." Undated. [My thanks to Browne's widow, Barbara Browne.]

[100] Undated clipping in the collection of Richard Sheffield.

[101] *Ibid.*

[102] See Cremer, p. 29-31.

[103] Browne, "Bela."

[104] Though the screening with *The End of the Affair* has been called a double feature, it appears in advertisements as if a potential audience member had to buy a separate ticket to see *Bride of the Atom*. That would also help explain Wood's poor sales, as *The End of the Affair* may well have gotten a good crowd. Also, at times people who attended like Paul Marco and Maila Nurmi have indicated the screening took place at the El Capitan. They are correct; the Hollywood Paramount later became the El Capitan.

[105] Advertisement. *Los Angeles Times* 11 May 1955.

[106] "*Atom* Preem Profits Accrue to Lugosi." *Variety* 3 May 1955: 2. Also, "Bela Lugosi Benefit." *Variety* 11 May 1955. [*Variety* also gave credit to Tony McCoy and theatre operator Marco Wolff for having the idea for the benefit.]

[107] "Lugosi Benefit Slated Tonight." *Los Angeles Times* 11 May 1955.

[108] Wentink, David. Interview with Maila Nurmi. 19 May 2006.

[109] Wentink, David. Interview with Paul Marco. 13 May 2006.

[110] "Roundup of Filmland and Broadway News." *Oakland Tribune* 21 May 1955.

[111] Gordon, Alex. "Further Memories of Ed Wood, Jr.: Part Two." *Fangoria* Issue 65. 1987: p. 61. [In this article, Gordon refers to the planned film by the title *The Phantom Ghoul*. However, as articles from the period show, at this moment Wood was promoting what seems to have been the same script (perhaps with some changes) as *The Ghoul Goes West*.]

[112] *Ibid.*, p. 61.

[113] "*Bride of the Atom*." *Variety* 1 June 1955.

[114] Grey, Rudolph. *Nightmare of Ecstasy: The Life and Art of Edward D. Wood, Jr.* Los Angeles: Feral House, 1992.

[115] Bosquet, "Film Friends to Help Lugosi in Dope Fight."

[116] Cremer, p. 35.

[117] See "Whittier RC Gray Ladies Help Mentally Ill Recover." *Los Angeles Times* 12 Sept. 1954: H10. Also, "Class Cheers Patients on Visits to Hospital." *Los Angeles Times* 10 Apr. 1955.

[118] The many volunteer services Red Cross "Gray Ladies" provided are covered in "Whittier RC Gray Ladies Help Mentally Ill Recover." Also, see "Downey RC Gets Wagon, Appeals for Drivers." *Los Angeles Times* 20 May 1956.

[119] Lugosi made these remarks to Senator Price Daniel and the Senate Subcommittee on Narcotics at Los Angeles hearings held during November 14-16, 1955.

[120] *Ibid.*

[121] Johnson, James Bond, MD. Email to Gary D. Rhodes. 30 Aug. 2005.

[122] In Cremer (p. 17), Szittja speaks about visiting Lugosi at the County Hospital. And a quotation from Ed Wood (p. 17-18) speaks about seeing him in a "ward" that sounds as if it was Metropolitan, but he could have been meaning the County Hospital.

[123] Cremer, p. 33. [This man's name was Saul Resnick.]

[124] "Whittier RC Gray Ladies Help Mentally Ill Recover," p. H10.

[125] "Bela Lugosi Plans Quick Return to Movie Work." *Los Angeles Times* 4 Aug. 1955.

[126] Untitled clipping from August 1955 in the collection of Richard Sheffield.

[127] Browne, "Bela."

[128] Lugosi, "How I Beat the Curse of Dope Addiction."

[129] *Ibid.*

[130] "Lugosi May Be Freed Next Week." *Syracuse Herald-Journal* 30 July 1955.

[131] Lugosi, Bela. Interview filmed on 16mm. 1 Aug. 1955. [This interview is archived at the UCLA-Hearst Archives in Los Angeles. The reporter actually mentions that Lugosi would be leaving the hospital "tomorrow," which would be August 2, but this was either stated in error (perhaps confusing his hearing date with his release date). Or, the reporter might have said "tomorrow" intentionally in anticipation of a slightly later date of broadcast.]

[132] "Lugosi Drug Cure Progresses." *New York Times* 3 Aug. 1955.

[133] "*Dracula* of Films to Leave Hospital as

Drug Cure Ends." *Chicago Tribune* 3 Aug.
1955.

[134] "Cured." *Newsweek* 8 Aug. 1955: 43.

[135] Untitled clipping from August 1955 in
the collection of Richard Sheffield.

[136] Browne, "Bela."

[137] Loosz had possibly moved his things
out of the Carlton Way apartment while
Lugosi was at the County Hospital or during
his early days at Metropolitan. Given
Lugosi's financial situation, it seems unlikely
that he was paying rent each month to keep
the Carlton Way apartment while living at
Metropolitan.

[138] "Bela Lugosi Leaves Hospital to Begin
Movie Comeback." *Los Angeles Herald-
Examiner* 6 Aug. 1955. [This clipping men-
tions that Lugosi's son Bela Jr. was also there
to greet him. Cremer (p. 36) mentions that
Loosz was there.]

[139] Lugosi, "How I Beat the Curse of Dope
Addiction."

[140] "Bela Lugosi Plans Quick Return to
Movie Work." *Los Angeles Times* 4 Aug.
1955.

[141] "Lugosi Out of Hospital." Undated
clipping in the scrapbook of Richard
Sheffield.

[1] Sheffield, Richard. Emails to Gary D. Rhodes. 18 Oct. 2005; 14 Apr. 2006; 9 June 2006.

[2] See Halberstam, David. *The Fifties*. New York: Ballantine, 1993: 472-473. Also, Segrave, Kerry. *Drive-in Theatres: A History Since Their Inception in 1933*. Jefferson, NC: McFarland, 2006.

[3] Rhodes, Gary D. Interview with David Katzman. 14 June 2005. Also, Sheffield, Richard. Email to Gary D. Rhodes. 17 Apr. 2006.

[4] West's song was titled "Criswell Predicts." See "Ida Deglamorizes Self for TV Role." *Los Angeles Times* 11 Mar. 1955: 26.

[5] Sheffield, Richard. Email to Gary D. Rhodes. 29 Mar. 2006.

[6] DeBasso, Michael. Email to Gary D. Rhodes. 27 June 2006.

[7] Sheffield, email to Rhodes, 17 Apr. 2006.

[8] Sheffield, email to Rhodes, 29 Mar. 2006.

[9] Rhodes, Gary D. Interview with Carleton Savell. 14 June 2005.

[10] Sheffield, Richard. Email to Gary D. Rhodes. 3 July 2006.

[11] Rhodes, interview with Katzman.

[12] Lugosi, Bela. Letter to Hope Lugosi. Aug. 1955. [Original in the collection of Dennis Phelps.]

[13] Sheffield, Richard and Gary D. Rhodes. Interview with Hope Lininger. 22 Mar. 1996.

[14] Laro, Frank. "Bela Lugosi to Wed Tonight." *Los Angeles Mirror-News* 24 Aug. 1955: 18.

[15] "Bela Lugosi, 73, Marrying His Hospital Pen Pal, 40." *New York Post* 24 Aug. 1955: 62.

[16] Laro, p. 1.

[17] *Ibid.*, p. 1.

[18] Sheffield and Rhodes, interview with Lininger.

[19] Hope claimed to have been married twice before she took her wedding vows with Lugosi (Mank, Gregory W. "Dracula's Last Bride" *Dracula: The First Hundred Years*. Ed. by Bob Madison. Baltimore, MD: Midnight Marquee, 1997: 113). But on the marriage certificate for their wedding ("Certificate of Registry of Marriage." Local Registrar's Number 21658. Filed 26 Aug. 1955. Book 3844: 63) she listed

Lugosi and Hope Lininger just before getting the marriage license.

zero prior weddings. Sheffield believed that she had never been married before or after Lugosi, that the other key men in her life were not actually husbands (Sheffield, email to Rhodes. 7 July 2006).

[20] Sheffield and Rhodes, interview with Lininger.

[21] *Ibid.* [That Jim Delaney worked for the police and his wife Pat worked for the city jail was mentioned in clippings, as well as in Sheffield, email to Rhodes. 18 Oct. 2005.]

[22] "Bela Lugosi to Wed Film Studio Clerk." *Hollywood Citizen-News* 24 Aug. 1955.

[23] Lugosi, Bela, as told to Lloyd Shearer. "How I Beat the Curse of Dope Addiction." *Parade*. 12 Aug. 1956.

[24] "Dracula to Wed Tonight." *Los Angeles Herald Express* 24 Aug. 1955.

[25] Sheffield and Rhodes, interview with Lininger. [Hope's alleged age of 39 strangely became 40 in some newspapers that ran the Associated Press and United Press articles on the wedding. See, for example, "Movie Menace Weds No. 1 Fan." *Tacoma News Tribune* (Tacoma, WA) 25 Aug. 1955.]

[26] "Actor Bela Lugosi, 72, Takes His Fifth Bride, 39." *Los Angeles Times* 25 Aug.

1955. [Hall's home was at 2308 North Hillhurst Avenue.]

27 *Ibid.* [Existing photos show Hope without the hat, so she must have removed it before everyone had cake and champagne. More curious is the fact that the *Los Angeles Examiner* ("Bela Lugosi, 72, 'Dracula' Actor, Married to One-Time Fan, 39." 25 Aug. 1955) claimed that Hope wore a "blue-and-gray silk print" and that Lugosi wore a "gray business suit." Both descriptions contradict the *LA Times* article of 25 Aug. 1955.]

28 *Ibid.* [Specifically, Dale Buffington was a technician at RKO and his wife Phyllis was head of the RKO Research Department. This article also mentioned the presence of "singer Jo Wiley" and "Gilbert Olson." They don't seem to have been friends of Lugosi's; more likely they were either friends of Hope's or Manly P. Hall's. Afton Farnsworth's attendance was something that Richard Sheffield (who heard about it after the fact) confirmed in his Letter to Gary D. Rhodes. 23 June 1987.]

29 Wentink, David. Interview with Paul Marco. 13 May 2006.

30 Wentink, interview with Marco.

31 "Actor Bela Lugosi, 72, Takes His Fifth Bride, 39."

32 *Ibid.* [In Wentink, interview with Marco, Paul Marco suggested he didn't recall the incense.]

33 Photos of Lugosi and Hope with champagne glasses and the wedding cake appeared in "Actor Bela Lugosi, 72, Takes His Fifth Bride, 39" and "Bela Lugosi, 72, 'Dracula' Actor, Married to One-Time Fan, 39." That Lugosi and Hope chose the apartment at 5620 Harold Way might have to do with the fact it was inexpensive. But there was also the fact that the area was apparently a Hungarian enclave. Harris, Lee. Email to Gary D. Rhodes. 7 Dec. 2006.

Incidentally, in Sheffield and Rhodes, interview with Lininger, Hope claimed that they returned that night to the North Serrano apartment. However, this seems to contradict Wentink, interview with Marco, in which Paul Marco clearly describes arriving at a new and largely empty apartment. Likely Hope made a slip of the tongue, conflating the Harold Way apartment they had when they were married with the apartment where they first met, which was at Béla Loosz's on North Serrano.

34 Wentink, interview with Marco.

35 *Ibid.*

36 Sheffield and Rhodes, interview with Lininger.

37 Rhodes, Gary D. Interview with Teddi Figge. 9 Feb. 2006. [Teddi is Bob Figge's widow.]

38 Rhodes, Gary D. Interview with Steve Buscaino. 7 June 2005.

39 Armstrong, Carl. Email to Richard Sheffield. 19 Sept. 2006.

40 Shomer, Bob. Email to Richard Sheffield. 20 Mar. 2006.

41 Rhodes, interview with Katzman.

42 Rhodes, Gary D. Interview with Mike Spencer. 23 May 1996.

43 Sheffield, Richard. Letter to Gary D. Rhodes. 23 June 1987.

44 Rhodes, interview with Figge.

45 Sheffield, letter to Rhodes, 23 June 1987.

46 Rhodes, interview with Katzman.

47 Sheffield and Rhodes, interview with Lininger.

48 Rhodes, Gary D. Interview with Richard Sheffield. 7 June 2005.

49 "Sennett to 'Star' at Gala Reopening." *Hollywood Citizen-News* 2 Nov. 1955.

50 "Unique Film Theater Given Big Send-Off." *Los Angeles Times* 5 Nov. 1955: 14. Also, "Old Time Movie Has Big Night!" Clipping in the personal scrapbook of Richard Sheffield.

51 Sheffield and Rhodes, interview with Lininger.

52 Rhodes, interview with Spencer.

53 The RKO Hillstreet ran *Dracula* (1931) and *The Black Cat* (1941) on 7 Jan. 1956, and then the 1934 version of *The Black Cat* (under the title *The Vanishing Body*) on 8 Jan. 1956. See Advertisement. *Los Angeles Times* 7 Jan. 1956.

54 Rhodes, interview with Spencer.

55 Rhodes, Gary D. Interview with Bob Shomer. 21 Mar. 1996.

56 Schallert, Edwin. "*Ransom!* Terrific Kidnapping Movie."

57 Armstrong, email to Sheffield.

58 Rhodes, interview with Shomer.

59 Rhodes, interview with Katzman.

60 Spencer, Michael. *Repeat Performance.* A carbon copy of the original is in the possession of Michael Spencer.

61 Rhodes, interview with Spencer.

DRAMA BY HYPNOTISM!

IT STARTED as a publicity gag, developed into a sensational experiment. At Universal Studios Bela Lugosi allowed himself to be hypnotized, and enacted a scene for *Black Friday* while in a trance. Director Arthur Lubin conceived the notion, Manly P. Hall carried it out by hypnotizing Lugosi. These photos show what happened.

Manly P. Hall has put Lugosi to sleep, above. He holds a sofa cushion behind the actor's head to keep it from lolling back

Hall leads the hypnotized actor to a door on the set, tells him he is locked in a closet and is stifling. Lugosi believes this firmly

Lugosi fights to escape from the "closet," sobs for mercy and tries with all his strength to turn the locked doorknob. A moment later he tried unsuccessfully to break the door down

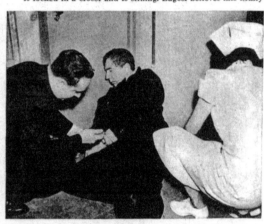

Shortly after the photo at left was taken, Lugosi, still in a trance, collapsed. Dr. George Esker took his pulse, found it 160—twice normal. This condition is usual under hypnotism

Hall wakes up the rumpled Lugosi. Contrary to popular belief, it is usually not difficult to waken a hypnotized person. If left alone, they'll wake up normally within several hours

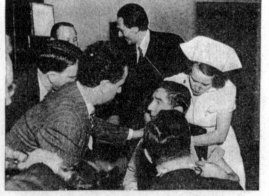

Lugosi is conscious now, feels no ill effects. Hypnotism is not "mysterious" or particularly dangerous when performed by an expert, but is an authentic psychological phenomenon

Publicity in an unknown magazine covering Lugosi's alleged hypnotism for Universal's
Black Friday (1940). *(Courtesy of Dennis Phelps)*

CHAPTER TWELVE FOOTNOTES

[1] Fidler, Jimmie. "Jimmie Fidler in Hollywood." *Nevada State Journal* (Reno, NV) 7 Mar. 1956.

[2] Sheffield, Richard. Email to Gary D. Rhodes. 17 Feb. 2006.

[3] Crocker, Harry. "Behind the Makeup." *Los Angeles Times* 2 May 1946.

[4] Rhodes, interview with Spencer.

[5] Wilk, Ralph. "A Little from 'Lots.'" *The Film Daily* 17 Oct. 1930: 6.

[6] *Krassó Szörényi Lapok*. 20 Aug. 1933. [An article on Lugosi in this publication gathered information about his early life from people like his schoolmate chum Zoltán Litsek.]

[7] *Ibid.*

[8] Again my thanks to Petrina Calabalic. This data emerges from the Béla Blaskó information on the Baptismal Register for the Roman Catholic Church of Lugos, the Death Register at the same (for István), the Lugos school registers from 1893 to 1895 (now housed in Timisoara at the National Archives of Romania).

[9] My thanks here to Gaidos Oliviu, whose expertise on Lugos architecture made him an invaluable source in finding Lugosi's birth home. Also, I would like to thank Petrina Calabalic, who independently verified the site of Lugosi's birth home.

In *The Immortal Count* (Univ Press of KY, 2003), Arthur Lennig claims that Lugosi was born on Templom Street (p. 16). This is partially correct, as it is the same physical street as Kirschengasse. However, the street was not known as Templom until circa 1890, some eight years after Lugosi was born. The German name "Kirschengasse" translates "church lane," whereas the Romanian "Templom" translates "Temple," as in "Temple Street." Their meaning is then much the same, but the use of "Templom" by 1890 suggests a growing Romanian population on what had been the German side of town. At any rate, the street was formally known as Kirschengasse in 1882.

The Death Register of the Roman Catholic Church of Lugos lists Lugosi's father István's death as being September 11, 1894; that document lists the family's address as being on Templom No. 7. Either the family moved from No. 6 to No. 7, or—as Gaidos Oliviu and Petrina Calabalic suggest—the change of street name from Kirschengasse to Templom brought about a different numbering system. For Lugosi's family, that meant still living at the same home, with a change of number from 6 to 7.

[10] Thanks here to Florin Iepan and his remarkable research into the Lugos of the 1880s and 1890s.

[11] When my friend Michael Lee and I visited a "history laboratory" at Lugosi's old school in Lugos during 2003 (which by that time was held in a different building than in Lugosi's day), we saw an enormous portrait of Vlad on the classroom wall that depicted him as a hero. For more information on Vlad's life (as well as the German stories about his cruelty), see Treptow, Kurt W. *Vlad III Dracula: The Life and Times of the Historical Dracula.* Portland, OR: Center for Romanian Studies, 2000.

[12] Mok, Michael. "Horror Man at Home." *New York Post* 19 Oct. 1939.

[13] My thanks here to Florin Iepan, the Romanian filmmaker, who is an expert on the superstitions of Lugos (now Lugoj) and the surrounding area.

Advertisement from the February 1, 1922 issue of New York's *Szinházi Ujság*.

[14] Wilk, Ralph. "Hollywood Flashes." *The Film Daily* 2 July 1931.

[15] Lugos school registers from 1893 and 1894 show Lugosi's grades. These are now at the National Archives in Timirsoara. My thanks to Petrina Calabalic for his help in locating and translating these.

[16] The school register shows Lugosi attending classes in 1894, but not 1895. Exactly when he left Lugos is unknown, but perhaps it was late 1894 or early 1895.

[17] A very interesting examination of Lugosi's early years appears in Cremer, Robert. *Lugosi: The Man Behind the Cape.* New York: Henry Regnery, 1976: 37-51.

[18] In *The Immortal Count* (p. 494), Lennig questions Lugosi's early use of the name "Lugosi" that comes one day after he appeared onstage as "Blaskó." This was first printed in my earlier book Lugosi (Jefferson, NC: McFarland, 1997: 153). He also questions the spelling of "Lugosi" at such an early period, rather than "Lugossy." Lennig writes: "In my search through the Hungarian theatre poster collection, I found no posters to confirm these dates. The performances I cite stem from playbills I examined personally."

I imagine by "Hungarian theatre poster collection," Lennig means to suggest those at the Országos Széchényi Könyvtár in Budapest. Elsewhere in *The Immortal Count*, Lennig writes that their theatre collection contains, "320,000 playbills and posters from all the towns in the old Austro-Hungarian Empire. In these wrinkled and decaying posters Lugosi's theatrical career lies hidden. The only way of checking his early years early years is to go through all the boxes. A thorough check would take months... (p. 21)."

I agree with Lennig's discussion of the breadth of the their collection of theatre posters. And I agree that it would take some time to examine all of them. What this means is that Lennig simply didn't examine the same posters that I have.

I too have conducted research at the Országos Széchényi Könyvtár, holding in my hands dozens and dozens of early Lugosi theatrical posters. I have also enlisted help in years past not only at that collection, but at other archives like the Vasváry Collection at the Somogyi Könyvtar in Szeged. For example the latter collection seems to have a far more complete collection of theatre posters for the 1910-1911 season in Szeged than any other archive.

I would stand by my findings printed in my first book regarding the time Lugosi's change of stage names from "Blaskó" to "Lugosi." Moreover, my research trip to Budapest in 2006 yielded many more Lugosi stage performances than I previously catalogued in my *Lugosi* (Jefferson, NC: McFarland, 1997), or that Lennig suggests when he vastly underestimates the number of Lugosi's Szeged performances in the autumn of 1910 (p. 22).

My belief now is that not only did Lugosi make the change of name as I once wrote, but that the spelling of "Lugosi" varied far more than Lennig suggests. Rather than a linear evolution from "Lugossy" to "Lugosi," it was back-and-forth. Even "Lugosy" appears on some handbills and in some theatrical publications (as in both of the articles written by Béla Kálmány for *Szinházi Ujság*, one on 30 Oct. 1910 and one on 14 May 1910).

Some of this may have been due less to Lugosi's choice than to the person who typeset the posters, but for whatever reason the spellings varied. Take Temesvár, where Lugosi appeared in 1903-1904. Lennig (p. 21) suggests quite rightly that Lugosi was billed as "Lugossy" when he appeared at the Ferencz József Városi Szinház. But "Lugossy" wasn't *always* his billing at that theatre during the 1903-1904 season. A thorough examination of Temesvár posters reveals that at times he was *also* billed as "Lugosi," as can be seen on the poster for *A Titok* (10 Sept. 1903), and as "Lugossi," as can be seen on the posters for *Klo-Klo* (25-26 Oct. 1903 and 8 Nov. 1903).

This variance of spelling factors into Lugosi's time in Debrecen as well. More often than not, his name in that city was spelled "Lugosi" on posters for at least thirty plays, some of which were staged more than once. This would include everything from *A Tanitóno* (29 Sept. 1909) through *Csöppség* (16 May 1910). But he was billed as "Lugossy" for *Tavasz* (30 Sept. 1909), and as "Lugossi" for *Kiz Czykros* (17-19 Mar. 1910).

And then in Szeged, in direct contrast to Debreczen, Lugosi generally appeared as "Lugossy" on posters, though as noted earlier the press sometimes called him "Lugosy."

[19] Lugosi's application for a change of name (and its approval) are noted in a 1917 addition made to the Baptismal Register of the Roman Catholic Church of Lugos.

[20] Lugosi appeared in Temesvár as Masodik in *Az ember trajédiája* on 1-2 Nov. 1903; as Ottó in *Bánk bán* on 10 Nov. 1903; as Tom Bátya in *Bob herczeg* on 11-12 Oct. 1903, 17 Nov. 1903, 4 Jan. 1903, 24 Jan. 1904, 21 Feb. 1904, and 27 Mar. 1904; and as Gecko in *Trilby* on 29 Dec. 1903 (with Lajos Réthey as Svengali and Anna T. Hadrick as Trilby).

[21] Lugosi sang in *Tannhäuser* on 7-9 Mar. 1904, 14 Mar. 1904, 18 Mar. 1904, 24 Mar. 1904, and 28 Mar. 1904.

[22] Lugosi worked with Gyula Gal in *Elnémult harangok* on 19 Apr. 1910, and with Sandor Góth in *Baccarat* on 3 May 1910. Surviving posters for these performances bill Gal and Góth's names above the titles of the plays.

[23] Lugosi appeared with top-billing as Armand Duval in *Kámeliás hölgy* (13 Apr. 1910, 4 May 1910). He also received top-billing for his role of Gusztav Balnai in *Czifra Nyomoruság* (21 Mar. 1910 and 22 Apr. 1910) and for his role of Róbert Károly in *Zach Klára* (24 Apr. 1910 and 26 Apr. 1910).

[24] Lugosi appeared as Adam in *Az ember tragédiája* on 27-28 Mar. 1910.

[25] Kálmány, Béla. "Lugosy Béla." *Szinházi Ujság* 30 Oct. 1910. [Lennig (p. 23) mistakenly claims this article was published on 14 May 1911. He is correct that a Kálmány article appeared on Lugosi that day in *Szinházi Ujság*, but that was a *different* article. It is almost as if Lennig has conflated the two, as he includes information from both while citing only the 14 May 1911.]

[26] "Szinház." *Szegedi Napló* 3 Sept. 1910.

[27] In Szeged, Lugosi appeared as Joska in *Az obsitos* on 5-6 Sept. 1910, 17 Sept. 1910, 23 Sept. 1910, 25 Sept. 1910, 25 Sept. 1910, 11 Oct. 1910, 10 Nov. 1910, and 8 Dec. 1910. He appeared as Rachel in *Bilincsek* on 16 Sept. 1910, 24 Sept. 1910, 26 Sept. 1910, and 30 Oct. 1910. He appeared as Frigyes Gentz in *A sasfiok* on 23-24 Nov. 1910, 7 Dec. 1910, 4 Mar. 1911, and 19 Mar. 1911. He appeared as Cassio in *Othello* on 9 Mar. 1911, and as George in *Richard III* on 20 Dec. 1910 and 10 Jan. 1911.

[28] Lugosi appeared as Rochermartel in *Trilby* on 8 May 1911, and as "Egy zászlös ur" in *Bánk bán* on 12 Nov. 1910. Lugosi appeared as Armand Duval in *Kámeliás hölgy* on 7 Sept 1910, 5 Oct. 1910, and 3 Apr. 1911.

[29] Lugosi appeared with top-billing in *Sárga liliom* on 14-15 Feb. 1911, 17 Feb. 1911, 22 Feb. 1911, 1 Mar. 1911, 14 Mar. 1911, 29 Mar. 1911, and 16 Apr. 1911. He appeared as Max in *Anatol* on 20 May 1911; it was his farewell performance in Szeged.

[30] Posters of both of Lugosi's Szeged performances as Romeo exist in the Vasváry Collection at the Somogyi Library in Szeged.

[31] I am very much indebted to the help of Mária Kórász at the Vasváry Collection at the Somogyi Könyvtar in Szeged. Their collection of theatre publications and Szeged posters includes materials not available at the Országos Széchényi Könyvtár in Budapest. The result has meant compiling a much more complete catalog of Lugosi's appearances in Szeged.

[32] "Szinház." *Szegedi Napló* 21 Sept. 1910.

[33] Lugosi played Count Vronsky in *Anna Karenina* on December 17, 18, and 27, 1910, as well January 26, 1911 and April 17, 1911. In "Szinház," a critic for the *Szegedi Napló* (18 Dec. 1910) wrote: "Bela Lugosi, playing the role of the passive Vronsky did show some qualities, with warmth expressed here and there in his speech, which instead of a proper articulation, was sometimes too rushed."

[34] Kálmány, "Lugosy Béla."

[35] "Szinház." *Szegedi Napló* 20 May 1911.

[36] For a wonderful examination of Budapest in this period, see Lukacs, John. *Budapest 1900: A Historical Portrait of a City and Its Culture*. New York: Grove, 1990. I would also thank Noémi Saly, who is an expert on the café culture of Budapest.

[37] Lugosi appeared as Tybalt in *Romeo and Juliet* at the Nemzeti Szinház on 7 June 1918. And he appeared as Duval in *Kaméliás Hölgy* on 7 Apr. 1918.

[38] I would add that—especially in the years between 1904-1908—Lugosi may have had many more important roles in famous plays than we have yet discovered. He may indeed

have played Cyrano or Hamlet, as he claimed. Also, I fear that we have tended to view Lugosi's early stage roles through Western eyes. In other words, many of us have often thumbed through the pages of his stageography looking for plays by writers like Shakespeare. Our eyes quickly scan past the many Hungarian plays that are unknown to us. But Hungarian audiences of the time would have considered many of them classics and many of them important, modern works. Take for example Lugosi's 1910-1911 season in Szeged. Forgetting even the importance of the roles he played, the Szegedi Városi Szinház programmed very few Shakespearean or Western plays; the bulk of Lugosi's appearances were in Hungarian plays.

[39] *Gabriel Von Wayditch: The Caliph's Magician*. Oakhurst, New Jersey: Musical Heritage Society. Undated.

[40] A photograph of Star's studio and its many buildings is in the collection of the Hungarian Film Institute in Budapest.

[41] Review in the *Orai Ujság*, reprinted in *Mozgófenykép Hiradó* 21 Apr. 1918.

[42] *Szinházi Élet* 27 Jan. 1918.

[43] I am very grateful to Gyöngyi Balogh at the Hungarian Film Institute for this data.

[44] Advertisements for Star films appear repeatedly in the German trade publications of the time.

[45] Gay, Peter. *Weimar Culture: The Outsider as Insider*. New York: Norton, 2001.

[46] Kracauer, Siegfried. *From Caligari to Hitler: A Psychological History of the German Film*. Princeton, NJ: Princeton Univ. Press, 1947: 47.

[47] Kracauer's *From Caligari to Hitler* remains a key study of Expressionist film. Another cornerstone text is Eisner, Lotte. *The Haunted Screen: Expressionism in the Cinema and the Influence of Max Reinhardt*. Berkeley: Univ. of CA, 1974.

[48] "Hypnose." *Film-Kurier* 4 Jan. 1920.

[49] "*Der Tanz auf dem Vulcan* [sic]." *Lichtbild-Bühne* 10 (1920).

[50] "*Lederstrumpf*, Cooper, & Co." *Film-Kurier* 15 Sept. 1920.

[51] *Szinhazi Ujság* 1 Jan. 1922.

[52] See, for example, *Küföldi Magyarság* 1 Oct. 1921; *Szinházi Ujság* 15 Sept. 1921; *Szinhazi Ujság* 1 Feb. 1922; *Amerikai Magyar Ujság* 3 Feb. 1922; *Szinházi Ujság*

15 Feb. 1922; and *Szinházi Ujság* 23 Mar. 1922.

[53] More details (including the full cast list) for *The Red Poppy* can be found in Rhodes, *Lugosi* (p. 165-166).

[54] Woollcott, Alexander. "The Reviewing Stand." *New York Herald* 12 Dec. 1922.

[55] Hammond, Percy. "The Theaters." *New York Tribune* 21 Dec. 1922.

[56] MacGowan, Kenneth. "The New Play." *New York Globe* 21 Dec. 1922.

[57] "German Club to Present Play." *Barnard Bulletin* (New York, NY) 23 Nov. 1923.

[58] Program for *Die Sorina*. Columbia University Archives.

[59] *Ibid.*

[60] See *Amerikai Magyar Népsava* 24 Jan. 1925 and *A Hét* 14 Feb. 1925.

[61] *A Hét* 16 May 1925.

[62] See, for example, the cover story on Kerekjarto in *Szhinázi Ujság* 1 Nov. 1921.

[63] "Business Records." *New York Times* 15 July 1924: 11.

[64] H. U. "A Sheik, a Lovely Lady, and a Grand Duchess on Parade." *New York Herald Tribune* 25 Oct. 1925.

[65] *Ibid.*

[66] See, for example, W. M. "*Arabesque* Presented as Expensive Spectacle." *New York Herald-Tribune* 21 Oct. 1925. Also, Woollcott, Alexander. "The Stage." *New York World* 21 Oct. 1925.

[67] "*Open House* a Naïve Play." *New York Times* 15 Dec. 1925.

[68] Atkinson, J. Brooks. "The Play." *New York Times* 30 Dec. 1926. ["As the chief bandit, Mr. Lugosi acts with an authority and a cadence worthy of better things."]

[69] Collins, Charles. "Oh How European the Clark Street Drama is Getting!" *Chicago Evening Post* 4 June 1924.

[70] "*The Silent Command*." *The Film Daily* 9 Sept. 1923: 10.

[71] "*The Rejected Woman*." *Moving Picture World* 3 May 1925: 85.

[72] "*The Midnight Girl*." *Moving Picture World* 28 Mar. 1925: 355.

[73] "*Daughters Who Pay*." *The Film Daily* 10 May 1925.

[74] "Bela Lugosi in Talkers." *Los Angeles Times* 21 Nov. 1928.

[75] A more thorough examination of the possibility that Lugosi appeared in *He Who Gets Slapped* appears in Rhodes, *Lugosi* (p.

372-375). In brief, Lugosi was in Chicago in the stage play *The Werewolf* in late May 1924. The play opened on June 1, 1924, and Lugosi received two favorable notices. The *Chicago Evening Post* (4 June 1924) called him "exceedingly good"; the *Chicago Daily News* (4 June 1924) said he was "efficient." But within a week of the opening, actor Vincent Serrano replaced him. The only reference to this in the local press came in the *Chicago Daily Tribune* (2 June 1924), which vaguely mentioned that Lugosi would be "relieved later in the week." They added, "Mr. Lugosi, evidently a good actor, was a bit heavy, and his dialect was not a beneficence in a cast which varied uncommonly in its attitude toward English diction."

And so Lugosi either chose to leave the cast or was asked to leave. *He Who Gets Slapped* shot in California between June 17 and July 28, 1924. With *The Werewolf* behind him, Lugosi's had no other known stage or film opportunities in Chicago or New York. His exact whereabouts that summer are unknown, so it is entirely possible he could have gone to California, however briefly.

After all, he likely was in need of work and none was apparently being offered elsewhere. The only press mention of his name during that summer seems to be an item in the *New York Times* ("Business Records." 15 July 1924) regarding Lugosi's unpaid debt to the Feszek Club, Inc. He may have owed the debt for some months before they filed a lien against him. But perhaps his nonpayment that summer and their filing the lien came out of the fact that he had left the city and wasn't physically there to try to work out a payment plan.

At any rate, in *The Immortal Count*, Lennig (p. 496) doubts Lugosi's appearance in *He Who Gets Slapped*, and to be sure there is no evidence outside of Dick's memory and two existing photos that show someone who resembles Lugosi. But Lennig's argument against Lugosi's appearance is problematic in many ways.

For one, he mentions that Lugosi was named in a review of *The Werewolf* dated June 24, 1924, which he takes to mean that Lugosi must have been in Chicago near that date rather than in California. He doesn't cite the source, but he apparently used Rhodes, *Lugosi* (p. 231), as he unknowingly repeats a typographical error in my earlier book without footnoting my work or examining the primary source himself. *The Werewolf* review in question was actually printed on June 4, 1924, *not* June 24. Thus his argument fails on this point; once replaced by Serrano, Lugosi never returned to *The Werewolf*.

He further questions why would Lugosi leave Chicago and go to Los Angeles. The answer is to find work, of course; none seems to have been available elsewhere. Lennig also suggests he had "no command of the English language and no money." But the reality is that we have no idea how many US dollars were in his pocket in June 1924; if anything, he presumably was paid for his week of work in *The Werewolf*. At the time of his departure from that play, Lugosi may well have had more money in hand than when he went to Chicago from New York days or weeks earlier. And bad English skills hadn't kept him from getting from New York to Chicago.

"If he did go there [California], would he even know how to get to the MGM studio?" Lennig also asks. Lugosi found his way from Louisiana to New York after first arriving in the US. And then he found his way to Chicago from New York; once there, he found the Adelphi Theatre where *The Werewolf* was staged. Presumably he also stayed in a Chicago hotel, which he must have found or had help in finding. So Lugosi *was* capable of purchasing a train ticket and getting to particular locations in a US city that he had not previously visited. Just because his English was very limited does not mean that he was incapable of getting off a train, hailing a taxi, and saying the three letters "MGM."

Finally, Lennig asks "Would have he waited around in hopes of becoming an extra, paid perhaps five dollars a day and rendered unrecognizable under the makeup? This seems unlikely." Lennig is correct; that course of events seems particularly unlikely. But Lennig has framed the argument too narrowly. Lugosi may have gone to Los Angeles in hopes of larger roles; after all, he had scored an important part in the East Coast production of *The Silent Command* (1923). Indeed, he may have been offered some role in a film that was no longer available once he physically arrived in California.

If so, that would help explain his early departure from *The Werewolf*. Or, if he didn't leave the cast of *The Werewolf* by his own choice, he may have been desperate to find work. Going to California might have held the promise of employment in a city where, unlike New York, he didn't owe anyone money.

None of this is to suggest with certainty that Lugosi was in California in June or July 1924, or that he definitely appeared in *He Who Gets Slapped*. Maybe he simply did go back to New York City. But Lennig's argument against Lugosi's appearance *He Who Gets Slapped* does not consider all the many variables and thus can't be viewed as solving this mystery.

[76] Lugosi's earlier film *The Veiled Woman* (1928) was available from Fox in a silent version and a synchronized sound version. However, it seems the synchronized version featured recorded music (and perhaps sound effects), but no dialogue. See, for example, "*The Veiled Woman*." *Harrison's Reports* 29 June 1929

[77] Schallert, Edwin. "Part Talkies Are Ridiculous." *Los Angeles Times* 14 Oct. 1928.

[78] Soanes, Wood. "Jane Fooshee Will Open Special Fulton Season Following Lugosi Week." *Oakland Tribune* 6 June 1930.

[79] "Howling Dogs at *Dracula* are Actors Woof-Woofing." *Los Angeles Times* 1 July 1928: C13.

[80] "'*Dracula* Kiss' to be Popular Among Villains." *Los Angeles Record* 1 June 1929.

[81] Hall, Gladys. "The Feminine Love of Horror." *Motion Picture Classic* Jan. 1931.

[82] Sylvester, Margaret. Letter to Bela Lugosi. Circa early 1930s.

[83] Jaskelainen, Irja. "Praise for Bela Lugosi." *Chicago Daily Tribune* 5 June 1932.

[84] Kendall, Read. "Around and About in Hollywood." *Los Angeles Times* 23 Dec. 1935: 11.

[85] Oldfield, Barney. "Theatre Topics." *Lincoln Sunday Journal and Star* (Lincoln, NE) 1 Sept. 1940. Also, Edmonds, Anne. "Hitch-hiked on the Road to Hollywood." *Oakland Tribune* 15 Sept. 1940.

[86] Meeker, Oden and Olivia. "The Screamy-Weamies." *Collier's* 12 Jan. 1946: 42.

[87] "'Medic' Callas for Real One after Stabbing." *Los Angeles Times* 23 Sept. 1953.

[88] Addison, George. "Man Was Once Much Wiser." *Los Angeles Times* 25 Aug. 1935.

[89] "Movie Stars May Have to Predict Own Futures." *The Hammond Times* (Hammond, IN) 16 Nov. 1942.

[90] Garrison, Carroll. "Behind the Scenes in Hollywood." *The Daily Independent* (Monessen, PA) 27 Nov. 1939.

[91] Fidler, Jimmie. "Jimmie Fidler in Hollywood." *The Chronicle Telegram* (Elyria, OH) 5 Jan. 1938. Also, Barney Oldfield's Stand-In. "Theatre Topics." *Lincoln Sunday Journal and Star* 4 May 1941.

[92] "Romantic Roles His for Years on Stage; Now He's Marked." *Montgomery Advertiser* (Montgomery, AL) 6 Feb. 1944.

[93] Fidler, Jimmie. "Fiddler in Hollywood." *Nevada State Journal* (Reno, NV) 15 July 1941.

[94] Winchell, Walter. "Walter Winchell on Broadway." *The Zanesville Signal* (Zanesville, OH) 14 May 1943.

[95] Snell, George R. Letter to Gary D. Rhodes. 7 Apr. 2006.

[96] *Ibid.*

[97] *Newark Advocate and American Tribune* 12 Sept. 1931.

[98] *Intimate Interviews*. 1932 short subject in which Dorothy West interviews Bela Lugosi. Available as a bonus feature on the DVD of Rhodes, Gary D. *Lugosi: Hollywood's Dracula*. Documentary Film. Spinning Our Wheels, 1997.

[99] MacDonnell, Dallas. "Society in Filmland." *Hollywood Citizen-News* 25 Nov. 1931.

[100] "Russian Buffet Supper Served Last Wednesday." *Los Angeles Times* 27 Nov. 1932.

[101] "Film Veteran Celebrates Thirtieth Year of Service as Screen Impresario." *Los Angeles Times* 1 Mar. 1936.

[102] Kilgallen, Dorothy. "The Voice of Broadway." *Mansfield News-Journal* (Mansfield, OH) 23 Apr. 1940.

[103] "Whitney-Taylor Rite Solemnized." *Los Angeles Times* 16 Jan. 1941.

[104] An example would be Lugosi's "midnight supper" for this group of friends, as described by Reine Davis in "Hollywood

Parade." *Los Angeles Times* 4 Dec. 1935. Also, see "Nyiregyházi to Mark 25th Anniversary." *Los Angeles Times* 25 Feb. 1940. [The "Nyiregyházi" clipping covers an event at the Ambassador Hotel Theatre attended by Lugosi, Ilona Massey, George Cukor, and Michael Curtiz."]

[105] Rhodes, Gary D. Interview with Michael Spencer. 23 May 1996.

[106] "Olympiad Bid Goes on Air." *New York Times* 22 May 1932. Also, Palmer, Zuma. "Radio." *Hollywood Citizen-News* 21 May 1932.

[107] "Hungarians to Hold Festival Sunday." *Los Angeles Times* 7 Sept. 1939. Also, "Festival Tomorrow." *Los Angeles Times* 9 Sept. 1939.

[108] "Opera and Concert Programs of the Week." *New York Times* 9 Nov. 1947.

[109] "Lopez Again Defends Mat Title Against Szabo at Olympic Tonight." *Los Angeles Times* 13 Nov. 1935.

[110] "Picture Notables Sponsor Various Athletic Groups." *Los Angeles Times* 28 Mar. 1935. Also, Ward, Arch. "Talking It Over." *Chicago Daily Tribune* 23 Oct. 1935.

[111] See, for example, "Quartet of Local Survivors in State Cup Tie Hook Up in Soccer Bill Today." *Los Angeles Times* 27 Jan. 1935; "Lighthorsemen Engage Hollywood Team in Crucial Soccer Battle at Loyola." *Los Angeles Times* 3 Feb. 1935; "Cup Posted By Lugosi." *Los Angeles Times* 17 May 1936; "Rovers Battle Flyers Today." *Los Angeles Times* 30 Oct. 1938; "Scot-Rover Cup Tussle Today." *Los Angeles Times* 2 Nov. 1941; and "Scots in Wild Rally to Edge Magyars' Soccer Team, 2-1." *Los Angeles Times* 31 May 1943.

[112] "Sheiks Bow to Vikings." *Los Angeles Times* 25 Mar. 1935.

[113] "Ex-Theater Man Held for Bail in Check Case." *Los Angeles Times* 5 Mar.
1936. Also, "Bela Lugosi to Testify Against Friend of Years." *Los Angeles Times* 17 Mar. 1936.

[114] Merrick, Mollie. "Lowell Sherman Just Now Is Pet of Movie Fates." *Dallas Morning News* 28 Apr. 1931.

[115] "Fiend Tries to Kill Bela Lugosi's Dog." *Hollywood Citizen-News* 21 Nov. 1935.

[116] "Three 'Werewolves' Licensed as Actor Races Death." *Los Angeles Daily News* 12 Mar. 1938.

[117] Fidler, Jimmie. "Jimmie Fidler in Hollywood." *The Appleton Post-Crescent* (Appleton, WI) 27 Jan. 1939. Also, Fidler, Jimmie. "Jimmie Fidler in Hollywood." *The Chronicle-Telegram* (Elyria, OH) 14 May 1948.

[118] Harrison, Paul. "Harrison's Hollywood." *The Fitchburg Sentinel* (Fitchburg, MA) 11 Apr. 1942.

[119] Mention of Lugosi's sculptures appears in the *Los Angeles Examiner* 10 Apr. 1932.

[120] Fidler, Jimmie. "Jimmie Fidler in Hollywood." *Syracuse Herald-Journal* (Syracuse, NY) 28 Jan. 1941.

[121] "Britannia Rules the Waves, but the Waves Rule Margaret." *Oakland Tribune* 17 Sept. 1939. Also, Fidler, Jimmie. "Jimmie Fidler in Hollywood." *Los Angeles Times* 2 June 1939: A10.

[122] Christoph, M. Oakley. "For Your Information." *Hartford Daily Courant* 11 Apr. 1930. Lugosi quoted the same proverb to George Snell, as mentioned in Snell, George. Letter to Gary D. Rhodes. 7 Apr. 2006.

[123] Sheffield, Richard. Email to Gary D. Rhodes 4 May 2005.

[124] Sheffield, Richard. Email to Gary D. Rhodes 29 Nov. 2005.

[125] "In Character." *Shock SuspenStories* 17. Oct.-Nov. 1954.

[1] "Actor to Testify." *Bridgeport Post* (Bridgeport, CT) 18 Aug. 1955.

[2] "Narcotic Dilemma." *Time* 3 Oct. 1955. [Curiously, Daniel seemed to back away from his statement about using the death penalty in "Death on Third Conviction of Dope Smuggling Urged." *Los Angeles Times* 16 Nov. 1955: 2.]

[3] "Senate Group to Hear Bela Lugosi Dope Story." *Los Angeles Mirror-News* 18 Aug. 1955.

[4] "Lugosi Drug Cure Progresses." *New York Times* 3 Aug. 1955. [This article claims that "he will remain under the jurisdiction and supervision of the Department of Mental Health for a year."]

[5] Lyon, Richard L. "Dope Witness Seized on Hill." *The Washington Post and Times Herald* 29 Sept. 1955: 3.

[6] "Narcotics Probers Going to California." *The Washington Post and Times Herald* 20 Oct. 1955: 33.

[7] The Senate Subcommittee on Narcotics held hearings in Los Angeles on November 14, 15, and 16, 1955. Lugosi testified on one of those three dates, but it is difficult to determine exactly which day it was; the surviving transcript doesn't say.

[8] Lugosi spoke these words to the Senate Subcommittee in Los Angeles between November 14-16, 1955.

[9] An example would be "Actor Stresses Narcotic Danger." *Reno Evening Gazette* (Reno, NV) 16 Nov. 1955.

[10] Lugosi, Bela, as told to Lloyd Shearer. "How I Beat the Curse of Dope Addiction." *Parade* 12 Aug. 1956.

[11] Weaver, Tom. Interview with Bob Burns. 24 July 2006. [My estimate of late 1955 or early 1956 comes from the fact that a United Artists studio biography of Lugosi circulated in the summer of 1956 mentions the appearance. "(Lugosi) was acclaimed on a network television program and given an award," it says, meaning it must have happened before the release of *The Black Sleep*. Of course the studio biography seemingly implies with the word "network" that the show was seen nationally, which it wasn't.]

[12] Duggan didn't begin his show in Los Angeles until April 2, 1956, so Lugosi's appearance would have happened sometime between that month and his death in August of that same year. [Ames, Walter. "Chicago Commentator Becomes Local Spieler." *Los Angeles Times* 5 Mar. 1955.]

[13] "TV Man's Wife Shoots Lock Off His Girl Friday's Door." *Los Angeles Times* 31 May 1956: 1.

[14] Cremer, Robert. *Lugosi: The Man Behind the Cape.* New York: Henry Regnery, 1976: 230.

[15] "TV Man's Wife Shoots Lock," p. 1. [Duggan's wife was named Ann Goss, due to the fact that Duggan's own surname was actually Goss.]

[16] "TV-Radio News." *Indiana Evening Gazette* (Indiana, PA) 14 Mar. 1956.

[17] According to the American Film Institute website, *The Man with the Golden*

Lugosi testifying before the Senate Subcommitte on Narcotics.

Arm premiered in December 1955 and went into general release in January 1956.

[18] The fact Sinatra sent $100 to the Bela Lugosi Benefit in March 1955 means that he must have had some other interest or interests in helping Lugosi as well, as that happened before he signed to do *The Man with the Golden Arm*. Perhaps Sinatra was a fan of Lugosi's movies; perhaps he was exhibiting a kind of generosity to another entertainer that he had on many other occasions. Perhaps it was both.

[19] Rhodes, Gary D. Interview with Michael Spencer. 23 May 1996. Also, Rhodes, Gary D. Interview with David Katzman. 7 June 2005.

[20] Mosby, Aline. "Bela Lugosi's Story Beats Film's Horror." [Clipping from Spring 1956. Pasted in Dick Sheffield's scrapbook.]

[21] Rhodes, interview with Spencer.

[22] Lugosi, "How I Beat the Curse of Dope Addiction."

[23] The Hungarian Revolution occurred from October 23 to November 4, 1956, shortly after Lugosi's death. But before his death, newspapers in 1955 and especially 1956 closely followed the growing changes and strategic importance that Hungary played in geopolitics.

[24] Lugosi spoke these words to the Senate

Lugosi as Casimir in *The Black Sleep*.

Subcommittee in Los Angeles between November 14 and 16, 1955.

[25] Sheffield, Richard and Gary D. Rhodes. Interview with Hope Lininger. 22 Mar. 1996.

[26] Hopper, Hedda. "Bogey Men-About-Town." *Washington Post* 14 Jan. 1940.

[27] Sheffield and Rhodes, interview with Lininger.

[28] *Ibid.* [In this interview, Hope claimed Lugosi "got" the maid for her, suggesting that he paid for her work. That is possible, given that he was claiming Social Security and had other, more sporadic income as well.]

[39] Cremer, p. 235.

[30] *Ibid.*, p. 235.

[31] Sheffield and Rhodes, interview with Lininger.

[32] *Ibid.*

[33] Rhodes, Gary D. Interview with Ruth Sheffield. 25 Mar. 1996.

[34] *Ibid.*

[35] Rhodes, interview with Ruth Sheffield.

[36] Sheffield and Rhodes, interview with Lininger.

[37] *Ibid.*

[38] Lugosi spoke these words to the Senate Subcommittee in Los Angeles between November 14 and 16, 1955.

[39] Lichello, Bob. "For 20 Years Hope Lininger Was a Fan! Then... 'I Married Dracula! And HE Was Afraid of ME!" *National Enquirer* 17 Nov. 1957. [This article deserves comment. On one hand, it was published in the *National Enquirer*. But on the other hand, the tone and content of Hope's comments seem very close to her remarks in the interview with Sheffield and Rhodes. That would also be true of Paul Marco's comments in Lichello and later in life. Though Lichello misspells his name as "Markle," the quotations attributed to him are strikingly similar to those he made even in his last interview (Wentink, David. 13 May 2006.)]

[40] Laro, Frank. "Bela Lugosi to Wed Tonight." *Los Angeles Mirror-News* 24 Aug. 1955: 18. [In this article, Lugosi claimed that after first meeting Hope, "it dawned on me, suddenly, that she believed in a Higher Power I believed in, too."]

[41] Rhodes, Gary D. Interview with David Katzman. 14 June 2005. [Katzman recalled that he saw burned pieces of wood in the

sink at the Harold Way apartment. He learned that Hope had been writing someone's name in the air with the sticks as their tips burned.]

[42] Rhodes, interview with Spencer.

[43] Sheffield and Rhodes, interview with Lininger. [Hope was definitely aware of her own bitterness. "Just the word 'Lugosi' sets my teeth on edge," she wrote in a 1 Mar. 1987 letter to Gary D. Rhodes. But her awareness doesn't necessarily help in separating the bitterness from her memories, or to understand her feelings as they existed in 1955 and 1956.]

[44] Sheffield and Rhodes, interview with Lininger.

[45] Rhodes, Gary D. Interview with Forrest J Ackerman. 4 Mar. 1987.

[46] Rhodes, Gary D. Interview with Rose Marie Kerekjarto. 20 Sept. 2005.

[47] Hopper, Hedda. "Looking at Hollywood." *Chicago Daily Tribune* 9 Mar. 1948: 25.

[48] These lots are mentioned in the "Last Will and Testament of Bela Lugosi," dated 12 Jan. 1954 and filed on 26 Sept. 1956 at the County Clerk's office for Los Angeles County.

[49] The nineteen lots (1, 2, 3, 4, 5, 10, 11, 15, 16, 17, 18, 19, 21, 22, 23, 24, 25, 26, and 27 in Block D of Rancho La Laguna, Lake Elsinore, County of Riverside, California) are listed in *Lillian A. Lugosi vs. Bela Lugosi*, D-152810. In the Superior Court of the State of California in and for the County of Los Angeles. 17 July 1953.

Given that Lugosi's will was finalized on 12 Jan. 1954, it is conceivable that Lugosi and Lillian, by mutual consent and with the assistance of her father Stephen Arch (as directed by *Lugosi vs. Lugosi*), could have sold one or more lots between that time and Lugosi's death in August 1956.

[50] Cremer, p. 232.

[51] *Ibid.*, p. 234.

[52] Sheffield, Richard. Letter to Gary D. Rhodes. 23 June 1987.

[53] For years, Dick Sheffield and I labored over how to describe this argument with appropriate caution and respect. Regrettably, another biographer published this story in a more graphic form, and did so even though Dick told him it was "off the record" and not to be published.

[54] Rhodes, interview with Ruth Sheffield.

[55] Lugosi, Bela. Interview filmed on 16mm. 1 Aug. 1955. [This interview is archived at the UCLA-Hearst Archives in Los Angeles. The reporter actually mentions that Lugosi would be leaving the hospital "tomorrow," which would be August 2, but this was perhaps stated in error (possibly confusing his hearing date with his release date). Or, the reporter might have said "tomorrow" intentionally in anticipation of a slightly later date of broadcast. Regardless, Lugosi likely meant that he quit drinking in 1953, as that was when he told Lillian he had his drinking under control. See Chapter Three.]

[55] Weaver, Tom. Interview with Ted Gargano. 17 Aug. 2004. [The man accompanying Lugosi to buy liquor is unknown, but Gargano described him as "old man." So it probably wasn't Ed Wood. Likely it was the older man that Hope remembered Lugosi meeting at AA.]

[56] Weaver, interview with Gargano.

[58] Rhodes, interview with Katzman.

[59] Lugosi spoke these words to the Senate Subcommittee in Los Angeles between November 14 and 16, 1955.

[60] Rhodes, Gary D. Interview with Forrest J Ackerman. 4 Mar. 1987.

[61] Rhodes, interview with Spencer.

[62] Cremer, p. 216.

[63] Sheffield and Rhodes, interview with Lininger.

[64] Rhodes, interview with Katzman.

[65] Fidler, Jimmie. "Fidler in Hollywood." *Nevada State Journal* (Reno, NV) 1 Mar. 1956.

[66] "Atomic Age Creatures Dispense Cinema Horror." *Los Angeles Times* 6 Jan. 1956: B6.

[67] Gagnard, Frank. "New Trends in Store for Horror Fan." *Dallas Morning News* 15 Dec. 1955.

[68] "TV Notes and Jars." *The Charleroi Mail* (Charleroi, PA) 22 Jan. 1955.

[69] "Television Programs." *The Gettysburg Times* 10 Feb. 1956: 16. [Station WTTG-Channel Five was running *Bela Lugosi Presents* from 9:30-11PM EST on Saturday evenings.]

[70] Rhodes, Gary D. *Lugosi: His Life in Film, on Stage, and in the Hearts of Horror Lovers.* Jefferson, NC: McFarland, 1997. [This book contains a chapter entitled "Advertising Lugosi." It also includes a pho-

tograph of Lugosi promoting KOOL cigarettes.]

[71] Wilson, Earl. "The Man of the Hour (After Midnight)." *Syracuse Herald-Journal* (Syracuse, NY) 7 Nov. 1950.

[72] Ryon, Art. "Ham on Ryon." *Los Angeles Times* 24 Oct. 1955.

[73] No available documentation (such as the *Players Directory Bulletin from the Academy of Motion Picture Arts and Sciences*) links Lugosi's name with the Herdan-Sherrell Agency in 1955 or 1956.

[74] Wentink, interview with Marco.

[75] Rhodes, interview with Ruth Sheffield.

[76] Koch, Howard W. Letter to Gary D. Rhodes. 8 Feb. 1988. [Koch also remembered that Bel-Air went over budget by $6,000, putting the final cost of the film at $235,000.]

[77] Koch, letter to Rhodes.

[78] Le Borg's prior horror movies included *Calling Dr. Death* (1943), *Dead Man's Eyes* (1944), *Jungle Woman* (1944), *The Mummy's Ghost* (1944), and *Weird Woman* (1944).

[79] Schallert, Edwin. "*Don Quixote* Project Mushrooms; O' Shea Sets Budget of $22,500,000." *Los Angeles Times* 16 Jan. 1956: B11.

[80] The most thorough production history and critical examination of this film is certainly Weaver. Tom. "*The Black Sleep.*" *Bela Lugosi: Midnight Marquee Actors Series.* Eds. Gary J. and Susan Svehla. Baltimore, MD: Midnight Marquee, 1995.

[81] Johnson, Erskine. "Hollywood Today." *Ironwood Daily Globe* (Ironwood, MI) 16 Mar. 1956.

[82] Mosby, Aline. "Bela Lugosi's 'Real' Story." *The Monassen Daily Independent* (Monassen, PA) 16 Feb. 1956.

[83] Deschin, Jacob. "National Show: Many Staged Attractions Planned at Armory." *New York Times* 18 Feb. 1951: 97.

[84] "The Man in the Shadows" radio show was broadcast over WCBS from 9:30-10PM EST on 10 Sept. 1949; radio listings do not show it being an episode of a regular series. ["Programs on the Air." *New York Times* 10 Sept. 1949: 28.] In terms of *The Black Cat* (1941), Rathbone receives topbilling on-screen, while Lugosi gets fourth-billing under him, Broderick Crawford, and Hugh Herbert.

[85] Such films would include: *The Death Kiss* (1933), *Night of Terror* (1933), *The Gorilla* (1939), *Black Friday* (1940), *The Black Cat* (1941), *The Wolf Man* (1941), *Night Monster* (1942), *The Body Snatcher* (1945), *One Body Too Many* (1944), and *Glen or Glenda* (1953). Granted, in some of these films his characters play important roles in their respective narratives; for example, his small role as Bela in *The Wolf Man* really causes the action of the film to unfold after he inflicts the curse of the werewolf on Lawrence Talbot (Lon Chaney, Jr.). But at the same time, these were all small parts with limited screen time.

[86] Advertisement. *Los Angeles Times* 5 May 1956: 8. [KHJ-TV broadcast *The Body Snatcher* on their "First-Run Movie Playhouse" at 7PM PST on 5 May 1956.]

[87] Mosby, "Bela Lugosi's 'Real' Story."

[88] Le Borg, Reginald. Letter to Gary D. Rhodes. 2 Apr. 1987.

[89] Koch, letter to Rhodes. Apparently Herbert Rudley in 2005 suggested in an interview with Lawrence Fultz, Jr. that Koch and Schenck were mistaken in their depiction of Lugosi on the set. But years earlier in an interview with Tom Weaver ("Herbert Rudley." *Attack of the Monster Movie Makers: Interviews with 20 Genre Giants.* Jefferson, NC: McFarland, 1994: 312), Rudley claimed he did not "socialize" with Lugosi at all. He made no other comment about him, and had little recollection of any cast members other than Basil Rathbone, with whom he shared so many scenes. Rudley's recent memories challenging Koch and Schenck seem somewhat at odds with what he said to Weaver.

[90] Weaver, Tom. "Classic Creatures Revisited." *Fangoria* 147. Oct. 1995. [Schenck (in "Classic Creatures Revisited"), Koch (Letter to Rhodes), and Le Borg (Letter to Rhodes) suggested that they believed Lugosi was on drugs during the shoot. This seems extremely unlikely. Instead, they probably misconstrued his poor health, nervousness, and his overuse of alcohol as drug use given his "numb" appearance and the 1955 publicity over his drug rehabilitation.]

[91] Weaver, "Classic Creatures Revisited."

[92] Mank, Gregory W. *Karloff and Lugosi: The Story of a Haunting Collaboration.* Jefferson, NC: McFarland, 1989

[93] Le Borg, letter to Rhodes. Also, Sheffield, Richard. Email to Gary D.

Rhodes. 22 June 2006. [Le Borg's memory of this event suggests that Lugosi was much more upset than what Sheffield recalls, especially in his article "Lugosi's Last Years: The Boy Who Befriended Bela" (*Famous Monsters of Filmland* 133. Apr. 1977: 50) where he recalled Lugosi took it "gracefully." Perhaps it is possible Chaney lifted him up on more than one occasion, with Lugosi giving a more displeased reaction the second time?]

[94] Le Borg, letter to Rhodes.

[95] Rhodes, Gary D. Interview with Louanna Gardner. 5 Nov. 2005.

[96] Weaver, Tom. *It Came from Weaver Five.* Jefferson, NC: McFarland, 1996.

[97] Rhodes, interview with Katzman. Also, Sheffield, 22 June 2006.

[98] Sheffield, 22 June 2006.

[99] Rhodes, interview with Ruth Sheffield.

[100] This publicity scheme happened while *The Black Sleep* was still shooting. A note in *Variety* on 29 Feb. 1956 claimed that the movie "continues filming." Presumably shooting finished in March, perhaps early in that month.

[101] Sherman, Gene. "Cityside." *Los Angeles Times* 1 Mar. 1956: 2. [Unfortunately Sherman doesn't give the exact date of the luncheon. He claims it was the "other noon," placing it in late February.]

[102] See "Film 'Hall of Fame' to Start Road Tour." *The Morning Press* (Santa Barbara, CA) 30 Dec. 1932. Also, "Maker of Wax Models Tells How It's Done." *The Morning Press* 10 Jan. 1933. [Stubergh's wax figure of Lugosi as Dracula was on display at Charles E. Pressley's "Motion Picture Museum and Hall of Fame" in Hollywood, where it appeared in the short subject *Hollywood on Parade* (No. A8, 1933). In 1933, the Lugosi wax figure toured to a variety of cities, including San Francisco, Portland, Seattle.]

[103] Taylor, Al and Sue Roy. *Making a Monster: The Creation of Screen Characters by the Great Makeup Artists.* Crown, 1980: 40. [Bau, who had also been a makeup artist for *The Black Sleep*, created life-size wax figures of Lugosi, Chaney, Rathbone, Tamiroff, Carradine, and Louanna Gardner at a cost of $20,000 (*Hollywood Reporter* 9 May 1956). Taylor and Roy suggest that Bau lost money on the flat-rate deal he accepted to create the figures.]

[104] Taylor and Roy, p. 40.

[105] Heffernan, Harold. Qtd. In Weaver, "*The Black Sleep.*"

[106] Sheffield, Richard. Email to Gary D. Rhodes. 10 Oct. 2004.

[107] "Bela Lugosi–Biography." United Artists Press Release. 1 Mar. 1956: 2.

[108] "*Black Sleep* Well-Made Horror Film Production." *Hollywood Reporter* 7 June 1956: 3.

[109] "Alfred Hitchcock Plans Two Features." *Los Angeles Times* 4 June 1956: A8

[110] See Hulburt, David. "Talk Around Town." *San Francisco Chronicle* 5 June 1956. [Printed the day before the horror stars arrived in San Francisco.] Also, "Terror Trio Have a Novel, Light Lunch." *San Francisco News* 7 June 1956: 23. [Printed the day after the press luncheon.]

[111] Advertisement. *San Francisco Call-Bulletin* 7 June 1956.

[112] Frankenstein, Alfred. "Hungarian Quartet Brilliant." *San Francisco Chronicle* 7 June 1956. [The quartet performed to much acclaim on June 6, 1956, received strong notices, and were to continue concerts through June 26, 1956.]

[113] Koch, letter to Rhodes. [Koch also told Moses to put a handcuff on Lugosi and get on a plane with him home. Perhaps he did say that, but the group (including Lugosi) travelled onto Portland instead. And Moses was not constantly keeping an eye on him; a newspaper story (Marks, Arnold. "Stage and Screen." *Oregon Journal* 6 June 1956: 3) claimed he was spending part of his time in Portland looking for a "young actress–a shapely beauty who can not only act, but ride horseback and swim."

As for Moses's own memory of these events, in Gregory William Mank's *Karloff and Lugosi: The Story of a Haunting Collaboration* (Jefferson, NC: McFarland, 1990: 302), he claims that in Portland Lugosi was "shaking–he looked like a man who was dying. I okayed a shot of alcohol. Meanwhile, the press was waiting in a restaurant across the street! So we came up with a very dramatic act. I told Bela, he wasn't really well, he had to go home, and the best way to do this was to put on a little show for the press, in which he would not be subject to questions–he couldn't answer them. So, he came into the room for the press, and–as planned–he collapsed. In actuality, Lugosi *really* collapsed [author's emphasis]–but it was planned that way, and Lon Chaney, his good friend and a prince of a guy, carried him out. Then we sent him home."

What did the others do? Allegedly the remaining group went on to Seattle, but if they did their publicity was nonexistent. A careful check of the Seattle newspapers (the *Seattle Post* and *Seattle Times*) for the three weeks after the Portland appearance (which had come *immediately* after the San Francisco appearance) has absolutely no mention of them or even a screening of *The Black Sleep*. If they did go onto Seattle–which seems very doubtful–Moses failed to generate *any* publicity whatsoever.

[114] Johnny Legend told this memory to *Fangoria* (Issue 22, 1981). Legend claimed that Tor not only noticed Lugosi's depression, but grew so tired of hearing him saying he "just wanted to die" that he held him out of window and shouted "Is this what you want, you miserable Hunkie [*sic*]? Tor's behavior in this story seems at odds with the fact they were close friends. Given that this is a second hand memory, one wonders if it changed in retellings.

[115] Marks, p. 3.

[116] Larson, Herbert. "Chiller-Thriller Film Reunion Staged in Portland by Fearsome Foursome." *The Oregonian* (Portland, OR) 8 June 1956.

[117] *Ibid.*

[118] Clipping from 1956 in the personal scrapbook of Richard Sheffield. [In *The Immortal Count* (Univ of KY Press, 2003), Arthur Lennig incorrectly claims that no press coverage of Lugosi's collapse in Portland occurred. But Dick preserved a copy of this original clipping in his scrapbook, as accessed/photocopied by Gary D. Rhodes in 1995.]

[119] *The Devil's Paradise*. Program. 1956.

[120] Rhodes, Gary D. Interview with James B. Leong, Jr. 25 Mar. 1996. [Regrettably Leong Jr. had no knowledge of *The Devil's Paradise*, or any materials from his father about it. When Leong Sr. was still alive, a fire unfortunately destroyed many of his stage and screen mementos and papers.]

[121] *The Devil's Paradise* program. 1956.

[122] Kid Mitchell had been acting in the LA area since at least the 1930s. See Kendall, Read. "Around and About in Hollywood."

Los Angeles Times 18 June 1937. And Marilyn Zack's work on TV is chronicled in "San Fernando High Presenting 1954 Follies Tomorrow." *The Valley News* (Van Nuys, CA) 21 Oct. 1954. Others listed in the cast included Leo Como, who appeared in a 1957 LA stage version of *Around the World in 80 Days* ("*Around the World* Stage Version Cleverly Done." *Los Angeles Times* 19 June 1957). Also Helen Scott, who appeared in a 1953 LA stage version of *The Curious Savage* (Von Blon, Katherine. "*The Curious Savage* Intriguing Comedy." *Los Angeles Times* 12 June 1953) and Sally Jones, who appeared in a 1956 LA stage version of *A Room Full of Roses* (Von Blon, Katherine. "*A Room Full of Roses* Offered at Call Board." *Los Angeles Times* 17 Nov. 1956).

[123] *The Devil's Paradise*, program.

[124] Sheffield and Rhodes, interview with Lininger. Also, Sheffield, Richard. Email to Gary D. Rhodes. 6 Oct. 2005.

[125] Rhodes, Gary D. Interview with Evelyn Bunn. 9 Mar. 2006. [Bunn was also certain that she was the *only* Evelyn Bunn working as an actress in the LA-area in 1956.]

[126] Rhodes, Gary D. Interview with Sally Jones. 4 Apr. 2002. [Jones was also certain that she was the *only* Sally Jones working as an actress in the LA-area in 1956.] Also, Rhodes, Gary D. Interview with Howard Amacker's daughter. 28 May 2005. [Amacker was listed on the program as having one of the lead roles.]

[127] I made a thorough search of the *Hollywood Citizen-News* (which I consider the "most likely candidate" because the play was staged in Hollywood), as well as all of the other LA-area newspapers. No advertisement or review seems to have ever been published.

[128] Weaver, Tom. "Kelton the Cop Sez: Don't Knock on Wood." *Fangoria* 64. June 1987.

[129] Wood, Edward D., Jr. Response to "Questionnaire" sent to him by Fred Olen Ray. Undated.

[130] Grey, Rudolph *Nightmare of Ecstasy: The Life and Art of Edward D. Wood, Jr.* Los Angeles: Feral House, 1992: 78.

[131] *Ibid.*, p. 78.

[132] Wood, "Questionnaire."

[133] Sheffield, Richard. Email to Gary D. Rhodes. 17 Sept. 2006.

[134] I am not the first to suggest that Wood shot this footage on two different days. Grey (p. 172) claims that Wood shot some of the Lugosi footage in April 1955 and some in June 1956. I don't know where he obtained the date April 1955. Given the "Cityside" column listed in the next footnote, I'm much more confident about the November 1955 date.

[135] Sherman, Gene. "Cityside." *Los Angeles Times* 27 Nov. 1955. [A more precise way to date the cemetery footage would be a headline from the San Fernando newspaper that Wood and others have mentioned that claimed "Ghouls Invade Cemetery." Wood claimed the headline appeared in the "San Fernando newspaper" (Grey, p. 78). But when Lugosi collector David Wentink made an exhaustive search of *The Valley News* (which would have been the key San Fernando-area newspaper of the time) for November 1955, June 1956, and July 1956, no such headline appeared. A search of a digital archive of the same newspaper for 1955-1956 also found no results. Was this an invented anecdote? Or was it printed in another newspaper that was much further geographically from the cemetery?]

[136] "Horror Bill Starts Run Today." *Los Angeles Times* 28 June 1956: 32. [The theatres included the Orpheum, the Uptown, the Fox Hollywood, the Fox Inglewood, the El Rey in Culver City, the United Artists in East Los Angeles and—according to this clipping—"several suburban theatres and drive-ins." Though the article was published on June 28, the films already had been screened on the night of June 27]

[137] Lillian continued to be linked with Donlevy in the press. Walter Winchell wrote that the two were "Hollywood's latest duet" ("Winchell on Broadway." *Nevada State Journal* 24 May 1957), later writing "Bela Lugosi's widow says she isn't Brian Donlevy's companion." ("Winchell on Broadway." *Nevada State Journal* 4 June 1957). In 1966, Lillian and Donlevy married.

[138] Koch, letter to Rhodes.

[139] Rhodes, interview with Ackerman. Also, Sheffield, Richard. Email to Gary D. Rhodes 22 June 2006.

[140] Haines, Jimmy. Email to Gary D. Rhodes. 13 May 2006.

[141] "Bela Lugosi–Biography," p. 5.

[142] "Toughened Dope Bill Made Law."

Washington Post 19 July 1956: 17.

[143] Lugosi, "How I Beat the Curse of Dope Addiction."

[144] Rhodes, Gary D. Interview with Steve Buscaino. 7 June 2005.

[145] Sheffield and Rhodes, interview with Lininger.

[146] *Ibid.*

[147] Haines, email to Rhodes.

[148] Weaver, interview with Gargano.

[149] Maila "Vampira" Nurmi has often mentioned a publicity event that she recalls at the end of Lugosi's life. It was a trip to Inglewood, California just a few weeks before Lugosi's death to promote *Bride of the Atom* (which by then was known as *Bride of the Monster*); she went in a hearse with Lugosi and Tor Johnson. Some hoodlums "messed up the hearse" while they were inside the theatre, and so they took a taxi home. Then hoodlums (presumably the same people) followed the cab, which eventually stopped, with Tor scaring them into going home. She described this story for Rudolph Grey (*Nightmare of Ecstasy*: 107, 109.). She repeated it to Steve Randisi ("Interview with the Vampira." *Filmfax* 106. Apr./June 2005.), and again to David Wentink (Interview with Maila "Vampira" Nurmi. 19 May 2006).

However, absolutely no newspaper advertisements for this screening show up for Inglewood during the last three months of Lugosi's life; nor does any such ad appear in Torrance, a city that Nurmi has also mentioned as being where the event occurred. Either it happened much earlier (as in January 1956, when *Bride of the Atom* (rechristened *Monster*) played on a double bill with *Ransom!* (1956) at a number of theatres (see Schallert, Edwin. "*Ransom!* Terrific Kidnapping Movie." *Los Angeles Times* 26 Jan. 1956), or the live appearance in Inglewood was not at all advertised, or–more likely–she confused this event with the LA opening of *The Black Sleep*.

She saw Lugosi on June 27, 1956 at the New Fox Theatre for the opening of *The Black Sleep*, but quickly moved on with Tor to a 9:30PM PST screening at the Fox Inglewood, the last of four screenings they attended that night (Advertisement. *Los Angeles Times* 27 June 1956). Perhaps the events she described happened that evening, and she confused Lugosi's appearance in

Inglewood with the fact she saw him at the New Fox. This seems even more probable given that she told Grey that it was part of a "tub-thumping" (p. 109) series of screenings they attended; she and Tor did make it to three screenings of *The Black Sleep* before appearing Inglewood.

Added to all of this is that some of Nurmi's other memories, such as seeing Lugosi roller skate down Hollywood Boulevard (Wentink, interview with Nurmi) are spurious at best.

[150] *The Hollywood Reporter* (10 Aug. 1956) claimed *The Black Sleep* and *The Creeping Unknown* double bill had earned more than $1,600,000 at the box office. Together, both had cost less than $400,000.

[151] Sheffield, Richard. Letter to Gary D. Rhodes. 20 Mar. 1989.

[152] "Best TV Bets Today." *Los Angeles Times* 1 Aug. 1956: C11.

[153] Rhodes, interview with Ruth Sheffield.

[154] Boyle, Hal. "Boyle's Column." *The Kerrville Times* (Kerrville, Texas) 27 May 1952.

[155] Sheffield and Rhodes, interview with Lininger.

[156] "Bela Lugosi Jr., now 17, is studying to be a lawyer." This information was printed in Winchell, Walter. "Winchell on Broadway." *Nevada State Journal* 18 Oct. 1955.

[157] Lugosi, "How I Beat the Curse of Dope Addiction." [This article and accompanying photograph may well have been prepared weeks before it was published on 12 Aug. 1956.]

[158] Rhodes, interview with Ruth Sheffield.

[159] Sheffield, Richard. Letter to Gary D. Rhodes. 14 Dec. 1986.

1 Sheffield, Richard and Gary D. Rhodes. Interview with Hope Lininger. 22 Mar. 1996.

2 "Bela Lugosi Collapses, Dies at Home Here." *Los Angeles Examiner* 17 Aug. 1956.

3 Sheffield and Rhodes, interview with Lininger.

4 Certificate of Death for Bela Lugosi. Registration District No. 7053. Registrar's No. 15906. Date entered by registrar, 4 Sept. 1956. [That an autopsy was to be performed is mentioned in "Bela Lugosi is Dead at 73 After Conquering Drug Habit." *New York Post* 17 Aug. 1956.]

5 "Lugosi Dies; Plans Burial in 'Dracula' Garb." *Hollywood Citizen-News* 17 Aug. 1956.

6 Wood told this story to his wife, Kathy (Grey, Rudolph. *Nightmare of Ecstasy: The Life and Art of Edward D. Wood, Jr.* Los Angeles: Feral House, 1991: 109). He told the same tale to Lugosi biographer Robert Cremer (*Lugosi: The Man Behind the Cape.* New York: Henry Regnery, 1976: 238). And he wrote about the event, even going so as to claim the script was opened to page six (Wood, Ed., Jr. *Hollywood Rat Race.* New York: Four Walls Eight Windows, 1998: 32). But Hope denied any knowledge of *The Final Curtain* (Sheffield and Rhodes, interview with Lininger).

7 That Hope must be trusted on this point does pose a possible difficulty. In Sheffield and Rhodes, interview with Lininger, for example, Hope told a few untruths herself. She claimed that her only wedding gift had come from Frank Sinatra, which was not true. She claimed that she had only mailed Lugosi a single letter while he was in the hospital, which was also false; along with the wide array of newspaper stories speaking about her letters, Lugosi's own correspondence to Hope after he was released refers to them in the plural as well.

8 Wood, Brett. *The Haunted World of Edward D. Wood, Jr.* Documentary film. Chatsworth, CA: Image Entertainment, 1996.

9 "Bela Lugosi Collapses," p. 16.

10 This was a ring that Lugosi had worn in *Abbott and Costello Meet Frankenstein* (1948).

11 Wood, *The Haunted World.* [In Sheffield and Rhodes, interview with Lininger, Hope confirmed this, claiming that "I knew nothing about that (decision to bury him in his cape)."]

12 For examples, see "Lugosi Dies; Plans Burial in 'Dracula' Garb." *Hollywood Citizen-News* 17 Aug. 1956. Also, "Bela Lugosi Shroud to Be Dracula Cape." *Los Angeles Times* 18 Aug. 1956. Also, "The Cloak of Dracula, Symbol of His Career, Will Shroud Lugosi." *New York Post* 19 Aug. 1956. Also, "Transition." *Newsweek.* 27 Aug. 1956: 72.

13 Sheffield, Richard. Letter to Gary D. Rhodes 5 July 1990.

14 Sheffield and Rhodes, interview with Lininger.

15 "Bela Lugosi Rights Attract Few Notables." *Los Angeles Times* 19 Aug. 1956.

16 "Hollywood Publisher Judge Palmer Dies." *Los Angeles Times* 26 July 1956: 24.

17 See "Silent Star Bonnie Earle Dies at 69." *Los Angeles Times* 23 Jan. 1952: 23. Also, "Albert Austin's Death Recalls Film Career." *Los Angeles Times* 19 Aug. 1953: 23. Also, "Final Rights Conducted for Skeets Gallagher." *Los Angeles Times* 25 May 1955: 2. Also, "Frankie Bailey, Former Toast of Broadway, Dies." *Los Angeles Times* 9 July 1953: A7.

18 "Services Set for Actor Harry Walker Soursby." *Los Angeles Times* 25 Sept. 1952: A2.

19 Rhodes, Gary D. Interview with David Katzman. 7 June 2005. [Regrettably, Katzman's photos have been printed and reprinted, occasionally licensed by Hollywood memorabilia dealers who have made money from his work. He has never been compensated or credited with taking some of the most famous photographs of horror film history.]

20 "Bela Lugosi Rights Attract Few Notables."

21 The funeral book was signed by 137 names. However, Lillian, Bela Jr., and Hope did not sign the book; nor did makeup man Harry Thomas, who claimed to have been at the funeral (Rhodes, Gary D. Interview with Harry Thomas. 15 Mar. 1996). Perhaps others who attended didn't sign either. Conversely, it is possible that some signa-

tures represent those who viewed the body on 17 Aug. 1956, but didn't actually make it to the funeral.

[22] At the time, Korda was editor of the Hungarian film trade publication *Mozihét.*

[23] These names are all listed in the funeral book.

[24] Rhodes, Gary D. Interview with Dallas E. Turner. 20 Feb. 2006.

[25] Rhodes, Gary D. Interview with Mike Spencer. 23 May 1996.

[26] "Bela Lugosi Rites Attract Few Notables."

[27] *Ibid.* Also, Sheffield, letter to Rhodes.

[28] "Bela Lugosi Rites Attract Few Notables."

[29] Sheffield, letter to Rhodes. Also, Rhodes, interview with Spencer. Also, Sheffield and Rhodes, interview with Lininger.

[30] Sheffield and Rhodes, interview with Lininger.

[31] See Marlowe, Don. *The Hollywood That Was.* Fort Worth: Branch Smith, 1969. However, it should be noted that a variety of historians have taken issue with Marlowe's Lugosi memories.

[32] A listing of Lugosi's agents appears in Rhodes, Gary D. *Lugosi: His Life in Film, on Stage, and in the Hearts of Horror Lovers.* Jefferson, NC: McFarland, 1997.

[33] Calhern died on May 12, 1956. He is buried at the Hollywood Memorial Cemetery in the Abbey of the Psalms, Abbey Foyer, Niche 308, Tier 3, South Wall.

[34] Lugosi's plot is in the Grotto, L120, 1. He is buried next to Bing and Dixie Lee Crosby, and his grave is located very near actress Sharon Tate's.

[35] Sheffield and Rhodes, interview with Lininger. [Hope assumed that Ralph Staats had planned the route down Hollywood Boulevard.]

[36] Rhodes, Gary D. Interview with Steve Buscaino. 7 June 2005.

[37] "Bela Lugosi Estate Valued at $2,900." *Los Angeles Times* 27 Sept. 1956: 4.

[38] Creditor's Claim Probate 382569 in the Matter of the Estate of Bela Lugosi. [Hope paid for at least $216.62 of the cost through the Lugosi estate. The casket cost $496, with the remainder of the $738.12 bill covering tax on the casket ($9.92), flowers and tax ($52.00 and $57.20), a vault ($78.00), a "vault charge" ($5.00), notices ($25.00), and a fee for the priest ($15.00).]

[39] Rhodes, Gary D. Interview with David Katzman. 7 June 2005.

[40] Lyon, Herb. "Tower Ticker." *Chicago Daily Tribune* 15 Nov. 1956. [At times comedian Joey Bishop has been credited with saying the punchline to this joke. (See Boller, Paul F. Jr. and Ronald L. Davies. *Hollywood Anecdotes.* New York: Ballantine, 1987: 289). However, Bishop is not mentioned in this 1956 article.]

[1] This filmography does not include non-fiction short subjects/newsreels, stage productions, radio shows, or television programs. A thorough listing of those projects can be found in Gary D. Rhodes's *Lugosi* (Jefferson, NC: McFarland, 1997).

[2] *A régiséggyujto* was a comedy short subject about a woman who cheats on her husband. Alfred Deésy directed Pál Forró's scenario for the Star film company. Along with Lugosi (under the name Arisztid Olt), the cast included Kamilla Hollay and Norbert Dán. See *Mozihét 5* (1918, p. 9) *Mozi-Világ 1918* (1918, p. 13), and *Belügyi Közlöny* (1920, p. 1261).

[3] In his book *The Immortal Count: The Life and Films of Bela Lugosi* (Univ. Press of Kentucky, 2003: 471), Arthur Lennig does mention *Ihre Hoheit die Tänzerin*, mistakenly believing it was an alternate title for *Der Tanz auf dem Vulkan*. However, censorship records make clear those are two *distinct* projects, both of which included Lugosi in their casts. *Der Tanz auf dem Vulkan* was released in 1920; it had a well-publicized premiere at the Ufa-Palast am Zoo in February 1920 (Advertisement. *Film-Kurier* 22 Feb. 1920). *Ihre Hoheit die Tänzerin* was not filmed until after February 1920, and perhaps not edited until after Lugosi had left Germany. It was a six-act feature whose cast was similar (but not identical) to *Der Tanz auf dem Vulkan*. Censorship record B.06712 makes clear that it was deemed "forbidden" to screen.

[4] *Lichtbild-Bühne* [LBB] 37 (1920) printed a review of *Das ganze Sein ist flammend Leid*. It clearly mentions that a fourth-billed Lugosi was in a cast that also included Fritz Greiner, Anton Ernst Rückert, and Alice Matay. Also in the cast were Ruth von Mayers and Carl Sick. Ottomar Ostermayr directed Alfred Schirokauer's screenplay, which was based on the novel by Gustav Meyrink. Theaters screened the film starting in September 1920.

[5] Along with the questionable film appearances I discuss in the main text, rumors of a few other Lugosi film appearances have circulated amongst fans and film historians. Allegations that he appeared in the film *The Lady of Scandal* (1930) are false. Equally incorrect are the allegations that he appeared in bit parts in *Frankenstein* (1931) and *Dracula's Daughter* (1936).

[6] A lengthy discussion of *Casanova* appears in Rhodes, *Lugosi* (p. 370-372). My research in the time since that volume was published suggests that–once Lugosi was replaced in the title role by Deésy–he didn't appear in the finished film at all.

[7] In Rhodes, *Lugosi*, I mistakenly claimed that *Lili* (1918) was a Phönix film (p. 70); however, I've since learned that it was without doubt a Star film, as confirmed by the many ads for the movie that appeared in the pages of the Hungarian film trades. For examples, see the ads in *Mozgófénykép Hiradó* 2 Sept. 1917; 13 Jan. 1918; 31 Mar. 1918; 7 Apr. 1918; 14 Apr. 1918; and 28 Apr. 1918. This is in addition to data housed at the Hungarian Film Institute, which includes a photograph of a color movie poster created for *Lili*'s premiere in October of 1917.

Lugosi as Roxor in *Chandu the Magician* (1932).

Lennig, *The Immortal Count* also makes this error (p. 469); perhaps we were both provided with the same incorrect data from the Theatre Collection at the Országos Széchényi Könyvtár in Budapest. I am surprised that neither of us earlier noticed the problematic discrepancy of Lugosi appearing in a Phönix film under the pseudonym Arisztid Olt, a name that he used only for his

Star films.

[8] Advertisement. *Der Film* 18. 1919: 120.

[9] *Lichtbild-Bühne* 17 July 1920.

[10] "Luna-Film." *Lichtbild-Bühne* 7 Aug 1920: 45. (*Die Silbermine* was also mentioned as an upcoming Lugosi film in *Der Kinematograph* 709. 1920.

[11] My thanks to Olaf Brill at CineGraph-Hamburg for his hard work in pursuing Lugosi's possible affiliation with these films.

[12] See Chapter Twelve for an investigation of *He Who Gets Slapped*. Also, Rhodes, *Lugosi*, (p. 372-375).

[13] See Rhodes, *Lugosi* (p. 381-383) for an investigation of *Lock Up Your Daughters*.

[14] For his Hungarian films, the trade *Mozihét*, *Mozgófénykép Hiradó*, *Mozi-Világ*, and *Szinházi Élet* have been key sources, as has the Hungarian Film Institute. For his German films, censorship records and the film trades *Der Film*, *Der Kinematograph*, *Film-Kurier*, and *Lichtbild-Bühne* have been key sources, as has the German Film Institute. For his US films, copyright records, trade publications like *Variety*, *The Hollywood Reporter*, *The Film Daily*, *Motion Picture Herald*, and *Motion Picture Daily*, and city newspapers like the *New York Times*, the *Chicago Daily Tribune*, and the *Los Angeles Times* have been used.

[15] Again, the release dates printed in this filmography for Lugosi's Hungarian and

Top: A Belgian movie poster for *Return of the Ape Man* (1944). *(Courtesy of Lynn Naron)*
Bottom: Lugosi and the cast of *The Whispering Shadow* (1933).

German films correct errors that appear in such places as Rhodes, *Lugosi*; Lennig, *The Immortal Count*; Cremer, *Lugosi: The Man Behind the Cape* (New York: Henry Regnery, 1976); imdb.com; etc. I would thank Gyöngyi Balogh at the Hungarian Film Institute and Olaf Brill at CineGraph for their help in this regard.

[16] See Rhodes, *Lugosi* for the exact dates on which his US films were copyrighted, as well as the official copyright numbers for each.

[17] Though it appeared in Rhodes, *Lugosi*, this film has generally not been listed in Lugosi filmographies. See *Mozgófénykép Hiradó* 19 Aug. 1917 for an ad and a lengthy plot summary.

[18] In some Star advertisements, *Az élet királya* was referred to as simply *Élet királya*. See ads in *Mozgófénykép Hiradó* published on 7 Apr. 1918, 14 Apr. 1918, 21 Apr. 1918, and 28 Apr. 1918,

[19] Rhodes, *Lugosi* (p. 67, 69) and Lennig, *The Immortal Count* (p. 467, 468) both incorrectly list *A Leopárd* as being a different film from *Küzdelem a létért*. In reality, they are two titles for the same film.

[20] A two-page ad in *Der Film* 49 (1919) and a review in *Film-Kurier* (4 Jan. 1920) use the title *Hypnose*. But in an ad in *Der Film* 48 (1919), the film is listed as *Sklaven fremden Willens*. Then, in an ad that appeared in *Film-Kurier* (18 Jan. 1920) listed both titles, with *Hypnose* in parenthesis. Rather than a subtitle, it appears as if to mention a former or alternate title. I privilege *Hypnose* because it was reviewed under that title.

[21] In *The Immortal Count* (p. 37 and 470), Lennig refers to the film as *Die Frau im Delphin oder Tage auf dem Meeresgrund* (*The Woman in the Dolphin, or Thirty Days on the Bottom of the Sea*). But this is not how the film was generally discussed or advertised at the time; instead, it was known simply as *Die Frau im Delphin*. For examples, see the article in *Der Kinematograph* 684 (1920), the ad in *Lichtbild-Bühne* 6 (1920), the ad in *LBB* 9 (1920), the ad in *LBB* 45 (1920, which also has a cast list), the article in *Der Film* 46 (1920), the article in *Der Film* 49 (1920), the ad in *Der Film* 41 (1920), the ad in *Der Film* 45 (1920), the articles in *Film-Kurier* (26 Oct. 1920, and 29 Oct. 1920), and the ads in *Film-Kurier* (29 Jan. 1920, 30 Jan. 1920, 31 Jan. 1920, 5 Feb. 1920, and 6 Feb. 1920). None of these publications use the alternate title. It does

Grego (Pat McKee, left) and Toby (John Carradine, third from left) bring Stella Saunders (Louise Currie) to Dr. Richard Marlowe (Bela Lugosi) in *Voodoo Man* (1944).

not seem that Lennig worked with primary sources regarding Lugosi's German film career; he offers no footnotes for the limited space he gives to Lugosi's time in that country, and for his filmography he relied on Gerhard Lamprecht's *Stummfilme 1920* (Berlin: Deutsche Kinemathek, 1968).

[22] The film was mentioned by the title *Schrecken* in *Lichtbild-Bühne* 5 (1920), *LBB* 7 (1920), *LBB* 9 (1920), and *LBB* 18 (1920); it was also under the title *Schrecken* in *Film-Kurier* (29 Apr. 1920). Ads using the title *Schrecken* appeared in *Der Kinematograph* 701-702 (1920), *LBB* 21 (1920, three different ads), *LBB* 21 (1920), *LBB* 23 (1920), *LBB* 25 (1920), and *Film-Kurier* (30 Apr. 1920), among others. An ad for the film as *Der Januskopf* appeared in *Der Film* 36 (1920). An article in *LBB* 35 (1920) used that title, as did a review in *Film-Kurier* (27 Aug. 1920).

[23] Articles in *Lichtbild-Bühne* 35 (1920) and *LBB* 43 (1920), as well as a full-page ad in *LBB* 37 (1920) used the title *Wildtöter*, as did an ad in *Film-Kurier* (1 Sept. 1920), an ad in *Der Film (*29 Aug. 1920), and an article in *Der Film* 43 (1920). But a review in *Film-Kurier* (1 Nov. 1920) used the title *Wildtöter and Chingachgook,* as did reviews in *Der Film* 44 and 46 (1920). At times (as in an article in *Der Film* 1. 1920, and a full-page ad in *Der Kinematograph* 688-689. 1920) *Wildtöter* was referred to as *Der Pfadfinder.* I privilege the title *Wildtöter und Chingachgook* because it was reviewed under that title.

[24] Unless otherwise noted, the films in this section were produced in the US. They are ordered chronologically using the dates copyright records were filed.

[25] No US copyright was filed for this serial.

[26] No US copyright was filed for this serial.

[27] No US copyright was filed for this serial.

[28] No US copyright was filed for this film.

[29] No US copyright was filed for this film.

[30] No US copyright was filed for this film.

INDEX